AF477028

FROM WAR TO PEACE

A PHOTOGRAPHER'S VIEW OF BRITISH AVIATION DURING THE 1940s

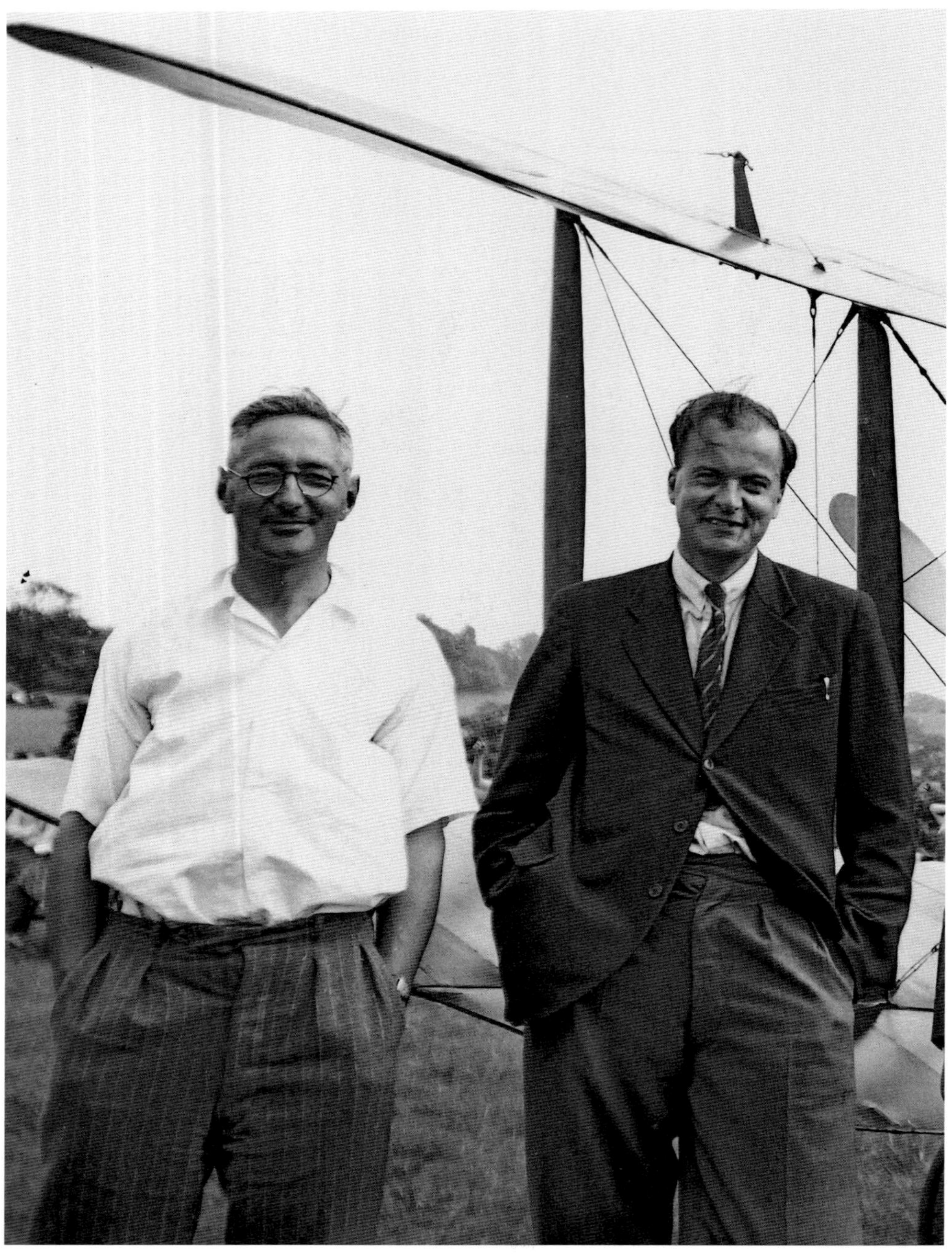

A. J. Jackson and E. J. Riding standing in front of the Shuttleworth Sopwith Pup G-EBKY at Elstree on the occasion of the air display held there on 27 July 1947.

FROM WAR TO PEACE

A PHOTOGRAPHER'S VIEW OF BRITISH AVIATION DURING THE 1940s

RICHARD RIDING

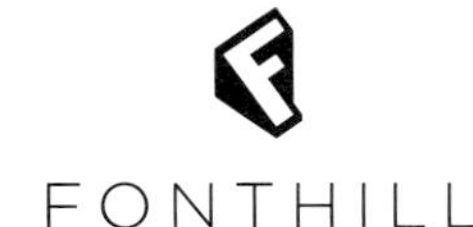

FONTHILL

In loving memory of Jan Chamberlain (1940–2014)
daughter of Flt Lt Douglas Harry Nock, former Herts & Essex Flying Club
and pre-war flying instructor, killed in an Airspeed Oxford
in South Africa on 15 November 1941.

This book is affectionately dedicated to my father E. J. 'Eddie' Riding
(1916–1950) and his pal A. J. Jackson (1911–82) who between them pioneered
an interest in recording and photographing British civil registered aircraft.

I am indebted to my old friend Ray Hankin, a staff member of The Aeroplane
during its final years in the late 1960s, for running his critical eye over the text.
Any errors or howlers are mine alone.

Richard Riding
Radlett 2016

Fonthill Media Language Policy

Fonthill Media publishes in the international English language market. One language edition is published worldwide. As there are minor differences in spelling and presentation, especially with regard to American English and British English, a policy is necessary to define which form of English to use. The Fonthill Policy is to use the form of English native to the author. Richard Riding was born and educated in England therefore British English has been adopted in this publication.

Fonthill Media Limited
Fonthill Media LLC
www.fonthillmedia.com
office@fonthillmedia.com

First published in the United Kingdom
and the United States of America 2016

British Library Cataloguing in Publication Data:
A catalogue record for this book is available from the British Library

ISBN 978-1-78155-331-2

Typeset in 10.5pt on 13pt Sabon
Printed and bound in England

Contents

Introduction

This book is a sequel to *A Flying Life: An Enthusiast's Photographic Record of British Aviation in the 1930s*, an account of my father's first ten years as an amateur aircraft photographer, published by Fonthill Media in 2013.

E. J. 'Eddie' Riding was born at Little Heath, Charlton, south-east London, in the Royal Borough of Greenwich, in February 1916. In 1920 the family moved to Chorlton-cum-Hardy, a suburb of south-west Manchester. His home was close to Wythenshawe and Woodford and when Barton opened in 1929 E.J.R. began keeping a log of all aircraft that passed over his home.

After acquiring a camera the same year he began taking photographs at local aerodromes and with the acquisition of a push bike, later ventured further afield to Hooton Park, Blackpool and all points north. Still later, in company with his pal Jimmy Ellison (J.G.E.), he toured the country in a trusty Austin Seven and by the outbreak of war in 1939 had accumulated a considerable collection of photographs, mostly of British civil-registered aircraft. This collection, together with those taken by J.G.E., formed the basis of *A Flying Life*.

In 1939 there was a parting of the ways. E.J.R got married and moved south to Middlesex, his family having already relocated to Dorset. J.G.E. remained 'north of Watford', to work for F. Hills & Sons in Manchester. After the war he moved to Stockton-on-Tees while E.J.R. remained in Middlesex, living in Hayes, near to Fairey Aviation's factory, his initial posting as an inspector for the Aeronautical Inspection Directorate (AID). After being transferred by the AID to London Aircraft Production at Leavesden in 1942, E.J.R. moved to Hendon where he remained for the rest of his short life. Although the two pals kept in contact, meetings were few and far between, both having started families. E.J.R. continued photographing aircraft but J.G.E. took very few after the outbreak of the Second World War.

He thought he was alone in his quest to add to his collection until he received a letter from another like-minded individual that heralded a new source of photographs and the start of a firm friendship. In March 1943 E.J.R. received a letter from A. J. Jackson (A.J.J.) and I can do no better than quote from his reply, dated 27 March:

Dear Mr. Jackson,

I was very glad to get a letter from you. We seem to have heard about each other since the early part of 1939. I wish to God we could have met in those days (when there was something to photograph). What yards of film we could have got through together!

Since 1929 I have been taking photographs of civil aircraft, and Service types when they cropped up, and that only at rare intervals in those days. But my interest has always been in something with registration letters on it. My first batch was taken with a film pack 'Brownie' at the Manchester 'Airport' (temp) Wythenshawe. I won't bore you with descriptions of those good old days except to mention a respect and affection for Avro 504Ks, which has neither faded nor diminished throughout the years.

The first lot of photos consisted of the D.H. 9C G-EBIG, Genet Avro Avians G-AACF and 'DL, Avro 504Ks G-EBKB and 'EASF. The last pictures I took (officially) were at Broxbourne just before war started—the Tomtit G-AEXD and the Dart Kitten G-AEXT.

However, to get to the crux of the matter: Will you let me have a list of all my stuff that you require? I think I can manage to let you have the stuff within a few weeks as my stock of photographic material is fairly good and I still do a considerable amount for illustrating articles and books.

I keep intending to re-organise my collection and run it along the same lines as yours, i.e. in alphabetical registration order, but the nearest I've got to that is to have them in book form, postcard size, with details attached to the back of each photo. So far I've done around 150, but what with long hours etc. the going is rather hard.

The collection as it stands consists of five albums. One is a historical record, consisting of *Flight* and *The Aeroplane* photos, and other dubious sources. John Yoxall [*Flight's* photographer], being a friend of mine, permits me to browse amongst their negatives and prints them for me at one-third reduction.

The others are arranged in alphabetical order of aerodromes visited, these being only my own photographs, and are contained in two large 24-inch × 18-inch albums. The other two are: a collection of individual types and a historical record of joy-riding firms, which is my prize possession.

I managed to visit 74 different aerodromes before war started, but I fancy this looks pretty elementary against what I heard concerning your activities in this direction.

Could you by any chance revise your decision regarding the process of swapping? Activities are so curtailed now in our particular line that the only recreation permissible, and the only way in which one can enlarge ones collection, is by finding someone else who is interested. I already have one of yours—a side view of the old Cygnet 'MB at Brooklands—Walton gave it to me in '39. Mine are mostly the same size—(116), a size which, in my opinion, is about the most suitable for this type of work.

I once cycled 95 miles to get a picture of S.E.5A G-EBIB—probably do it again tomorrow in spite of the pain it would entail! In later years we [E.J.R. and J.G.E.] acquired a very ancient and dilapidated Austin 7 for the magnificent sum of £4, which enlarged our scope considerably. In 1937 we did a tour covering 1,300 miles in our ten days holiday and managed to get to over 20 'new' aerodromes. After the war we had a vehicle each and used to visit separate localities each weekend, comparing notes and, if it was worthwhile, vice versa the following weekend.

We hadn't quite risen to the heights that you and Mason had reached in doing visits by air. In the Manchester district it was a real achievement to 'bum' a ride, even in 1939, to anywhere but within the locality.

I wish we could arrange a meeting some time. I suppose you spend all your leave with your people. I go to South Marston, near Swindon, about once a month and that seems well on the way to Colerne. I wonder if anything could be done about it next time?

Must wind up now; hoping to hear from you again.

A.J.J. replied in the first week of April 1943, enclosing a list of 'wants' taken from the list of 'bags' E.J.R. had sent him. A.J.J. suggested that the two should meet in Bath, easy for E.J.R. to get to by train and not far for A.J.J., who was stationed at RAF Colerne where he was a Sergeant at No. 39 Maintenance Unit. In an eight-page letter dated 14 April E.J.R. began:

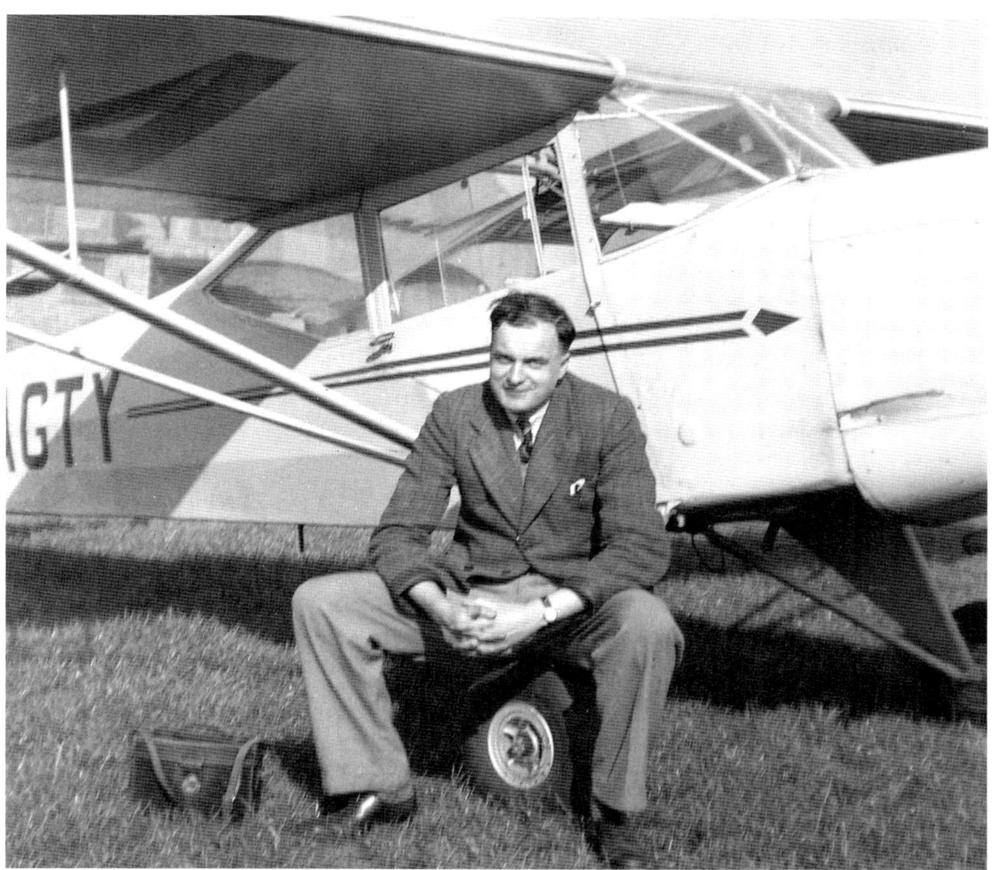

E. J. Riding photographed with Auster Autocrat G-AGTY at Rearsby on 26 March 1946.

Your interesting reminiscences bode well for the time we shall waste in the very near future. I have taken your tip and have arranged to stand for two hours and ten minutes on the 11.15 a.m. from Paddington on Saturday 17th, arriving at Bath at 1.25 p.m. You can no doubt guess how much I'm looking forward to it.

Thus, on the date arranged, E.J.R. and A.J.J. met for the first time, beginning a close friendship that lasted until E.J.R.'s death in April 1950.

Because photography during the war was difficult and often illegal, E.J.R. concentrated on hunting down photographs of pre-war aircraft by writing to likely sources such as *Flight*, *The Aeroplane*, press agencies, old pilots and aircraft manufacturers. Even this innocent pastime had its hazardous moments. In April 1944 he wrote to a photographer in Morecambe, asking for photographs of Avro 504Ks taken the 1920s. In a letter to A.J.J. he wrote:

The arm of the law reached out and grabbed E.J.R. last week. The photographer at Morecambe handed my letter to the local constabulary (anything dealing with aeroplane photographs nowadays is liable to suspicion—1928 vintage included). The result was a cop in plain clothes, notebook in hand, at No. 17 last Monday week. Needless to say he went away quite satisfied with my insanity.

Added to this oversensitivity regarding photography, film and photographic paper was in short supply. In the same letter E.J.R. gave a useful tip to Sgt A.J.J.:

I've heard that Kodak will send films to Service men (HQ are in London, no doubt you have the address). What about spinning them the old story: i.e. miles from civilisation, wife and two babes etc., etc.? I could use a couple of 116 Verichromes right now!

Meantime, E.J.R. had sent A.J.J. a list of J.G.E.'s predominantly pre-war negative collection and all three were fast adding to their respective stockpiles. In addition, E.J.R. advertised in *The Aeroplane* of 4 June 1943 for like-minded collectors to contact him. At that time a small core of British civil aircraft enthusiasts kept in touch, keeping up to date with the Air Registration Board's (ARB) British Civil Register via Leslie T. Mason (known as the 'Masonic Gentleman'), who subscribed to the register. Before the war Mason and Jackson used to visit Croydon every fortnight; the former taking photographs, the latter scribbling away in a notebook. Mason too served in the RAF during the war, but was not demobbed until 1947. Whilst he was serving in Italy the ARB registers were sent to E.J.R.

Two other enthusiasts were N. H. B. Walter, known as 'Nim', and a chap called Nicholson. Later on Chris H. Barnes joined the circle, the possessor of some 4,000 aircraft photographs. Though he specialised in an earlier era, Barnes was later to produce definitive histories of Short Brothers and Handley Page for the Putnam's aeronautical list. Another member was C. Nepean Bishop, a former RAF flying instructor in Rhodesia, who after the war worked in a bank and looked the part.

In appearance he was not unlike Captain Mainwaring of 'Dad's Army'. But at weekends he morphed into one of the country's foremost aerobatic display pilots, usually flying Tiger Moths with the Redhill-based Tiger Club. The club even named one of its Tigers *The Bishop* in his honour. Another latecomer to the circle was former RAF pilot Alec Lumsden, like Bishop also a member of the Redhill flying club.

E.J.R. also continued his visits to the *Flight* negative library at Dorset House, spending hours—and lots of cash—on prints, reporting to A.J.J.:

> Will try and get a few hours at *Flight's* office next week—then you'll see the money going up the spout! Boy, when I get in that place discretion goes to the winds—so does Madge's house-keeping money!

Thirty years later, as editor of *Aeroplane Monthly*, the author had the run of the *Flight* photographic library, plus the photographic archive of its defunct weekly predecessor, *The Aeroplane*, for which he was custodian. During the course of a couple of years every negative box in both collections was opened and examined, in many instances E.J.R. having probably been the last to do so.

After their first meeting in April 1943 E.J.R. and A.J.J. met as frequently as possible. The continuing passion for their hobby is well illustrated by a line from a letter written subsequently by E.J.R. to A.J.J.:

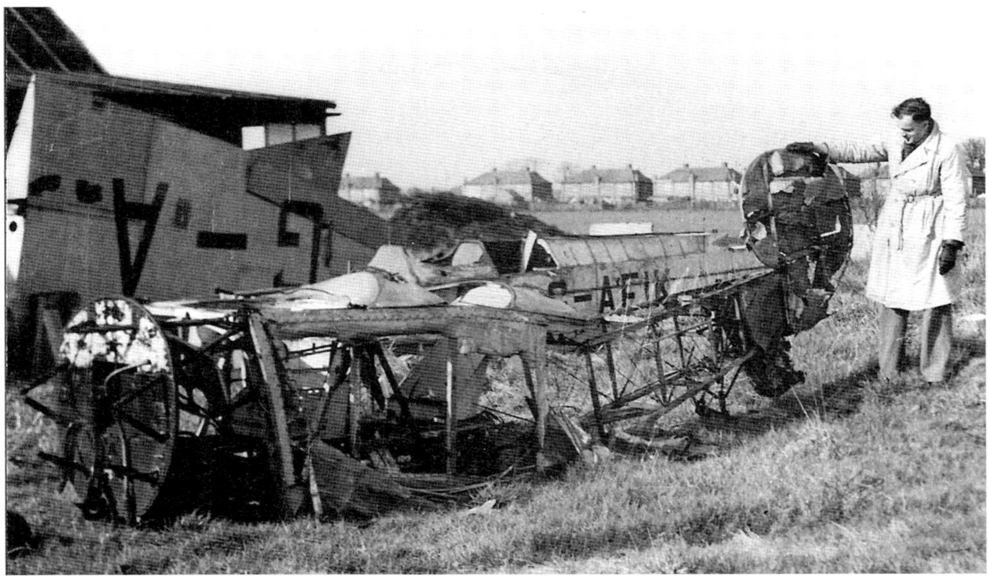

E. J. Riding photographed by A. J. Jackson examining the mortal remains of an anonymous Avro 504K at Hanworth in 1947. In the background can be seen the wings and fuselage of dumped B.A. Swallow 2 G-AFIK, first delivered to Blackburn Aircraft Ltd at Brough in 1938 and later acquired by the Peterborough Flying Club before joining the London Air Park Flying Club's large fleet at Hanworth on the eve of war in 1939.

I shall be like a cat on hot bricks until we hear from Blackburn's; if only we can land G-EBLA [an Avro 504K once based at Brough]. I shall go to church every Sunday for the rest of this year [it was then June].

A. J. Jackson

Aubrey Joseph Jackson, known as 'Jack', Jacko or A.J.J. (his Christian names were a closely guarded secret), was born in Manor Park, London, on 19 October 1911 and educated at Southend High School for Boys. He was fascinated by aircraft from an early age and his interest in civil aircraft and aircraft registrations was fired by one particular photograph printed in *The Meccano Magazine*, of which he was an avid reader in the early 1920s. The photograph featured one of the first British aircraft to carry a civil registration and since the letters on the fuselage puzzled him, he decided to find out about them. Thus the seeds were sown for a life-long obsession.

Like E.J.R., from the age of 15 he kept a spotting notebook. He too had a father who was a keen amateur photographer and soon A.J.J. combined the two interests that evolved into one of the most complete photographic records of British civil registered aircraft. His ultimate aim was to collect a photograph of every single British civil aircraft and to record its history. Unbeknown to him, up in Manchester E.J.R. had embarked on the same plan, though A.J.J. had a head start of several years.

A.J.J. trained as a teacher, taking up a post at East Ham School. When war broke out in September 1939 the school was evacuated to Weston-super-Mare and A.J.J. joined the RAF. Stationed at No. 39 Maintenance Unit at RAF Colerne, Wiltshire, he worked on Spitfires and it was from here that he started corresponding with E.J.R. Early in their association they found they had something else in common—each had a wife named Marjorie. When the Ridings and Jackson families first met the author and eldest son David Jackson, both under a year old, shared a pram for an afternoon. Seventy-three years on we are still in contact, but not quite so intimately!

After the war A.J.J. settled at Leigh-on-Sea, Essex, and at nearby Rochford aerodrome (later called Southend) in 1947 learnt to fly on Tiger Moths, a type that remained dear to his heart and on which he became an authority. The author recalls being told that during one instruction flight A.J.J. was ordered to climb straight ahead to 5,000 feet. The retort to his instructor was: 'You're no longer in the RAF and as I'm paying we'll level out at 1,000 feet!' He later set up the Rochford Hundred Flying Group at Southend, operating Auster types originally, and was an enthusiastic and active member of the Redhill-based Tiger Club.

E.J.R. encouraged and commissioned A.J.J. to write for *Air Review* and other publications from the Eaton Bray-based Harborough Publishing Company in the post-war period. They also drove and flew to airfields all over the country at weekends in pursuit of their hobby. E.J.R. was fortunate in that aviation was still very much part of his job; A.J.J. on the other hand had gone back to full-time teaching.

In 1948 both were dismayed when the fortnightly *Aeroplane Spotter* newspaper ceased publication in July. First published as a weekly in January 1941, the publication survived wartime paper rationing and the extraordinary ban on advertising in new publications started during wartime. Both men had been contributing letters and photographs to this revered paper from time to time and its demise left a void in the aircraft spotters' world. The penultimate issue carried a whole page announcing the formation of Air-Britain on 1 July (with the motto 'The Air is our Concern') that was to be administered by a full-time staff and charging *7s 6d* for membership. A.J.J. was instrumental in its birth and began editing the organisation's *British Civil Aviation News* (*BCAN*). That led to his Register Review column in *Air Pictorial* that ran for more than 30 years. He is best known for his epic British *Civil Aircraft* series of books, first published by Putnam & Company in 1959 as a two volume set and later revised and expanded to three volumes so that the scope for each ran from 1919 to 1972. They are recognised as the standard references on the subject and the first editions were dedicated to 'Eddie Riding'.

After E.J.R.'s death in April 1950 the Jackson and Riding families kept in regular contact. Following in the slipstream of *British Civil Aircraft*, A.J.J. produced *De Havilland Aircraft since 1909*, *Avro Aircraft since 1908* and *Blackburn Aircraft since 1909*, all while still holding down a full-time teaching job. The writing task was made all the more easier by the support he received from wife Marjorie, entrusted with the mammoth task of typing the manuscripts. A.J.J. also found time to write a children's book for MacDonald Educational, entitled *Air Travel*.

His seemingly irrepressible enthusiasm juddered to a temporary halt in July 1974 with the sudden death of Marjorie, but his life-long interest pulled him out of the abyss and in time he returned to his typewriter and camera with vigour. He remarried in 1978 and was in the middle of revising his 'bible' on Blackburn Aircraft when he succumbed to a heart condition that had stopped him from flying solo in the 1970s, passing away peacefully while watching snooker on TV on the evening of 27 October 1982.

The enduring legacy of the unique A. J. Jackson aircraft negative collection is housed at the Brooklands Museum, under the charge of his eldest son, Wg Cdr David Jackson (RAF Ret'd).

Collecting Continues

By the late 1940s there was intense activity amongst members of the circle to build up their individual collections, new contacts being tracked down and cajoled into parting with yet more photographs. While both E.J.R. and A.J.J. had ambitions of securing photographs of every pre-war British civil aircraft, fate stopped the former from realisation whereas A.J.J. continued collecting right up to his death, 32 years after the loss of his pal.

Following E.J.R.'s death in April 1950 my mother had the good sense to hang on to the invaluable collection of negatives and prints accumulated over a period of 21 years. This became a constant reminder to me of my father's passion for aeroplanes and not unnaturally I caught the bug. In later years I realised that though my father had kept detailed records of many of his activities there appeared to be no comprehensive record of his negative collection, giving dates and locations of his hundreds of visits to aerodromes.

When A.J.J. died in 1982 his collection was administered by his younger son, Roger, until his own tragic early death in 2004. Shortly after Roger's funeral, the Jackson family presented me with a parcel. On opening it, I was overjoyed to discover that not only did it contain my father's letters to A.J.J., but also a book recording chronologically details of every aircraft E.J.R. had photographed since 1929. Shortly before his death he had obviously lent it to A.J.J. and it had laid gathering dust for more than 50 years. Needless to say, this treasure trove has been invaluable in compiling the second of two volumes that together chart the 20 plus years of what some would argue were the golden years of aviation in Britain.

This pictorial account of the second decade of E.J.R.'s aviation life story begins in January 1940 and the start of his wartime employment with the AID when seconded to Fairey Aviation's Hayes factory, where Swordfish and Albacores were being produced for the Royal Navy's Fleet Air Arm. Surreptitiously or otherwise and whenever able, he captured for posterity a fascinating kaleidoscope of aircraft of the era. Now, with this book, it is my pleasure to be able to share just some of his pictures with others.

Richard Riding

1

From 'Apple Cores' to 'Streamlined Bricks' (1940–45)

> I now manage to fly in every machine I sign out as
> airworthy, which is of course as it should be.
>
> Letter from E. J. Riding to A. J. Jackson.

The last occasion that E. J. Riding (E.J.R.) photographed aircraft before war was declared on Germany on 3 September 1939 was at Broxbourne and Maylands, Essex, on 27 August, where he added Dart Kitten G-AEXT, Hawker Tomtit G-AEXE and D.H. 83 Fox Moth G-ABVI to his rapidly expanding collection of photographs of British civil registered aircraft. Rather than risk being arrested for pursuing his hobby, E.J.R. relied subsequently on tracking down photographs of elusive aircraft by contacting other collectors or visiting the offices of *The Aeroplane* and *Flight*. By those means he managed to add some 200 or so 'new' aircraft to his collection during the war.

In the meantime he was still employed by the Aeronautical Inspection Directorate (AID) and in January 1940 was an inspector seconded to the Fairey Aviation Company Ltd at its Hayes, Middlesex, factory. Here he was engaged in the inspection of Swordfish and Albacore biplanes destined for the Royal Navy's Fleet Air Arm. After inspection aircraft were taken by road to Fairey's Great West Aerodrome (FGWA) and checked again before undergoing contractors' handling trials. Up to the beginning of the war E.J.R. had accumulated around 19 hours flying, but had to wait until 1941 before getting airborne once more.

Throughout 1940 E.J.R. was employed almost wholly on the inspection of Albacores. Designed to replace the Swordfish, and though an improvement in many respects, the Albacore was, according to Tony Taylor, former RAF test pilot and Air Transport Auxiliary (ATA) ferry pilot, 'an example of the over-development of a successful but long obsolescent formula.' Terence Horsley, a former Fleet Air Arm pilot, described it as a 'gentleman's Swordfish' with all 'mod cons'. Designed to meet Air Ministry Specification S.41/36 of February

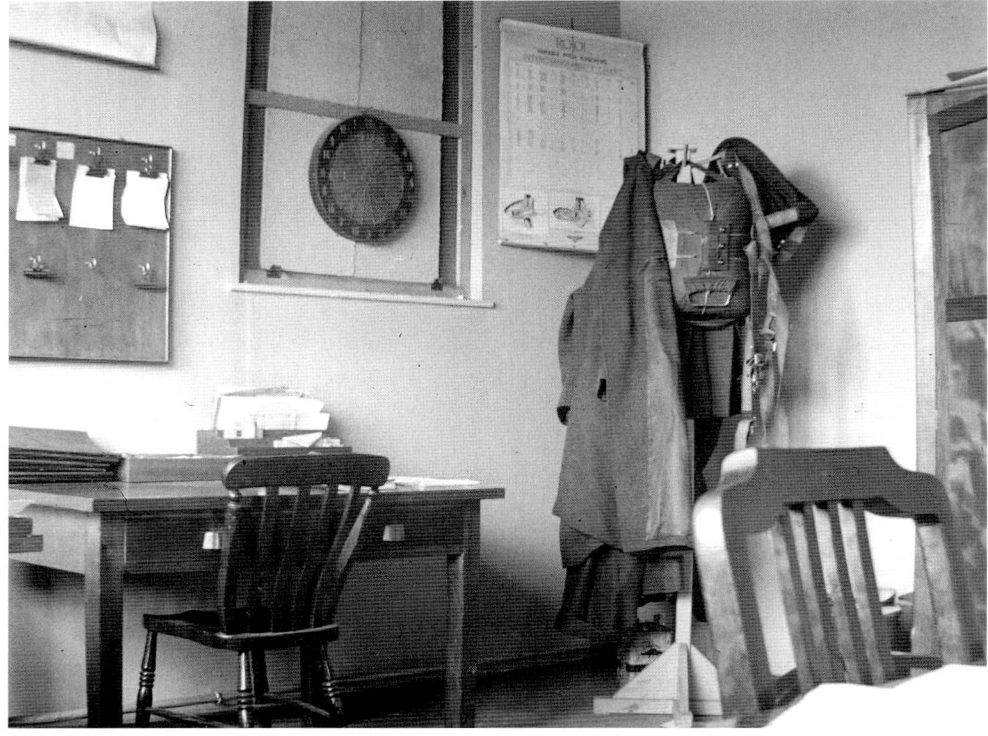

The spartan AID office at Fairey's Great West Aerodrome in April 1942. Note the dartboard and parachutes hanging on the coat stand.

1937, improvements included a heated enclosed cockpit, windscreen wiper, an automatic dinghy-launching system in case of ditching, a variable pitch propeller, hydraulically-operated flaps and even a lavatory of sorts!

The prototype Albacore, L7074, was first flown by Foster H. Dixon from FGWA on 12 December 1938. It received unfavourable comment following A&AEE trials of third prototype L7076 in the summer 1940. Of points in its favour good diving characteristics was one, though the elevators and ailerons were judged to be heavy. But the rear cockpit was cold and draughty despite cabin heating, and during summer the extensive glazing made the cockpit uncomfortably hot. Although the Albacore was virtually unspinable, certainly with the wing slots free, it had an uncomfortable stall, the wing dropping in either direction. But with slots locked the aircraft would not stall fully, remaining steady at a high rate of sink. The A&EE found the Albacore difficult for the pilot to climb aboard and pilots were later warned that the deck-arrester gear lever could easily be mistaken for the flap handle and if the hook was inadvertently dropped it could not be retracted again, with serious consequences.

Production of the Albacore began at Hayes in 1939 with L7076 later flown as a seaplane. Problems with the 1,065 hp Bristol Taurus II delayed initial production but these were resolved with subsequent upgrade to the 1,130 hp Bristol Taurus

XXII. Interestingly, E.J.R.'s flying logbook notes that the horsepower of these engines was 1,050 hp and 1,030 hp respectively. He was involved with aircraft in the X8940-9290 and BF584-777 serial range, all built at Hayes. Of the total 800 produced, including prototypes, only one example survives; a composite of N4389 and N4172 is exhibited statically at the Fleet Air Arm Museum at RNAS Yeovilton.

Armament consisted of a fixed forward-firing gun in the upper starboard wing, and single or twin gas-operated Vickers K guns in the rear cockpit. The Albacore could carry an 18-inch 1,600 lb torpedo or four 500 lb (or six 250 lb) bombs on wing racks.

The first unit to receive the Albacore was No. 826 Squadron at RNAS Ford in March 1940; it was also the first squadron to use the type on operations. The first squadrons to embark Albacores on a carrier were Nos 826 and 829, on HMS *Formidable* in November 1941. They escorted convoys to Cape Town and took part in the Battle of Cape Matapan in March 1941. Most Albacore squadrons had been re-equipped with Barracudas by the end of 1943.

Altogether, Albacores were operated by 14 FAA plus two RCAF squadrons. The Swordfish on the other hand remained in first line service with nine FAA squadrons until the beginning of 1945, the last until June. E.J.R. flew on more than 40 Albacore contractor's handling trials, all from FGWA, with Fairey test pilots Vernon Gorry-Wilson, Foster H. Dixon and Christopher Staniland, between March 1941 and April 1942. Most flights were of short duration to check for left or right wing low flying characteristics and consisted essentially of dives and stalls. Fairey's Great West Aerodrome (later Heathrow).

The Great West Aerodrome came into being because Fairey Aviation was forced to move from RAF Northolt, where it had been flight-testing aircraft built at its Hayes factory, to a more suitable location on which to build an airfield for its exclusive use. In 1928 a large tract of prime market garden land was purchased south of the A4 Bath Road, not far from the village of Heathrow. Known initially as Harmondsworth Aerodrome, the all-grass field was opened officially in June 1930 and had a maximum run of 3,300 ft with Fairey accommodated in the north corner in a hangar reputed at the time to be the world's largest. The aerodrome was soon to witness a steady stream of aircraft on test, ranging from Fairey IIIFs to Swordfish and Albacores. The airfield also played host to pre-war Royal Aeronautical Society garden parties, an important showcase for the country's aviation industry, normally held each year in May.

In 1943 the airfield was requisitioned, ostensibly to be developed into a 'Transport RAF Terminal Station'. In fact, the airfield and much of the surrounding land was earmarked as a future London Airport and by acquiring FGWA and the area around it for military purposes a public enquiry was averted. Fairey Aviation's plans to move its factory from Hayes to FGWA were thus scuppered. Eventually it moved to Heston from where, in 1947, it was again evicted by the Air Ministry moving its factory finally to White Waltham.

Ownership of what had now become known as Heathrow passed from the Air Ministry to the Ministry of Civil Aviation on 1 January 1946, by which time its

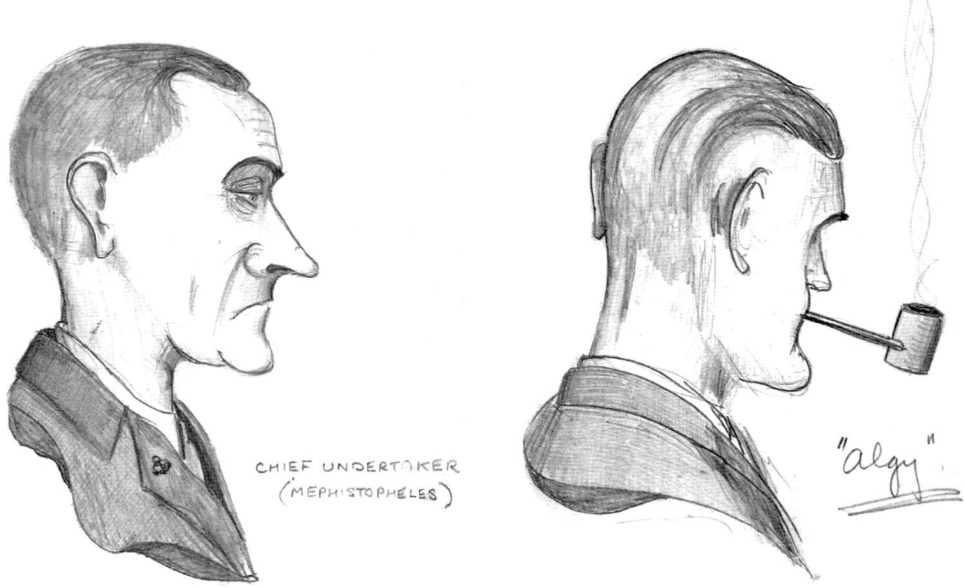

Above left : 1941 pencilled caricature by E.J.R. of an unidentified member of the AID at Fairey Aviation, Hayes, entitled *Chief Undertaker (Mephistopheles).*

Above right: Another 1941 pencilled caricature by E.J.R., this time of colleague 'Algy' Watson from the AID office at Fairey Aviation.

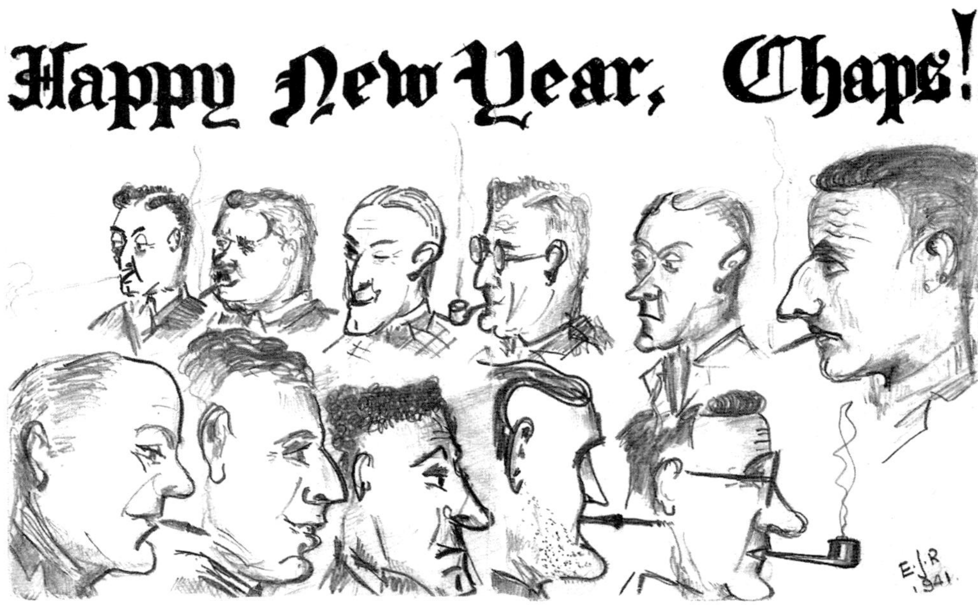

For New Year 1941 E.J.R. produced pencilled caricatures of his colleagues working in the AID department at the Fairey Aviation Company Ltd., at Hayes, Middlesex. The only person recognisable is 'Algy' Watson, bottom row, second right.

development into an international airport was far from complete. The official opening took place on 31 May when the site was still a shambolic muddy mess littered with tents and prefabricated huts masquerading as offices and passenger terminals. Finally, by 1947, the three new runways were in operation and a four-phase plan was executed to provide an improved North Terminal. This work was completed by the early 1950s, by which time plans were afoot for further expansion.

E.J.R.'s association with FGWA began when he accompanied Chris Staniland on two short test flights in Fairey Albacore N4285 on 2 March 1941. His final flights from the aerodrome were made on 12 April 1942 with Foster H. Dixon in Albacore BF636.

Whilst E.J.R. worked away at Fairey's, significant events were happening in aviation and in the wider world. On 24 February 1940 the first flight took place of the Sabre-engined Hawker Typhoon, P5212, flown by Philip Lucas and on the 27th the prototype Blackburn Firebrand, DD804, took to the air for the first time.

On 10 May Prime Minister Neville Chamberlain resigned and the war took a turn for the worse when Germany invaded Holland, Belgium and Luxemburg. The Dutch capitulated on the 14th and the following day the RAF mounted its first large-scale raid on German industrial targets in the Ruhr. On 30 May the evacuation from Dunkirk began and was completed on 3–4 June. Of more particular interest to Fairey Aviation were the first operational sorties by Albacores of No. 826 Squadron FAA and their bombing of road and rail communications at Westende and attacks on E-boats off Zeebrugge.

British morale took a knock on 8 June when the aircraft carrier HMS *Glorious* was sunk by the *Scharnhorst* and *Gneisenau* whilst returning from Norway. Two days later Italy declared war on the Allies.

The war was brought a step nearer home during 30–31 June with the occupation of Jersey and Guernsey by Germany, ending British communication with the islands. On 23–24 July a Bristol Blenheim made the first wartime flight by a British aircraft over Berlin, though it was made in error and no bombs were dropped.

The newly formed British Overseas Airways Corporation (BOAC) began operations and on the following day Lord Beaverbrook was appointed Minister for Aircraft Production. German bombs fell on Central London for the first time during the night of 24–25 August and on 13 September Buckingham Palace was bombed; although the King and Queen were in residence they were unhurt.

On 17 September Adolf Hitler postponed *Operation Sea Lion*, the planned invasion of Britain, until the spring of 1941. On the night of 14–15 November the Luftwaffe launched a massive attack on Coventry with more than 400 bombers.

The first flight of W4050, bomber version of the D.H.98 Mosquito, took place on 15 November and there was mild excitement at FGWA when test pilot Chris Staniland got airborne for the first time in the dreadful Fairey Barracuda prototype, P1767, Britain's first all-metal monoplane torpedo bomber for carrier operation.

1941

The New Year got off to a bad start when national heroine and aviatrix Amy Johnson, now a First Officer with the Air Transport Auxiliary (ATA), was lost on 5 January. When ferrying Airspeed Oxford V3540 from Squires Gate, Blackpool, to Kidlington, Oxford, she was seen to emerge from cloud and come down in the Thames Estuary. Her former husband, Jim Mollison, always maintained that Amy was shot down by an enemy raider, but it is more likely that, contrary to ATA regulations, Amy was flying above cloud and simply got lost, ran out of fuel and was looking for somewhere to land when she broke cloud. Although some of her effects were recovered subsequently, her body was never found.

On 9 January Avro Lancaster prototype BT308, a converted Manchester III fitted with four Rolls-Royce Merlins instead of the Manchester's two Vultures, made its first flight.

On 4 February E.J.R. had his first wartime flight, in Stinson SR. 10C Reliant G-AFVT, from FGWA with Foster H. Dixon with whom he was to make many flights over the ensuing months. 'VT was owned by Fairey Aviation throughout the war and flown on communications duties. Dixon was born on 14 July 1912, joined the RAF in 1932 and flew with No. 1 Squadron from 1933–36. He took part in the RAF Hendon Displays of 1935 and 1936 and joined Fairey in 1936, becoming chief test pilot in 1942. Dixon was killed flying Fairey Gyrodyne G-AIKF when the helicopter suffered rotor head failure, crashing at Ufton near Reading on 17 April 1949. His flight observer, Derek Garraway, was also killed.

During the first week in March E.J.R traded in his old Austin Seven (See *A Flying Life*) and acquired Austin '65' AXN352, clocking up 800 miles in the first month! Earlier, on 2 March, he had the first of many Albacore flights—two short test flights in N4285 with Christopher Staniland.

Christopher S. Staniland (1905–1942) was born on 7 October 1905, joining the RAF in 1924 and serving with No. 41(F) Squadron before a posting to the RAF High Speed Flight in 1928. Well known in motor cycle and motor racing circles, he almost beat the Brooklands track record of 143 mph in 1935. Joining Simmonds Aircraft Ltd as a test pilot in 1929, Staniland moved to Fairey Aviation in a similar role. He piloted several prototype Fairey types on first flights, including G.4/31 K3905, S.9/30 S1706, TSR.II (Swordfish prototype) K4190, Fantome F-6/G-ADIF, Battle K4303 and Barracuda P1767. He was killed testing the second Firefly prototype, Z1827, on 4 June 1942 following elevator over-balance and collapse of the tail unit at low level, possibly caused by the cockpit hood detaching and hitting the empennage.

During the night of 11–12 May the first Halifax bombing raid was carried out by No. 35 Squadron on targets at Le Havre. The previous night Rudolf Hess, Germany's Deputy Fuhrer, acting as a personal and unauthorised peace emissary, had flown a Messerschmitt Me 110 from Germany to Scotland, bailing out near Glasgow. For his efforts he was imprisoned in the Tower of London.

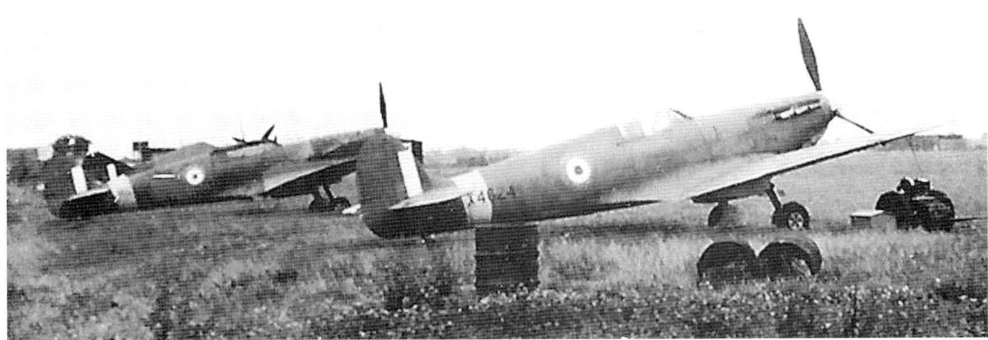

Supermarine Spitfire I X4624 at FGWA in July 1941. A former 54 Squadron aircraft this Spitfire was an aerodrome defence aircraft until it was transferred to 52 OTU later that year. It was built at Woolston, Southampton and first flown in October 1940. It was taken off RAF charge in March 1945 and probably scrapped.

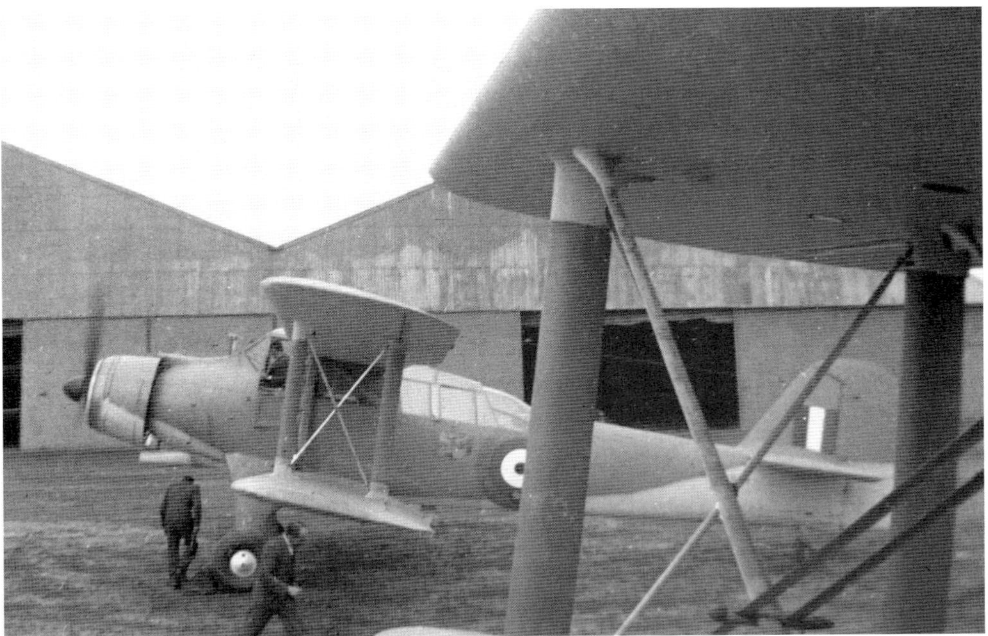

Photographed from another Albacore at Fairey's Great West Aerodrome in January 1942, X9151's 1,050 hp Bristol Taurus has been started prior to an early test flight. Built at Hayes at the end of 1941, X9151 was delivered to No. 820 Squadron FAA in January 1942 and subsequently served with Nos 831 and 783 Squadrons.

On 15 May the first flight of W4052, fighter version of the D.H. 98 Mosquito, was made from a field adjacent to Salisbury Hall, Hertfordshire, by Geoffrey de Havilland Jnr. In the evening of the same day P. E. G. Sayer made the first flight of Gloster E.28/39 W4041 from RAF Cranwell. It lasted 17 minutes and the jet age, for Britain at least, had arrived. Yet the RAF's first jet fighters, Gloster Meteor Is of No. 616 Squadron, would not enter service until July 1944.

On 10 June W4051, the third Mosquito variant, made its first flight. This photo-reconnaissance version was the first of the breed to enter service with the RAF and also the first to fly operationally.

On 12 September E.J.R. had his first flight with Fairey test pilot Vernon Gorry-Wilson. They flew in Tipsy 2-seater F-0222, accompanying a Fairey P4/34 to Farnborough, probably K7555, used as a flying mock-up for the Fulmar, and which in 1941 K7555 was fitted with retractable Fairey-Youngman flaps and was flown to RAE Farnborough. Of all the Fairey test pilots with which he flew, Gorry-Wilson was the one for which E.J.R. had the most respect.

Capt. Vernon Gorry-Wilson (1902–42) was born in Stockport on 12 July 1902. He began his aviation career apprenticed with A. V. Roe, joining the RAF in 1919 and serving until 1930, initially flying marine aircraft at home, later flying in Iraq as an instructor. On leaving the RAF Gorry-Wilson joined Imperial Airways, flying the Karachi–Darwin sector of the first England–Australia air mail. He was the pilot and only survivor when flying boat Short S. 8 Calcutta G-AASJ *City of Khartoum* crashed into the sea off Alexandria after running out of fuel on the night of 31 December 1935. Gorry-Wilson later flew with International Air Freight before joining Jersey Airways Ltd at the end of 1938, remaining with the airline until German occupation of the Channel Islands in 1940. He then joined Fairey Aviation as a test pilot and was killed on 6 November 1942, aged only 40, when the 18th production Fairey Barracuda I (P9661) he was testing spun in near Ringway.

On 12 September DG597, the prototype Airspeed Horsa troop-carrying glider, built at Salisbury Hall and assembled at FGWA was first flown by Airspeed test pilot George Errington. DG597 later underwent further towing trials at FGWA towed by Whitley V P5104 flown by Flt Lt 'Nick' Carter. The glider was afterwards used for RATOG trials.

On 3 October 1941 E.J.R. transferred from Fairey's Hayes factory to FGWA to supervise assembly of Albacore Is. He was responsible for all electrical tests and inspection of completed aircraft prior to flight test and final despatch.

As an interlude from his work on Albacores, during the afternoon of 30 October E.J.R. cadged a ride in A. W. Whitley P5104 with T. W. Woods on a test flight following a 60-hour overhaul. Two dives and a circuit were made over Hanworth Air Park.

During November E.J.R. began regular test flights in Albacores with Foster C. Dixon and Vernon Gorry-Wilson. The flights lasted anything from five to 50 minutes but mostly averaged 10 minutes following correction of minor snags, such as left or right wing low, tail heaviness etc.

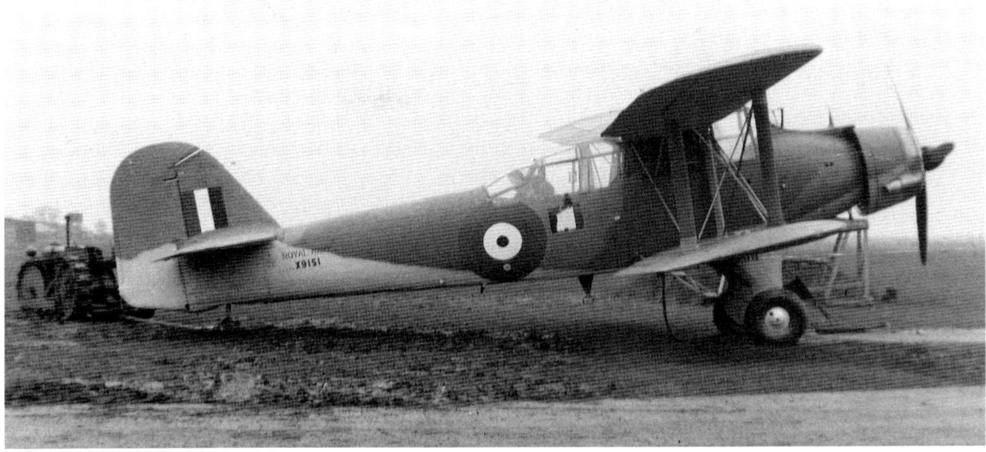

Fairey Albacore I X9151 awaiting initial flight testing at Fairey's Great West Aerodrome in January 1942. Note the glazing below the rear cockpit and forward of the roundel, providing a clear view through the aircraft's fuselage.

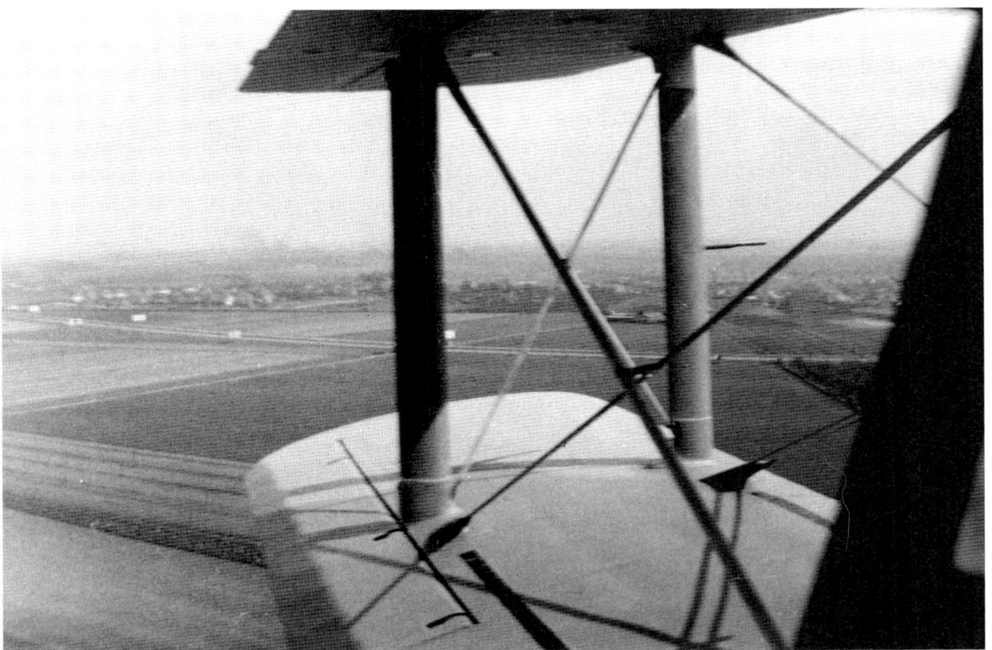

View from the rear cockpit of a Fairey Albacore shortly after take-off from Fairey's Great West Aerodrome in April 1942. The Great West Road is visible in the distance.

British morale received a savage blow on 12 November with the sinking of the aircraft carrier HMS *Ark Royal*, torpedoed and sunk by a German submarine east of Gibraltar.

On 7 December the bombing of Pearl Harbor by Japanese carrier-based aircraft marked the start of war with the USA and Great Britain, both formally declaring war on Japan the following day. Ten days later E.J.R. had a one-hour test flight in Swordfish I L2717 with Foster H. Dixon, taking 30-minutes to attain 10,000 ft. This Swordfish was retained by Fairey and used for dingy stowage and gun trials before passing to E Flight at the RAE and ending its flying career on dive recovery trials with the A&AEE.

On the 22nd prototype Fairey Firefly Z1826 was first flown by Christopher Staniland.

1942

The New Year began with an intensive Albacore test and delivery workload; during the first two months E.J.R. had more than 20 Albacore flights. On 8 February he had the first of many flights with ATA pilot and aviation artist Second Officer Stanley Orton Bradshaw who arrived at FGWA in Fairchild Argus HM177 with an overheating Warner Scarab engine. The problem fixed, Bradshaw gave E.J.R. a couple of circuits by way of reward and from that moment the two men became firm friends.

On 13 February E.J.R. had a third and final flight with Flt Lt Carter in Whitley P5104 from FGWA, towing Horsa DG597 to 6,000 ft for further tests. On the following day he had a 15-minute trip from FGWA with South African Flt Lt George Duff in No. 104 Squadron Vickers Wellington W5431 EP-W based at RAF Driffield. Sadly Duff was killed in the same aircraft on 10 March, the Wellington crashing at Driffield on returning from a raid on Essen.

While E.J.R. was busy clearing Albacores during March, he had more pressing matters on his mind. His wife Madge was overdue with their first child, the author arriving finally with some reluctance, a couple of weeks late on 25 March at nearby Hayes, reportedly during an air raid!

Stirling Work

E.J.R.'s last Albacore test flights took place on 12 April with Foster Dixon in BF636. Five flights were made in this aircraft on contractor's trials to give it a thorough testing. The following day E.J.R. was posted to S. E. Opperman Ltd at the Stuart Works, Borehamwood, Hertfordshire, and the company's factory on the North Circular Road, Stonebridge Park, London, NW10. Now promoted to senior examiner/inspector-in-charge AID, he checked Short Stirling undercarriage assemblies and gear boxes and was responsible additionally for supervision of the North Circular Road factory. Although a step in the right direction, no flying was involved.

The first flight of Miles Martinet LR241 took place on 24 April and during 27–28 April the first operational sorties by Mosquito fighters were made by Mk IIs of

No. 157 Squadron. Another morale booster for Britain occurred on the night of 30–31 May when RAF Bomber Command launched its first Thousand Bomber raid, dropping more than 1,455 tons of bombs on Cologne. During the day of the 31 May the first Mosquito bomber raid was made by the Mk IVs of No. 105 Squadron, also on Cologne.

Following E.J.R.'s work re-location to the north of London the family moved from West Drayton to Hendon, less than a quarter of a mile from the RAF airfield and directly beneath the approach to one of the runways, which pleased E.J.R. greatly, but probably not his wife. Because of frequent air raids houses in the area were not hard to find, many residents having upped sticks and evacuated to quieter areas. When visiting Hendon aerodrome to photograph Jack Savage's skywriting S.E.5As before the war E.J.R. had no inkling that within five years he would migrate from Manchester to settle in the area.

The prototype Avro York, LV626, was first flown on 5 July sporting two fins only, three becoming standard from the third prototype. Tragedy occurred on 25 July when Air Commodore HRH Duke of Kent and all occupants except the tail gunner were killed when their Short Sunderland flew into hills near Wick, Caithness, in poor visibility when on its way to Iceland.

On 2 September the prototype Hawker Tempest V HM595, a converted Typhoon, was first flown and on the 12th the prototype Miles Messenger U-0223, converted from the prototype Miles M.28 Mercury, had its maiden flight from Woodley, Reading.

On 12 December E.J.R. had a 45-minute flight in Short Stirling I R9271 from South Marston with A. L. 'Tom' Brooke-Smith. During the flight, a contractors' handling trial, 'Brookie' took the Stirling to 4,500 ft over Lyneham and Wroughton and attained 260 mph in a dive. R9271 went missing during a raid on Essen on 6 March 1943 when with No. 90 Squadron. E.J.R. had flown previously with Brooke-Smith on 7 May 1939 from Gatwick in a Short Scion. Many years later 'Brookie' visited the author's office at *Aeroplane Monthly* and signed his name in the appropriate columns in E.J.R's flying log book.

1943

For the first six months of 1943 E.J.R.'s feet remained firmly on *terra firma* and his camera in its case for the entire year. On 4 February the unarmed prototype Bristol Buckingham DX249 was first flown and the first flight of a Gloster Meteor, fifth prototype DG206, was made by Michael Daunt from RAF Cranwell on 5 March.

A welcome fillip to morale for beleaguered Britain was news of the successful bombing of three German dams. On the night of 16–17 May 19 Avro Lancaster bombers of No. 617 Squadron, led by the legendary Wg Cdr Guy Gibson, bombed successfully the Mohne, Eder and Sorpe dams. Eight aircraft and 54 RAF crewmen were lost and Gibson was awarded the Victoria Cross for his heroism.

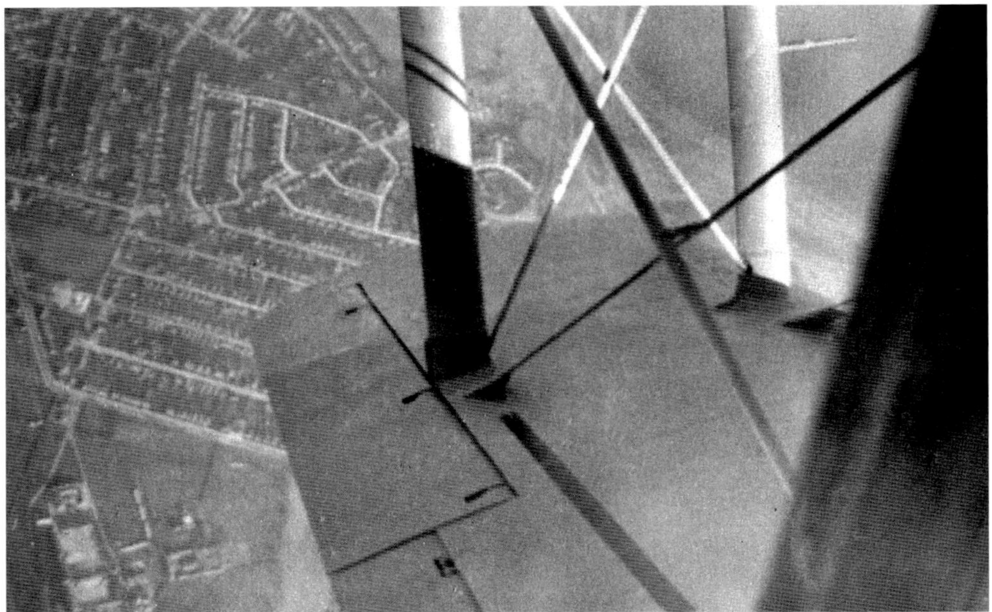

Staines and the adjacent reservoir seen from an Albacore at 6,000 ft in a climbing turn. Test flights lasted anything from 5 to 15 minutes depending on what checks had to be carried out. Invariably short flights followed correction for left or right wing low. Contractor's handling trials were usually of 15 minutes duration.

As a taste of things to come E.J.R. had his first flight in a Handley Page Halifax on 19 June, from Radlett with Sqn Ldr T. V. Mitchell, carrying out contractors' handling trials on Mk II HR921. During the flight they climbed to 7,000 ft and reached 330 mph in the ensuing dive, E.J.R also recording a landing speed of 110 mph.

In the aftermath, E.J.R. wrote to A. J. Jackson (A.J.J.) eulogising about the experience:

Last Saturday p.m. (19 June 1943) was the epitome of bliss. I had a ride in a Halifax Mk II Series 1A (HR921). It lasted 50 minutes and we went down beyond Reading, almost as far as Newbury. I climbed into the dorsal turret after the take-off and stayed there until asked to go forward for the trimming trials, finishing up in the bomb-aimer's seat in the nose. It was a lovely day and we skimmed down valleys of clouds, taking some like hurdles and ploughing through the big ones. There were only three of us on board including the pilot, one Sqn Ldr Mitchell. Only one complaint—it was too darned hot. I sat up in my bird cage roasting slowly. They ought to put ventilators in these kites. Anti-climax; on getting home, full of the joys of living, I burst into Madge with the news—you can guess the rest. I dunno, but these women don't seem to have any soul.

And talking of Handley Page and Radlett, the firm's futuristic H.P. 75 Manx, H-0222, made its first flight on 25 June in the hands of James Talbot. Sadly, Talbot was to lose his life in the crash of Handley Page Hermes G-AGSS on its maiden flight on 2 December 1945.

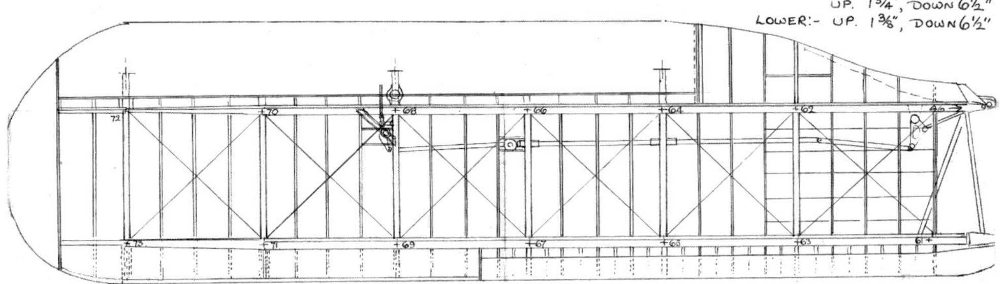

FRONT SPAR.

JT.	SPAR	RIB	SPAR.
61	82'55	X	82'55
63	82'74	82'87	82'74
65	82'74	82'67	82'74
67	82'75	82'87	82'74
69	82'86	82'86	EYE BOLT
71	M.2 44 M. 33	2 M.32	M.34 M.45
73.	M.31 M.32	M.31 M.42	

JT.	SPAR	RIB	SPAR.
46	X	X	X
62	82'74	82'87	82'74
64	82'74	82'88	82'74
66	82'75	82'87	82'75.
68	82'79	82'86	EYE BOLT
70	M.33.	M.32	M.33.
72.	M.31 M.32.	M.31 M.32.	M.33 HEAD REAR

E.J.R.'s plans of the starboard upper and lower mainplane from one of his handwritten AID Fairey Albacore notebooks. After inspection of Albacore parts and equipment for which he was responsible, E.J.R. applied his personal AID stamp (A.I.D. 14. K.) so that in the event of a crash or malfunction the inspector responsible for checking the aircraft's structure could be traced.

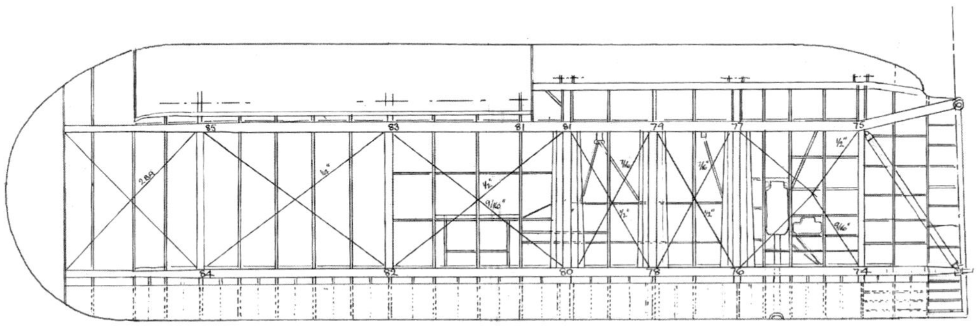

FRONT SPAR

JT	SPAR	RIB	SPAR.
74	H 45.	D.76320 STB 82/87	82'85.
76	82'75	82'87	82'75.
78	82'75	82'87	82'75.
80	82'75	82'810	82'85.
82	82'86	82'86	EYE BOLT.
84	2 M.32.	2 M.32	2 M33.
WING TIP	2 M.35	2 M.31.	

REAR SPAR.

JT.	SPAR	RIB	SPAR.
75	82'55	82'88	82'75
77	82'85	82'87	82'75
79	82'75	82'87	82'75
81	82'75 89	82'87	82'85.
83	82'69.	82'88	EYE BOLT
85	M.33 M.47.	3 M.32	M.33 M.47
WING TIP		2 M.31.	2 M35

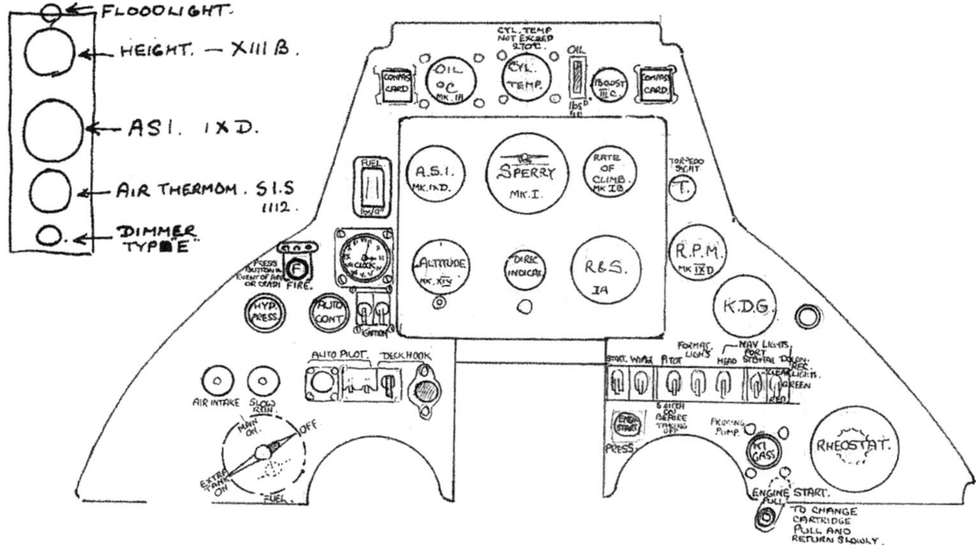

E.J.R.'s rough hand-drawn diagram of the instrument panel taken from one of his Fairey Albacore notebooks.

Another futuristic shape took to the air for the first time on 10 July in the form of the all-wood, tandem-winged Miles M.39B Libellula, a five-eighth scale test model of the company's bomber project.

On 24 August E.J.R. had another flight in a Short Stirling with Tom Brooke-Smith, this time in EF508 from South Marston and again on contractors' handing trials. As well as climbing to 7,000 ft for stall tests Swindon and its famous railway works were overflown at low level.

Leavesden and the London Aircraft Production Group

On 6 September E.J.R. was posted again, this time to London Aircraft Production Group (LAPG), Leavesden Aerodrome and tasked with inspection of Handley Page Halifax IIs and IIIs prior to flight.

Leavesden was built on a 300-acre site purchased from Watford Corporation by the Government in 1940. A 3,033 ft runway was laid and two large factory complexes and adjacent hangars erected. No. 1 Factory was leased to LAPG to assemble an eventual 710 Halifax IIs and IIIs. The first Leavesden-assembled example took to the air on 8 December 1941, the last, B Mk III PN640 named *London Pride*, was rolled out on 16 April 1945.

The second factory complex, No. 2, built and run by de Havilland, was leased to the Second Aircraft Group (SAG) where D.H. 98 Mosquito Mks III, 30, 33 and 36 were assembled. The first Leavesden-born Mosquito, T.III W4075, was rolled out in January 1942 and flown to nearby Hatfield for further testing. Mosquito production at Leavesden totalled 1,390, ending with a batch of 163 Mosquito NF.36s, the last being delivered in March 1947. When military contracts ceased in 1946 the airfield was later turned over to civilian use, mainly the servicing and repair of de Havilland aircraft and engines. Beginning in 1954 Leavesden produced both piston engines and gas turbines, continuing to do so when de Havilland was absorbed into Hawker Siddeley. In 1961 the site was sold to Bristol Siddeley Engines and passed eventually to the Rolls-Royce Aero Engine Division, producing mostly small gas turbines for helicopters, though the airfield was still leased by the Ministry of Defence via a property agency.

During its later years Leavesden was also a publicly-licensed airfield and home to many flying clubs, maintenance companies and charter companies. By the 1990s Rolls-Royce was receiving fewer orders for engines and spares, announcing closure of its Leavesden factory in May 1991 and moving out completely by June 1993. The airfield became unlicensed and the last recorded operational movement was in March 1994. Today the entire site is occupied by Warner Bros. Studio, having become one of the largest film production studios in Europe and spawning the highly successful Harry Potter series of feature films.

When E.J.R. arrived at LAPG Halifax IIs in the JN serial range were being produced. His first flight on a contractor's trial was with T. W. Morton on 8 September in JN942, during which a climb to 7,000 ft was made followed by a 320 mph dive. E.J.R. was to have many such flights with Morton from Leavesden.

Born on 27 June 1905, Capt. Theodore William 'Sammy' Morton learnt to fly aged 19 and joined the RAF in 1921. He left the Service in 1931 to be a commercial airline pilot until 1940 when he became chief test pilot with LAPG. Famously, he started Morton Air Services (MAS) in May 1945, but was unable to start commercial flying until 1 January 1946, when restrictions on civil flying were lifted, with a fleet of Airspeed Consuls and D.H. 89A Dragon Rapides. MAS took over rival Olley Air Services in February 1953 and Morton resigned when his company was absorbed into British United Airways in 1968.

In a letter to A.J.J. on 19 September 1943 E.J.R. wrote:

The flying is going great guns. I went up for 45 minutes on Friday AM (Sept 17) in Halifax II JN952. We were above cloud most of the time, but as I was otherwise occupied I didn't see where we went. I have a suspicion it was a circular trip round London and back over Tilbury and Hatfield. The results (photographs) are quite satisfactory.

Sixteen months after the start of detail design, the prototype D.H. 100 Vampire, LZ548, was flown by Geoffrey de Havilland Jnr from Hatfield on 29 September. In another letter to A.J.J the day before, E.J.R. wrote:

I didn't get a single flight all last week, but on Monday (27 September) I had a real 'five bob' one. Halifax II JN960 was the hearse and we went up as far as the suburbs of Birmingham and back. Most of it was above cloud and all the scenery up there was really grand. I sat in the dorsal turret all the time and was thrilled to the marrow watching a Beaufighter creep up to within 200 ft of the tailplane and then proceed to 'cut us up' and generally demonstrate that we were standing still.

We had a dinghy blow out over Aylesbury last week. It hasn't been found yet and I guess the dinghy is probably making admirable hot water bottles for all the yokels for miles around.

And on 23 October:

Have just had another very fine trip—one hour in Halifax II JN111. We cruised backwards and forwards between Hemel Hempstead and Leighton Buzzard and managed to pinpoint poor old G-EBBS' [D.H. 34] last resting place at Ivinghoe. After the test part was over we hied down to Heathrow and shot them up and were 'attacked' by a Polish Spit from Northolt. He flew alongside and made rude gestures and then did mock attacks from the rear. Very interesting—many other good blokes have gone out the same way.

I now manage to fly in every machine I sign out as airworthy, which of course is as it should be.

On 10 November E.J.R. had the first of many flights with Flt Lt Eirik Sandberg of the Norwegian Army Air Force (its title until Spring 1944 until merged with Naval Air Service to form RNoAF). During a flight in Halifax II JP123 they had a 'fight' with a P-38 Lightning and hit a fence on landing back at Leavesden, but no damage was sustained. After the war Sandberg, who had been RAF trained and was a former Bomber Command pilot, became Norway's chief test pilot and was seconded to de Havilland aircraft at Hatfield after the war to oversee testing of Royal Norwegian Air Force D.H. 100 Vampires before delivery.

1944

E.J.R.'s New Year began with a flight in Halifax II JP186 with Sandberg on 2 January. On the 12th Michael Daunt made the first flight of the first production Gloster Meteor Mk.1 EE210/G.

On 5 April Miles Monitor prototype NF900 was first flown from Woodley, Reading. On the same day E.J.R. flew with 'Sammy' Morton in Halifax II JP297 on a re-flight.

During the following months E.J.R. was busy signing out Halifaxes and getting many flights, mostly with 'Sammy' Morton and Sandberg, until 2 June when he made his last flight with LAPG, in Halifax III MZ305 with Morton.

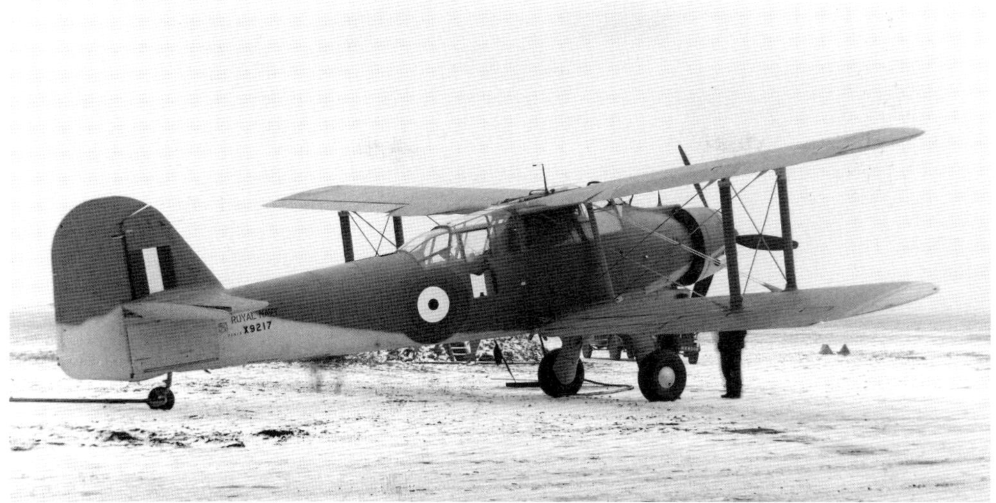

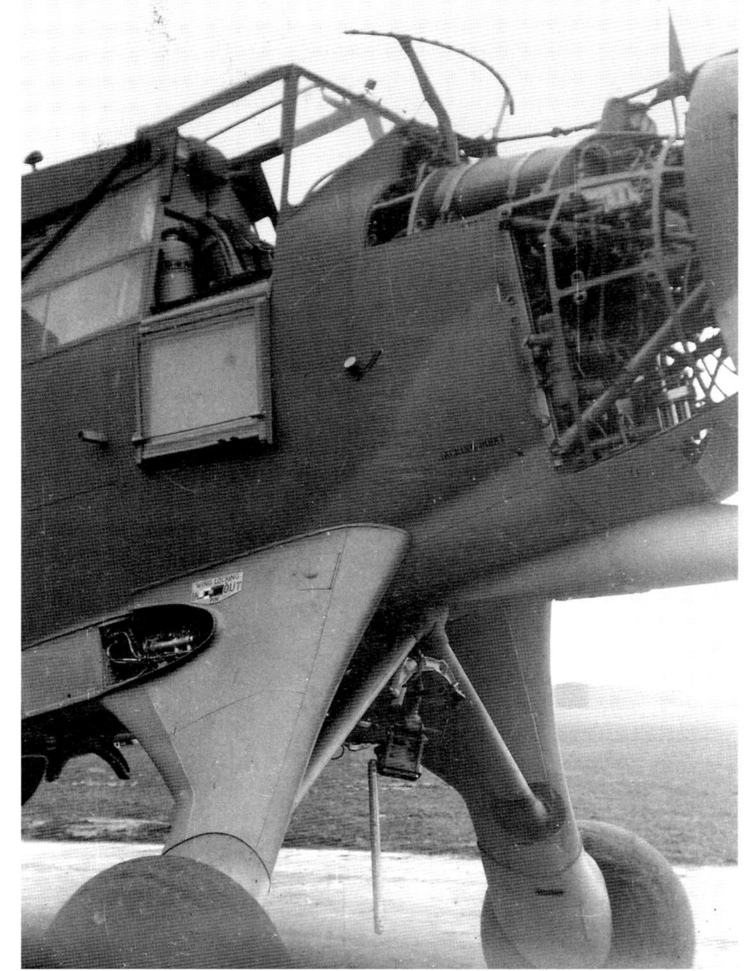

Above: Fairey Albacore I X9217 in snow at Fairey's Great West Aerodrome in January 1942 shortly after its first test flight. A few days later it was delivered to No. 76 MU, Wroughton, before being assigned to No. 796 Squadron FAA at Tanga in October 1942.

Right: Unidentified Fairey Albacore at Fairey's Great West Aerodrome during engine fuel flow tests in January 1942. Former test pilot H. A. Taylor's comment that 'In non-operational conditions the greatest danger for the pilot appeared to be related to the process of climbing aboard' is well illustrated. Note the spray bar in front of the windscreen.

Leavesden and the Second Aircraft Group

Three days later E.J.R. moved to the other side of Leavesden Aerodrome where de Havilland had set up the Second Aircraft Group (SAG) in the No. 2 Factory to produce D.H. 98 Mosquitoes. Like the LAPG, the SAG drew components from many sub-contractors around the country, ranging from coach builders and furniture manufacturers to small engineering concerns and cottage industries. More than 20 per cent of wartime Mosquito output was Leavesden-built, production continuing there until 1947.

On 6 June the nation waited with baited breath as D-Day, the Allied invasion of France, began. Three days later the prototype Avro Lincoln, PW925, was first flown from Ringway.

Morale took another shaking on 13 June with arrival of the first German V-1 flying bombs launched against Britain. The first fell near Swanscombe, near Gravesend, Kent. The following day E.J.R. had a couple of flights in D.H. 94 Moth Minor EO236 from Leavesden to Hatfield and return with B. Campbell. The flight was so bumpy that the occupants of the coupe Minor literally hit the roof! On the same day he had his first flight as an 'observer' in a Mosquito, Mk 30 MM696, with Sqn Ldr Jack Greenland, a de Havilland production test pilot. The two men became firm friends and the close relationship between the two families has lasted to this day. Indeed, this book has been written at the Greenland's former Radlett home.

On the 15th large scale V-1 attacks on Britain began in earnest and of around 150 launched half reached London. For the next two weeks nearly 100 V-1s fell on England daily and by 21 June 1,000 had been launched against London. This daily onslaught moved E.J.R. to write the following to A.J.J.:

I'm thinking of sending Madge and the offspring home [EJR's mother lived at Wimborne, Dorset] unless it gets a bit quieter (constant air raids). I shall then do my spell of nights at the aerodrome and be at home by myself during the day. It's a bit of a bind for her being there all day by herself and having to put up with it at night as well.

However, they reckon they've [the Germans] only got 14 days supply, so we'll see what happens after Thursday. In the meantime we can only grin and bear it, as, barring a series of 12,000 lb raids on the Pas de Calais, I can't see any solution—a balloon barrage if properly designed might do it, but to grow good roses, you put the manure at the roots—it seems to apply in this case.

And again on 28 June to A.J.J.:

Since a week last Thursday, we have been showered with devices called Fly-bombs, Buzz-bombs, Kivik rockets, or, to put it in the words of a certain gentleman at work 'Blarstards', which, I think, describes them to a 'T'. We average 10 or 12 daytime alerts and the usual all-night session until 4 a.m. So, for 'Southern England', read the

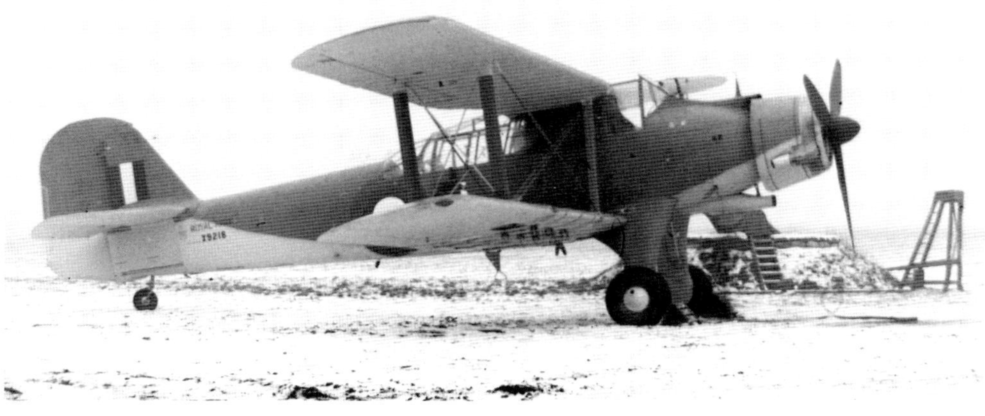

Fairey Albacore I X9218 in snow at Fairey's Great West Aerodrome in January 1942 awaiting air test. A few days later it was delivered to No. 76 MU, Wroughton, before going to No. 789 Squadron at Wingfield in April 1943. Later it was transferred to No. 799 Squadron, also at Wingfield.

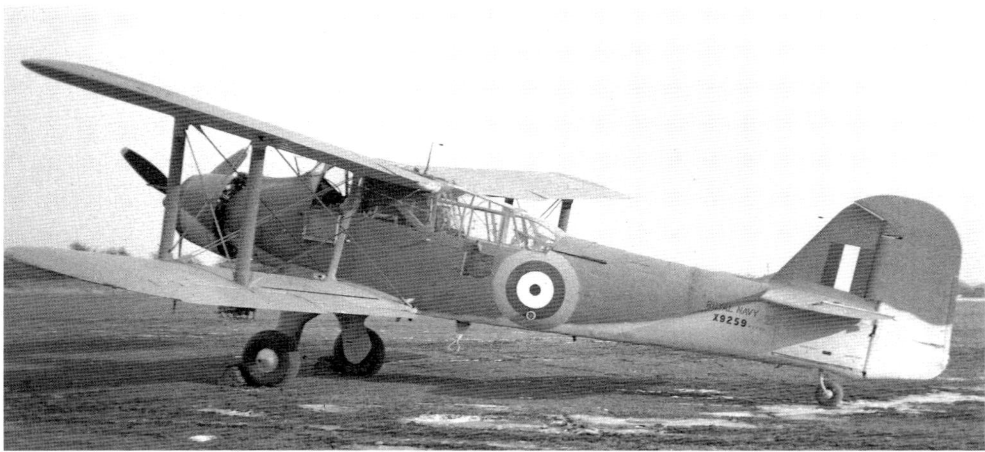

Above: Fairey Albacore I X9259 at Fairey's Great West Aerodrome in February 1942 awaiting collection for delivery to No. 76 MU Wroughton on the 8th. In November 1943 it was taken to the Royal Naval Aircraft Repair Yard, Nairobi, before going to the RAF Aden Communications Flight in December 1945. It was badly damaged following an overshot landing at Mafid that month.

Below: A couple of X-serialled Fairey Albacore Is in snow at Fairey's Great West Aerodrome in January 1942. The aircraft in the foreground is undergoing ground testing of its Bristol Taurus engine.

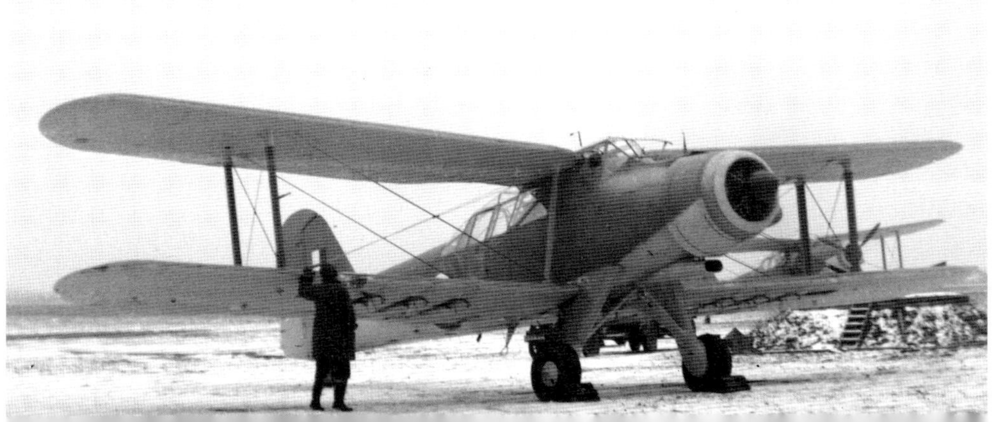

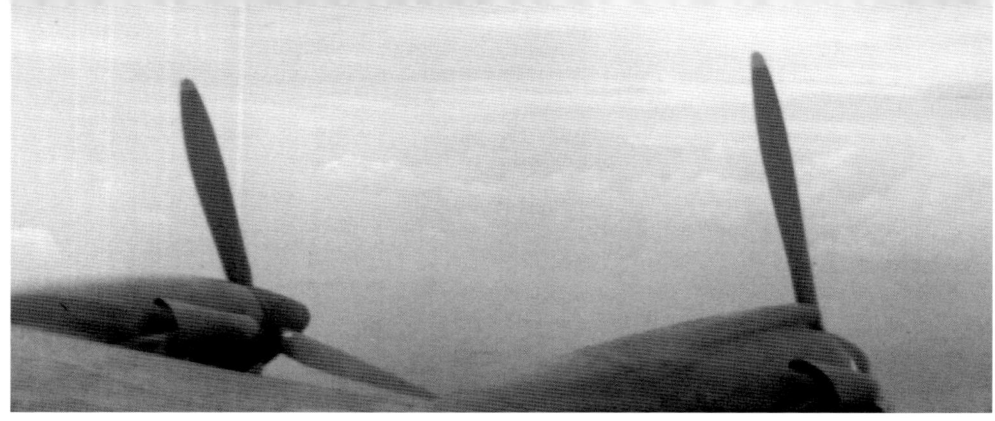

This series of views was taken from Merlin-engined Handley Page Halifax II Series 1A JN952 during a 45-minute test flight from Leavesden on 17 September 1943 with T. W. Morton in the left hand seat. Part of a batch of 250 Halifax IIs produced by the London Aircraft Production Group between July 1943 and June 1944, JN952 was delivered to No. 102 Squadron but went missing during a bombing raid on Magdeburg in January 1944, the month when the RAF all but destroyed this German city. Of particular interest is the photograph showing two of the Rolls-Royce Merlin XXIIs stopped. The log book comment by E.J.R. records: '*7,000ft, clouds 9/10th, dull. In dorsal turret all the way. Met Wellington near Henley.*'

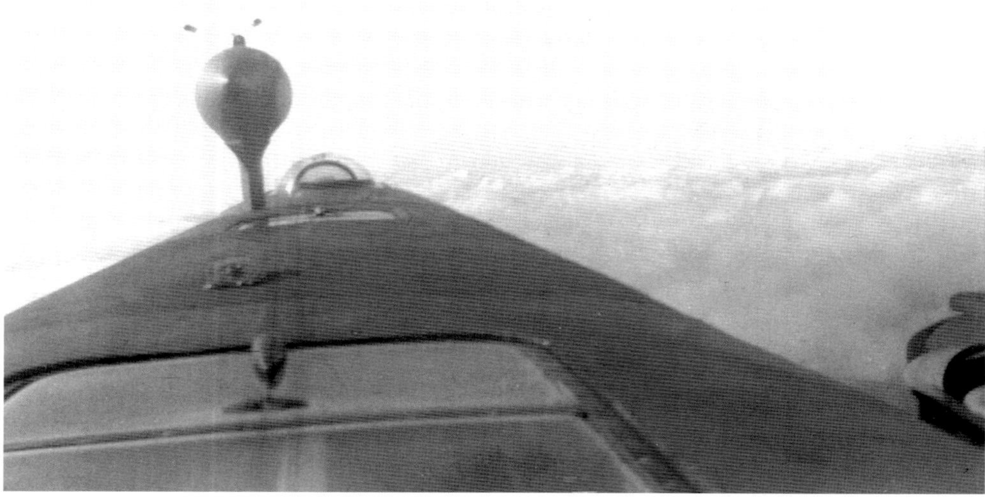

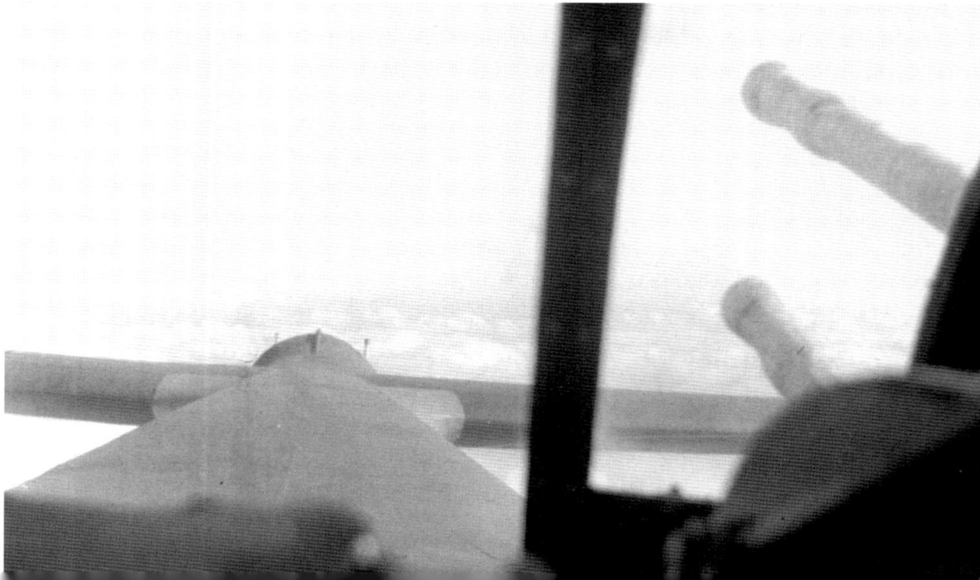

usual target and you won't be far wrong. Until this a.m. we'd had nothing within one and a half miles, but I gather that 'some damage and casualties have occurred' elsewhere. They sound like Trojan vans in flight, and when the propulsion unit starts coughing, you look around for a convenient hole and pull it in after you. Flying speed appears to be in the neighbourhood of 350, and the stalling speed 330. Result, straight in, bonk. The plumbers will no doubt be busy putting a few windows back when the originators run out of ammo. I saw one shot down by a Spit Vb over Harrow last week. The Gestapo [sensors]seem to be opening several outgoing letters recently—a woman down the road mentioned in a letter to her husband that she was 'sitting in the garden during an alert writing this letter', and they sent it back to her.

On 6 July Prime Minister Winston Churchill announced that 2,754 V-1s had been launched against Britain in the first month, killing 2,752 people, an average one person per bomb.

Three days later E.J.R. had a flight in a Halifax III from Leavesden to RAF Driffield with ATA ferry pilot Lettice Curtis. The delivery to No. 158 Squadron was made in 1 hour 5 minutes; E.J.R. returned to Sherburn-in-Elmet with Curtis in an ATA Fairchild Argus. In a letter to A.J.J. he wrote:

I went up to Driffield in Halifax MZ351 last Sunday fortnight (with woman driver— air frame) and from there got a Fairchild EV787 to Sherburn-in-Elmet, where lunch was served in the ATA mess.

Many years later I looked up these flights in Lettice's flying log book.

On 12 July the first Meteors entered RAF service with No. 616 (South Yorkshire) Squadron and were soon helping to destroy incoming V-1s. On the 28th the first flight of the magnificent D.H. 103 Hornet, RR915, took place at Hatfield.

The first of many flights E.J.R. had with First Officer W. A. 'Johnny' Jordan ATA, of Jordan Mills, Sandy, Bedfordshire, (member of the Jordan cereals/ cereal bar family) was on 5 August. Together they delivered and collected ATA personnel at Luton, Cambridge, Gransden Lodge, Upwood, Tempsford and back to Leavesden in Anson I NK810.

The first flight of the Hawker F.2/43 Fury NX798 by Philip Lucas took place on 1 September and a week later Duncan Sandys, Parliamentary Secretary, Ministry of Supply, declared that the Battle of London was over, 'except possibly for a few last shots.' During 80 days of bombardment the enemy had launched more than 8,000 V-1s, of which some 2,300 had got through to the London region. However, V-1s launched from Heinkel He 111s over the North Sea continued to fall on Britain. The day after the Sandys' announcement the first German V-2s hit Britain, falling on Chiswick and Epping.

The Arnhem landings, an airborne operation to capture the bridges over the Maas at Grave, the Waal at Nijmegen and the Neder Rijn and codenamed 'Operation Market Garden', began on 17 September and continued for more than a week, with very high casualties.

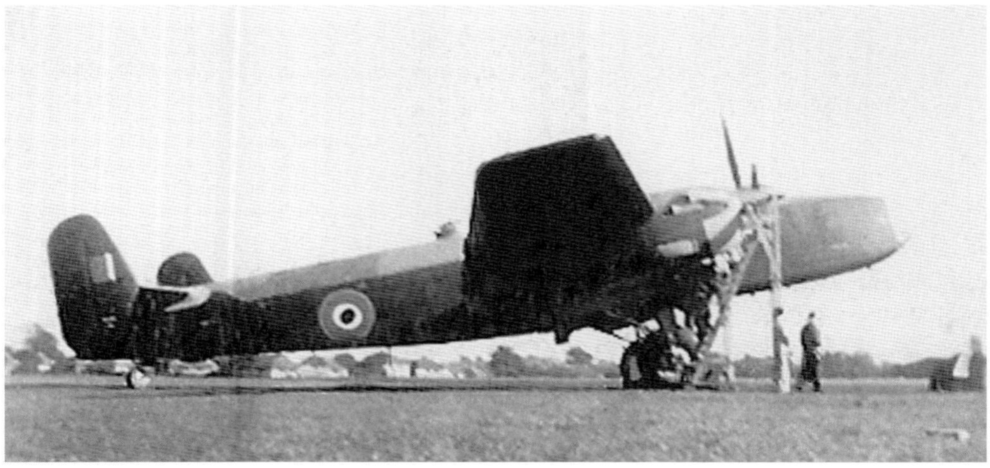

A poor photograph of Handley Page Halifax II JN952 at Leavesden on 17 September 1943 prior to the aforementioned test flight.

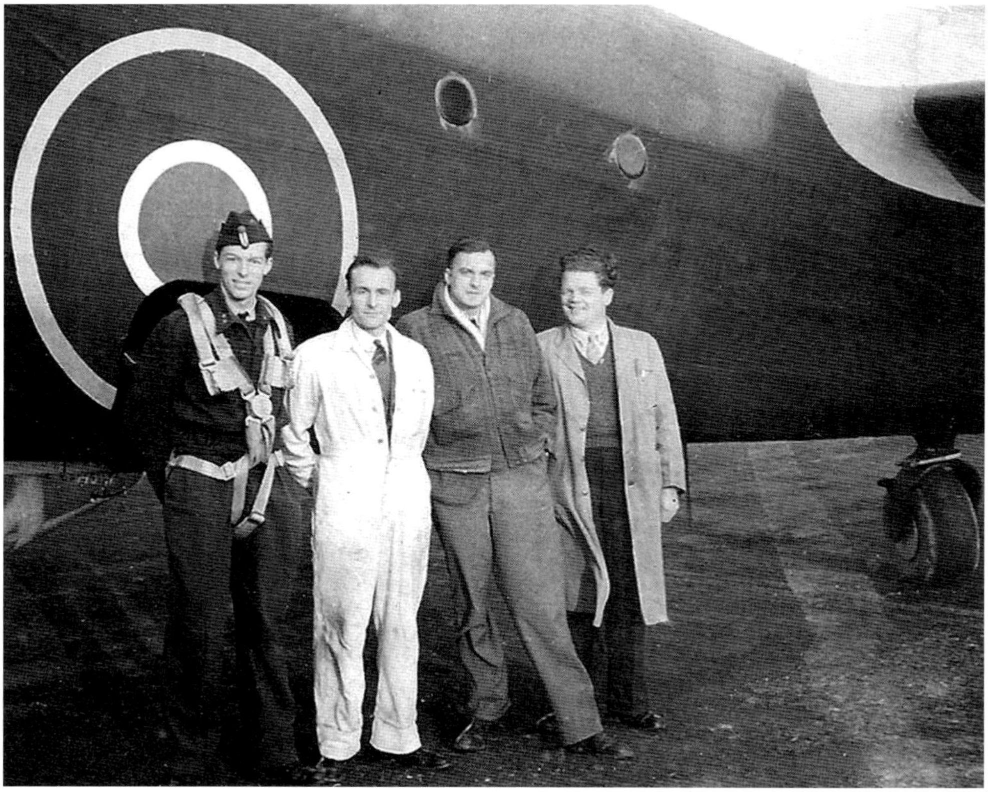

An LAP Halifax flight-test crew prior to taking-off from Leavesden in 1943 with E.J.R., second right, and John 'Tubby' Simpson to his left.

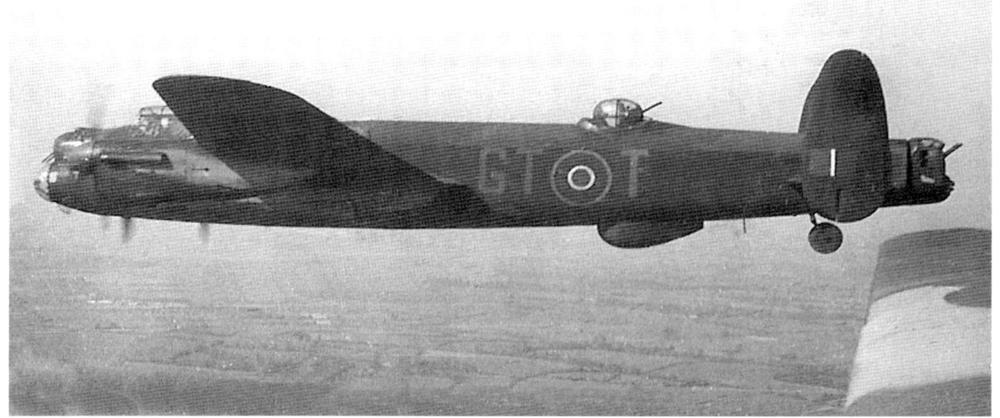

Above and below: Two views of Avro Lancaster GT-T of No. 156 Squadron taken over Tring, Hertfordshire, from D.H. 98 Mosquito N.F.30 NT604 on 13 April 1945. The Lancaster was bringing back POWs from liberated Europe.

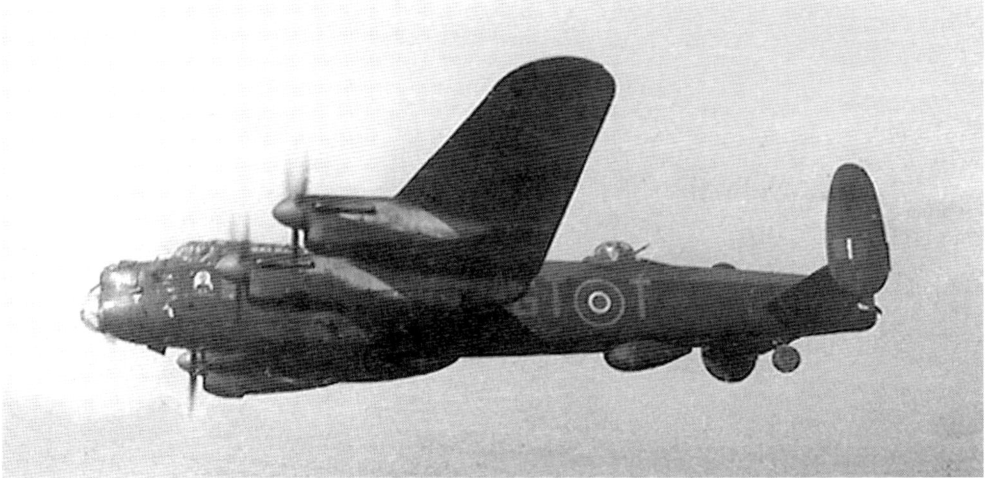

Below: This formation of 8th Air Force Curtiss C-46D Commandos, with 44-77643 nearest the camera, was spotted during the early part of 1945, location unknown. Completed in January 1945, this aircraft left the USA for the UK in February and stayed only a few months before returning to the USA in July 1945. The largest and heaviest twin-engine aircraft to see operational use with the USAAF, the C-46D could carry either 50 troops or 10,000 lb of cargo, all on the power of two 2,000 hp Pratt & Whitney R-2800 engines.

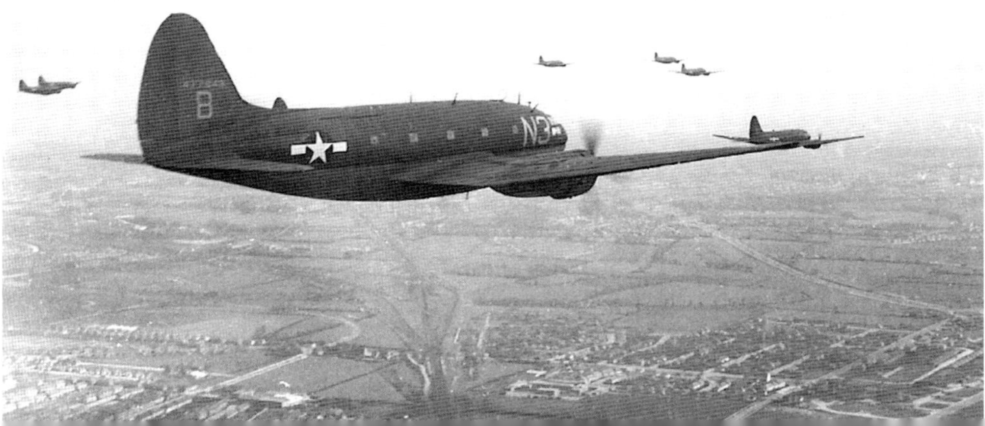

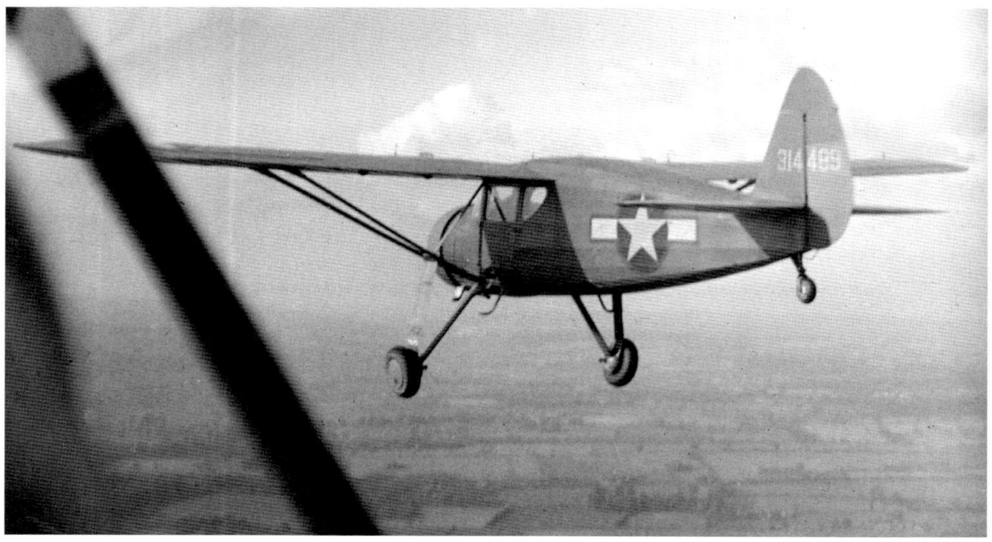

Fairchild C-61A Forwarder 43-14489 over St Albans on 27 October 1944, photographed from C-61A 43-14503 flying from Leavesden. '89 passed to the RAF, becoming FS572 and flew with No. 227 Group Communications Flight until taken off RAF charge in April 1945.

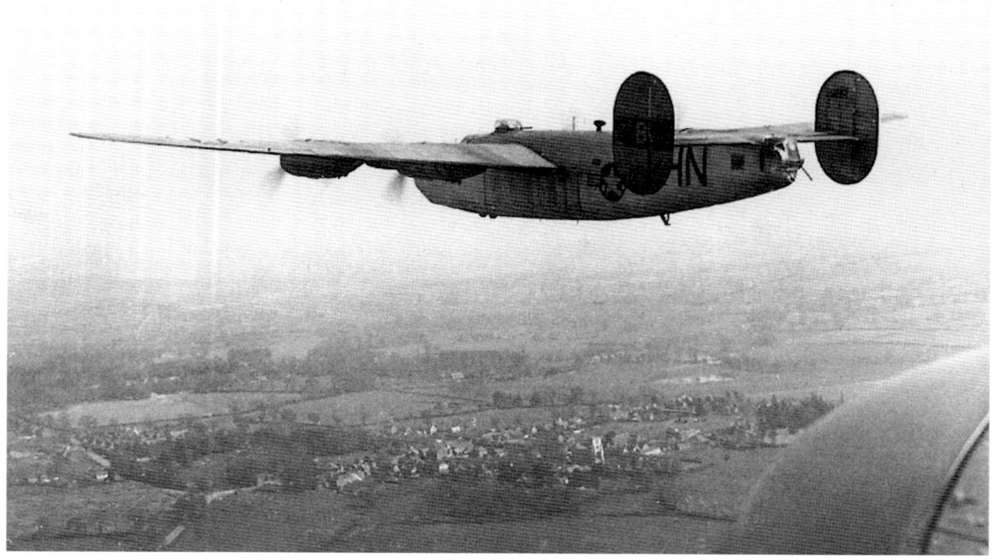

Whilst flying with Stan 'Fearless Freddie' Offord in D.H. 98 Mosquito N.F.30 NT604 on 13 April 1945 E.J.R. spotted this Consolidated B-24 Liberator in the vicinity of Cheddington, Buckinghamshire, closing on it for this photograph. The B-24 was assigned to the 446th Bomb Group's 705th Bomber Squadron, stationed at RAF Bungay (Flixton). The 705th's B-24s (the *Bungay Buckaroos*) had moved to Flixton in November 1943 and stayed until July 1945 before returning to the USA after their work in Europe was completed.

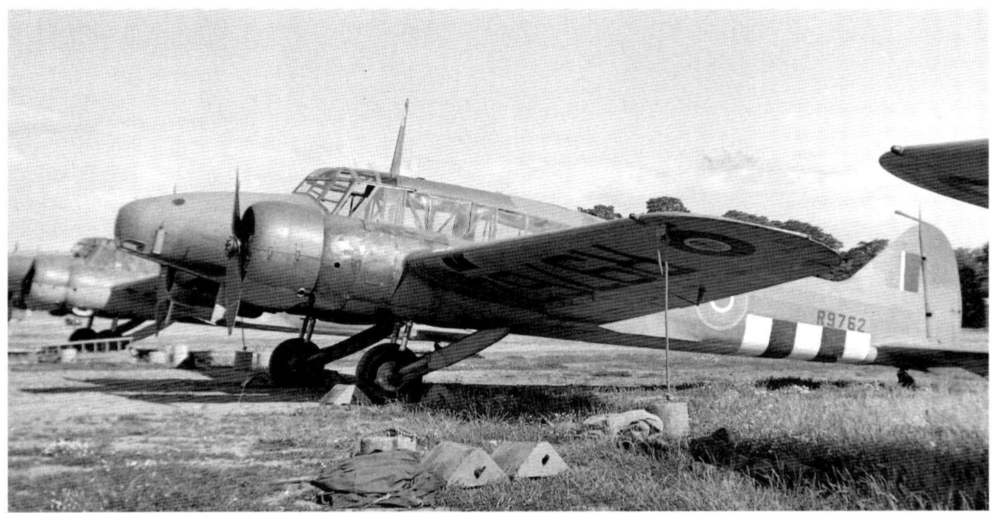

Tethered at White Waltham in July 1945 and bedecked in invasion stripes is Avro Anson I R9762. Built in 1940 and delivered to No. 3 Ferry Pool ATA, this Anson finished the war with No. 1 Ferry Pool, ATA HQ, White Waltham, before passing to the Signals School in November 1946.

In a letter to A.J.J. on 27 September E.J.R. wrote:

Went across to the old firm yesterday [LAPG] and bought a ticket for a Halifax ride—only 20 minutes to Henley and back but it made a change from the usual streamlined bricks [Mosquitoes]. We've had three prangs and two near misses over that trouble I told you about. Mollison's been in twice [Jim Mollison was then an ATA ferry pilot]—he's getting fat and you'd hardly recognise him.

And in another letter, dated 13 October, E.J.R. wrote:

One or two ATA drivers have been flying my '98s [Mosquitoes] to Colerne and picking up your Spits [A.J.J. was stationed at RAF Colerne working on Spitfires] for the return flight. I asked one of them to look out for you. I am in the running for a considerable amount of aviation by the looks of things. A small USAAF unit has been opened at our place under the command of Capt. R. Fowler. He did some joyriding on Jennies down Omaha way, so must know his job—and they have three Fairchilds, a P-47 and are expecting some others any day. He says they have a B-17 and two C.78s (Norsemen, in English). I have had 1 hour 10 minutes in Fairchilds and went out to collect a Cessna Bobcat with him today. We flew back in a tropical rainstorm hovering between seats and ceiling most of the way.

E.J.R. was referring to a small communications flight set up by the USAAF at Leavesden in October 1944 whose aircraft included three Fairchild C-61s, one Cessna C-64 Bobcat and a Norduyn Norseman. Throughout October E.J.R. had several flights from Leavesden with this unit in Fairchild C-61s 43-14489 and

43-14503, Cessna C-64 Bobcat 42-58439 and Norduyn Norseman 44-70351, with pilots Capt. Fowler, Capt. Talbot, Lt Owens and Lt H. X. Sullivan]

After the sobering failure of the Arnhem operation almost two months earlier there was better news on 12 November with the announcement that the German battleship *Tirpitz* had capsized in Tromsø Fjord, Norway, after being hit by three Tallboy 12,000 lb bombs delivered by Lancasters of Nos 9 and 617 Squadrons. On November 14 1944 E.J.R. wrote to A.J.J.:

Have done some aviating of late with the Americans—one and a half hours in Fairchild 43-14489, driver Lt Owens. Route, Leavesden to Panshanger, Panshanger to Boreham, Boreham to Panshanger and Panshanger to Leavesden. I nearly got lost navigating back from Chelmsford but was very fortunate in picking out a portion of the main LNER that was parallel with the Great North Road north of Welwyn which I remembered driving up many moons ago. By following southwards a few miles was able to find our own field just before it got dark.

Have just read the manuscript of a book passed to me for criticism by Russell [MD of Harborough Publishing Company and publisher of *Aeromodeller*]. It's called I Couldn't Care Less, by Anthony Phelps and is about the ATA. When published, this'll be a best seller, you mark my words.[E.J.R. subsequently supplied a number of his photographs for this wonderful book].

On 4 December E.J.R. wangled a visit to RAF Colerne with the intention of meeting A.J.J., writing him this letter the following day:

I came over [to 218 MU, RAF Colerne] with a pal of mine on Monday (4 December), Elliot of ATA in Mosquito 30 NT245 and got to Colerne at 11.40 and duly found our way to the reception hut and got your extension. You can imagine my disappointment on being told you were out for the day. It was a very sad and doleful E.J.R. that climbed into Mosquito XXX NT257'G and departed at 12.15pm for Hatfield, which we reached in 23 minutes! Union time being 35 minutes. The Anson was waiting at Hatfield and they very kindly gave me a lift back and I got in just in time for dinner being only away two-and-a-half hours. I rounded off the day by going up with Ft Lt Dodson in a dual control Mosquito III. We did a couple of rolls and I flew it for a stretch, weaving in and out of small clouds. When we landed the sun had set and I had another 1 hr 50 minutes to put down in the book.

Incidentally, I rather think that my wallet fell out of my greatcoat pocket when the pilot threw it down to me after we landed, so if you hear of anyone finding one, you'll know whose it is. Luckily there's no dough in it, only my official pass, identity card, driving licence, insurance and one or two papers and not dirty postcards as 'Whitey' the operations 'officer' at White Waltham suggested. [The wallet was subsequently found and returned intact].

On 9 December the 'black-out' regulations imposed on London were relaxed to a 'dim-out' because most of the attacks on Britain were now being made by pilotless aircraft and missiles.

1945

On January 21 E.J.R. wrote to A.J.J.:

> Have returned once more to Leavesden [he had been off for ten days with gastric flu] and the north east wind, sending streamlined bricks [Mosquitoes] in your direction [RAF Colerne MU]. You can take it from me that all those that you cast your weary eye during your velocifications around the perimeter track have meant much hard-got breath, aches, pains, hacked shins and frozen fingers to yours truly this last month of unmentionable weather.

On 26 January Tommy Rose made the first flight of Miles M.57 Aerovan U-0248/G-AGOZ from Woodley. The last V-2 rocket fell on Britain on 17 March at Orpington, Kent, killing one person. Statistics issued at the time reported that between 8 September 1944 and 27 March 1945 1,115 V-2s had arrived in England of which around 500 hit London, killing 2,855. And on 29 March the last German V-1 flying bomb was shot down near Sittingbourne, Kent. It was reported that no fewer than 9,200 V-1s had been launched against Britain between 13 June 1944 and 29 March 1945. Of this number nearly 4,000 were destroyed while still airborne. Fatalities attributable to V-1 explosions amounted to 6,139.

E.J.R. became reacquainted with Stanley Orton Bradshaw and was to accompany him on numerous ATA Anson taxi flights, the first of which was on 30 March in R9762, flying from Leavesden and calling at Watton, Foulsham, Oulton, Wyton before returning to Leavesden. A renowned aviation artist and journalist, Bradshaw (1903–1950) was born on 2 February 1903. He learnt to fly with the London Aeroplane Club at Stag Lane in August 1926. During the 1930s Bradshaw illustrated aviation books published by John Hamilton & Company, including some for W. E. Johns. He joined the ATA in April 1941 and served as a Second Officer until November 1945. After the war he continued painting and was a regular contributor to *The Aeroplane* on light aviation matters. He became Associate Editor of *The Light Plane* in the late 1940s and was killed in company with E.J.R. when flying Auster Autocar G-AJYM at Boston, Lincolnshire, on 7 April 1950.

The first of many adventurous Mosquito test and delivery flights with de Havilland production test pilot Stanley F. Offord occurred on 3 April. During the 30-minute flight in Mosquito III RR296 they shot up Esher, the home of E.J.R'.s aunt Edie, three times and showed off over Brooklands by flying past a Stirling with *both* props feathered!

On 30 April the day arrived for which the free world had been waiting six long years—the news that Adolf Hitler and his wife Eva Braun had died in their bunker beneath the Chancellery in Berlin. Meanwhile, E.J.R. continued inspecting and flying in SAG Mosquitoes. On 6 May he wrote to A.J.J.:

> I apologise for the delay in letting you know of my survival from the second hand Mosquito ride [Mk30 MM700'G FK-G delivery to No. 219 Squadron] ride of the

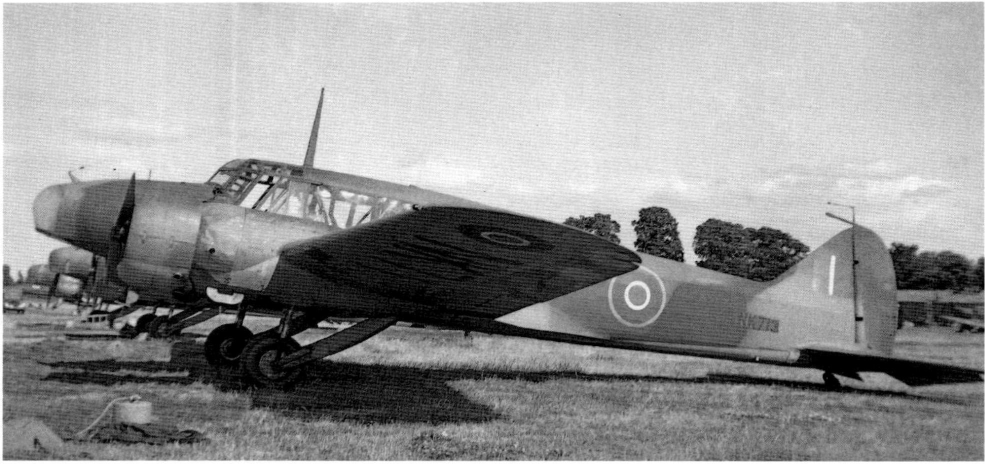

Avro Anson I NK713 was part of a batch of 800 Ansons turned out by A. V. Roe in 1944 and spent most of its active life as a ferry aircraft at the Air Transport Auxiliary's HQ at No. 1 Ferry Pool, White Waltham, where it is pictured in July 1945. This Anson was taken off RAF charge in January 1947.

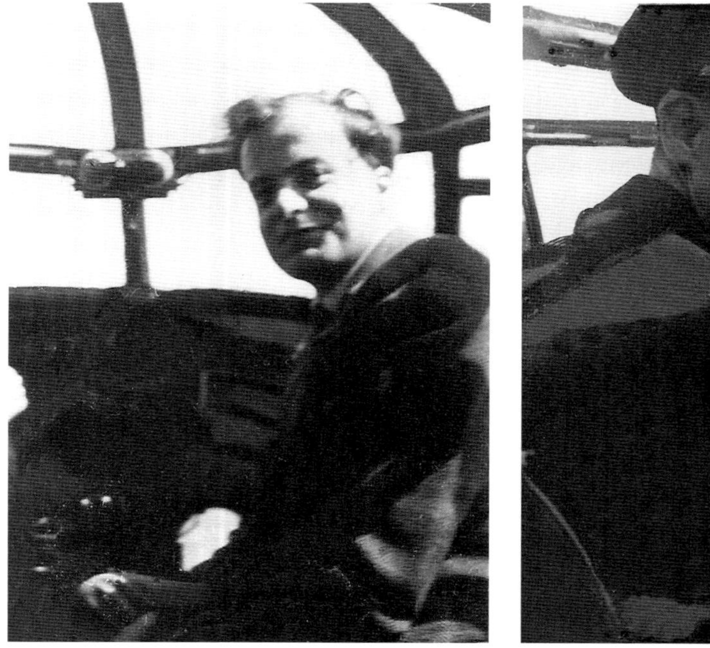

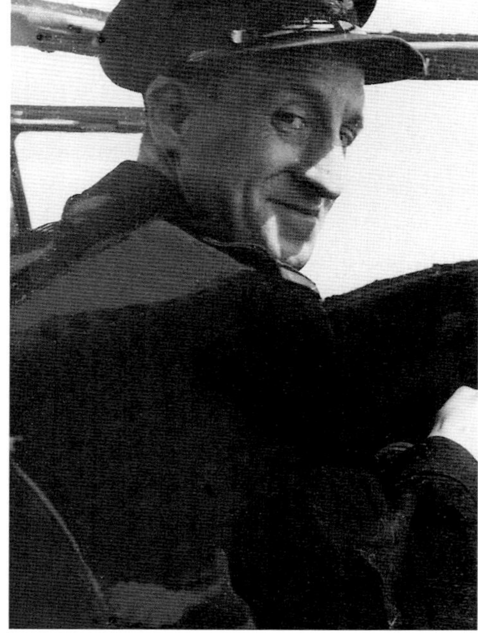

Above left: E.J.R. in the right hand seat of an ATA Anson I flown by First Officer Stanley Orton Bradshaw in 1945.

Above right: First Officer Stanley Orton Bradshaw flying an ATA Anson I in 1945. An accomplished aviation artist, Stanley learnt to fly with the London Aeroplane Club at Stag Lane in 1926. He and E.J.R. lost their lives on 7 April 1950 when the Auster Autocar in which they were flying crashed at Boston, Lincolnshire.

17th ultimo. A more uncomfortable journey I've yet to make, as apart from engine vibration and an impossibility to make more than 240 on the clock there was summat wrong with the cabin heating and by the time we reached Reading I was beginning to look back at regular intervals to see if we were on fire. At Chelmsford we were both frying in our own fat and they kept us circling for 15 minutes in the queue at Bradwell. However, the subsequent flight up to Cambridge and then back home in the Fairchild (HB622) with both windows open provided a very pleasant reviver. Apart from skidding along on one wheel and nearly cart wheeling at the end of the day, everything passed off well.

Following the death of Hitler, Winston Churchill announced the German surrender, total and unconditional, signed at General Dwight D. Eisenhower's HQ near Rheims, France. But the war against Japan continued in the east.

On 11 June E.J.R. wrote to A.J.J.:

I fear my trips to Colerne have ceased, at least for the time being as we are now producing Mossie Mk 36s and these seem to be going to Shawbury and St. Athan for the usual fitting out operations.

Within weeks of the ending of war in Europe new commercial airliners were materialising. On 14 June the first flight of Avro Tudor G-AGPF took place in the hands of S. A. Thorn and Jimmy Orrell and just over a week later J. 'Mutt' Summers got the prototype Vickers 491 Viking G-AGOK airborne from Wisley.

On 5 July Foster Dixon made the initial flight of RA356, the prototype Fairey Spearfish dive bomber, intended to replace the Barracuda, but the big brute of an aeroplane was too late for war service.

The following day E.J.R. wrote to A.J.J.:

I spent a day with Stanley Bradshaw yesterday, driving with him to White Waltham and being allotted Anson I NK713 for the day. We left at 12.45 and proceeded via Radlett, Luton, Henlow, Hucknall, Lichfield, High Ercall and Cosford back to White Waltham, whence we arrived at 17.30 hrs—three-and-a-half hours flying excluding stops at the above. We had the machine to ourselves after Henlow and climbed up to 6,000 ft above the clouds, twisting and turning amongst the avenues and tunnels etc. We came down through them right over Ratcliffe aerodrome and practically glided into Hucknall where we spent an hour waiting to pick up old Keith Jopp.

And on 9 July, in another epistle:

Boy, have I had a week of flying. As well as the trip to Plymouth in a D.H. 89A last week, I had a further three hours 50 minutes in another '89A going from Leavesden to RAF Stradishall, and from there to Shawbury and then to Thorney Island and back home. Perfect weather all the time with 40 miles vis. I could see your place from 5,000 ft over Swindon on the way down to Thorney Island at about 18.30 hrs.

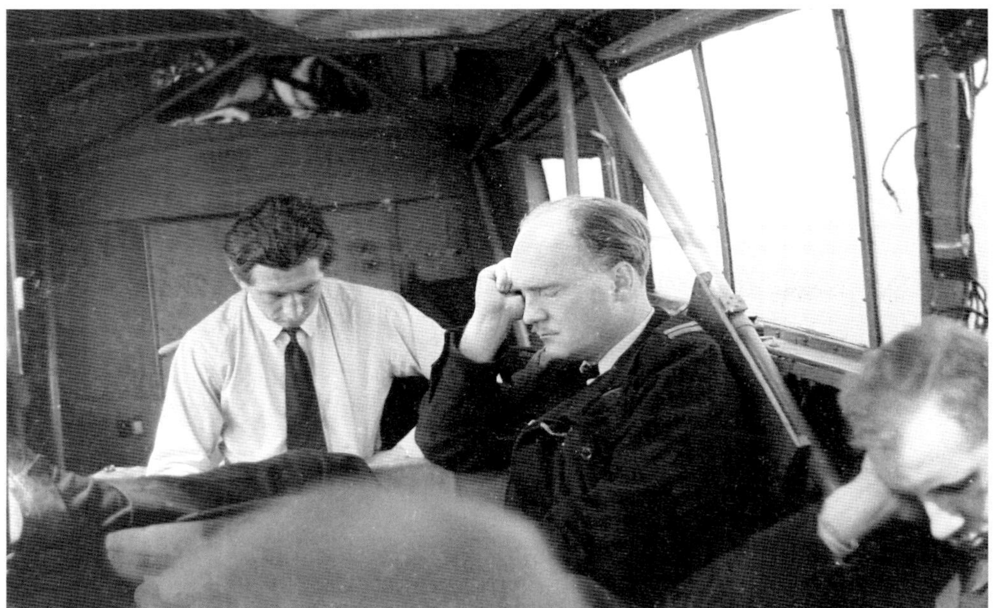

Homeward bound after a long day's flying. E.J.R. accompanied several ATA Anson taxi pilots on their rounds, sitting in the right hand seat. A typical day's flying was that on 13 June 1945 in Anson I NK810. Taking off from Leavesden at 11 a.m., pilots were dropped off or picked up at Hatfield, Lichfield, Shawbury, High Ercall, Cosford and Wolverhampton, returning to Leavesden in time for afternoon tea.

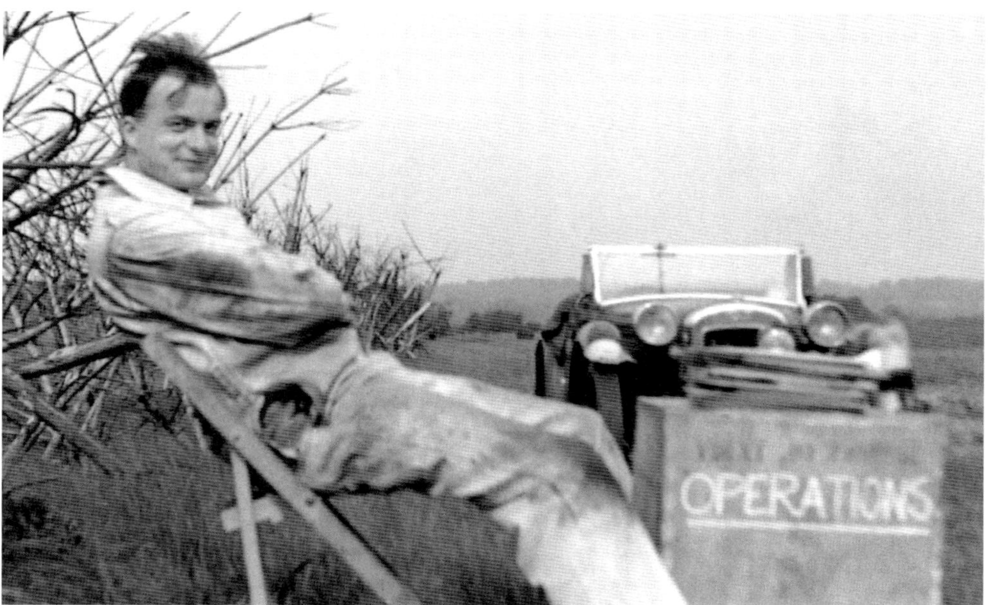

Taking a break from signing out Mosquitoes, E.J.R. awaits delivery pilots at ATA's Leavesden 'Operations' in May 1945. His 'desk' is an upturned tea chest and his Austin 'Chummy' is in the background.

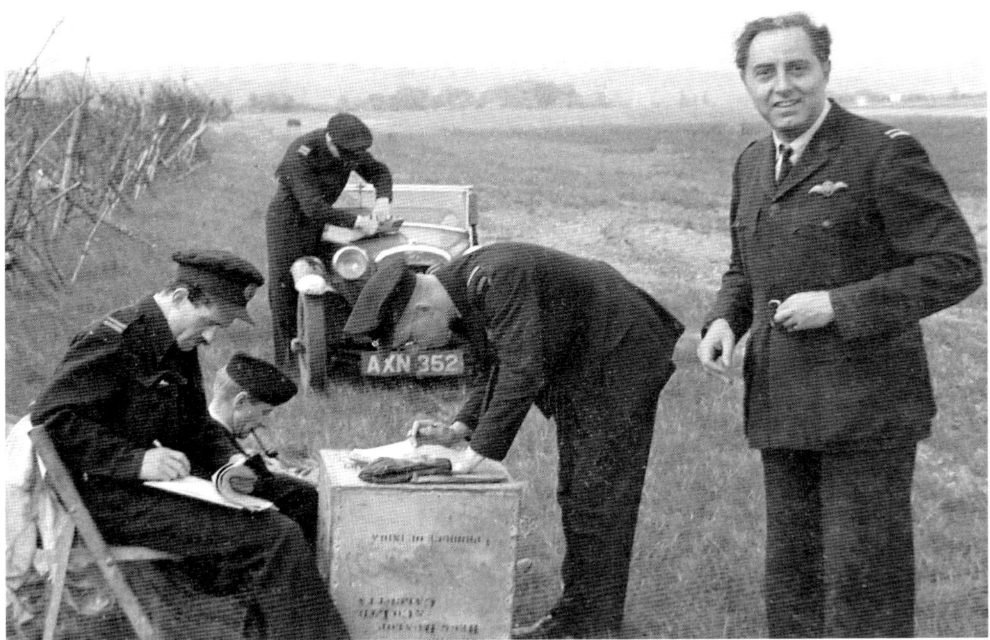

First Officers Victor Baxter-Jones, seated, and Austrian-born Stefan Karpeles-Schenker, standing right, signing delivery receipts at Leavesden's ATA 'Control' in May 1945. E.J.R.'s Austin 'Chummy' is again visible.

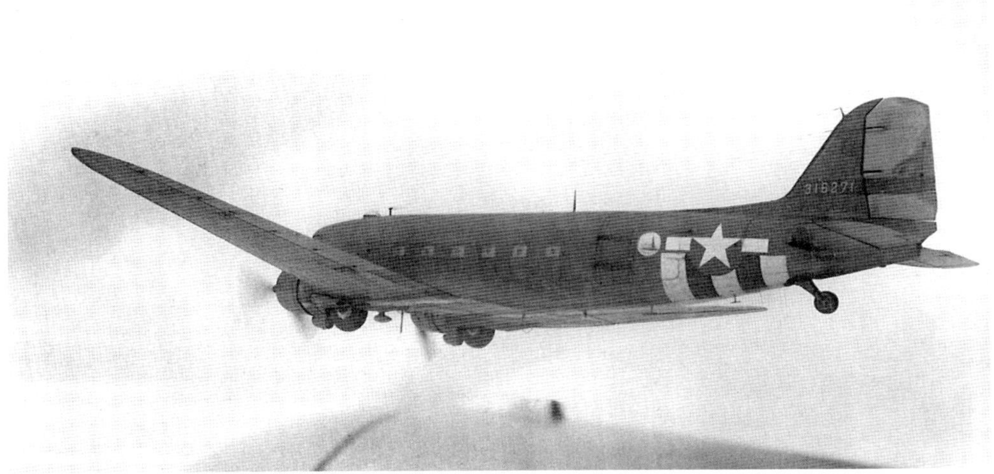

During an outing with Offord in D.H. 98 Mosquito N.F.36 RL181 on 24 July 1945 E.J.R. photographed this Douglas C-47B over Edgware; Offord could not resist rolling the Mossie twice as they flew alongside. After the war C-47 43-16271 remained in Europe and was sold to Swiss Alpair Air Traffic, becoming HB-ASA. It soon passed to Swissair, was re-registered HB-IRK, and put into service in 1948. On 18 June 1957 the aircraft stalled and spun into Lake Constance during a training flight. All nine occupants were killed.

I had a bread-and-butter flight in a Mossie Mk 36 yesterday afternoon. We headed due south and crossed the Channel at Shoreham, heading straight out to sea. We reached the French coast at St. Jouin-sur-Mer and flew along the cliff tops at ground level up as far as Etretat, where we turned out to sea again and flew back at 100 ft all the way, hitting the Isle of Wight at Brightstone and passing over Ryde and Thorney Island. Total time: 1 hour 35 minutes—test flight [*sic*].

And there was more that week:

Had the best flight of my life today—Leavesden to Roborough (Plymouth) return in D.H. 89A NR687. Three-and-a-half hours all told, via Winchester, Poole, Sidmouth and Torquay. Boy! It was grand flying down the coast about a quarter of a mile out watching the lucky sods sunbathing. The reason for this flight? To fetch a 10-gallon barrel of cider for the CO of the Communications Flight at our place! Oh my Gawd—and they pull us in for 'wasting' petrol on the road.

The transfer of aircraft and personnel of the 8th United States Army Air Force from Britain to the USA on its way to the Pacific war theatre was completed on 11 July. In 51 days 2,118 four-engine bombers had been flown across the Atlantic. Winston Churchill's government was defeated in the General Election of 26 July and the Labour Party came to power.

On 6 August the end of the war in the east became inevitable with the dropping of the first atomic bomb on Hiroshima, Japan, by a Boeing B-29 Super Fortresses of the 509th Composite Group, US 20th Army Air Force. A second bomb dropped on Nagasaki three days later led to Japan's unconditional surrender on 14–15th, announced at midnight by President Truman and Britain's Prime Minister Attlee.

Despite the return of peace E.J.R. continued to sign out Mosquitoes and was still getting a great deal of flying—not only in Mosquitoes.

On 4 September he wrote to A.J.J.:

Had another trip to Roborough in Rapide NR687 (30 August), this time to take back the empty barrel and pick up a new one! It was filthy weather when we left, with clouds down to 700 ft. I fully expected to spend the night there, especially as we didn't leave until 16.00 hrs. However, by the time we'd passed Upavon the clouds began to break and at Yeovil there was a perfect blue sky. We got back at 19.45.

I went with our pilot Offord to Staverton, Glos. [in D.H. 98 Mosquito 36 RL231 on 31 August] to have a look at an Alsatian pup which he wanted to buy—this in the course of a bread-and-butter Mosquito flight. The dog turned out to be a four year-old, standing about as high as a small pony. However, with much pulling and hauling we managed to get the darned thing into the cockpit—and ourselves on top of it and set sail for home. We lashed it to the scanner crate and expected to have a proper blood bath when the engines started; but for some reason or other it seemed to stun the dog into a state of coma, and it lay and dribbled all the way back. On top of this we got lost, and it was only when the W/T station at Rugby showed up that we got our bearings and headed southwards.

I went up to High Ercall in an Anson on Monday. By now there must be 300 Halifax IIIs and VIIs there being inhibited for long term storage together with an equal number of Spits and Hudsons. It's very depressing seeing all the empty aerodromes on the way up.

To much rejoicing the Second World War ended officially at 1.30 a.m. GMT on 2 September when Japan signed an unconditional surrender aboard the American battleship *Missouri* in Tokyo Bay.

On 12 September E.J.R. had a flight in Miles Martinet EM648 with First Officer R. Elliott ATA from RAF Shawbury to Leavesden after the pair had delivered Mosquito 36 RL213 to Shawbury. At nearby Hatfield the prototype D.H. 104 Dove (G-AGPJ) made its first flight on 25 September.

E.J.R. and Stan Offord flew D.H. 98 Mosquito III TV966 to the ATA Pageant/ Display at White Waltham on 29 September, opened by Lord Beaverbrook. Offord's performance in the Mosquito prompted *The Aeroplane* to comment: '... perhaps the most astounding display of the day was given ... by a de Havilland Mosquito III. After a spectacular show, much of which was flown on one motor, this Mosquito was brought across the aerodrome at well under 100 ft, with both motors dead; the pilot admitted afterwards he had never tried this before.' Another highlight that received mention was Alex Henshaw's breath-taking demonstration

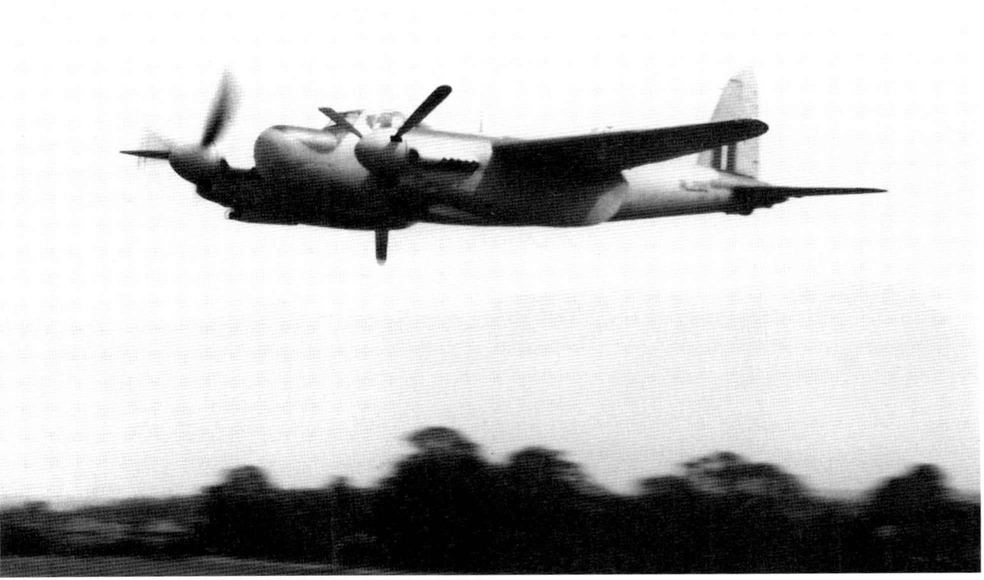

D.H.98 Mosquito N.F. 36 RL205 beating up Leavesden with one prop feathered after an early test flight, probably by Offord, on 17 August 1945. Freddie usually finished off his Mosquito air tests with a low level, single-engine barrel roll. A batch of 163 N.F.36s was delivered by D.H. Leavesden between May 1945 and March 1947. RL205 went to No. 85 Squadron and later passed to Nos 29 and 219 Squadrons before being assigned to a Signals School in June 1954.

of a Supermarine Seafire 47. Lettice Curtis brought in a Consolidated B-24 Liberator and there were six captured German aircraft on view. E.J.R. and Offord returned to Leavesden in Fairchild Argus HB592 flown by Stanley Bradshaw. Shortly after, on 30 November, ATA stood down at a ceremony at White Waltham. Between 1940 and 1945 the organisation had ferried more than 307,000 aircraft and by the end of the war comprised 734 air crew members of which 90 were women. In the Crypt at St Pauls an ATA memorial tablet reads:

> To the memory of the one hundred and seventy three men and women of Air Transport Auxiliary representing many nations who gave their lives in the Allied cause during the world war of 1939 to 1945. Remember then that also we in a moon's course are history

On 26 October George Miles made the first flight of the pretty Miles M.65 Gemini prototype, G-AGUS, built and flown with a fixed undercarriage.

On 8 November E.J.R. was at RAE Farnborough taking photographs of German aircraft for Harborough Publications that were used eventually in *Aircraft of the Fighting Powers—Volume VII*, edited jointly by E.J.R. and Owen Thetford, with magnificent three-view scale drawings by E.J.R.

On Sunday 2 December C. F. Uwins made the first flight of the prototype Bristol 170 Freighter G-AGPV and on the same day tragedy struck at Radlett when Handley Page Hermes prototype G-AGSS, flown by Flt Lt J. R. Talbot, crashed soon after take-off, killing the pilot and his crew. The cause of the accident was the result of elevator overbalance leading to Talbot losing control.

During that week *The Daily Telegraph's* air correspondent, Air Commodore G. S. Payne, caused uproar when he advocated that BOAC should buy American aircraft. To back up his argument, he contended: 'It is fair to say that there are no British commercial long-range landplanes now available, and few contemplated comparable with existing American types. Nor will there be any obtainable within a reasonable time which will be better than American planes likely to be available and already established.' Sir Roy Dobson, MD of A. V. Roe Ltd retorted that the Avro Tudor I could take 24 passengers across the Atlantic in great comfort faster and higher than any American aircraft, and that the Tudor II for Empire routes would be able to carry 60 passengers at high cruising speeds. He also stated that the Avro York was far more modern and satisfactory than many American types and then cited that the Lancastrian, carrying 13 passengers (actually nine), flew the Australian–London service in an elapsed time of 63 hours!

From October to December 1945 E.J.R. continued to sign out Mosquitoes and made a dozen or so more flights, including a number of first flights with Stan Offord.

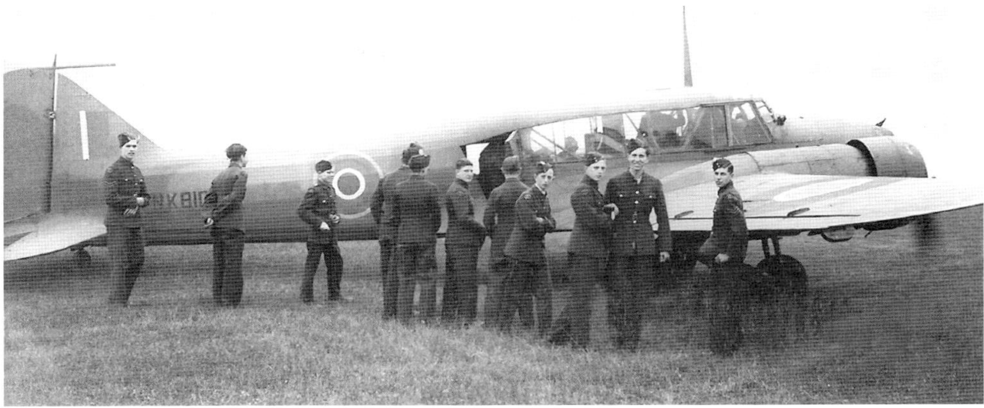

Stanley Orton Bradshaw taking up cadets from Nos. 2 and 3(F) ATC squadrons at Leavesden on 19 August 1945 in ATA Anson I NK210.

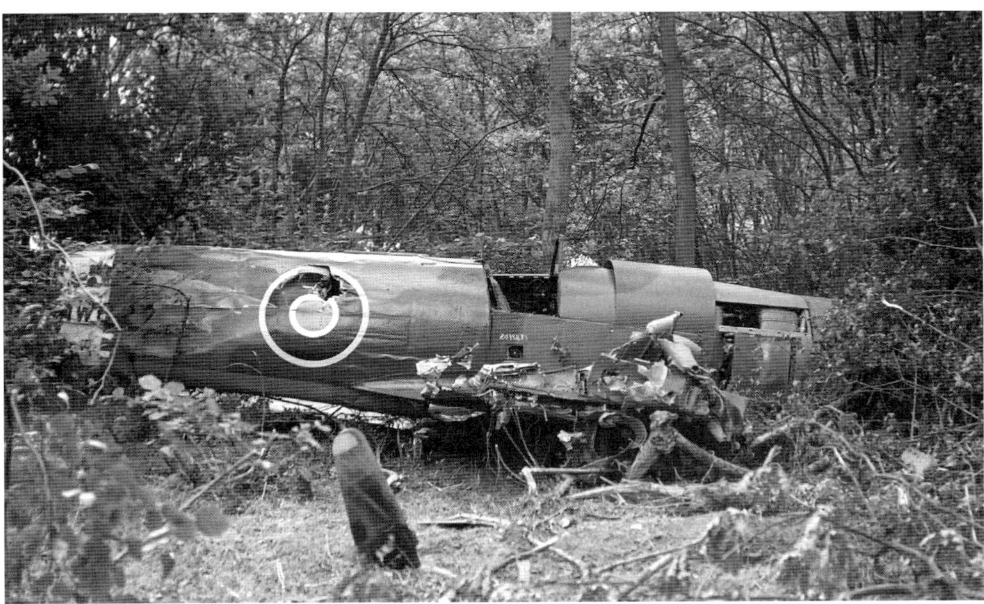

On 5 July 1945 First Officer Diane Ramsey took off from White Waltham, home of the ATA's No. 1 Ferry Pool, in Hawker Tempest II MW827 bound for RAF Henlow when the throttle stuck wide open causing the Tempest to career around the sky at 400 mph. Trying to lose speed by climbing resulted only in gaining a lot of altitude, so Ramsey turned back to White Waltham, cutting the engine on the approach but still arriving at high speed. On hitting the grass and bouncing over the far hedge the Tempest disappeared into a wood on Smewins Farm, leaving a trail of debris in its wake. When those who had witnessed Diane's arrival got to the Tempest it had shed most of its extremities, but there, sitting on top of the engine cowling, was the pilot, completely unscathed. E.J.R. took this photograph shortly after and it shows just how lucky the pilot was to escape with her life.

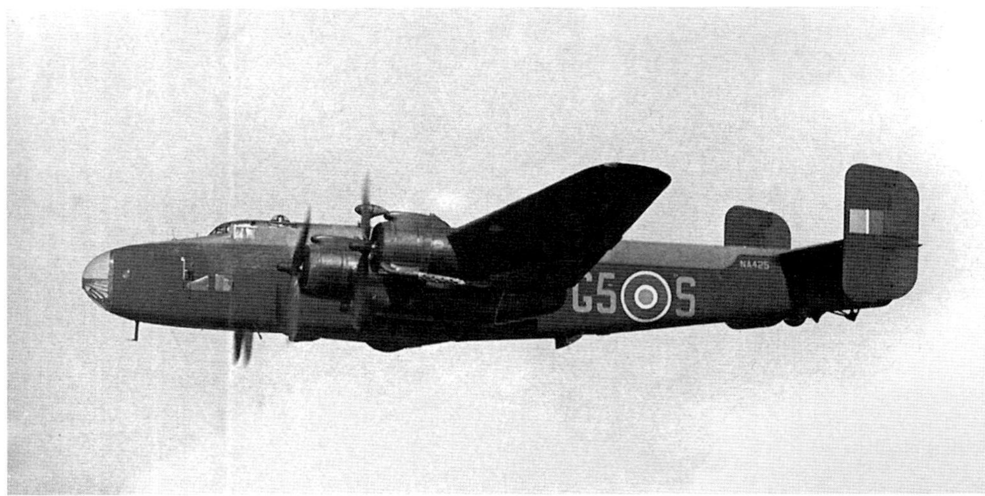

'Freddie' Offord and E.J.R. came across Handley Page Halifax VII NA425 while flying D.H. 98 Mosquito N.F.36 RL211 from Leavesden on 27 August 1945. NA425 was one of a batch of 122 Halifax VIIs built by Rootes at Speke, Liverpool, in 1945 and was delivered to No. 190 Squadron at Great Dunmow, passing to No. 295 Squadron before being struck off charge in December 1949.

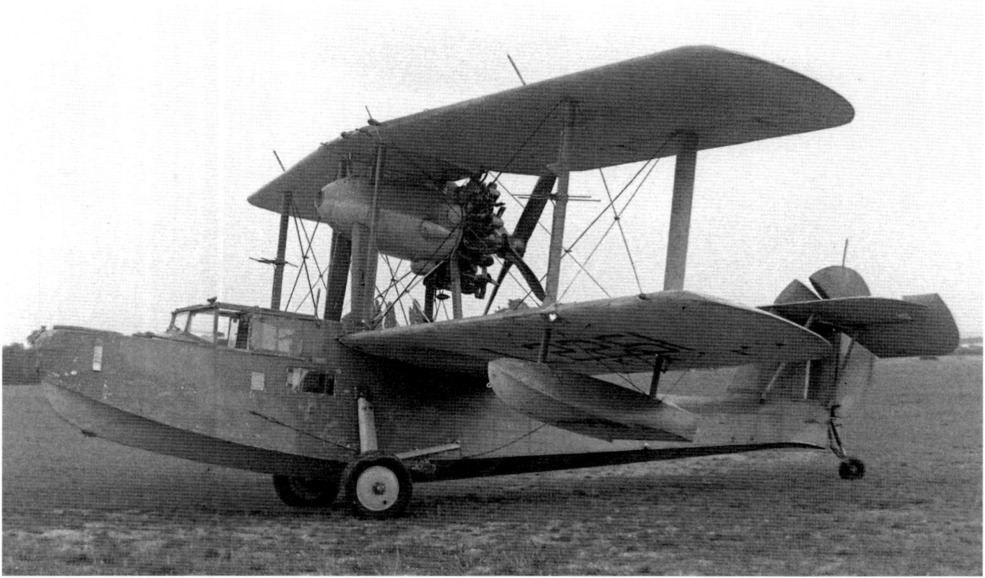

On 17 September 1945 Supermarine Walrus L2251 arrived at Leavesden. Built at Woolston in 1939, the amphibian was assigned to No. 751 Squadron RNAS Ford and served later with No. 772 Squadron and the MAEE at Helensburgh in 1944. Records do not throw any light on the amphibian's history after that date. The reason for its visit to Leavesden is not known.

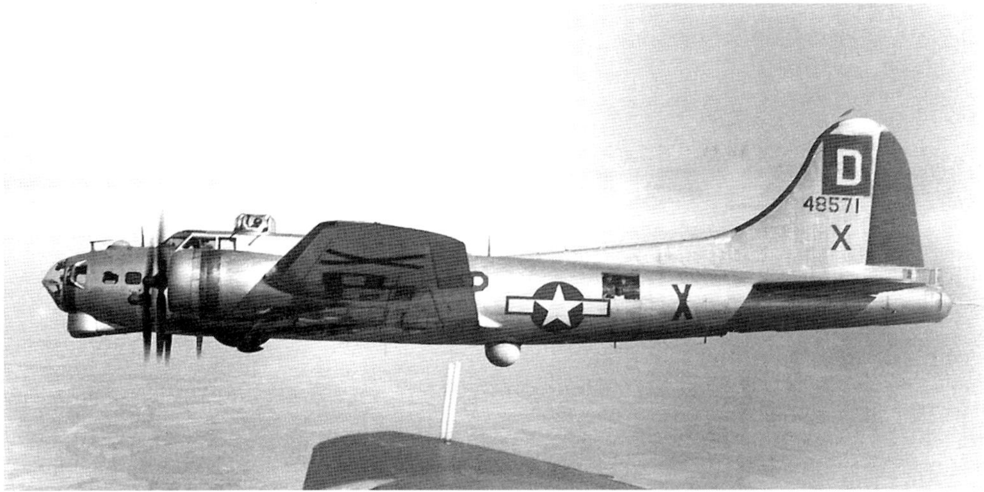

On the same 27 August flight Offord and E.J.R. also encountered Boeing B-17G Fortress 44-8571 EP-X and chased it around St Albans, much to the amusement of the bomber's crew – at least they didn't fire at the Mosquito! The Fortress had been delivered originally to the USAAF at Cheyenne in October 1944 and was assigned to 100 BG at Thorpe Abbotts. At the time it was accosted over St Albans the B-17G was stationed at Framlingham. After returning to the USA in October 1945 the aircraft was scrapped in January 1946.

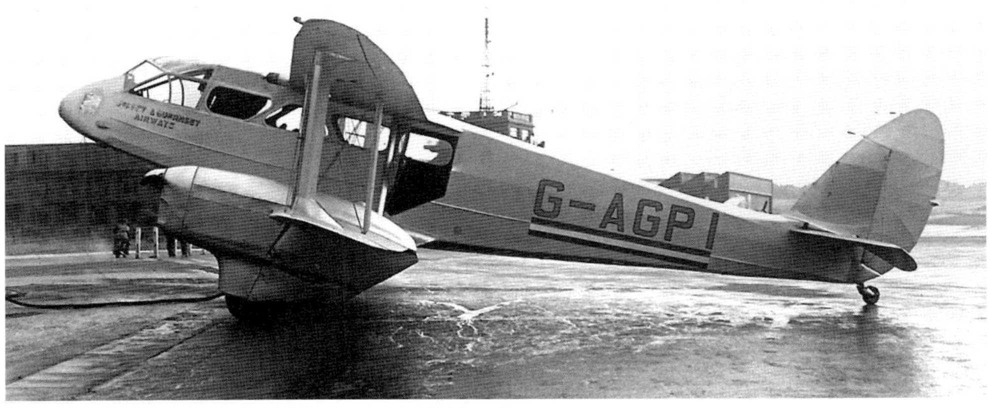

Built by Brush Coachworks Ltd at Loughborough in 1945, D.H. 89B Dominie I NR809 was sold in June to become Rapide Mk III G-AGPI and registered to Jersey Airways Ltd, passing later to Jersey & Guernsey Airways in whose livery the Rapide is seen at Croydon on 27 August 1945. The Rapide was subsequently registered to the Ministry of Aviation, BEA, and finally to Somerton Airways Ltd at Cowes, Isle of Wight, in May 1949. Shortly after, on 16 June, 'PI crashed at Somerton, Cowes, after it overshot on landing, hitting trees and a house. Though the pilot was injured the six other occupants were unharmed.

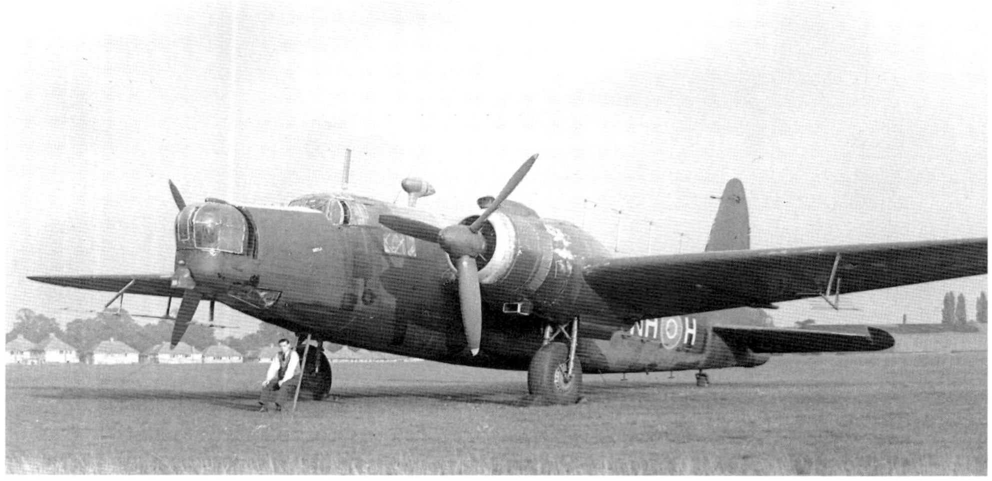

Vickers Wellington GR XIII MF639 was part of a batch of 600 built at Vickers-Armstrongs' facility at Squires Gate, Blackpool, and was photographed at Leavesden on 17 September 1945. It bears the code letters of No. 415 Squadron RCAF, based at Bircham Newton, but by the time this photograph was taken the squadron had disbanded in May that year. Note the stickleback radio aerials on the rear fuselage.

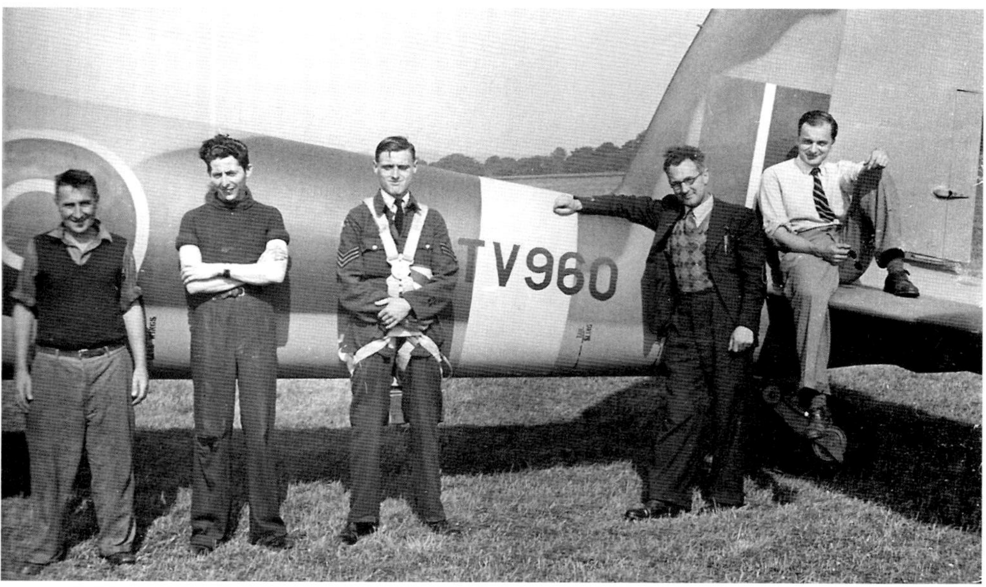

Another view of D.H. 98 Mosquito T.III TV960 taken on the same day. E.J.R. is sitting on the tailplane prior to the Mosquito setting off on a delivery flight in the hands of the young RAF officer kitted up and ready to go. The aircraft was delivered to No. 13 OTU at RAF Bicester and taken off RAF charge in June 1946.

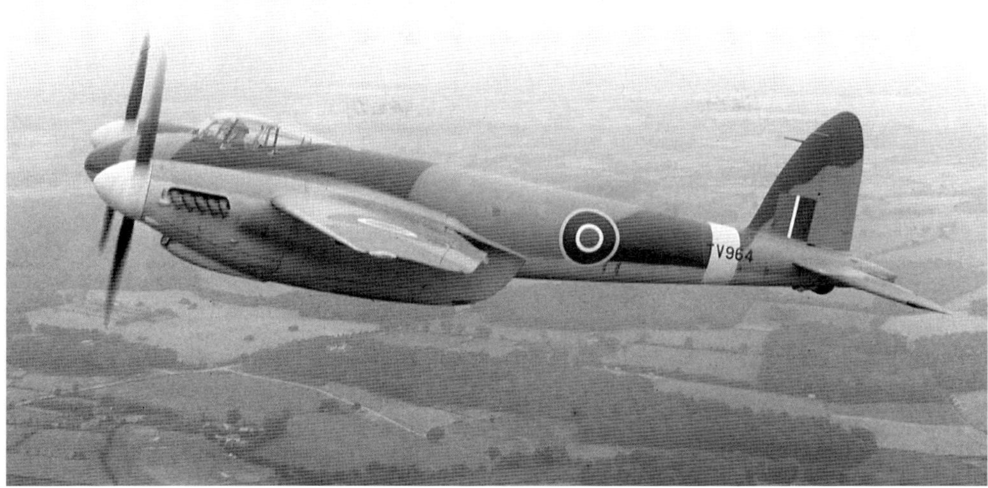

A masterpiece of flying skill and ATA co-operation: First Officer Peter Garrod coaxes D.H. 98 Mosquito T.III TV964 down to 95 mph in order to formate on ATA Fairchild Argus HB604, flown by First Officer Martyn Steynor on 26 September 1945 over Princes Risborough. E.J.R. accompanied 'Freddie' Offord on TV964's first flight on 22 September 1945. During the 45-minute flight Offord took the aircraft to 9,500 ft for test dives and 'shot up' Eaton Bray in Bedfordshire four times allowing E.J.R. take the controls to make steep turns. Three days later Offord and E.J.R. took sister ship TV966 to the memorable ATA Pageant at White Waltham.

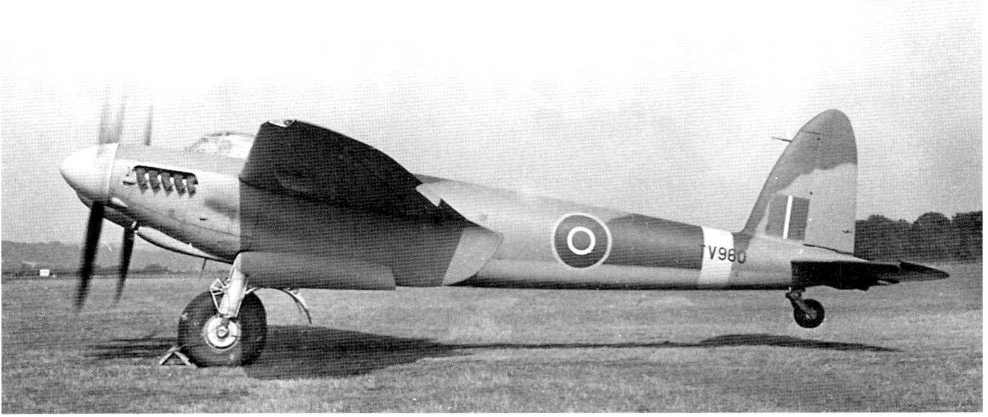

E.J.R. risking his career and the safety of the aircraft by running up D.H. 98 Mosquito T.III TV960 against the wheel chocks at Leavesden in September 1945, a practice frowned upon for obvious reasons. One of a batch of 50 T.IIIs delivered from Leavesden between July 1945 and May 1946, this aircraft was delivered to France's Armée de l'Air.

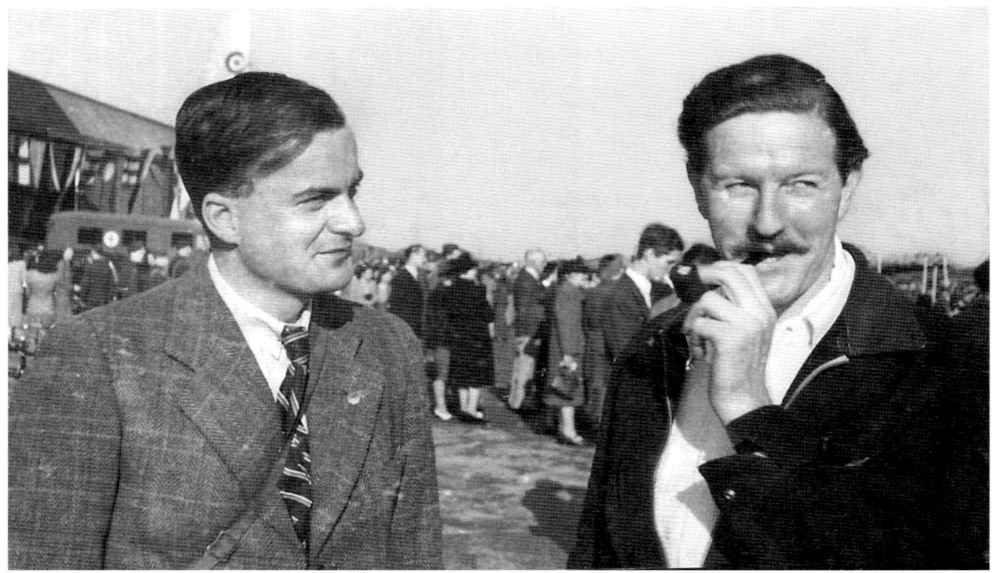

E.J.R. with the dashing Leslie Phillips look-alike Freddie Offord at the ATA Pageant at White Waltham on 30 September 1945.

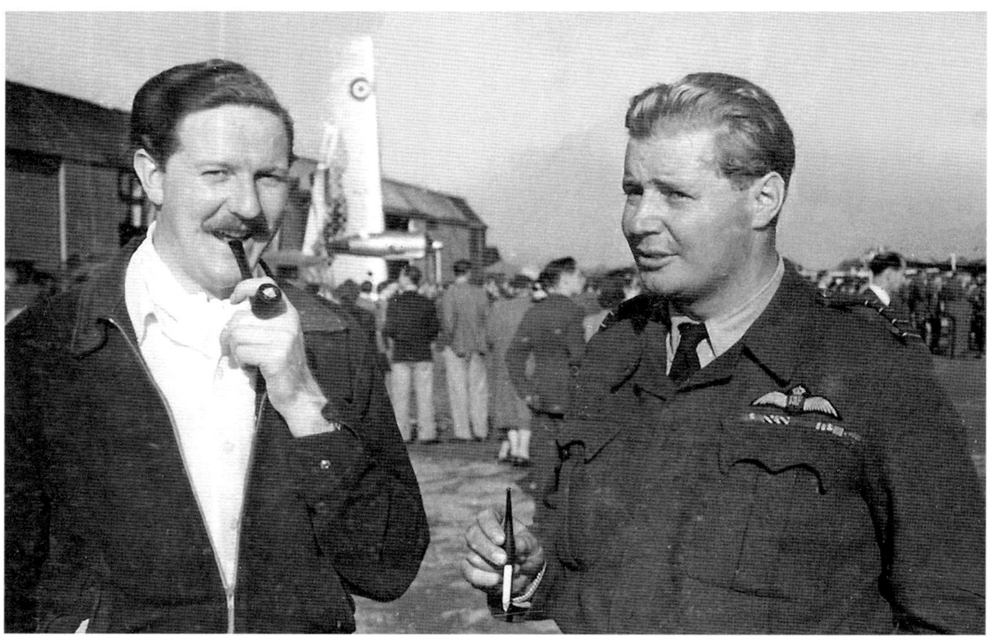

Offord and Wg Cdr Wykeham Barnes (1915–95)—he dropped the Wykeham in 1955—at the ATA Pageant at White Waltham on 30 September 1945. Offord and E.J.R. took D.H. 98 Mosquito T.III TV966 to the pageant from Leavesden. During what *The Aeroplane* described as 'a spectacular show', Offord flew the Mosquito mostly on one engine. He finished off with a high speed run across the aerodrome below 100 ft with both engines dead!

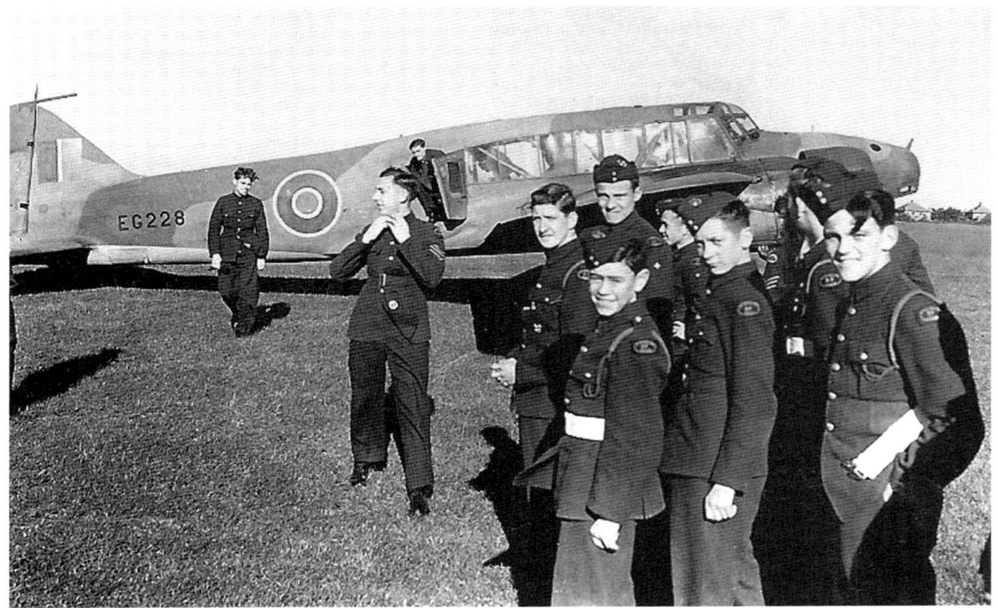

This group of Watford ATC cadets is about to take an air experience flight in ATA Anson I EG228 at Leavesden on 22 September 1945. E.J.R. and Stanley Orton Bradshaw organised such flights for ATC squadron cadets during 1945 in ATA aircraft flown over from White Waltham. The last flight of that particular day took five cadets, aeronautical artist C. Rupert Moore and E.J.R. on a 45-minute cloud-chasing sortie at 7,000 ft over London.

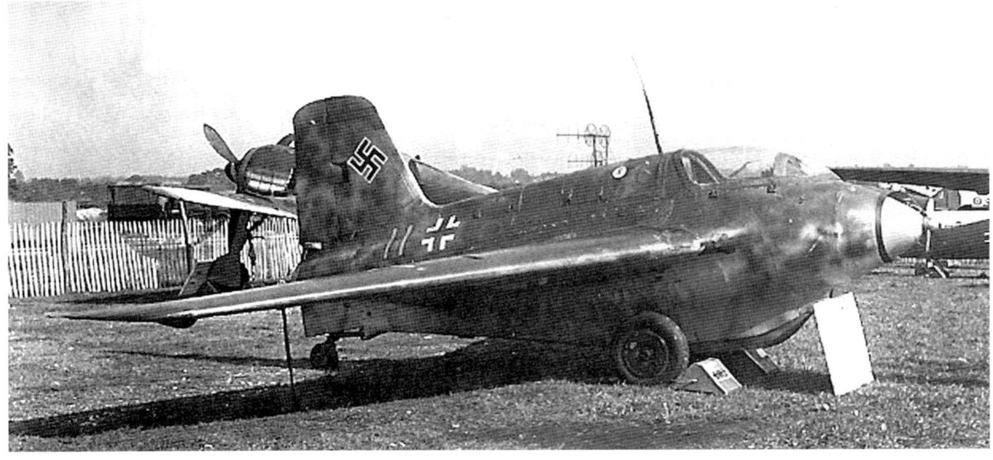

Seen at the ATA Pageant was Messerschmitt Me 163B-1 Komet 191454, previously on exhibition in London's Hyde Park during 16–22 September. Formerly 'Yellow 11' of JG 400, the fighter was surrendered at Husum and sent to RAE Farnborough, from where it passed to RAF Brize Norton. After exhibition in Hyde Park and at White Waltham the Me 163 was shipped to Canada in September 1946 and scrapped there *c.* 1957.

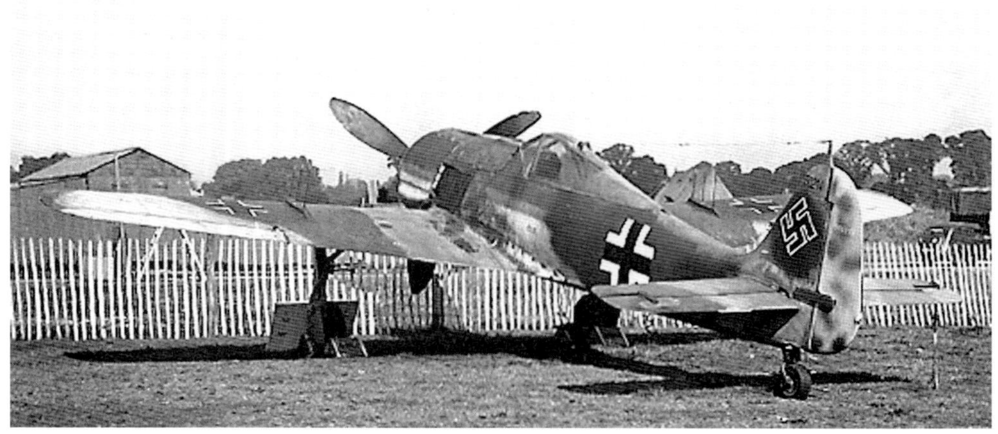

Also seen at the ATA Pageant was Focke-Wulf Fw-190A-6 wk nr 550214. Built at AGO Oscherleben, this was a trials aircraft and when captured at Leck was found to be equipped with FUG 217J Neptun–Liliput radar. Given the identification 'Min-10', the aircraft went to RAE Farnborough and after exhibition at Hyde Park and White Waltham was shipped to South Africa in 1946. It is now displayed at the South African National Museum of Military History, Johannesburg.

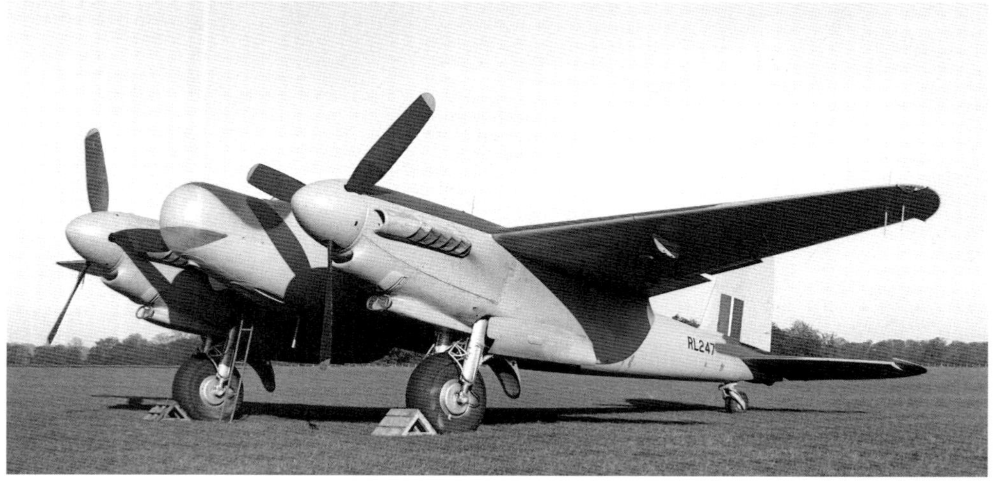

D.H. 98 Mosquito N.F. 36 RL247 at Leavesden on 27 October 1945, probably the day of its first flight. Part of a batch of 163 N.F. 36s delivered by de Havilland, Leavesden, between May 1945 and March 1947, RL247 was issued to No. 228 OCU at RAF Leeming where it was damaged in March 1949 following a forced landing due to engine trouble.

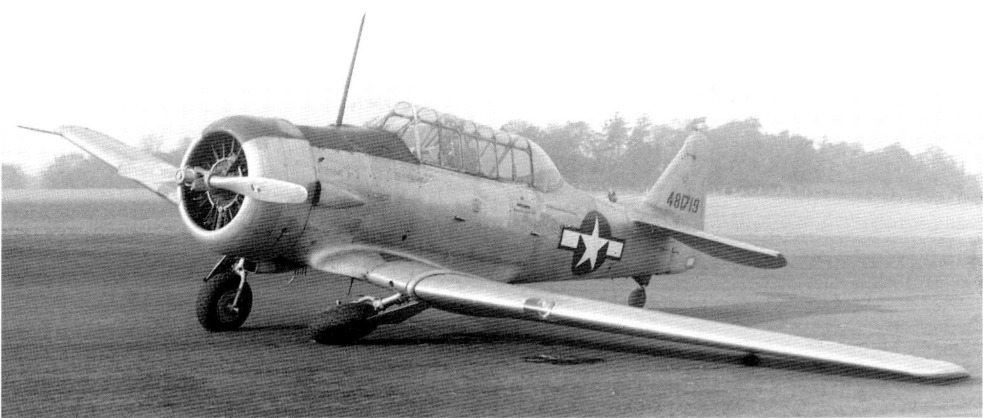

North American AT-6 Texan 44-81719 was practically undamaged after the port undercarriage leg retracted on Leavesden's runway on 31 October 1945. Post-war the Texan flew in Germany as D-IDOK and later D-FDOK before the registration was cancelled in January 1962.

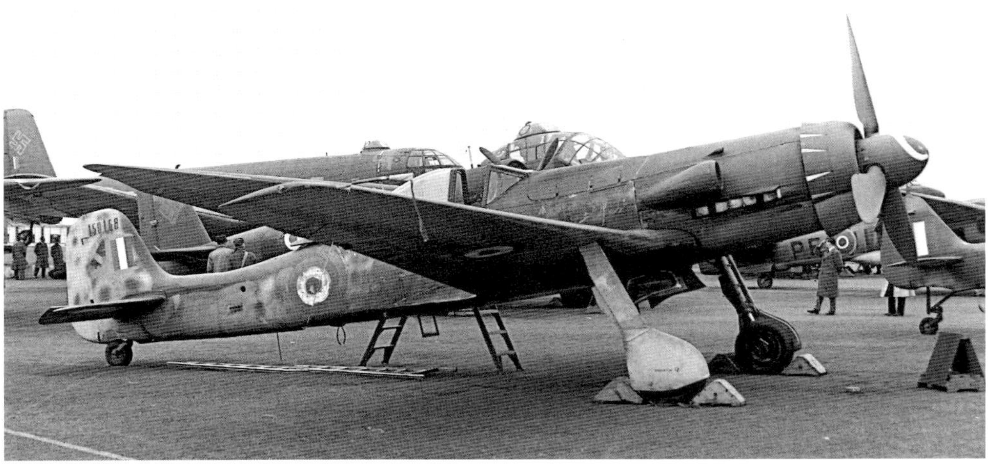

On 8 November 1945 E.J.R. visited the Exhibition of German Aircraft and Equipment staged by the Royal Aircraft Establishment at Farnborough. One exhibit was the Focke-Wulf Ta 152-H high-altitude fighter designed by Kurt Tank and about to enter quantity production when the war ended. A development of the Fw 190, with a 46 ft 6 inch wing span and lengthened fuselage, it was once described as 'looking like a Focke-Wulf 190 stretched in a distorting mirror.' Powered by a 1,700 hp Jumo 213E engine, the Ta 152 featured a pressurised cockpit complete with ultra-violet lighting! Ta 152 150168 also bore the temporary marks 'Air-Min 11' and was test-flown by Eric 'Winkle' Brown, before being scrapped in 1946.

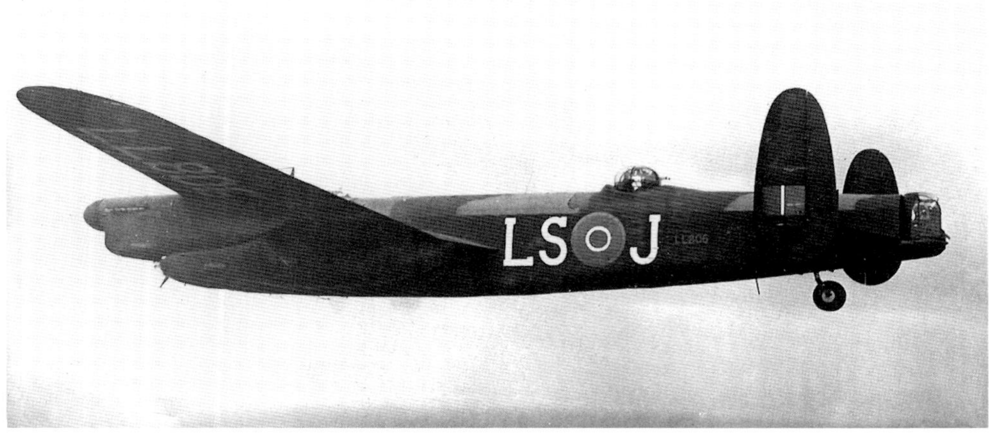

During another outing with Offord, on 9 November 1945 and this time in D.H. 98 Mosquito 33 TW230, E.J.R. came across No. 15 Squadron Avro Lancaster LL806. Unbeknown to Offord and E.J.R., 'J – Jig' was a veteran of no fewer than 134 operational flights, all flown within a space of one year. Offord 'shot up' the Lanc four times as he chased it to its RAF Mildenhall base. Perhaps, if he had known the bomber's pedigree, he would have paid it more respect. LL806 was taken off RAF charge in December 1945, a venerable bomber that should have been preserved for posterity.

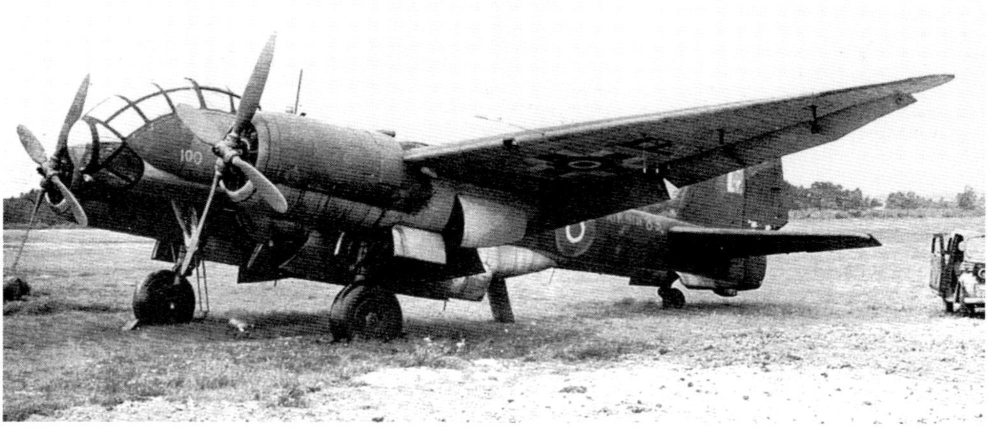

The final development of the Junkers Ju 88 was the Ju 388L-1. The example seen here at Farnborough on 8 November 1945 is wk no 500006 and came from Tarnewitz. On arrival in the UK in August 1945 it was assigned to the Air Ministry and marked 'Air-Min 83'. This photo-reconnaissance aircraft was coded PE+IF and '6' and bereft of bomb racks. After a limited amount of flying at Farnborough the aircraft passed to the College of Aeronautics, Cranfield, and was eventually scrapped. E.J.R.'s Ford car is seen right.

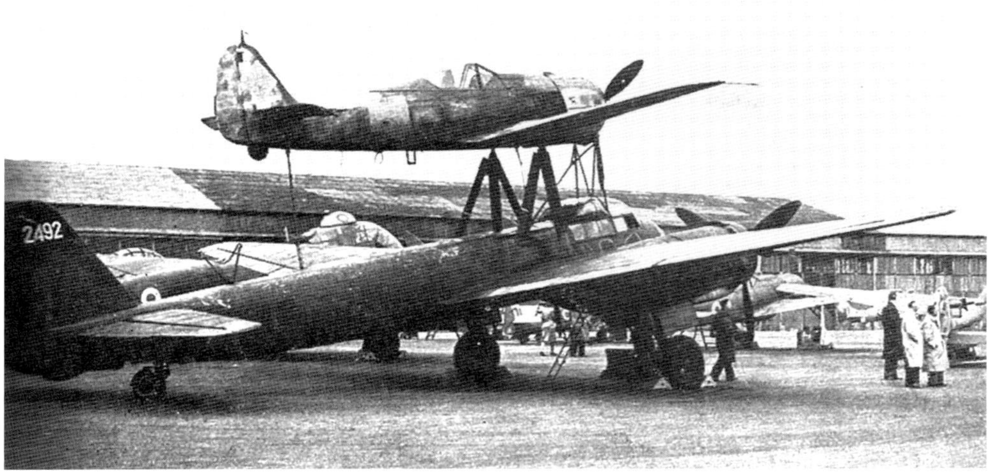

A centre of attraction at the German aircraft exhibition at Farnborough in November 1945 was the piggy-back combination of Junkers Ju 88A wk nr 2492 and Focke-Wulf Fw 190A wk nr 733759, known collectively as Mistel S 3A. Arriving separately at Farnborough in time for the exhibition, the combination was given the designation 'Air-Min 77'. The Ju 88 was scrapped at Farnborough the following year, the fate of the Fw 190 uncertain.

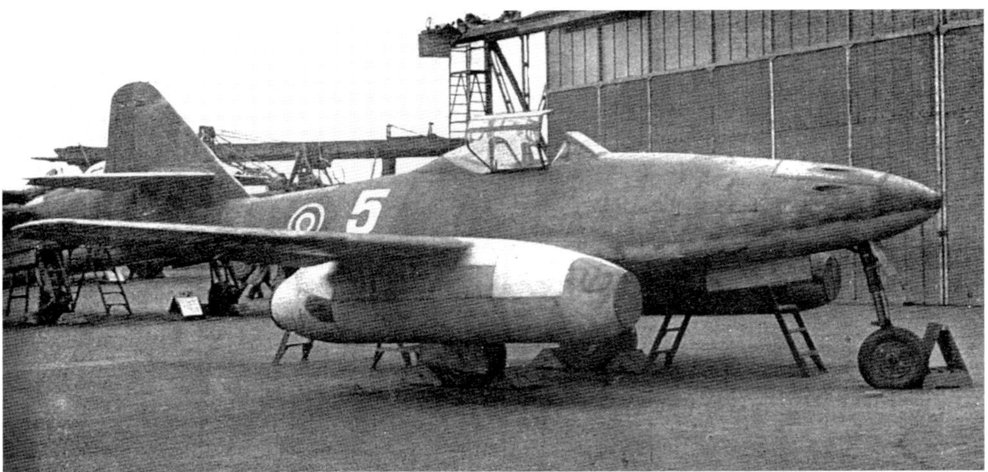

This Messerschmitt Me 262A-1 was surrendered at Fassberg, flown to RAF Manston and then on to Farnborough in August where it is seen on 8 November 1945. Coded 'White 5' of I/JG 7 and bearing the Air Ministry marks 'Air-Min 80', the 262 was shipped to Canada in mid-1946 but sadly was burnt out(?) in a fire-fighting exercise at Aylmer, Ontario, not long after. Today it would have been worth a fortune!

2

Back to Civvy Street
(1946)

> If I'd stayed on 'till Tuesday I could have had a three hour flight in the
> *Golden Hind*, which was due to have a new cooker fitted to
> serve up frozen food or something.
>
> Letter from E. J. Riding to A. J. Jackson in 1946.

On the first day of the New Year private flying was released from its wartime detention and resumed in the United Kingdom, but the future looked bleak. Oliver Stewart, editor of *Aeronautics*, got straight to the point in his editorial in the February issue:

> Contrary to popular belief and published proclamation, the ban on private and club flying was not lifted on 1st of January. All that really happened was that the privilege of flying, always enjoyed by Government officials and members of the Services, was shifted a little so that it took in men of extreme wealth and extreme prodigality. The Government said, in effect, 'we make flying free, but we keep fuel bound; we shall stop nobody from flying in the future; we shall only stop them from getting the petrol with which to fly.'

The Aeroplane's editorial for 4 January 1946 was equally dismissive and was headed 'Thanks for nothing'.

Also on 1 January the Ministry of Aviation (MoA) took over Heathrow from the Air Ministry, BSAA Avro Lancastrian G-AGWG leaving for a proving flight to South America, captained by AVM D. C. T. Bennett of Pathfinder Force fame. Elsewhere, the first peacetime private charter flight was made—from Cardiff Airport to Filton, Bristol, by Cambrian Air Services' Taylorcraft Auster G-AFWN.

In a raging blizzard Luton Aero Club reopened on 2 January after being closed for the duration of the war and Croydon Airport resumed operations.

E.J.R. made his second post-war visit to Croydon on 25 January, photographing a handful of Avro 652A Mk 19s and a couple of Dragon Rapides.

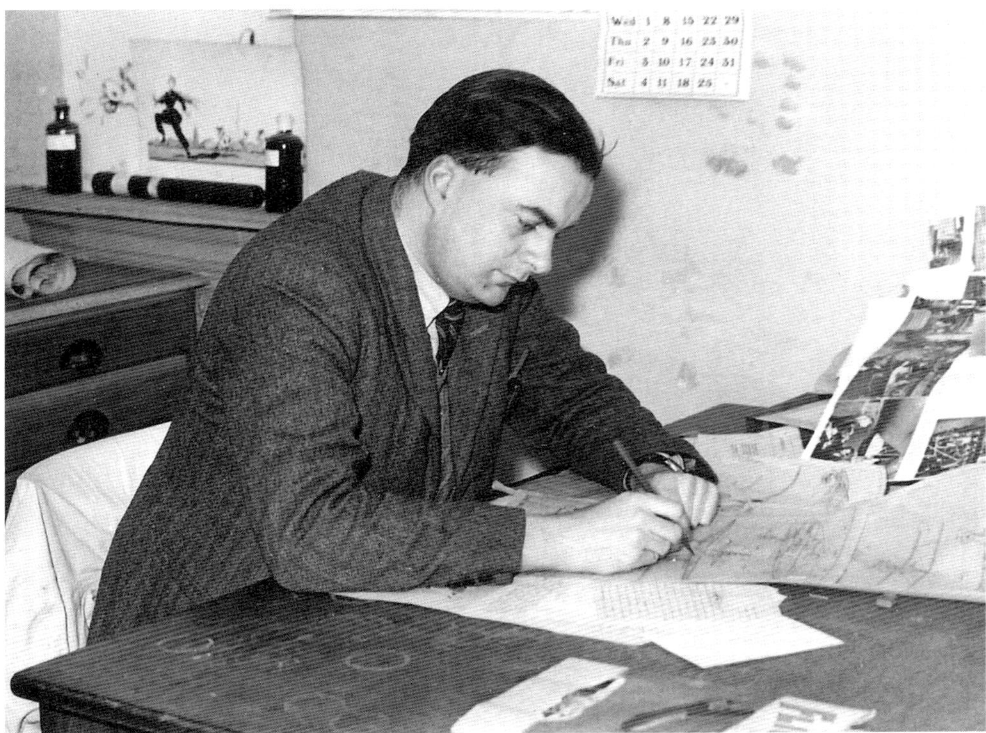

E.J.R. left the AID in February 1946 and joined the Harborough Publishing Company on 1 March where he worked on *Aeromodeller* and *Air Review* magazines and co-edited Vol VII of *Aircraft of the Fighting Powers* with Owen Thetford. He is seen here pretending to work in his Eaton Bray office for the benefit of a publicity photograph. Eaton Bray featured a model sportsdrome and had its own landing field.

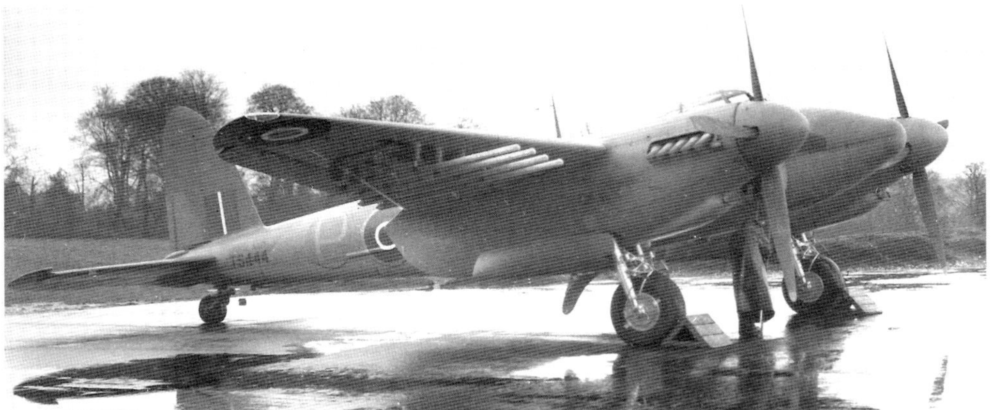

D.H. 98 Mosquito T.33 TS444 in the rain outside the Mosquito Flight Shed at Leavesden on 1 February, the day Offord and E.J.R. attempted to deliver it to A&AEE Boscombe Down for evaluation. Leaving at 10.30 and arriving 25 minutes later, Boscombe Down did not want the aeroplane. On the return flight to Leavesden the weather was so foul Offord lost his way and ended up over the Kent coast! The Mosquito finally landed back at Leavesden after a flight of 45 minutes via Gravesend and Hornchurch!

On 10 February he visited Radlett and attended a Display of British Civil and Military Aircraft arranged by HM Government for representatives of the United Nations Organisation (UNO) with the co-operation of the Society of British Aircraft Constructors (SBAC). A number of the latest British military types were on show, including the Gloster Meteor IV and the D.H. 100 Vampire F.1 jet fighters alongside the D.H. 103 Hornet, Supermarine Spiteful XIV and Avro Lincoln heavy bomber. That led *The Aeroplane* to comment: 'Propellers are not quite done with yet.'

The Royal Aero Club announced the formation of an Association of British Aero Clubs on 20 February, expecting 52 clubs to join.

On 28 February E.J.R. had his last flight with the AID, in D.H. 98 Mosquito 36 RL258 with a pilot rejoicing in the unlikely name Storm Back. January and February had been busy months with Mosquito production, E.J.R amassing almost 30 flights in Mks III, 30, 33, 36. On 1 March he began employment with the Harborough Publishing Company Ltd, based at the company's premises at Eaton Bray near Leighton Buzzard. In addition to compiling the last volumes of *Aircraft of the Fighting Powers* he doubled as photographer and draughtsman for *Aeromodeller* magazine and many of the company's other publications.

In March Northolt opened officially as a civil airport, on loan from the RAF to the Ministry of Civil Aviation (MCA). On 4 March 1946 the British European Airways (BEA) Division of BOAC began operating aircraft in civil markings with BOAC uniformed crews. From 6 March all BOAC aircraft operating on European routes reverted to peacetime civilian registrations and liveries.

Taylorcraft Aeroplanes (England) Ltd changed its name to Auster Aircraft Ltd on 8 March to dispel the idea that the Auster was an American aircraft built in England. The company went to great pains to stress that the design had been revised completely, having set up its own design and stress department for this purpose.

On 10 March Avro Tudor 2 G-AGSU made its maiden flight from Woodford, Cheshire. British South American Airways began a regular London–Buenos Aires service on the 15th and on 25 March Heathrow became London Airport officially.

E.J.R visited Aldenham airfield (later Elstree) for the first time on 30 March and on the following day, in a letter to A.J.J., wrote:

You'll laugh at this: Coming home from C. Rupert Moore's last night, my stooge (Norman Eastaff (ATC)) and I called in at the Aldenham House aerodrome [known later as Elstree] just to see what was doing and made the acquaintance of the owners of Auster Autocrat G-AGVT—Wing Commander Royce Wilkinson and an FAA cove called Forth. Anyway, after a spot of blarneying we arranged that for the sum of 12*s* 6*d*, Easy and I should be airborne for the magnificent time of 15 minutes! So saying, at 14.40 hrs 'VT took off downhill, with Messrs Forth, Riding and Eastaff on board and when about 100 ft up the second mentioned took over and headed towards Radlett, when two circuits of the Moore residence was made without going into a spin. We then returned to Aldenham and made three attempts at landing—I let Forth have it just as we muffed the third. S'no use, I can't get used to keeping the nose up with 40 showing on the clock, I keep wanting to come in at 90 with a mile or so to go.

On 27 March Percival Proctor III DX231 of the Metropolitan Communications flight, Hendon made a forced landing in Hyde Park, London at dusk on a flight from Holmesley South Aerodrome, Hampshire. Capt. L. T. Carruthers took the prototype Percival Prentice TV163 aloft for the first time from Luton on 31 March. On the same day some interesting statistics were revealed in answer to Parliamentary questions. During the period September 1938—September 1945 560 airfields were constructed, or had been taken over and extended, in Great Britain. The average cost in 1945 for a bomber airfield was £1 million and for a fighter airfield £850,000. On the 14th the author having not long celebrated his fourth birthday, had his first flight, from Elstree in Auster Autocrat G-AGXJ with R. Forth. The following day E.J.R. visited Yeovil and flew with Westland chief test pilot Harald Penrose, taking aerial photographs of Somerset. Later that day Westland test pilot Flt Lt J. 'Tommy' Thompson took him for a 1 hour 45 minute flight in veteran Westland Widgeon G-AAGH to photograph Dorset.

On 1 May E.J.R. travelled to Woodford for the first press demonstration flight of Avro Tudor I G-AGRC. The pilots were Jimmy Orrell and A. H. Cook. The Tudor was taken to 25,000 ft and the 1 hour 35 minute flight overflew Blackpool, Rhyl and Manchester.

A week later the prototype Handley Page Hastings TE580 was flown for the first time from RAF Wittering and on the 15th Geoffrey de Havilland Jnr made the first flight of the futuristic D.H. 108 TG283 from Woodbridge, Suffolk.

Initial flight of the Miles M. 60 Marathon U-10/G-AGPD took place on 19 May with Miles chief test pilot Ken Waller in command. Two days later E.J.R. flew to Renfrew from Croydon, returning the following day in Railway Air Services DC-3 Dakota G-AGZB, Capt. Hilary in command on both occasions.

Over in Toronto, Canada, W. L. 'Pat' Fillingham carried out the first flight of the prototype D.H.C.1 Chipmunk CF-DIO-X on 22 May, no one present imagining that dozens of Chipmunks would still be flying nearly 70 years later.

Former aircraft designer and ATA captain Geoffrey Wikner, partner in Foster, Wikner Aircraft started in 1936 and designer of the Wicko, left Hurn Airport on 24 May in H.P. Halifax G-AGXA with family and friends for his native Australia. On the 31st London Airport (Heathrow) opened officially to international traffic. Frequently engulfed in a sea of mud and providing only tents for handling passengers, the country's premier airport then boasted just one runway.

More than 300 aircraft from 35 RAF squadrons flew over London on 8 June, a national holiday to mark belatedly Victory Day and the war's end. Figures published a day or two earlier in a Government White Paper revealed that the conflict had killed a total 325,038 UK members of the armed forces and civilians between 3 September 1939 and 14 August 1945.

E.J.R. attended the Eastleigh Air Pageant on 22 June. Despite there being modern jets in the flying programme the low level antics of a BOAC Hythe Class Short

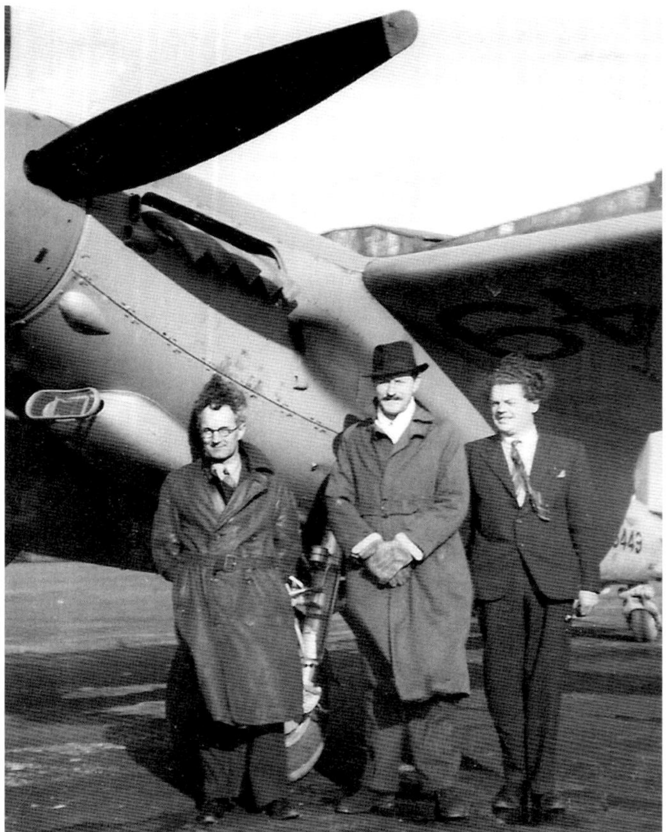

Offord, centre, with Leavesden's Mosquito Flight Shed foreman H. G. Harris to his right and Flight Shed superintendent John 'Tubby' Simpson, in his best suit, in front of D.H. 98 Mosquito TR.33 TS449. On 5 February Offord, accompanied by E.J.R., took this navalised version of the Mosquito, to 14,000 ft, performing four barrel rolls and two loops with a half-roll out of each. The flight ended with Offord giving E.J.R. some dual forced landing practice on a field near Sarratt in Leavesden's circuit.

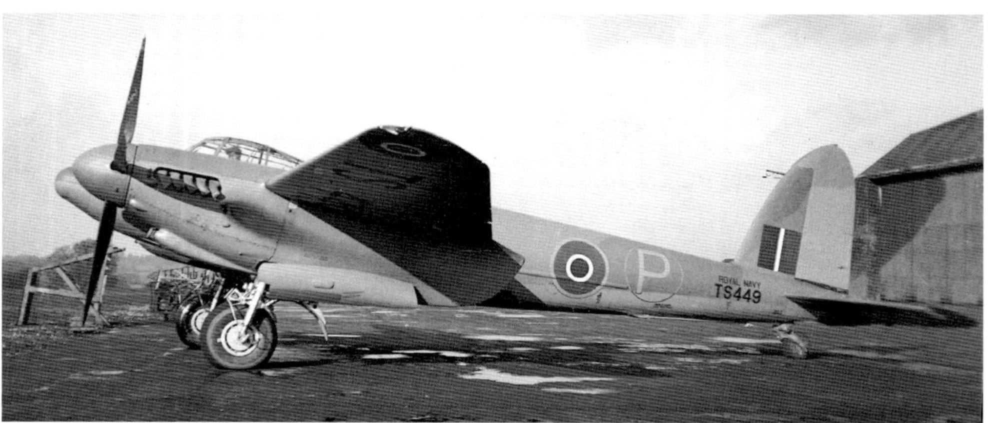

D. H. 98 Mosquito TR.33, TS449, outside Leavesden's Mosquito Flight Shed on 6 February. This second pre-production example of what became the Sea Mosquito for the Fleet Air Arm, had fixed as opposed to manually-operated folding wings found on later production versions and four-blade propellers. The same year it carried out RATOG trials with the RAE on HMS *Illustrious*. Later still, TS449 served with No. 790 Squadron FAA and finally with the Israeli Air Force. Remarkably, parts of the aircraft survive and are being incorporated into the restoration of Mosquito FB.VI TA122 at the de Havilland Heritage Centre at Salisbury Hall, Hertfordshire.

Sandringham stole the show. A few days later, during 27–30 June, the RAE put on a display of British aircraft, aero engines and equipment at Farnborough, not to be confused with the SBAC show at Radlett, held later in the year. On 29 June Shoreham Airport re-opened with a rally organised by the South Coast Flying Club.

Bernard Lynch carried out the first live ejection from an aircraft on 24 July, exiting during trials Gloster Meteor III EE416 flown by Capt. J. Scott of Power Jets from Martin-Baker's airfield at Chalgrove.

The prototype Supermarine Attacker TS409, known by the aviation press as the 'jet Spiteful', made its first flight in the hands of Jeffrey Quill on 27 July. On 1 August British European Airways Corporation and British South American Airways Corporation (formerly British South American Airways Ltd) were established formally.

In the absence of a 1946 King's Cup air race the 58-mile Folkestone Aero Trophy Race proved to be a worthy substitute. Held at Lympne, Kent, during the weekend of 31 August—1 September and organised by the Cinque Ports Flying Club, it was won by John Grierson flying Supermarine Walrus G-AHFN at a stately 121 mph. The most exciting event of the weekend was the Lympne High Speed Handicap race, reportedly the fastest held in Britain, not excepting the pre-war Schneider Trophy races, with a field of four of the fastest types in the military inventory: D.H. 100 Vampire, Hawker Fury I, D.H. 103 Hornet and Supermarine Seafang 31, flown respectively by Messrs Geoffrey de Havilland Jnr, Bill Humble, G. H. Pike and Mike Lithgow. Humble, flying the Fury, won the race, averaging 342 mph after de Havilland in the Vampire, which averaged 428 mph, was disqualified because he was flagged off mistakenly 30 seconds too soon.

During the first week of September the prototype Chrislea C.H.3 Ace G-AHLG was first flown from Heston by Rex Stedman. There were high hopes for this neat little light plane, but the novel flying controls were to be its downfall. A wheel controlled the ailerons, elevators and rudder but instead of twisting it left and right and pushing and pulling, the pilot was required to move the wheel up, down and sideways. Meanwhile, on 1 September, the Vickers Viking was introduced into service by BEA, G-AHOP leaving Northolt for Copenhagen, after being christened *Valerie*.

On the 7th Gp Capt. E. M. Donaldson, Commanding Officer of the RAF High Speed Flight, which had been re-established at Tangmere specifically for the purpose, broke the world's air speed record in specially prepared Gloster Meteor F.4 EE549, averaging 616 mph over a three-kilometre course between Worthing and Littlehampton.

The seventh and first post-war SBAC show was held at Radlett on 12–13 September, but because of a shortage of paper and limitations on working hours imposed by print unions coverage in the aviation weeklies was very limited. Highlights of the show were the Avro Tudor I, Gloster Meteor and Geoffrey de Havilland Jnr's breath-taking aerobatic display in the D.H. 108. He was to die in this aeroplane before the end of the month.

The price of aviation fuel was increased by a halfpenny on 16 September. Bulk retail prices rose to *2s 1d* for a gallon of 73 octane, *2s 2d* for 87 octane and *2s 4d* for 100 octane.

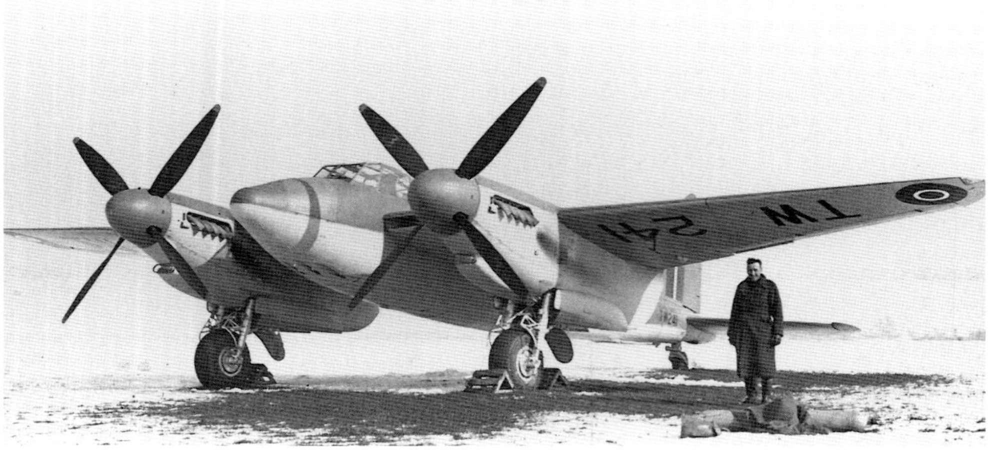

On 21 February E.J.R. and pilot Storm-Back dashed to Hatfield and back for lunch from Leavesden in D.H. 98 Mosquito TR.33 TW241, shortly after the aircraft's first flight. Both men took it out again the same day for a 30-minute test following a 'right wing low' correction, culminating with two low-level rolls and a shoot up near Luton. Powered by two 1,640 hp Rolls-Royce Merlin 25s, TW241 was the first Sea Mosquito brought up to full Naval specification, with folding wings and Lockheed oleo landing gear to aid rebound ratio for decking landing. It was later acquired by the Israeli Air Force.

E.J.R. had two flights in Airspeed A.S.65 Consul G-AIDY on 26 September, from Portsmouth to Christchurch return. The aircraft was on its second test flight, flown by Airspeed test pilot Ron Clear. A week later E.J.R. wrote to A.J.J:

The other day I went into Christchurch and visited our old friend Bud Fisher. Bud laid on a truly magnificent tour of his domain, and I was able to inspect all his fleet, which when assembled will be as follows: D.H. 60G Moth G-AAHI, two Miles Falcons (one belonged to Malcolm Douglas-Hamilton) for which he hopes to get brand new numbers, and which I hope he doesn't, two Magisters resplendent in coats of pillar box red paint, two Swallow IIs G-AEGN and G-AEVA, an Avro 631 Cadet G-ADFD, a Piper or Taylor Cub G-AFJP, and outside in the open were the remains of the Spartan G-ACAD. The latter has had it in a big way, and is little more than a collection of tea chests with lettering on them.

I left at lunchtime with an invitation to visit him at home in the evening. I then proceeded to Hythe, where after buggering about for two hours, I was ushered into the Line Manager's office and after a few minutes found me out on the tarmac with a motor boat and a guide at my disposal. The result of the escapade was the following [photographs]: G-AGJN, G-AGJK, G-AGKV, G-AHER and most of G-AFCT. If I'd stayed on till Tuesday I could have had a three hour flight in the Golden Hind, which was due to have a new cooker fitted to serve up frozen food or something.

Geoffrey de Havilland Jnr was killed in D.H. 108 TG306 on 27 September when it broke up over the Thames Estuary. The wreckage was located in shallow water at Egypt Bay, Isle of Grain.

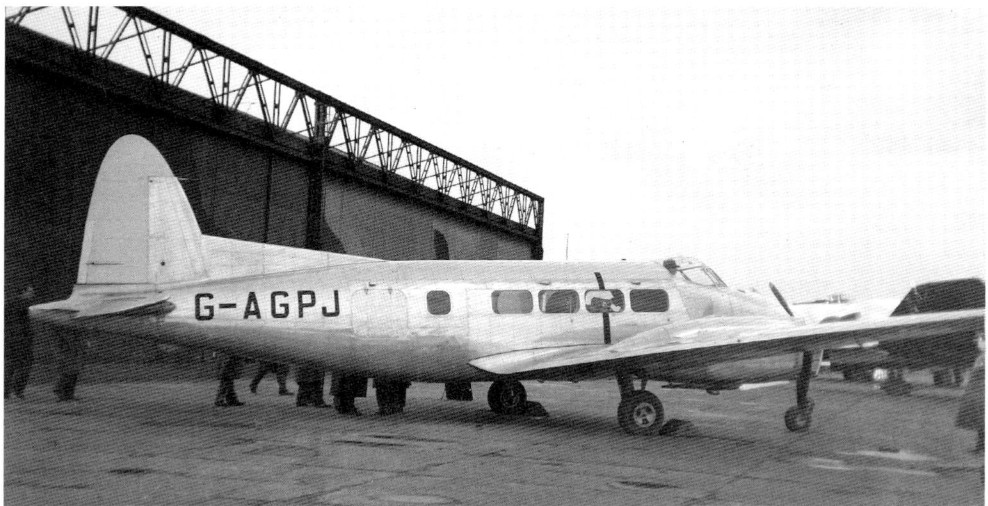

The prototype D.H. 104 Dove G-AGPJ at Radlett on 10 February. First flown on 25 September 1945 from Hatfield, and following trials at Farnborough, the Dove is seen fitted with a large dorsal fin to improve asymmetric control during single engine flight. This crude addition was replaced later with the more elegantly curved dorsal, characteristic of many subsequent de Havilland aircraft. 'PJ flew with the RAF for a couple of years as WJ310 before being exported to the Cape Verde Islands as CR-CAC in March 1956.

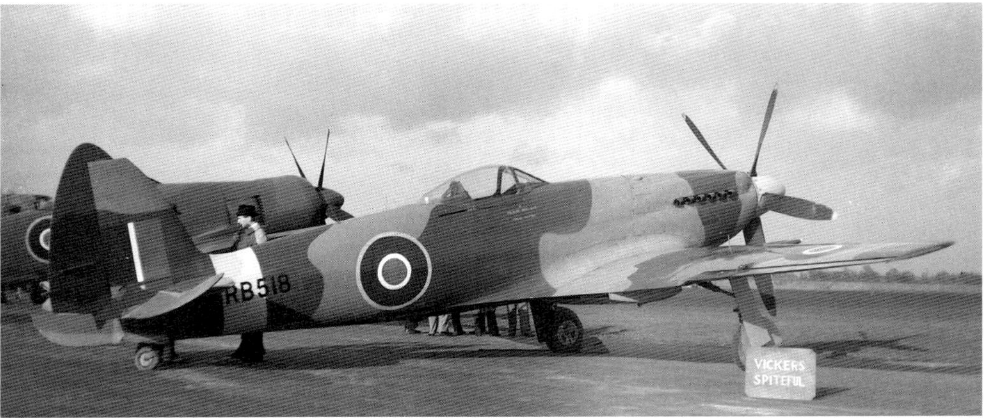

Also present at the Radlett UNO display was Vickers Supermarine Spiteful XVI RB518, fitted with a Rolls-Royce Griffon 101 engine driving a five-blade Rotol propeller. It once achieved 494 mph in level flight, though at the expense of the engine. Developed directly from the Spitfire, a laminar flow wing with straight leading and trailing edges replaced the classic elliptical shape.

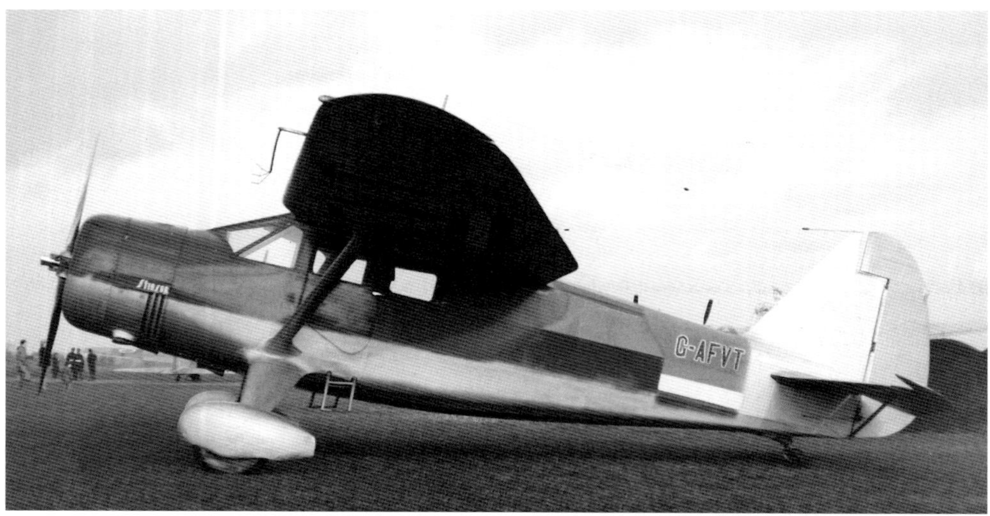

Another visitor to the UNO gathering at Radlett on 10 February was Stinson SR-10C Reliant G-AFVT, first registered in January 1940 and seen in wartime scheme with registration letters underlined with red, white and blue stripes. 'VT was operated for many years as a communications hack and, surviving a coming together with a Spitfire on the ground at Heston in April 1941, was sold in the USA in June 1968 to become N5913.

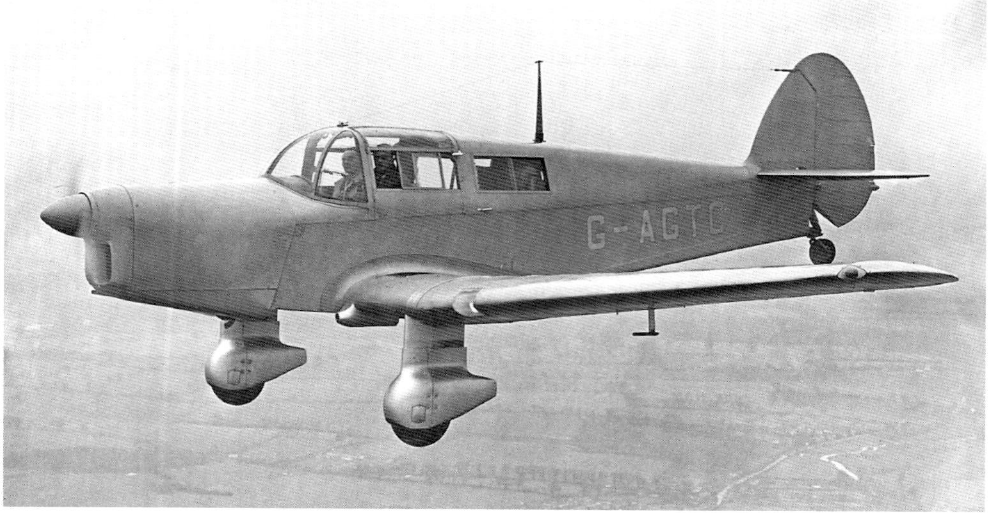

Luton-based Proctor 5 G-AGTC flown by Percival test pilot Capt. L. T. Carruthers, with aviation author Owen Thetford beside him, over Harpenden in morning mist on 22 March. 'TC was one of the first new civil aircraft to be registered when civil flying resumed officially on 1 January 1946. The Proctor 5 was a purely civil version of the RAF communications and training aircraft produced in large numbers, mostly by F. Hills & Sons Ltd at Trafford Park, Manchester. Many subsequently found their way onto the civil market. The four-seat Proctor 5 was powered by a 210 hp D.H. Gipsy Queen and cruised at 135 mph. Production ran to 150 of which 90 or so appeared on the British civil register. 'TC was damaged beyond repair at Malaga, Spain in May 1969.

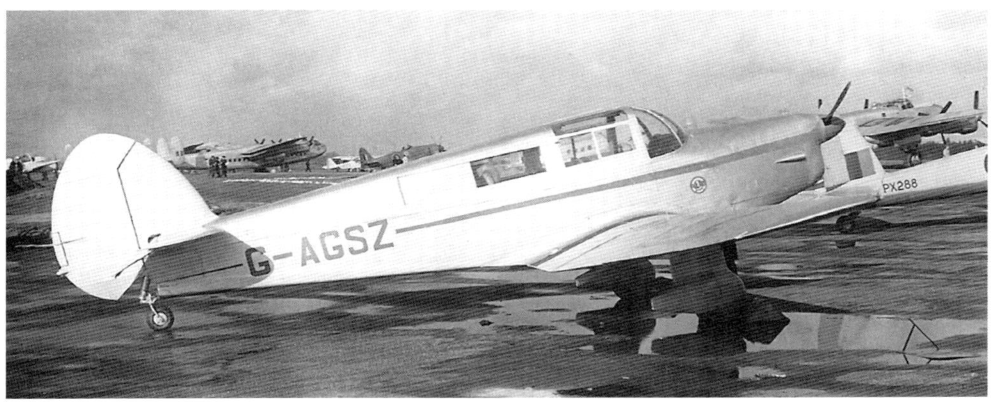

Towards the end of 1945 three low-hour Proctor IVs built by F. Hills and Sons, Manchester, in 1944 were sent to Percival Aircraft, Luton, to become prototypes for the civil Proctor 5. One of them was RM197 which became G-AGSZ, a demonstrator displayed at the SBAC-arranged display for UNO representatives at Radlett where it was photographed on 10 February. Subsequently registered to Hunting Air Travel Ltd, the Proctor was acquired by the Hon. Simon Warrender and flown to Australia during May and June 1949. Based at Melbourne and later registered VH-ADP, it was removed from the Australian register in 1959.

During October BOAC announced it was to use stewardesses for the first time, to begin with on the airline's Lockheed Constellations.

With a view to stimulating interest in lightweight aircraft and to encourage their design, construction and ownership (defined as powered aircraft with an all-up weight not exceeding 1,000 lb and engine not exceeding 75 hp) the Ultra Light Aircraft Association (ULAA) formed in London on 26 October, led by Messrs R. W. Clegg and Maurice Imray.

On 9 November BEA withdrew its Vickers Viking fleet temporarily because ice forming on the tailplane was causing stability problems.

A Gloster Meteor flown by former FAA Fairey Albacore pilot James Bridges on 12 December flew from Paris Le Bourget to Croydon in 23 minutes 37 seconds. On 16 December the first flight of the prototype Westland Wyvern TS371 was made by Harald Penrose from Boscombe Down. On the same day Nutts Corner, Belfast, opened to scheduled civil air traffic and on the 18th the first of BEA's Jupiter class Junkers 52s went into service on the London–Liverpool–Belfast route.

A NOTAM (Notice to Airmen) that month stipulated that 265 RAF and Naval airfields were 'totally prohibited' to civil aircraft, even in emergency. It was suggested darkly that explosives were stored on these aerodromes, or that runways were obstructed. It was common knowledge among pilots that many of the specified aerodromes were perfectly safe prompting *Aeronautics* to comment: 'Any sensible pilot who finds himself in a tight spot near a 'totally prohibited' aerodrome will doubtless go and have a look-see before deciding to crash elsewhere.'

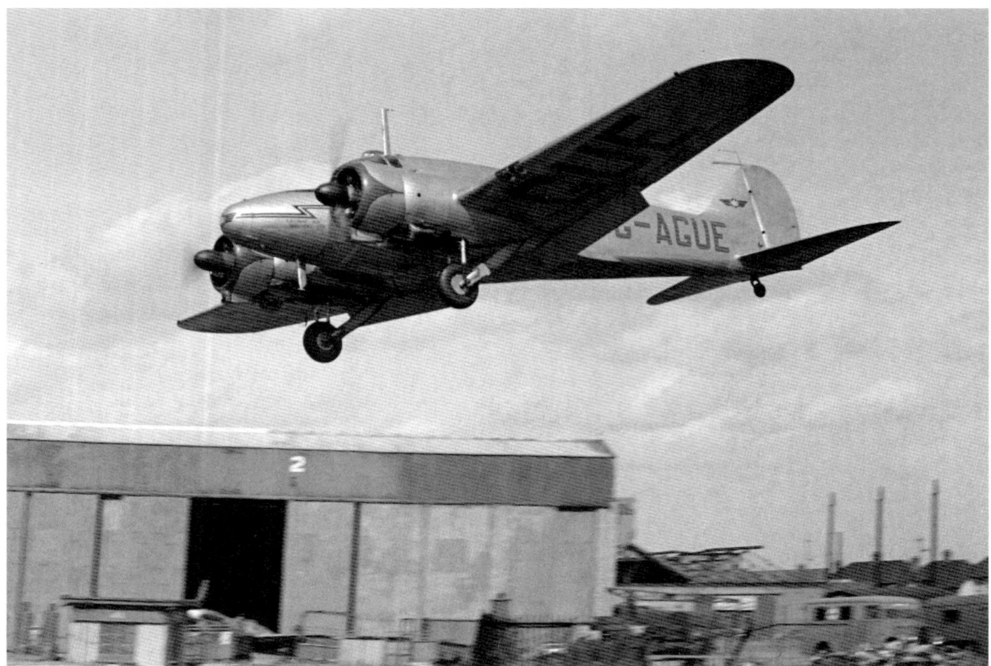

This evocative view of Railway Air Services' short-lived Avro 19 Series I Anson G-AGUE landing at Croydon was taken on 23 March. Converted from RAF aircraft VL361, it was registered in November 1945 but crashed and caught fire near Speke, Liverpool, in August 1946 while on an engine test flight, killing the pilot and injuring the two engineer passengers.

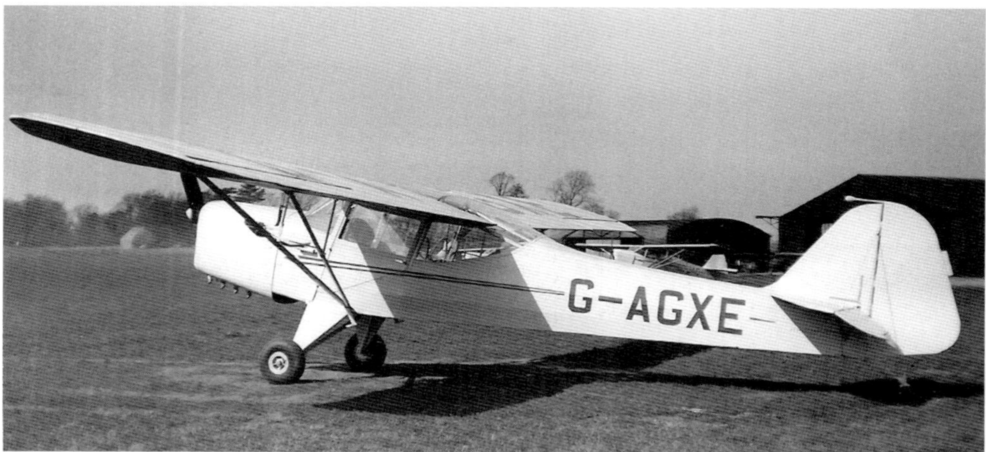

Brand spanking new Auster Autocrat G-AGXE, fresh from the Rearsby factory, on 26 March. Registered the same month, 'XE was exported to South Africa in April 1947 to become ZS-BPM. So prolific were Autocrats at the time that the entire G-AGX series of registrations, bar G-AGXA (a Halifax B. III), were taken up by the type.

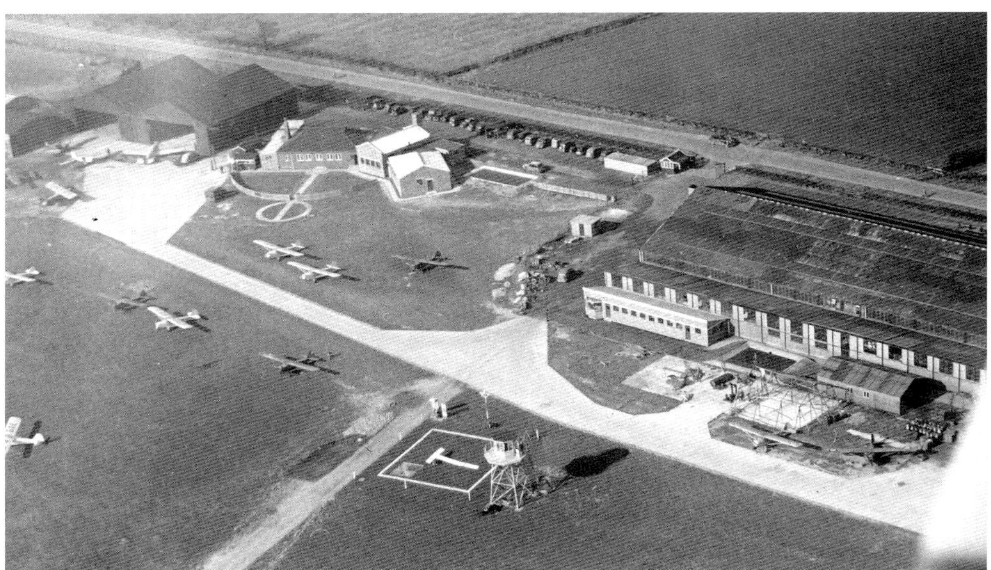

Aerial view of Rearsby, Leicester, photographed from Auster Autocrat G-AGTY on 26 March; the same month that Auster Aircraft Ltd was formed from Taylorcraft Aeroplanes (England) Ltd. Taylorcraft had been producing aircraft at nearby Thurmaston since 1939, flight testing them from Rearsby aerodrome, opened officially on 23 July 1938. Production of Austers continued at Rearsby for another 30-odd years, the company being absorbed into short-lived Beagle Aircraft Ltd in 1961. Sadly the aerodrome was closed in 1971 and although much of the factory area is still in use (by the automobile industry), much of the aerodrome has returned to agriculture with no sign that this plot of land was the birthplace of many hundreds of light aircraft.

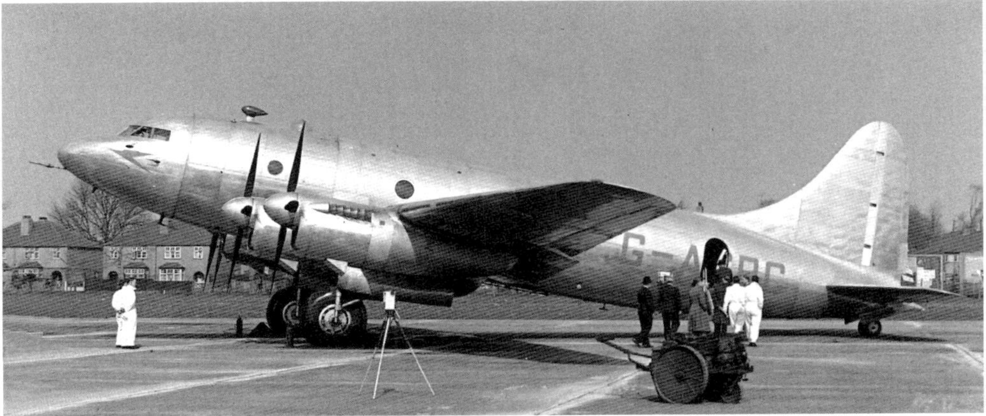

Avro 689 Tudor I G-AGRC at Heathrow on 25 March. First flown on 12 January 1946 the aircraft was owned by the Ministry of Supply and aircraft Production and was scrapped at Woodford in December 1948.

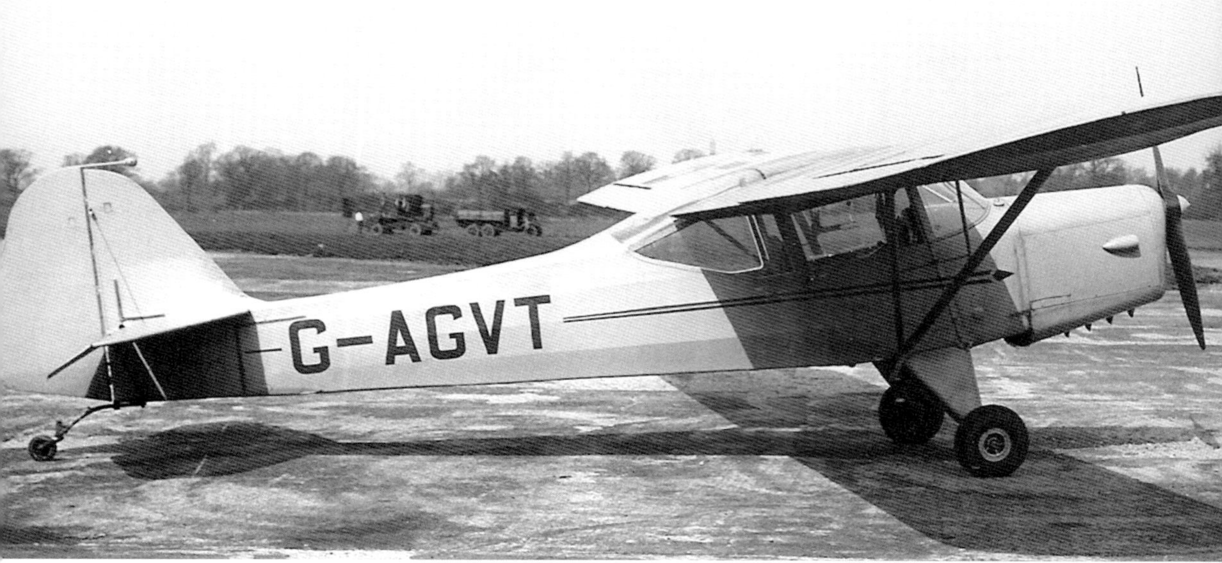

Above: Auster Autocrat G-AGVT was registered in February 1946 to London Motor & Aero Services at Elstree, formally known as Aldenham, where it is seen on 31 March. On 16 March the following year 'VT was damaged beyond repair at Heston.

Below: The sole example of an unnamed Auster type produced in 1945 as a successor to the pre-war Taylorcraft Plus C, a licence-built but modified monoplane built by the Taylorcraft Young Airplane Corporation of America. Regarded as the prototype of the two-seat Auster J-2 Arrow, G-AGPS was powered by a 65 hp Lycoming 0-145 B3 flat four engine and first registered in July 1945. It is seen at its Rearsby birthplace on 26 March and was used as a company hack until 16 March 1947 when blown over in a gale and destroyed.

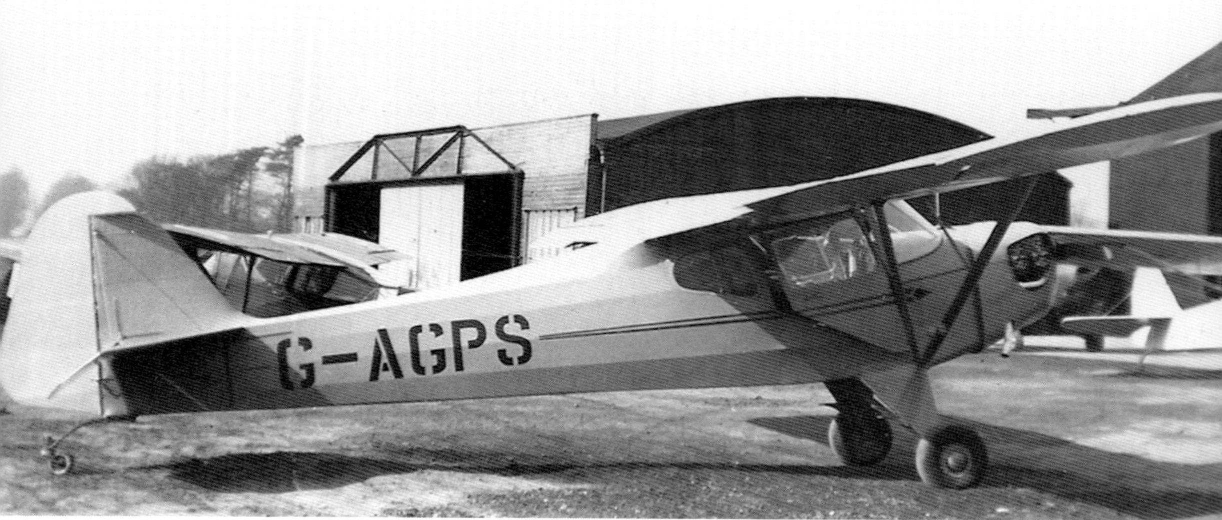

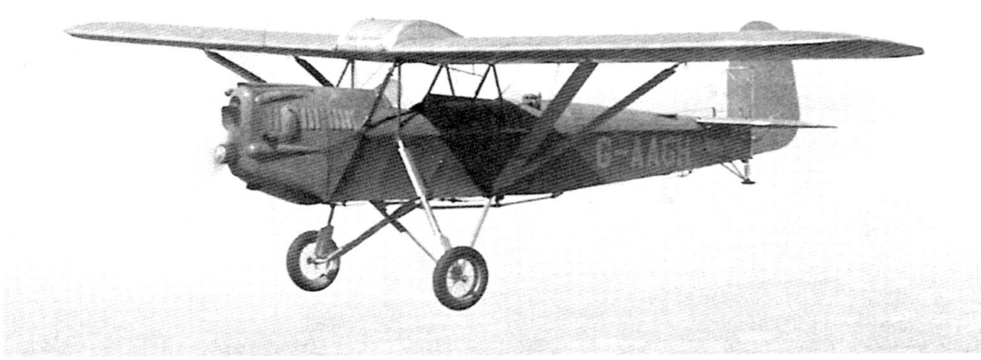

Westland Aircraft's white-helmeted chief test pilot Harald Penrose, loitering over Dorset in veteran Westland Widgeon IIIA G-AAGH on 16 April. The last Widgeon built, 'GH was registered to Westland in September 1930 and flew as a communications hack until destroyed in a pilotless take off from Merryfield, Somerset, on 27 July 1948, hitting a hangar and bursting into flames. Powered by a 105 hp Cirrus Hermes I engine, the Widgeon cruised at a stately 85 mph and was a popular turn at post-war displays, crazily but expertly flown by Penrose who skidded around the sky pumping an old motor horn as he went.

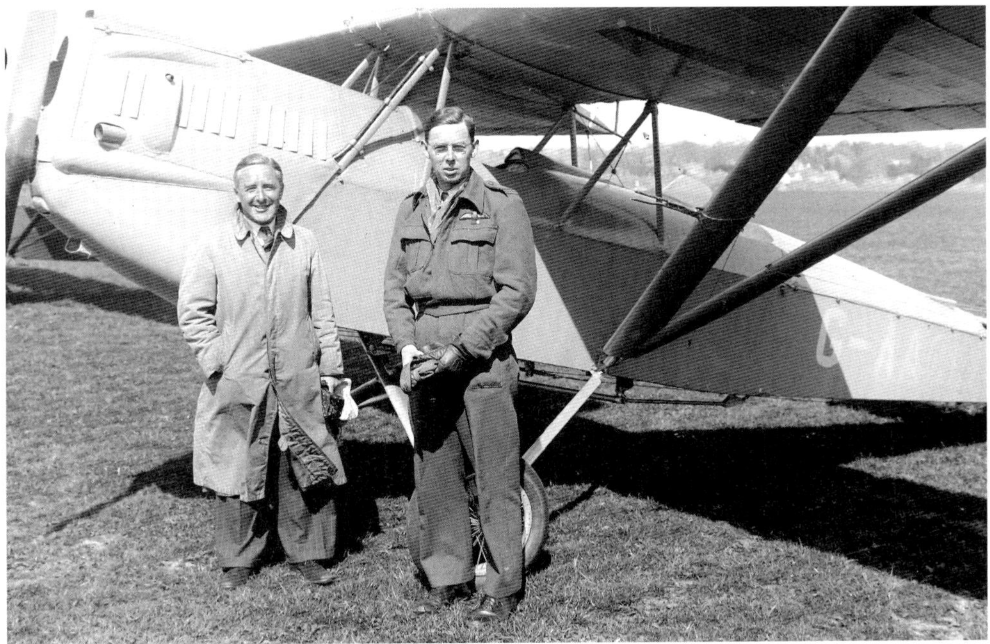

Westland Aircraft chief test pilot Harald Penrose and production test pilot Flt Lt J. B. 'Tommy' Thompson at Yeovil with Westland Widgeon IIIA G-AAGH on 15 April. Tommy, with E.J.R. as passenger, had just returned from a one hour 45 minute aerial tour of Dorset. The following day Thompson flew E.J.R. in Auster V TW516 to take air-to-air photographs of Penrose flying the Widgeon. The author met Thompson in 2011 and was able to present him with a copy of this photograph shortly before the pilot's death.

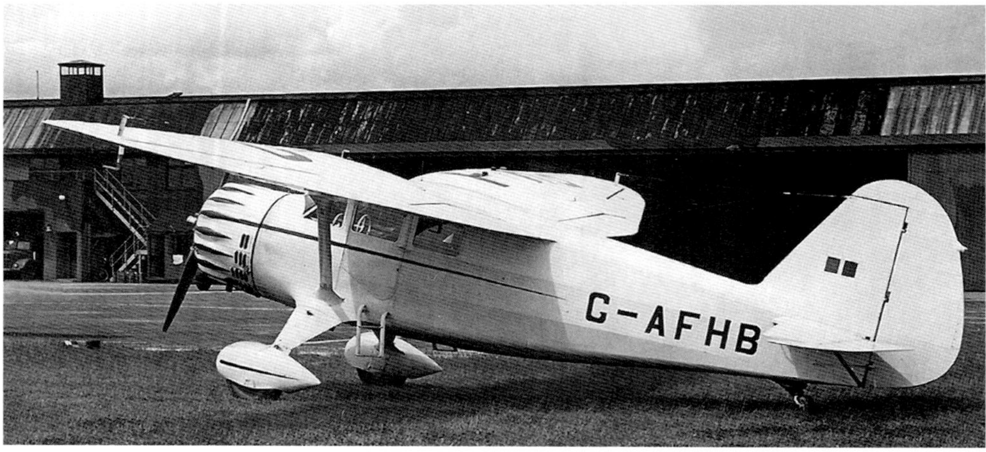

The American Stinson SR-10 Reliant was the ultimate model of this series of large four/five-seaters and first certificated in April 1938. It incorporated 25 structural and aerodynamic changes, mostly concerned with reducing drag. The economy model was the SR-10B, powered by a nine-cylinder 245 hp Lycoming R-680-D6. Several were exported to the UK, including G-AFHB seen at White Waltham on 29 May. Built at Wayne, Michigan, it was registered in July 1938 to A. Ellison and based at Castle Bromwich until impressed into the RAF as W7981 in February 1940. Assigned to No. 24 Squadron, presumably at RAF Hendon, the aircraft transferred to the station flight at RAF Andover in January 1943. After being taken off RAF charge in September 1944 the Stinson returned to the civil register in August 1945 and was acquired by test pilot Geoffrey Alington. He quickly sold it on to A. Noon who registered it in Kenya as VP-KDK, operating for Noon & Pearce Air Charters Ltd. The Stinson returned to the UK once more in 1949 and was finally reduced to spares in 1956.

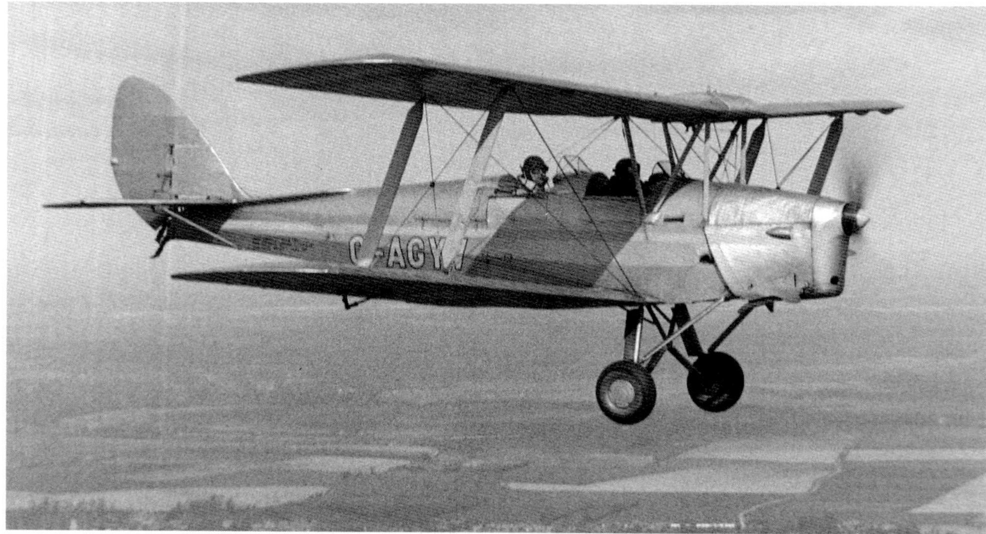

Flying over East Anglian fen country on 9 April is Marshall's Flying School D.H. 82A Tiger Moth G-AGYV on an instructional flight. At the time Marshall's had six Tigers on strength and instruction cost £3 per hour. Formerly N6751 with the RAF, 'YV was sold in Belgium three months after this photograph was taken and became OO-TWD.

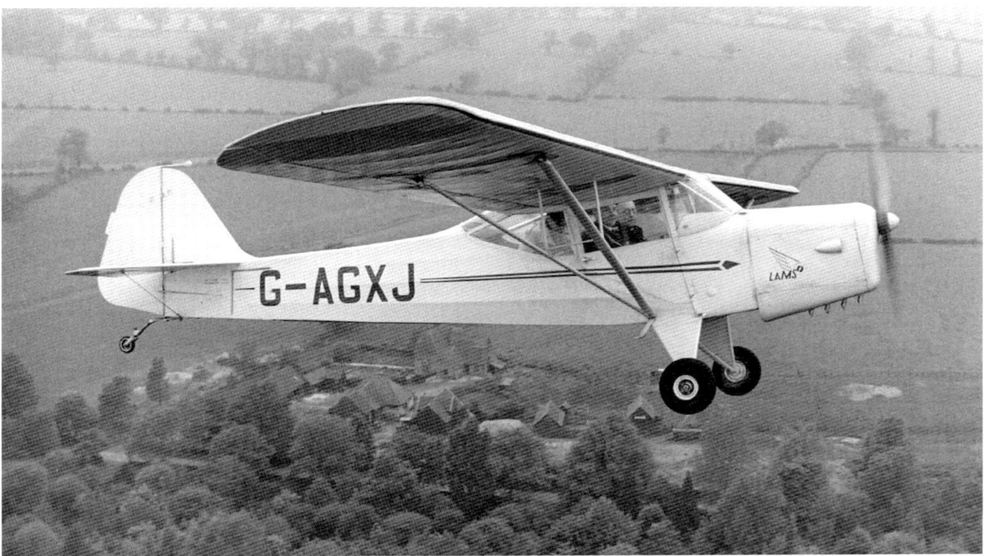

London Aero & Motor Services cream Auster Autocrat G-AGXJ, photographed after taking off from its Elstree base on 26 May flown by C. Nepean Bishop. The author had his first ever flight in 'XJ a few days before and didn't like it a bit. The entry in E.J.R.'s log book read: 'Dick's first flight—emergency landing!' Enough said. 'XJ was sold in France in August 1953 as F-BGRX.

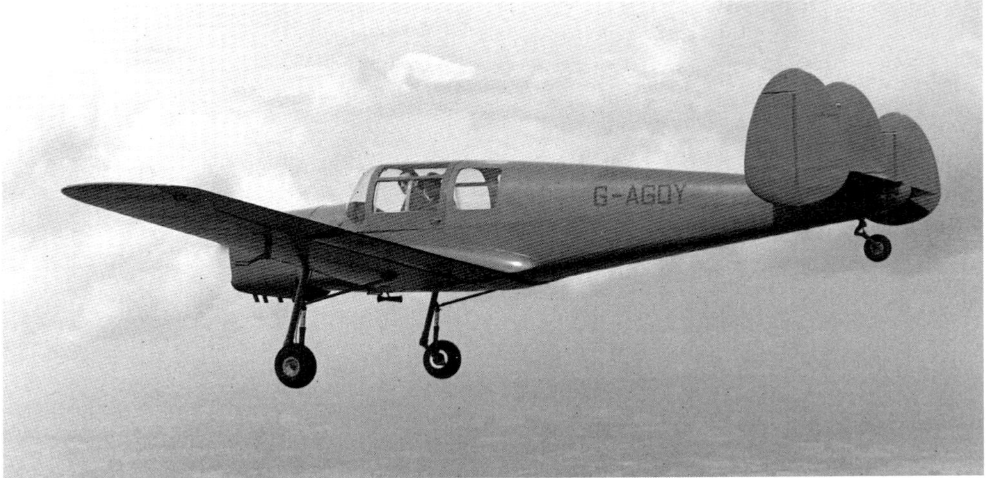

Miles M.38 Messenger Mk 3 began life during the war as a Miles M.48 and was flown in the Class B markings U-0247. Unusual in that it had fully-retractable flaps, the aircraft was given the new designation M.38 Messenger 3 and sold in Switzerland in August 1946, becoming HB-EIP. Two years later it returned to the UK and, flown by Walter Bowles, was based at Elstree until sold in Ireland as EI-AGE in 1953. It is seen flying from Woodley, Reading, on 29 May flown by Ken Waller and photographed from Miles M.18 U-3 piloted by Hugh Kendall.

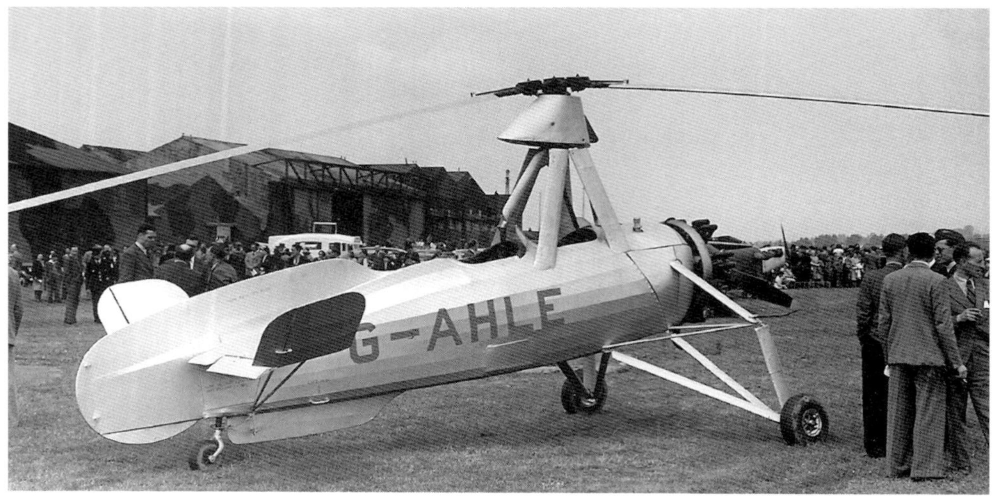

Surprisingly, several Cierva C.30 Autogiros were still airworthy in the UK after the Second World War. G-AHLE, seen at Eastleigh on 22 June, was built originally in 1934 as Cierva C.30A G-ACWH by Avro at Newton Heath, Manchester. It remained with Cierva at Hanworth until impressed into the RAF as DR623 when it flew with No. 74 Wing Calibration Flight at Duxford, 1448 Flight, and latterly with No. 529 Squadron at RAF Henley. It was sold in May 1946 and became 'LE, remaining with the Cierva Autogiro Company Ltd at Eastleigh until withdrawn from use in June 1947. It was scrapped at Shoreham in 1952 when in possession of the local ATC. At the Eastleigh display 'LE was flown in company with the prototype Cierva W.9A two-seat helicopter PX203.

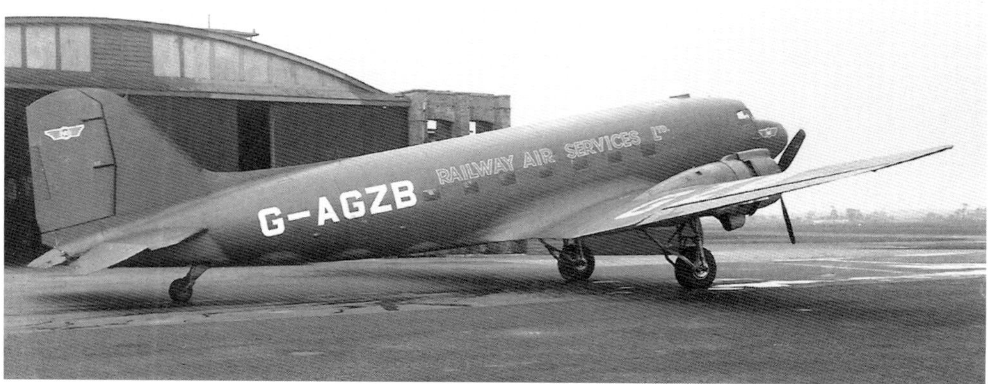

First flown in 1943 and formerly FZ624 with the RAF, this Douglas Dakota 3 served with Nos. 48 and 10 Squadrons before passing to No. 1336 Conversion Unit at Welford. It was sold to BOAC in February 1946 and transferred to Railway Air Services, in whose wartime camouflage scheme it is seen at Renfrew on 21 May. The company's winged badge is visible on the aircraft's nose and rudder. Together with other BOAC Dakota 3s G-AGZB became the nucleus of the BEA Pionair class fleet in 1947. Named *Robert Smith-Barry*, it crashed on St Boniface Down near Ventnor, Isle of Wight, on 6 May 1962 while flying from Jersey to Portsmouth in low cloud and drizzle, bursting into flames on impact and killing nine of the 18 occupants. See p. 83 for a later photograph.

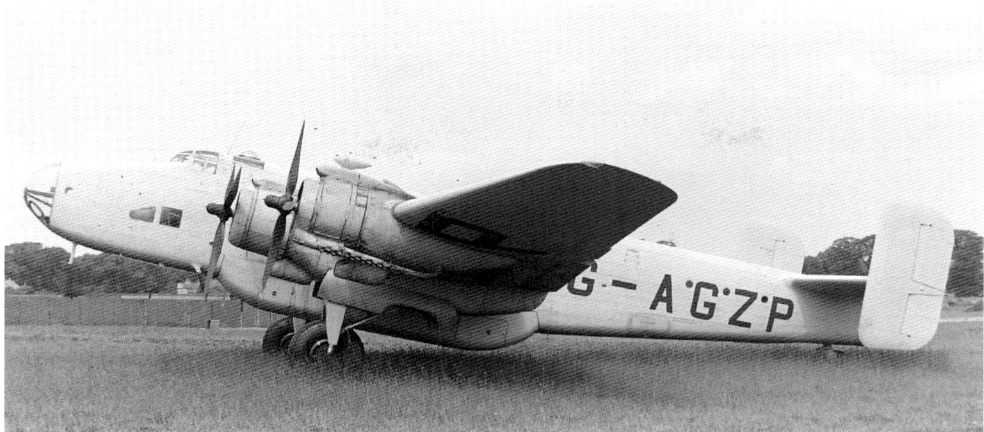

Parked at White Waltham on 29 May is Handley Page H.P. 70 Halton G-AGZP owned by the Maharajah Gaekwar of Baroda. Modified to VIP standard from a Halifax C. Mk 8, 'ZP was operated for the Maharajah by White Waltham-based British American Air Services Ltd. In 1947 the aircraft was modified further and flown to South Africa to become ZS-BTA with Alpha Airways (Pty) Ltd. In August 1949 the much travelled Halton returned to the UK and spent the rest of its life with the Lancashire Aircraft Corporation, based with other Haltons at Bovingdon until scrapped there in 1953.

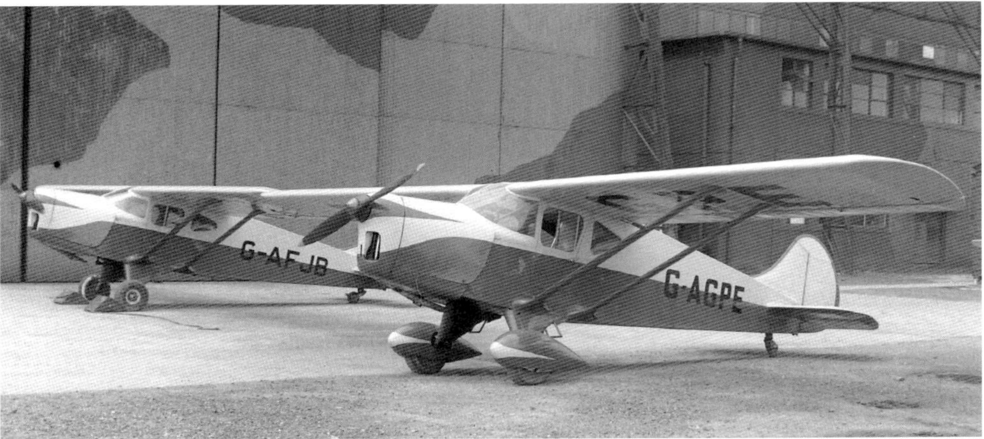

Built at Eastleigh and photographed there on 22 June, Foster Wikner Wickos G-AFJB and G-AGPE were on view during that day's air display. 'JB was delivered first to the Midland Aero Club in 1938 before being impressed as DR613 and flown as a communications hack by Cunliffe-Owen Aircraft Ltd, also based at Eastleigh. Philippa Bennett, former Flight Captain with the ATA, as was the aircraft's designer Geoffrey N. Wikner, used the aircraft as an air taxi in company with 'PE, formerly HM497 during wartime. 'PE was withdrawn from use in July 1948; 'JB passed to the Eastleigh-based Southampton Aero Club in 1956 and was withdrawn from use finally in 1963. John Dible acquired the airframe in 1998, Ron Souch and his team restoring the Wicko to airworthy condition to fly again in 2005.

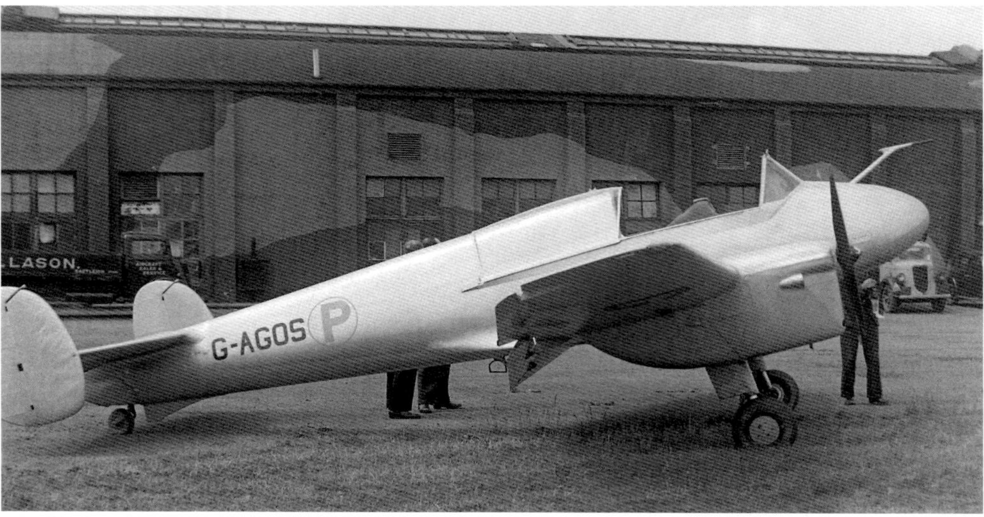

Better known for the manufacture of instruments and cameras, Reid & Sigrist of Desford, Leicestershire, produced two aircraft. The first, the curiously-named R.S.1 Snargasher, was a three-seat, twin-engine trainer, first flown in 1939. It was followed by the R.S.3, appropriately named Desford, a twin-engine, two-seat, twin-finned, low-wing monoplane powered by two 130 hp D.H. Gipsy Major I engines. First flown in July 1945, it was sold to the Air Council and modified for prone pilot experiments, for which it was re-designated R.S.4 Desford Trainer and fitted with 145 hp D.H. Gipsy Major 10s. During 1958 G-AGOS was used as a photographic aircraft by Film Aviation Services, continuing in this role with Kemp's Aerial Surveys Ltd into the early 1970s. Following a spell with the Strathallan Collection in Scotland, the Desford returned to its native county and is preserved by Leicestershire County Council Museums. 'OS is seen at Eastleigh on 22 June.

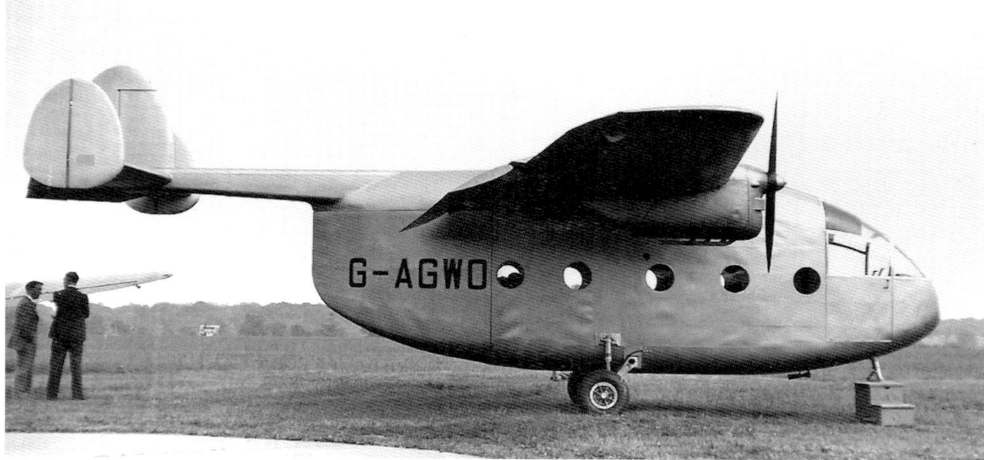

The sole Miles M.57 Aerovan Mk. 2, G-AGWO, initially Class B registered U-8 and built at Woodley in 1946, was first flown in March by Ken Waller and is seen at Eastleigh on 22 June. The second Aerovan prototype, it was configured for ten passengers, differing from the first by having a longer front fuselage and round instead of rectangular windows. After use as a company demonstrator 'WO was acquired by the Marquis of Londonderry in November 1946 and kept at Newtownards until it crashed on 2 July 1947.

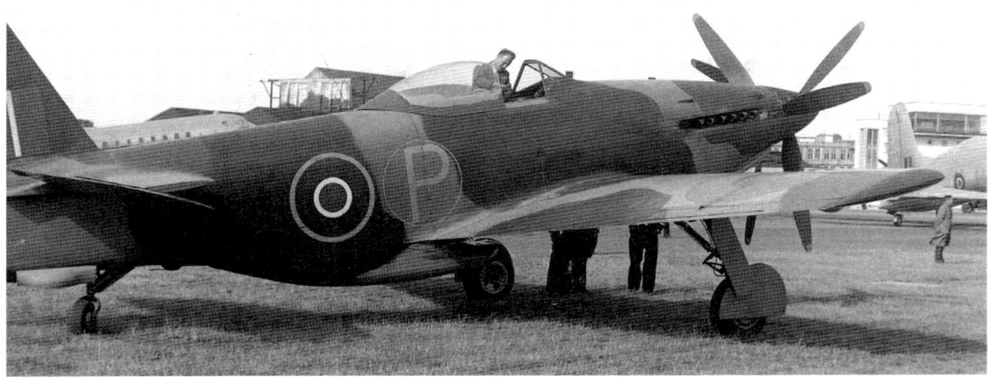

Present at the Display of British Aircraft and Equipment at Farnborough during 27–30 June was one-off Martin Baker M.B.5 fighter R2496, demonstrated memorably by Sq Ldr Jan Zurakowski. First flown from RAF Harwell on 23 May 1944, the M.B.5 was armed with four 20 mm cannon and powered by a 2,340 hp Rolls-Royce Griffon 83 engine, giving an impressive maximum level speed of 460 mph. One pilot who flew it described it as 'a cross between a Mustang and a V-2.' By the time it could have readied for RAF service jet fighters were the vogue and the war would have ended before production was in full swing. The fate of the M.B.5 is still shrouded in mystery though it is believed to have ended up as a target on a gunnery range, which would be par for the course!

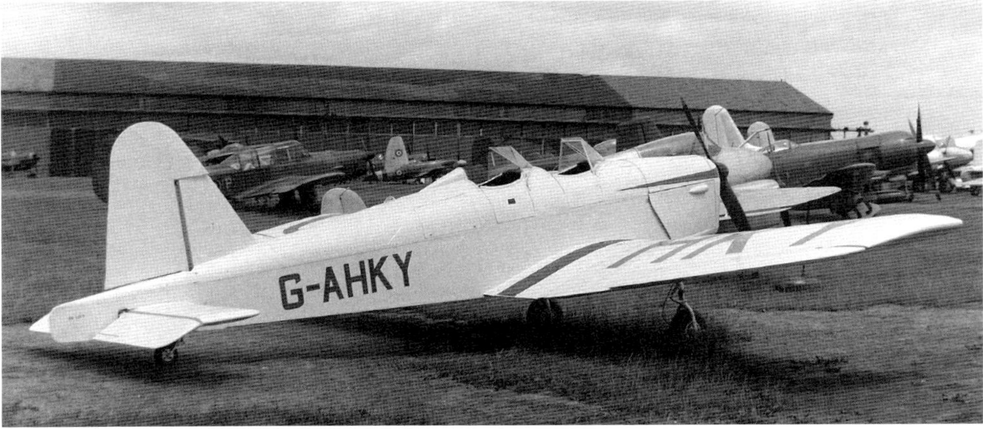

Looking somewhat out of place at the Display of British Aircraft and Equipment at Farnborough on 29 June was Miles M. 18 Mk 2 G-AHKY. Developed from the Mk 1 two-seat trainer first flown in December 1938 and registered G-AFRO, it was later converted to a single seater, fitted with a tricycle undercarriage and had the fin and rudder moved forward 22 inches. The two-seat Mk 2 appeared almost a year later with conventional undercarriage, but retained the forward positioning of the fin and rudder. Initially registered U-8 and later U-0224 whilst conducting Air Ministry acceptance trials, the Mk 2 was impressed as HM545 and used by Miles as a communications hack. Acquiring the G-AHKY registration in August 1946, the aircraft was owned and raced successfully for many years by Brian Isles, winning the coveted King's Cup in 1961 with an average speed of 142 mph. The aircraft is displayed currently at the National Museum of Flight at East Fortune, Scotland.

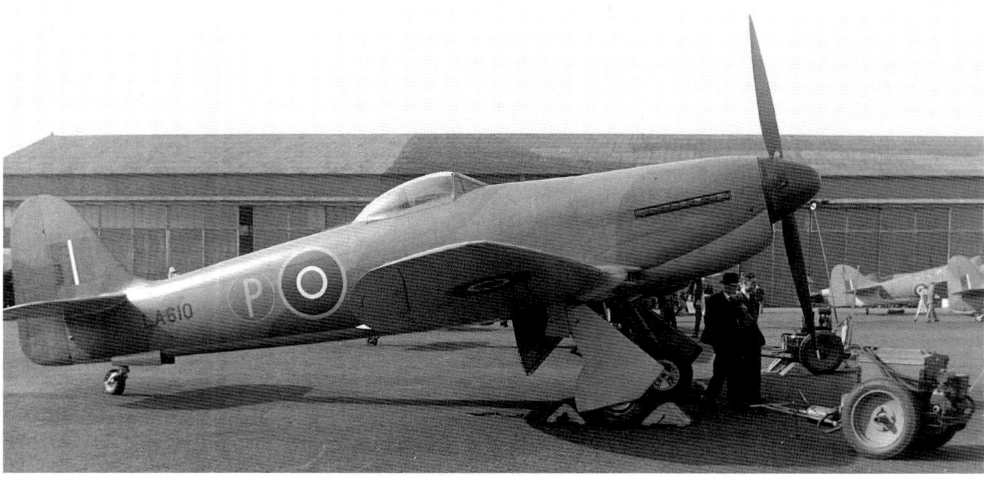

Hawker Fury F. I LA610 first prototype fitted with a 3,000 hp Napier Sabre VII engine at the Display of British Aircraft and Equipment at Farnborough on 29 June. Originally a Tempest III powered by a Rolls-Royce Griffon 85 driving a Rotol six-bladed contra-rotating propeller, the aircraft was first flown on 27 November 1944. Following conversion to Fury F.I configuration and powered by the Sabre VII, LA610 reached a level speed of 485 mph. In January 1948 Hawker Aircraft Ltd reserved for it the civil registration G-AKRZ, but the Fury was scrapped the following year.

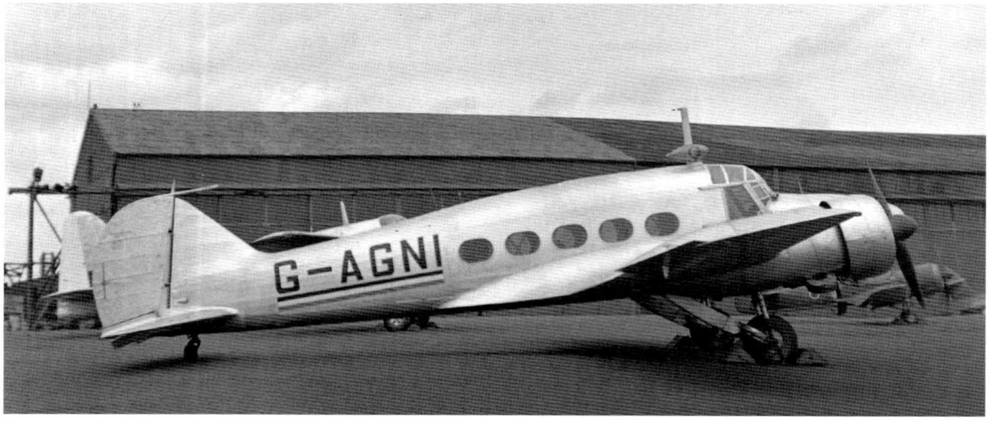

Avro 19 G-AGNI began life as Anson 12 MG159 at Yeadon in 1943, was delivered to A&AEE and later assigned to the Controller of Research and Development before returning to A.V. Roe. Modified to take nine passengers and cabin glazing changed to five oval windows per side, it became the first Avro 652A Nineteen. In this form it was registered 'NI in January 1945 to the Ministry of Aircraft Production and evaluated for feederliner operations. It is seen at the Display of British Aircraft and Equipment staged by the RAE at Farnborough during 27-30 June. In October 1947 it was acquired by Universal Flying Services, based at Eastleigh. On 11 June 1948, when flying from Barrow to Ronaldsway, Isle of Man, 'NI ran short of fuel and, becoming temporarily lost, was forced to ditch off Broda Head, Isle of Man. All seven occupants escaped but the Nineteen was written off.

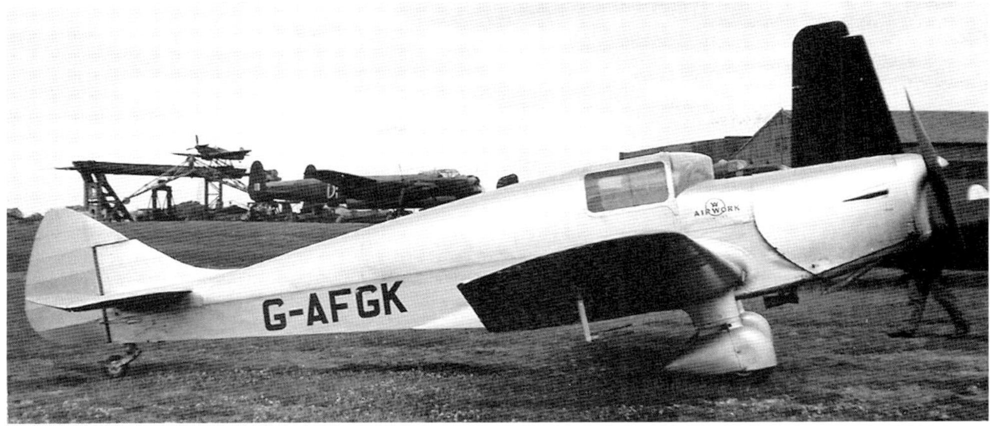

This is one of those photographs where the eye wanders off the main subject to the background. It was taken at Farnborough on 29 June and close inspection shows a Supermarine Seafire III sitting atop the 'P' catapult. Unbelievably, the Seafire was catapulted over the heads of the crowd. Miles M.11A Whitney Straight G-AFGK was first registered in April 1938 to Rosemary Rees. Although not impressed into RAF service, the aircraft flew throughout the war and for a time was fitted with the Maclaren Drift Undercarriage for trials at Farnborough during 1940–41. This device, operated from the cockpit, could set the undercarriage at an angle when landing into a crosswind. Although the aircraft was crabbing the wheels were set parallel with the flight path. Post-war G-AFGK had a succession of UK private owners, the last being Harold Best-Deveraux who sold the aircraft in 1977 to America where it was re-registered N72511.

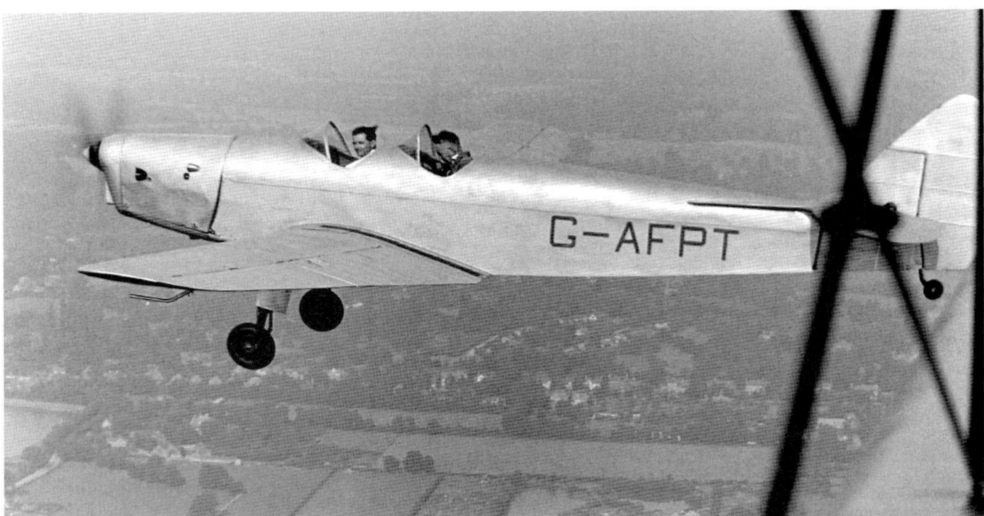

On 13 July, E.J.R. flew with Ian Forbes in D.H. 87B Hornet Moth G-ADNB to take air-to-air photographs of David Cotter flying A. J. Jackson in the West London Aero Club's D.H. 94 Moth Minor G-AFPT. First registered to the Edinburgh Flying club in 1939, 'PT was impressed into the RAF as BK831 in August 1940, turning up at the famous sale of surplus light aircraft at RAF Kemble in March 1946. The West London Aero Club restored the Minor to the register later that month and the Certificate of Airworthiness (C of A) was renewed in August. 'PT was wrecked in a crash at White Waltham on 17 September 1949.

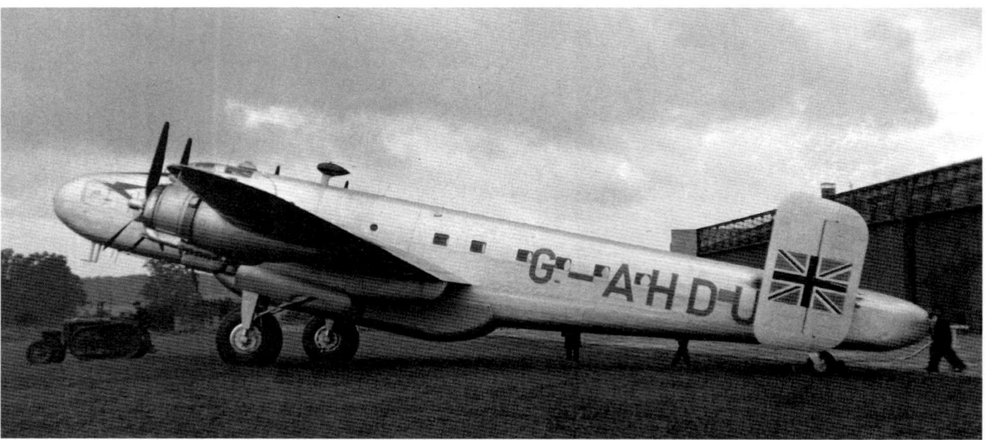

Handley Page H.P. 70 Halton G-AHDU had just received its first C of A and been christened *Falkirk* by Lady Winster when photographed at Radlett on 18 July. Formerly Halifax C. Mk 8 PP310, assembled at Radlett in 1945, it was sold in June 1946 to BOAC as the first of 12 Halton conversions for the airline. For a year BOAC operated Haltons on its London-Accra desert routes until the introduction of Canadair C-4s. 'DU passed to Aviation Traders Ltd in July 1948 and was in service with Bond Air Service Ltd until scrapped at Southend in July 1950.

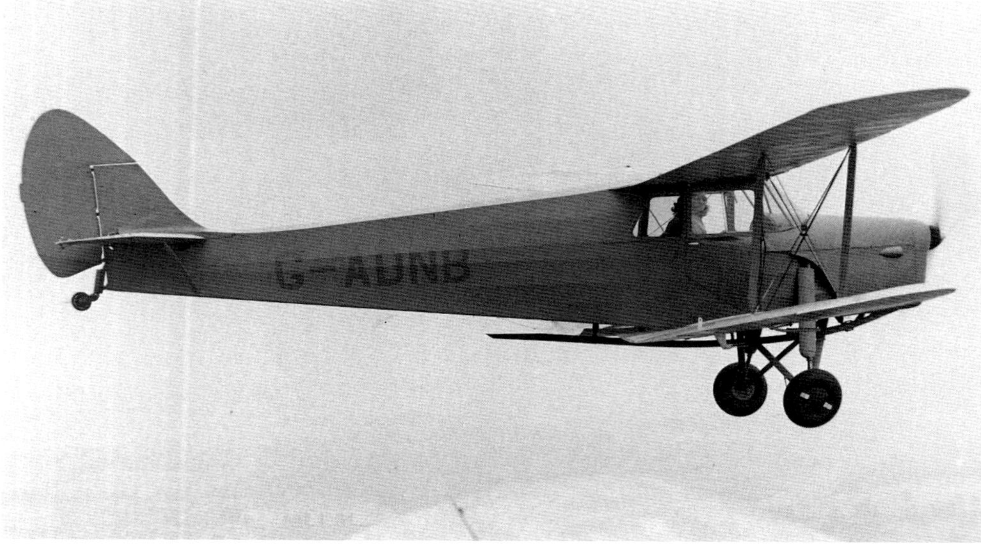

Ian Forbes flying the West London Aero Club's D.H. 87B Hornet Moth G-ADNB in the vicinity of its White Waltham home on 13 July. First registered in April 1936, 'NB was owned by the Plymouth & District Aero Club until impressed as W5772 in January 1940. It was used on Scarecrow patrols to frighten U-boats into diving and then passed to No. 7 Radio Servicing Section at Filton, Bristol. First post-war owner was Ben Bathurst, the Hornet Moth being restored to the register as G-ADNB by the West London Aero Club the same month this photograph was taken. In March 1972 'NB was shipped to the USA and became N36DH.

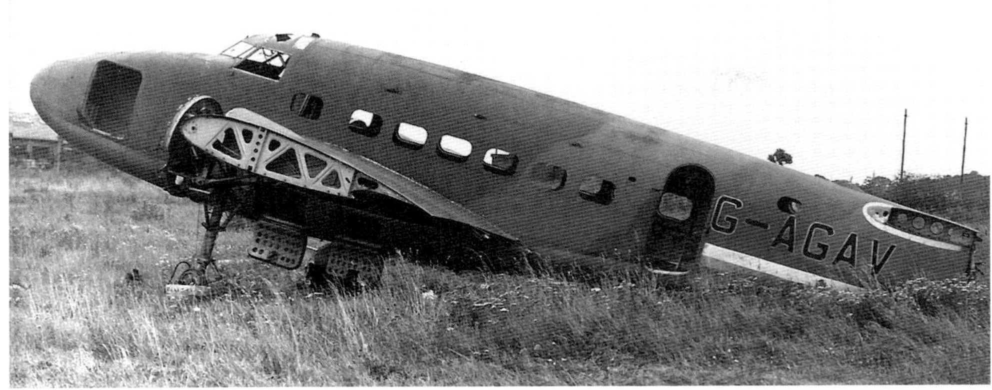

The mortal remains of Lockheed Model 14-H G-AGAV in long grass at Croydon on 10 August. Flown previously by the Polish airline LOT as SP-LMK and named *Lublin*, this Model 14-H flew to Bucharest after the German invasion of Poland on 1 September 1939 and was allocated the British registration for intended sale to Imperial Airways. A C of A renewal at Croydon in 1944 revealed that the aircraft was corroded badly and it was put out to grass still wearing camouflage and civil registration letters underlined in the red, white and blue style of the wartime period.

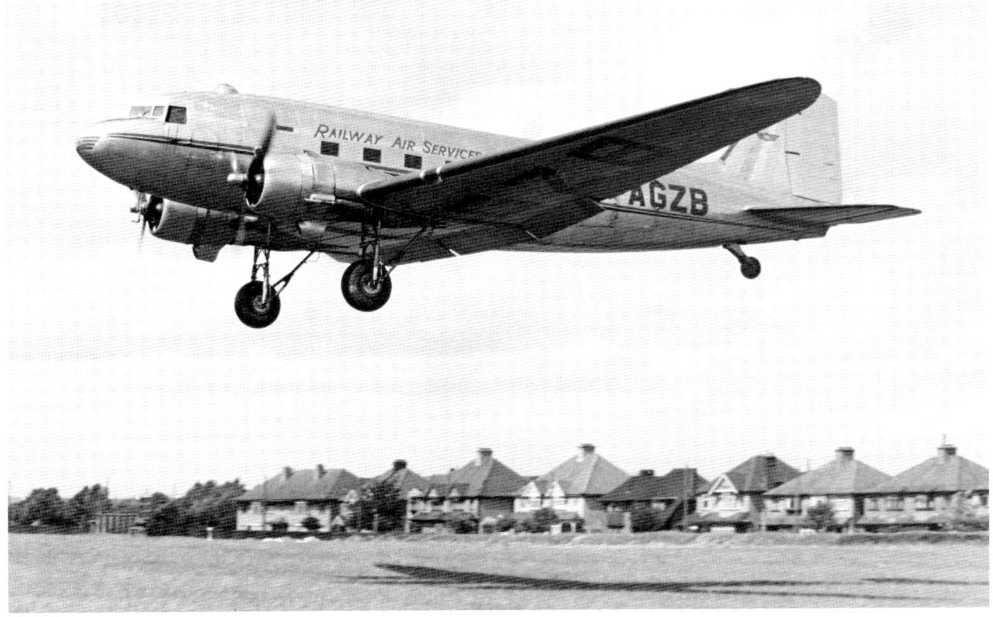

Another picture of Railway Air Services' Douglas C-47A Dakota 3 G-AGZB, this time about to touch down on Croydon's grass on 10 August. First flown in 1943 and formerly FZ624 with the RAF, this Dakota 3 served with Nos 48 and 10 Squadrons before passing to No. 1336 Conversion Unit at Welford. It was sold to BOAC in February 1946 and together with other BOAC Dakota 3s became the nucleus of BEA's Pionair fleet in 1947. See p. 76 for an earlier photograph.

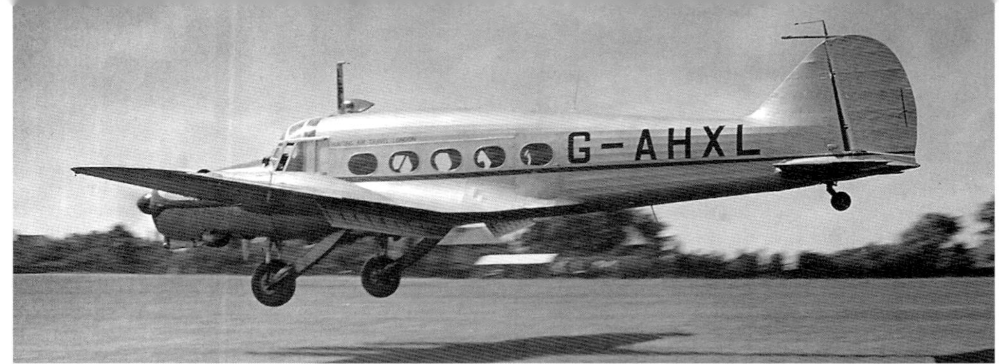

Just a couple of feet from touchdown, Hunting Air Transport's brand new Avro XIX Series 1 G-AHXL arrives at Croydon on 10 August. Registered a few days earlier, 'XL later passed to Airways Training Ltd at Aldermaston and then to BEA in November 1948 before migrating to Sweden where it became SE-BRP in July 1950. On 4 December that year it had an ignominious end, falling through the ice while landing on Lang Lake near Sundsvaal.

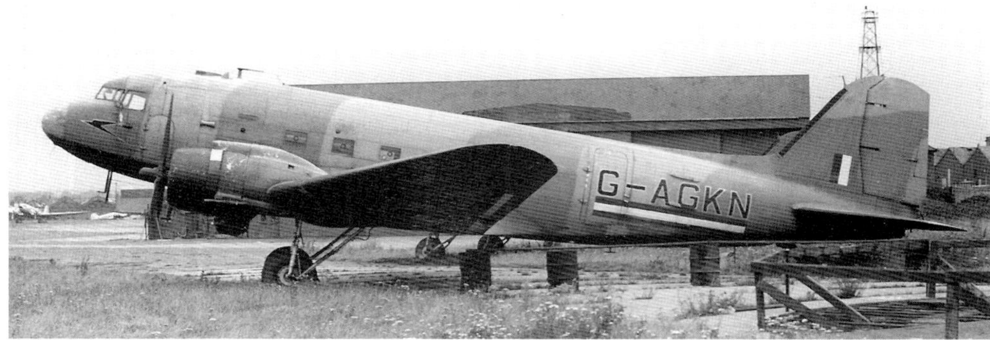

Above: Camouflaged Douglas Dakotas bearing civil registrations were a common sight at UK airfields early post-war. Pictured at Croydon on 10 August is Douglas C-47B Dakota 4 G-AGKN of BOAC, built in 1944 and formerly KJ990 of the RAF. While approaching Toulon Airport in low cloud on 14 July 1948 'KN crashed into a cliff killing all six occupants.

Below: Looking like something from a bygone age, D.H. 84 Dragon 2 G-AECZ was still plying its trade from Croydon after the war. Built in 1936 and delivered to Air Cruises Ltd at Hatfield, 'CZ was flying with Southern Airways Ltd at Ramsgate when war intervened. Impressed into the RAF as AV982, the Dragon was badly damaged at Castle Bromwich in September 1940 but was repaired as new and delivered to English Electric for communications duties. In June 1946 the Dragon was restored to the register and sold to Air Taxis Ltd in whose livery it is seen at Croydon on 10 August. In 1948 Wiltshire School of Flying became the next operator until March 1950 when it was sold in Ireland, becoming EI-AFK. Still airworthy, having been restored by Aer Lingus volunteers in celebration of the airline's 75th anniversary after several years grounded, the Dragon was flown again in February 2012.

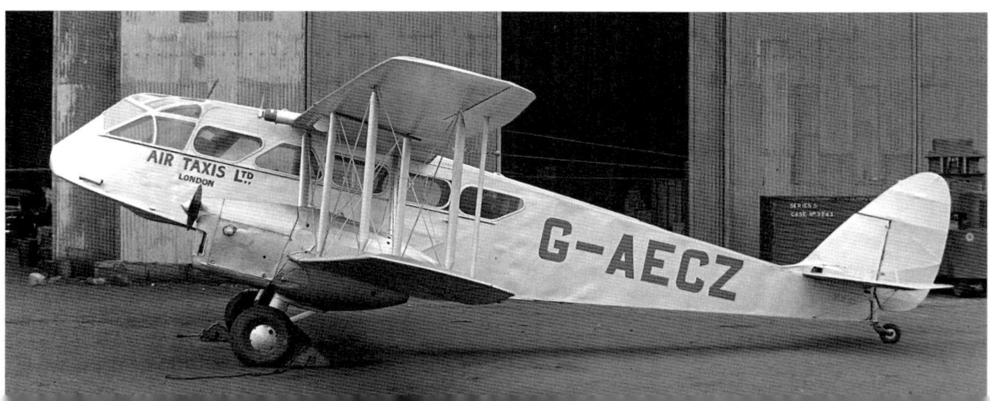

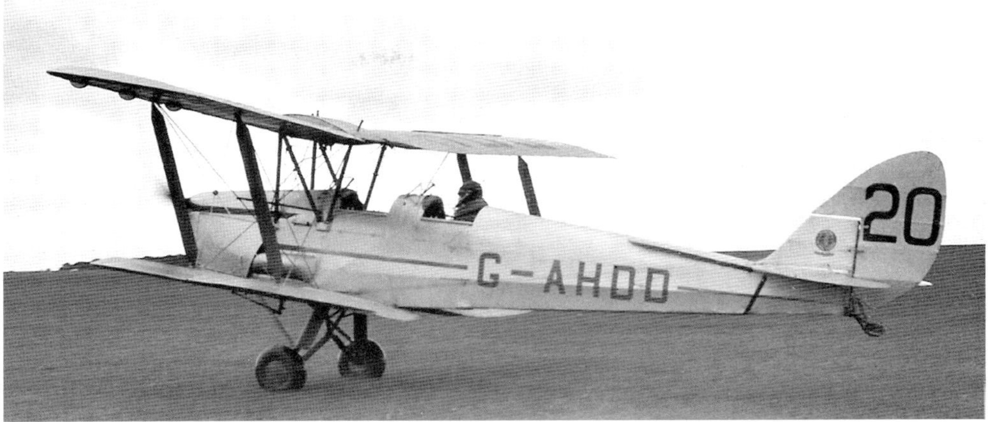

P. Sentance takes off from Lympne in Luton Flying club's D.H. 82A Tiger Moth G-AHDD during the second heat for the Folkestone Trophy on 31 August. Previously EM849 with the RAF, the aircraft served with No. 21 EFTS at Booker until sold in January 1946 and registered in March. In later life 'DD was owned by Chipperfields of circus fame before coming to grief in a crash at Calais, France, on 6 August 1955.

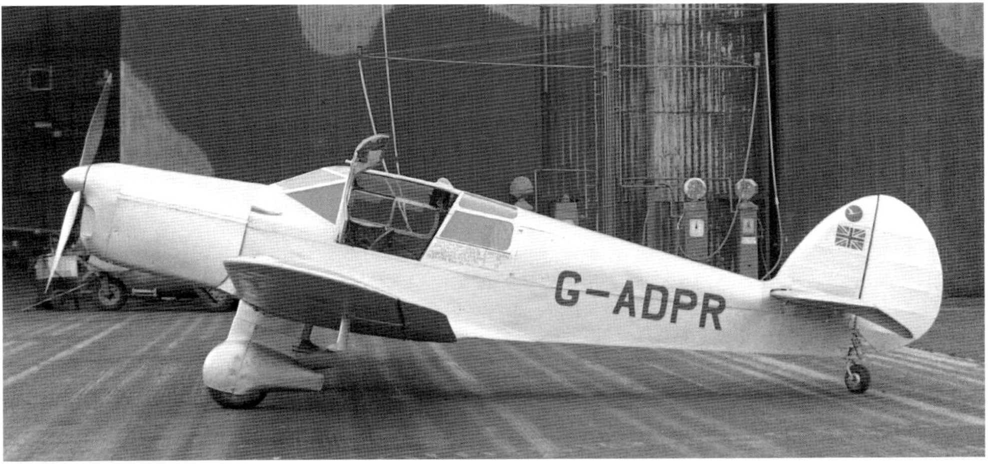

Can you imagine crossing the South Atlantic in a Percival Gull Six? That's what plucky New Zealander Jean Batten did in October 1935 flying G-ADPR, seen at Luton on 24 August. The following year, in the same aircraft, she flew from England to New Zealand, covering 14,224 miles in 11 days 45 minutes elapsed time, including a two-day stopover in Sydney. And when in October 1937 she flew the Gull Six from Australia to England in five days 18 hours 15 minutes she became the first person to hold both England-Australia out-and-back solo records. Built in 1935 this important record-breaker was impressed into RAF service as AX866 in July 1940, touchingly named *Jean* and used by the station flight at Ringway. It was then assigned to a glider instructor school before going to an advance flying unit, ending up at RAF Kemble and the famous post-war aircraft sale. Restored to the register in August 1946, *Jean* made a number of public appearances before joining the Shuttleworth Collection in April 1961. *Jean* made one further journey to New Zealand, this time by ship, and is now suspended above the duty free shop at Auckland International Airport.

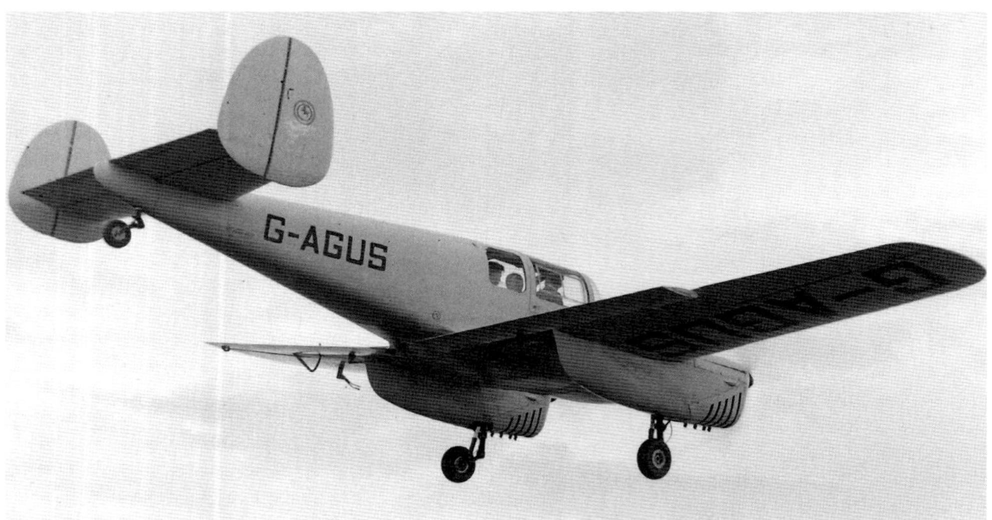

One of the big hopes for the post-war recovery of the British light aircraft industry was the Miles M. 65 Gemini. G-AGUS, the prototype, is seen in the vicinity of its Woodley birthplace on 29 August flown by J. Nelson and photographed from Miles M. 18 G-AHKY flown by Hugh Kendall. Maiden flight of the cream and red prototype was on 26 October 1945 by designer George Miles. Powered by two 80 hp Cirrus Minor 2 engines, unlike production examples 'US had a fixed undercarriage. In time-honoured Miles fashion production of the Gemini began at once and about 130 were built in a year. After much testing and following a European tour the Gemini prototype headed for Sweden where it became SE-BUY. In November 1953 it suffered engine failure on take-off at Alunda and was wrecked.

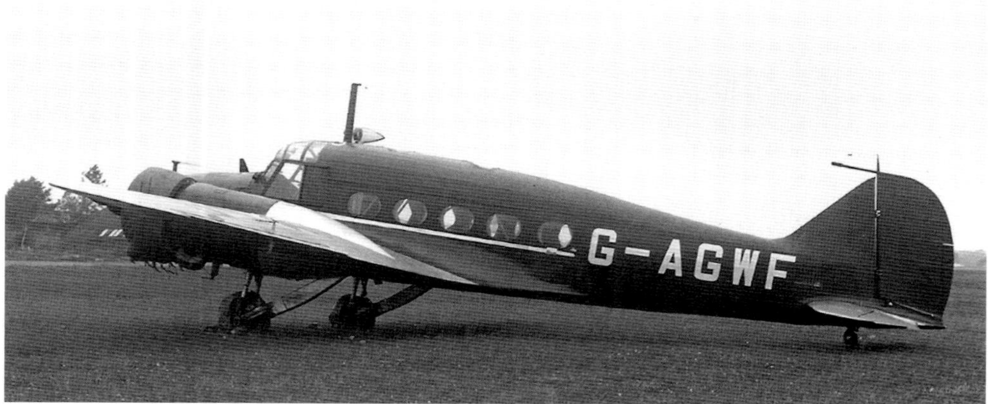

Built by A. V. Roe Ltd at Yeadon in 1946 as TX202 for the RAF, this Anson XIX was diverted to the Ministry of Aviation, registered G-AGWF in June 1946 and based at Gatwick where is seen on 10 August. In November 1951 it was acquired by the Sperry Gyroscope Company and then Fairways (Jersey) Ltd in October 1955. After its C of A expired in 1957 'WF donated various parts of its anatomy for spares before being scrapped in 1960.

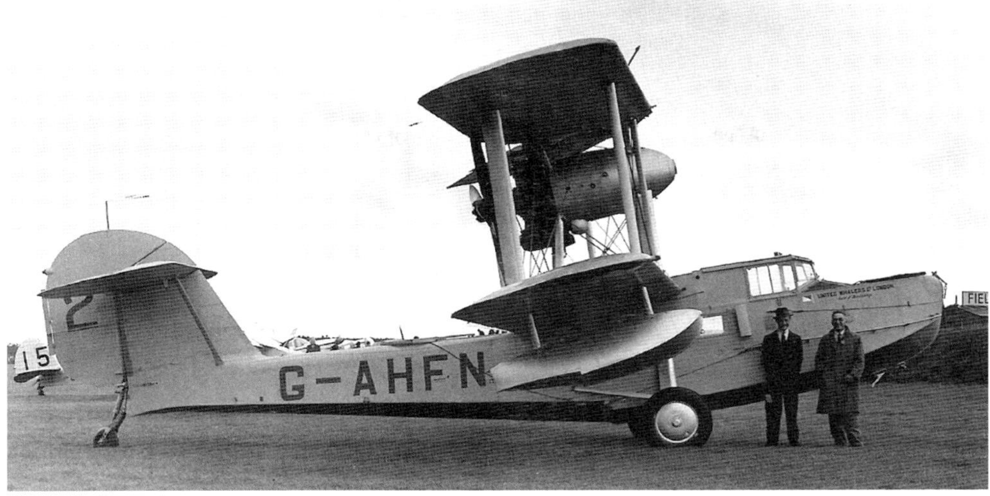

Not only did this Vickers-Supermarine Type 236 Walrus participate in the Folkestone Trophy race at Lympne during the weekend of 30-31 August, it won! G-AHFN, with sister ships 'FL, 'FM and 'FO among others, was one of 17 war surplus examples of the amphibian to be earmarked for conversion to civil use. They were adapted in 1946 and used by United Whalers Ltd, their exploits during a season's whaling in the Antarctic becoming the subject of *Air Whaler*, written by John Grierson, flight commander of the whaling factory ship *Balaena*. Before setting off on the whaling trip Grierson entered 'FN for the race. The handicappers were not sure how fast a Walrus would go and Grierson said later that their ignorance worked in his favour. He is seen crossing the finishing line having averaged 121.5 mph. The Walrus had been delivered to the Admiralty as L2336 in 1939 and passed to the RAF in December 1944. The civil registration came with its sale in August 1946. After storage at Prestwick 'FN was taken to Loch Ryan in June 1955 before being wrecked at Stranraer in a storm the following month.

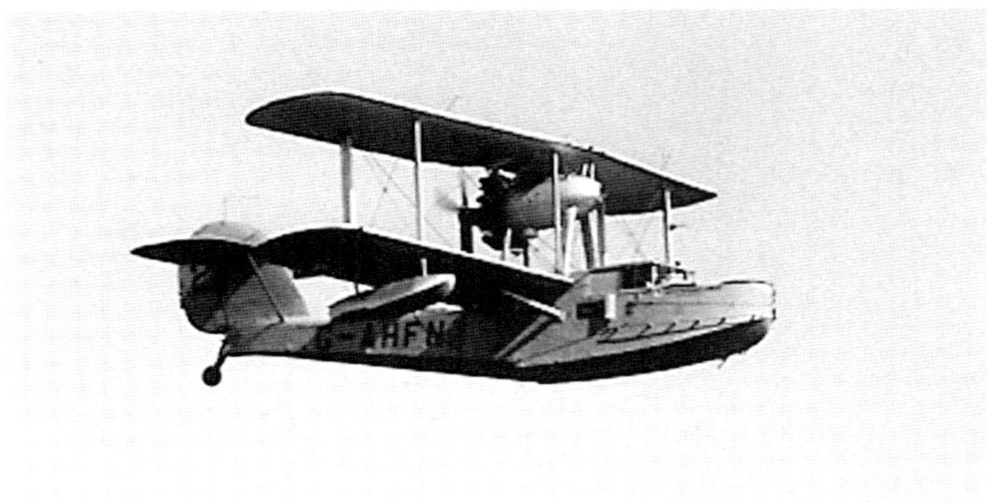

L. T. Mason and A. J. Jackson standing with Vickers-Supermarine Walrus G-AHFN at Lympne during the weekend of 30–31 August 1946.

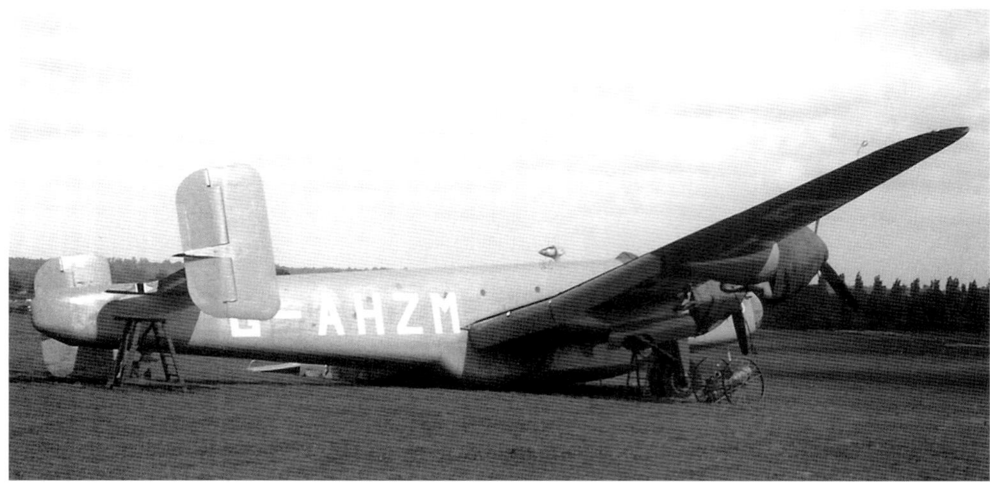

In 1945 six brand new, ex-Radlett, PP-serialled H.P. 70 Halifax C. Mk 8s came up for disposal and were acquired Dr Graham Humby, boss of London Aero & Motor Services Ltd (LAMS) at Elstree. Registered G-AHZJ to 'ZO and doped blue with white lettering, all had acquired C of As by the end of 1946, except 'ZM which had come to grief as it taxied out for its certification test flight on September 16. The port undercarriage leg collapsed and it remained a forlorn sight behind Elstree's main hangar until the early 1950s. Elstree was initially the LAMS maintenance base until the company moved to Stansted in 1947.

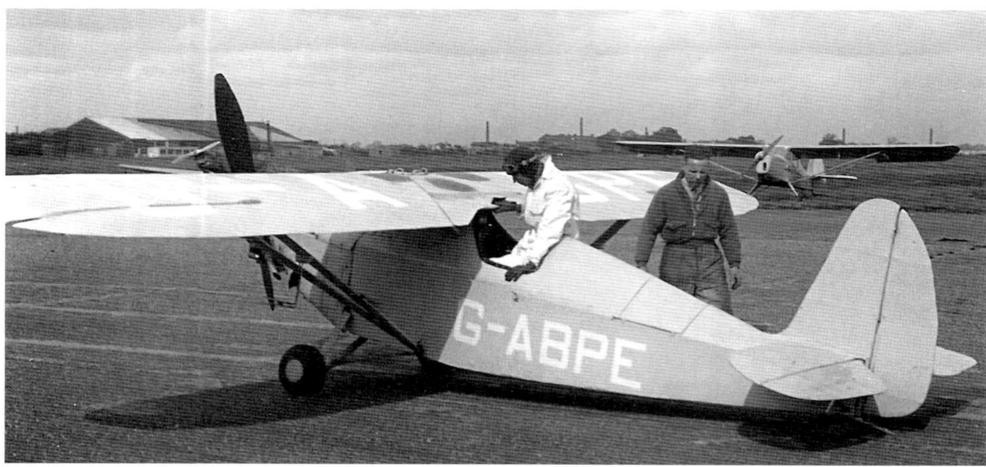

Built at Hooton Park in 1931, Comper CLA.7 Swift was owned first by Christopher Clarkson before being shipped to Kuala Lumpur for Dr. E. Robertson and named *Vital Spark*. 'PE returned to the UK in 1935 and passed through several ownerships until purchased by A. B. Golay in May 1944 and kept at Heston where it was photographed on 21 September. On 26 April 1947 Golay crashed the Swift near St Albans and one wing, the undercarriage and various other items were taken to E.J.R.'s Hendon home where they remained until the early 1960s.

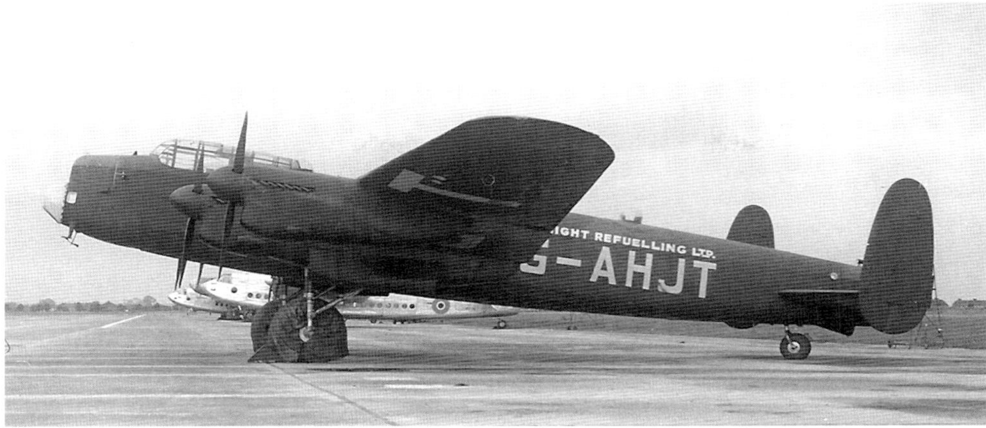

In August 1946 Flight Refuelling Ltd acquired four RAF Avro Lancaster 3s (LL809, LM681, LM639 and ED866) from the Ministry of Supply for use in-flight refuelling trials. Based at Ford, they were registered G-AHJT to 'JW respectively. After conversion the Lancaster quartet was paired off into two tankers and two receivers. Flights were made over the Atlantic in co-operation with former RAF Pathfinder chief Air Vice-Marshal D. C. T. Bennett and British South American Airways Corporation. Seen at Heathrow on 27 September is the yellow-lettered, all-black G-AHJT. Repainted silver overall, 'JT later flew on the Berlin Airlift, carrying fuel to the beleaguered city, before being scrapped at Tarrant Rushton, Dorset, in January 1950.

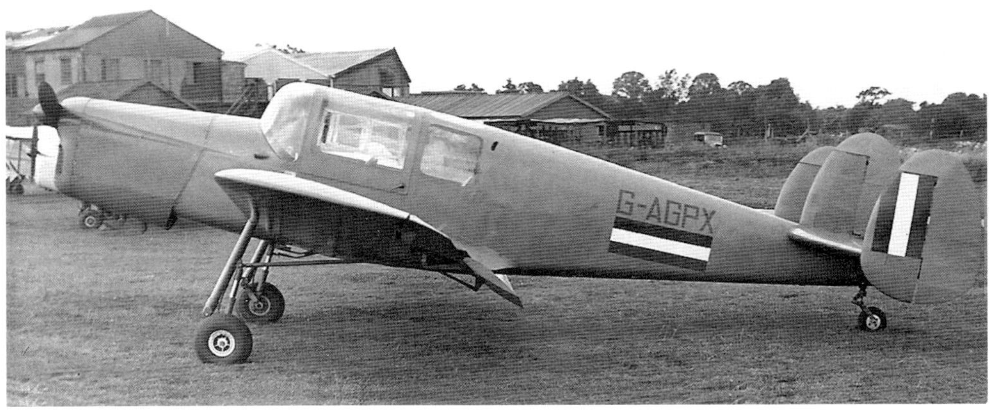

The three-seat Miles M.38 Messenger 2B G-AGPX at Woodley on 29 August, still bearing its wartime civil marks underlined in red, white and blue identification stripes. 'PX was first registered in November 1945 to Blackburn Aircraft Ltd at Brough and used as a test bed for the 155 hp Blackburn Cirrus Major 3. When the Messenger was withdrawn from use in 1962 it was owned by D. M. B. Carnegie and probably kept at Panshanger.

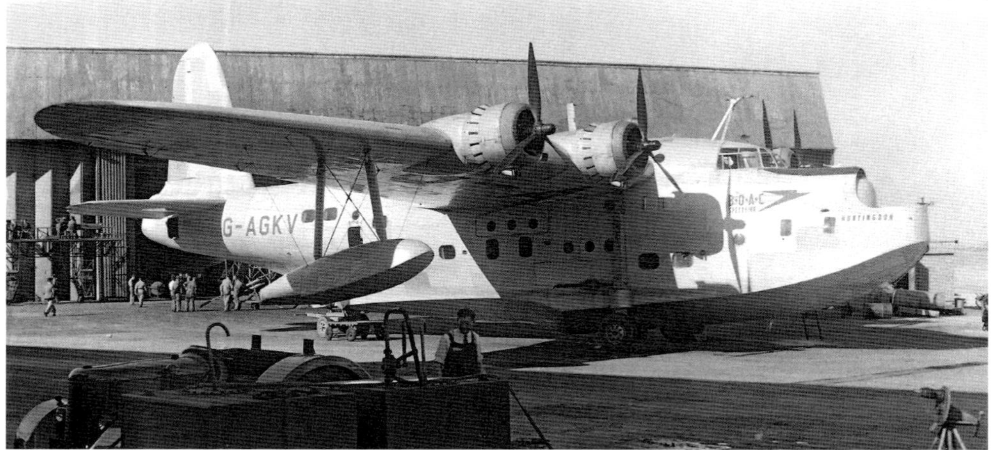

Short S. 25 Sunderland 3 G-AGKV *Huntingdon* outside the BOAC Hythe maintenance hangars on 27 September. Flown initially in joint RAF Transport Command/BOAC markings as ML786/OQZD, she was stripped of all armament, bulbous retractable fairings replacing the gun turrets as part of a cheap conversion to accommodate priority passengers and mail. As 'KV, the 'boat joined others of its class on BOAC's Poole-West Africa route. Later she was upgraded at Hythe with Bristol Pegasus 38 engines and fitted with more comfortable seating for 24 day or 16 night passengers. Known as the Hythe class, the 'boats reopened the all-important but rapidly-shrinking British Empire routes. Returned to Shorts at Belfast in December 1948, 'KV was withdrawn from use in 1951.

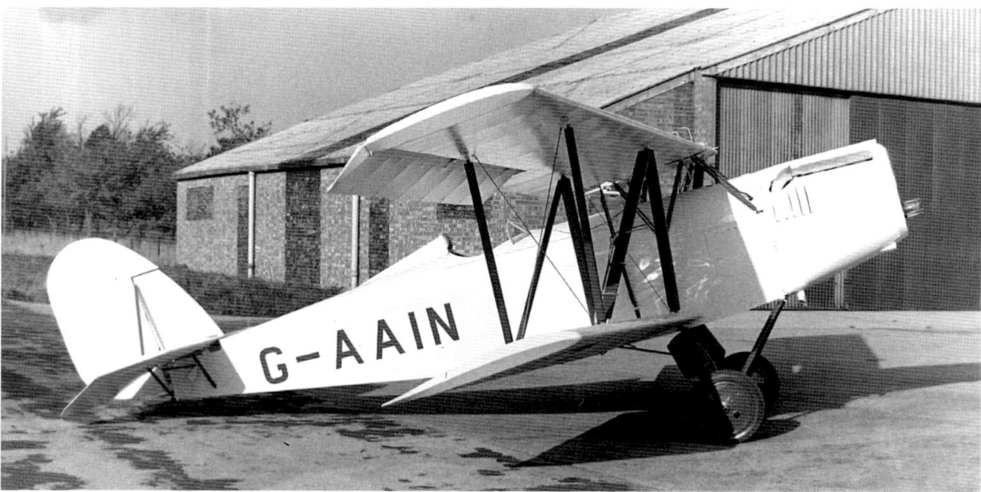

A familiar sight at Shuttleworth flying days at Old Warden for many years, the Parnall Elf G-AAIN was designed by Harold Bolas and was one of three built at Yate 1928-32. First registered in June 1932, 'IN passed to Lord Apsley at Badminton in 1934 and spent the war in storage. First post-war owner was W.J. Nobbs and it was under his ownership when photographed minus propeller at Kidlington, Oxford, on 28 October. The Shuttleworth Trust acquired the Elf in July 1951 where it remains. Powered by a 115 hp Cirrus Hermes II engine, the Elf was characterized by its solid-looking vee interplane struts in place of flying wires. Like most biplanes of the period the wings were foldable

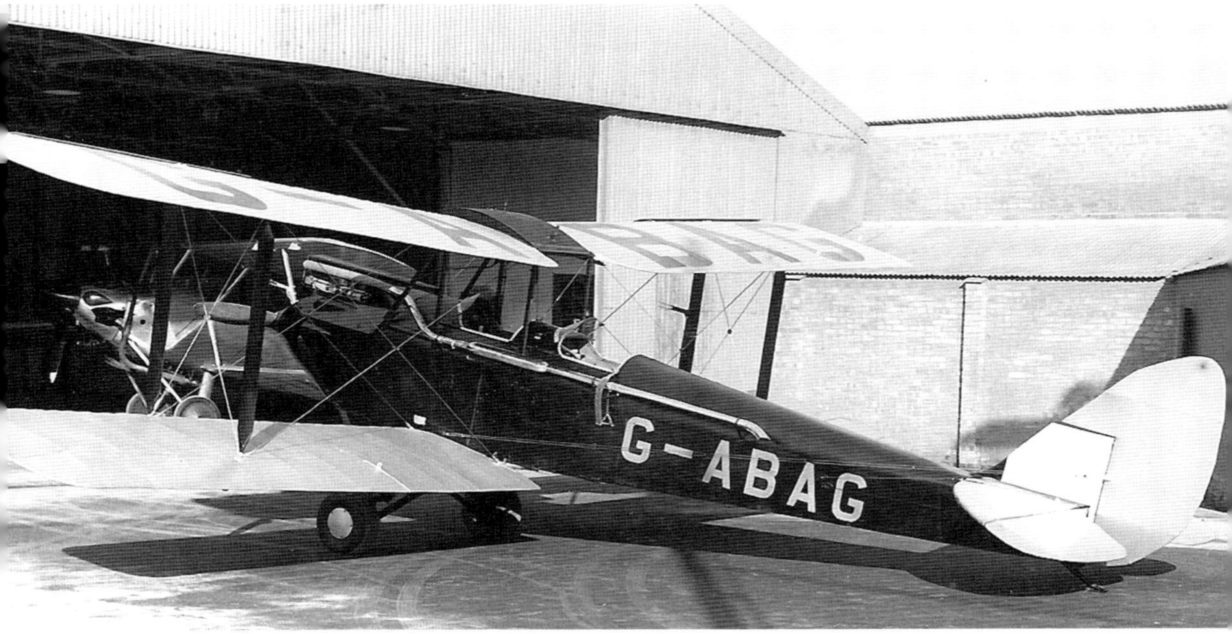

Another familiar sight at Shuttleworth flying days for many years was D.H. 60G Moth G-ABAG, also seen at Kidlington on 28 October, together with another current Shuttleworth aircraft, Hawker Tomtit G-AFTA, just visible in the hangar. 'AG was registered first in June 1930 to Bentley Motors Ltd and passed through several owners before acquisition by the Shuttleworth Trust, surviving a crash at Perth in February 1955. It is now owned by the Woods brothers.

An unusual view of British-built Tipsy Trainer I G-AFWT photographed from Auster Autocrat G-AHCN flying from White Waltham on 13 October. Delivered new to W. R. Trounson at Denham in the summer of 1939, 'WT passed to West London Aero Services Ltd at White Waltham in 1951 and is still extant today. Developed from the single-seat Tipsy S-2 and the two-seat Tipsy B designed by Belgian Ernest Tips, the Trainer was an improved version of the B incorporating washout on the tips of strengthened wings, a one-piece elevator and camber-changing flaps. First aircraft were built by Avions Fairey S.A. at Gosselies, Belgium, but with the intervention of war production was continued by the Tipsy Aircraft Company Ltd at the London Air Park, Hanworth. Powered by a 62 hp Walter Mikron 2 engine, the Trainer had staggered seats, similar in fashion to the D.H. 98 Mosquito.

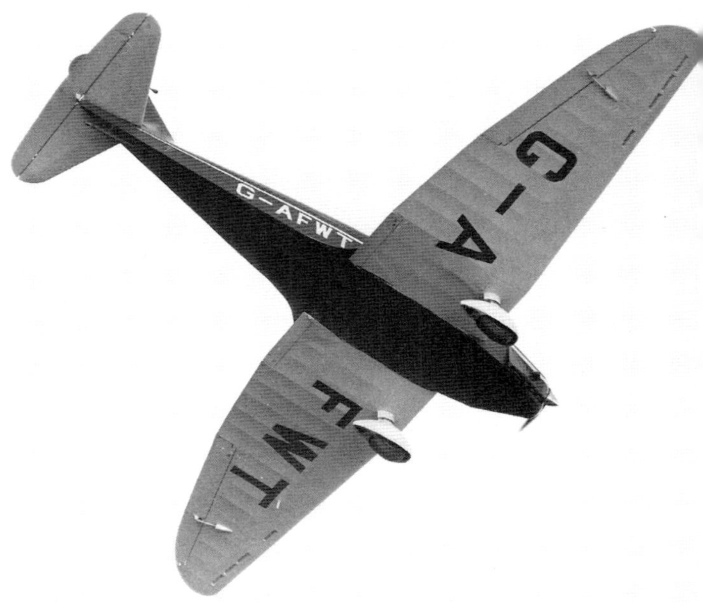

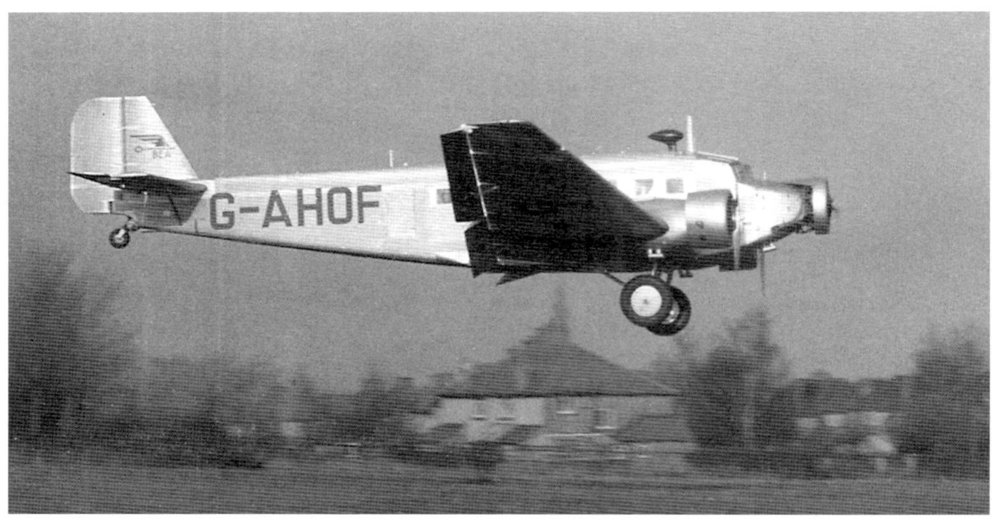

Immediately after the war in Europe ended 40 captured Luftwaffe Junker Ju/3m military transports were impressed in May 1945. Of these 12 were registered to BEA. Following civil conversion by Short Bros. and Harland at Belfast, some were used on internal routes from Croydon to Liverpool and on Scottish services from Renfrew. All-silver Junkers 52 G-AHOF, formerly VN729, is snapped landing at Croydon on 7 December. Most of the fleet, including 'OF, was scrapped at Warrington in February 1948.

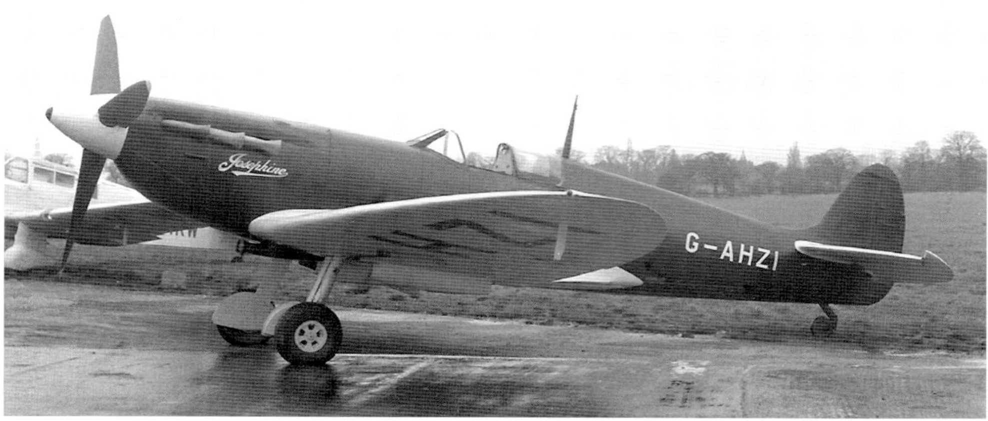

Probably the only Spitfire ever used for business trips, Mk II G-AHZI, seen here on 11 November, was based at Elstree in 1946–47 and flown by M. L. Bramson, a former S.E.5A pilot with the Savage Skywriting Company. His task was to arrange contracts and loads for the H.P. Halifaxes of Elstree-based London Aero & Motor Services Ltd. His mount began life as Spitfire IIB P8727 at Castle Bromwich where it was flown first on 16 July 1941 by Alex Henshaw. After a period with the Central Gunnery School at RAF Warmwell, Dorset, it moved to No. 276 Squadron before being taken off RAF charge in April 1945. At Marshalls, Cambridge, its Rolls-Royce Merlin II engine was exchanged for a 1,440 hp Merlin 45 and a C of A granted in October 1946. Named *Josephine*, 'ZI made frequent business trips to Europe until 15 April 1947 when it crashed taking off from Kastrup, Copenhagen.

West London Aero Club's D.H.87 Hornet Moth G-ADNE photographed from Taylorcraft Plus D G-AHXG in the vicinity of White Waltham on 16 November. At the outbreak of war 'NE was owned by the Yorkshire Aeroplane Club and impressed as X9235, but crashed near Penrith on its delivery flight to No. 2 Coastal Patrol Flight at Abbotsinch on 2 March 1940. It was repaired at Witney and moved around from one unit to another before restoration to the civil register by West London Aero Services Ltd at White Waltham in 1946. The veteran Hornet Moth is airworthy at the time of writing and flown by the G-ADNE Group.

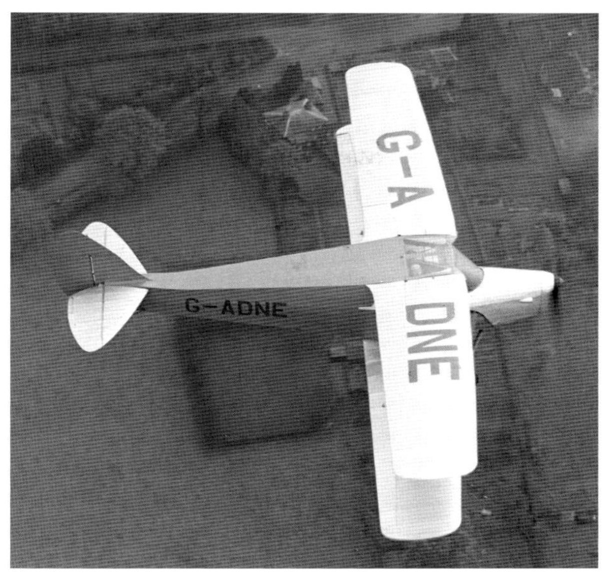

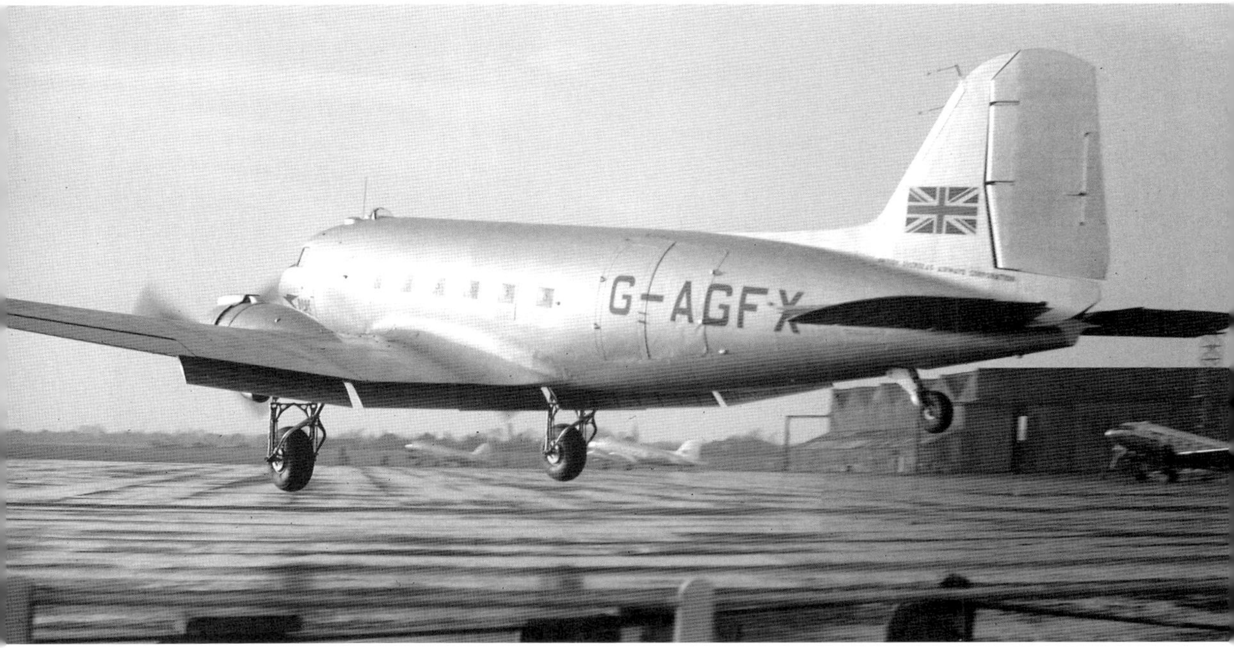

One can almost hear the throttled back Pratt & Whitney Twin Wasps as BOAC Douglas C-47 Dakota 3 G-AGFX just clears the fence at Croydon on 7 December. Dakota I FD769 was supplied to the RAF under lend-lease but was diverted to BOAC and registered in March 1943. Later upgraded to Mk 3 standard, 'FX was sold in South Africa as ZS-DCZ in June 1949.

3

Rebuilding Britain's Aircraft Industry (1947)

> For pity's sake grab a chair and get a load of this! In any case, I expect your palsied hands have by now caressed the enclosed three gems of aeronautical art.
>
> Letter from E. J. Riding to A. J. Jackson in 1947.

E.J.R. and A.J.J. were for ever searching new sources for photographs of British registered civil aircraft and every so often they struck gold. In a letter to A.J.J. dated 7 January 1947 E.J.R. wrote:

For pity's sake grab a chair and get a load of this! In any case, I expect your palsied hands have by now caressed the enclosed three gems of aeronautical art.

Today, a bloke came in and asked if he could take some photos of my twin-engined Sandringham [E.J.R. had built this scale model for exhibition at the Third National Model Aircraft Exhibition organised by the *Daily Express* in association with *Aeromodeller* at Dorland Hall in December–January 1946–47. Powered by two motors it was 'flown' round-the-pole in a purpose-built pool]. With a couldn't care less old boy attitude, I told Elwell [J. H. Elwell of the *Aeromodeller* research staff] to wade out and fetch it ashore and when he finished I asked him who he worked for and the reply was Topical Press, Red Lion Court, Fleet Street. Feeling a tinge of interest I said: 'I suppose the firm lost everything in the blitz'. 'Oh no', said he, 'we are the only press agency in town to have all our own plates intact since the last war.' Well, cockle, I dunno how my ague-shaken hand managed to work the ruddy rheostat [the Sandringham was electric powered] for the rest of this a.m., and at lunch time I bribed 'Wilbur' Wright to take over for the rest of the day and hared it hot foot for the tuppenny tube. Panting and breathless, (pausing for dramatic effect) I staggered up Red Lion Court and asked for the boss and ten minutes later was ushered into a dark dungeon lined with exciting looking boxes. There they were, 'undreds of the beggars: 'Aviation up to 1924', Aviation 1925, 26, 27, 28 ad lib—rows and rows, including a similar row of Accidents (Aviation) Pre 1924 and After'.

Feverishly I grabbed 'Accidents Pre-1924 and lifted the lid. 100,000 volts shot up my spine for the first photo in the box was G-EAXU [SE5A], crash, Waddon, one-off. Well, to cut a long story short, I went through everything up as far as 1935 during the next four hours and the results are listed herewith.

On 3 January the Air Ministry announced that the King's Flight was to be reconstituted and Air Commodore E. H. 'Mouse' Fielden's reappointment as captain of the flight that consisted of four Vickers Viking Is (VL245–VL248) based at RAF Benson. Two (VL246 and '47) were used to carry King George VI and Queen Elizabeth separately and had spacious and luxuriously-appointed interiors. The third aircraft was a staff aeroplane and the fourth equipped as a flying workshop that could deal with any problems encountered by the two VIP Vikings.

On 28 January E.J.R. popped over to Wisley for a 15-minute demonstration flight in BEA Viking G-AHPJ, flown by test pilot Sqn Ldr Robart, before inspecting Viking VL247 prior to preparing an article on the type for *Aeromodeller* magazine.

Earlier, on 18 January, E.J.R. attended the first meeting of the Informal Light Aeroplane Committee at White Waltham, chaired by Peter Masefield. Sponsored by the Ministry of Civil Aviation, purpose of the meeting was for the committee to have the opportunity of inspecting and flying as many new light aircraft as possible so as to gather evidence to form a basis for their discussions. Such luminaries as Richard Fairey of Fairey Aviation Ltd, Alan Butler of de Havilland Aircraft and

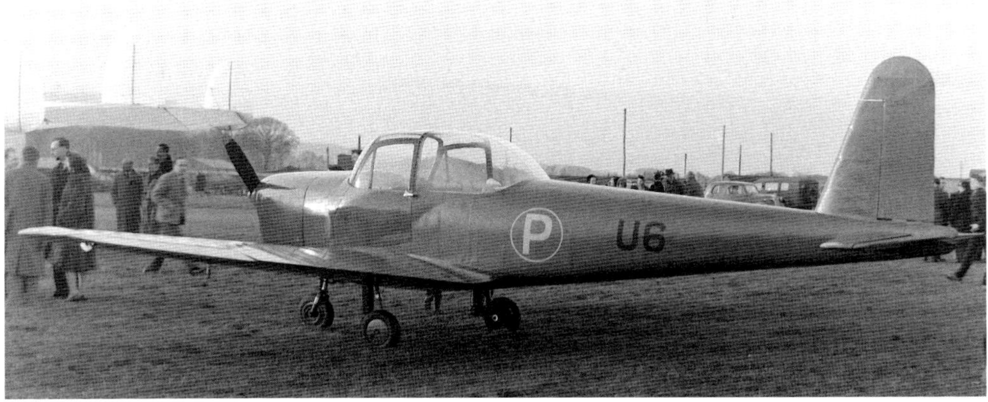

Also present at the Informal Light Aeroplane Committee's meeting and making its only public appearance, was the sole Miles M.64 U-6, first flown by George Miles on 3 June 1946. A promising design powered by a 100 hp Blackburn Cirrus Minor, the M.64, also known as the L.R. 5, (produced by employees of the Miles Liverpool Road factory) embodied many features that had become commonplace on light aircraft in the USA, such as a fixed tricycle undercarriage with steerable nose wheel, car-type doors, retractable flaps and excellent all-round vision. Sadly, the M.64 was a non-starter from the off. Design of the fuselage was such that it caused a large area of the wing to be in a stalled condition, particularly during slow flight, and because the company's resources were committed to production of the Gemini, Messenger and Aerovan, a redesign of the fuselage was not possible and the M.64 was abandoned.

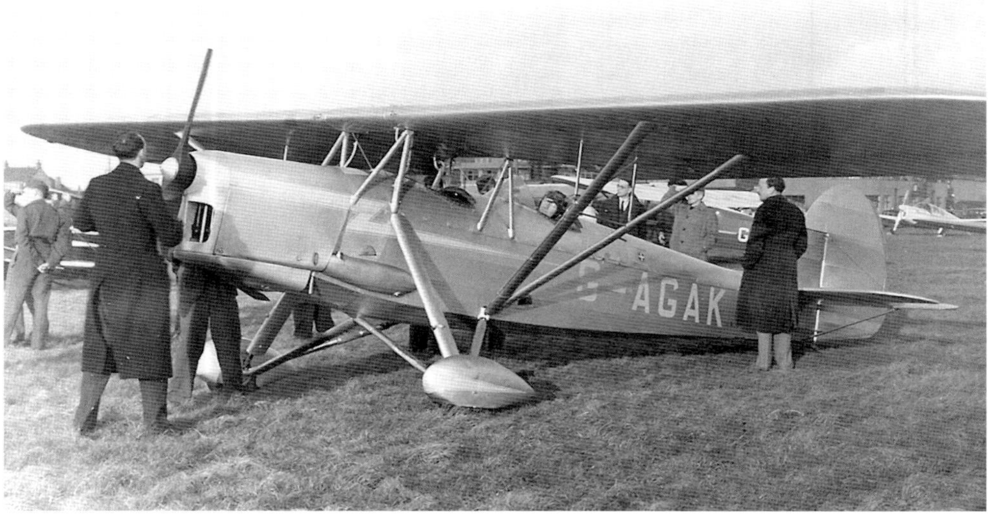

A visitor amongst the latest light aircraft market contenders at the Informal Light Aeroplane Committee's meeting was pre-war Hirtenberg H.S. 9A G-AGAK. This two-seater was built in 1937 by Hirtenberger Patronen Zundhutchen und Metallwarenfabrik A.G. at Hirtenberg, Austria, for J. H. Davies and registered OE-DJH initially. In July 1939 it arrived in the UK as D-EDJH and put on the British register in November before going into storage at Filton for the war's duration. 'AK surfaced again in October 1946 at Gatwick, remaining airworthy until it crashed in poor weather at Butser Hill, near Winchester, on 15 February 1955. Previously it had been raced and cherished by Don Robertson, former wartime test pilot and hovercraft inventor.

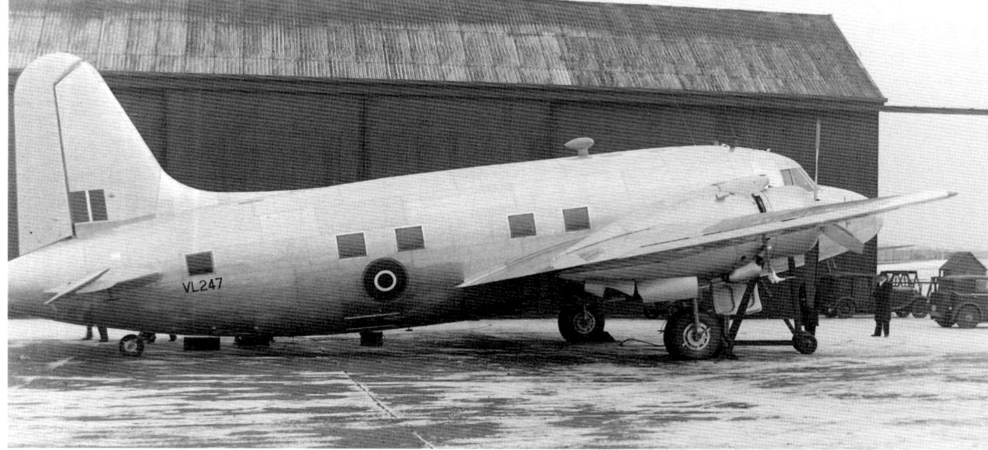

Fit for a King! Part of a batch of 16 Vickers Vikings produced by Vickers, Weybridge, in 1946–47, VL247, pictured in the snow at Wisley on 28 January, was one of four Viking C. Mk 2s delivered to the King's Flight, later the Queen's Flight. The spacious interiors of VIP Vikings VL246 and VL247 each had two lounge compartments, were blue carpeted, had pleated curtaining side walls and adjustable chairs stressed to 25g! King George VI and Queen Elizabeth were flown separately in the two VIP aircraft. VL247 was sold in 1958 and passed to Tradair Ltd at Southend before joining Channel Airways in December 1962. It was withdrawn from use at Southend in 1965.

C. G. Grey, editor of *The Aeroplane,* were present to help determine what future requirements were necessary to help the light aircraft industry and the private pilot. Lord Nathan, Minister for Civil Aviation, promised to do his utmost 'to see that the clubs and private flying got a square deal.' Of the 35 types on show there were many hopefuls, such as the Chrislea Ace prototype, the American Globe Swift and the D.H.C.1 Chipmunk, plus a lame duck or two, including the Miles M.64 that, on paper at least, seemed to embody the light plane pilot's requirements.

Incidentally, from 22 January until 17 March snow fell every day somewhere in the UK, and February was the coldest month on record up to that time.

On 1 February many of Britain's privately-operated internal air services were handed over to BEA, a process completed by 12 April. And, for the first time in more than 35 years, both *Flight* and *The Aeroplane* missed publication (of three issues, 14 February to 7 March), one impact of a national effort to save fuel (and therefore energy) due to a shortage of coal during the exceptionally cold winter.

On 21 February E.J.R. flew from Croydon to Nutts Corner, Belfast, in BEA Junkers 52/3m G-AHOG flown by Capt. Moynihan. From Nutts Corner he continued to Prestwick and on to Glasgow Renfrew in BEA Dakota G-AIOF. The return journey the following day was in BEA Dakota G-AGZF with Capt. Childs, the Prestwick to Northolt sector taking 2 hours 5 minutes, flown at 5,000 ft all the way where the outside temperature was minus 14 degrees C.

On 1 April the first flight of the prototype Blackburn B-48 RT651 was made from RAF Leconfield.

During 4–23 April E.J.R. holidayed on Jersey with his boss, Harborough Publishing's D. A. Russell, flying out from Croydon in Morton Air Services D.H. 89A Dragon Rapide G-AGWP flown by Capt. O'Brien, returning in a 35–40 mph gale in Rapide G-AGWR flown by Capt. Solomon. While on the island E.J.R. took air-to-air photographs of Island Air Services D.H. 89A Dragon Rapide G-AHPT over St Ouen from Percival Proctor G-AHVD.

The BEA Viking fleet returned to service on 21 April after joint tests with Vickers resolved the tailplane icing problems experienced in December 1946. E.J.R. had a 20-minute flight with a Mr Zenitz in Ercoupe OO-ERO from White Waltham on 11 May and was photographed (in colour!) while doing so by the doyen of aerial photographers, Charles E. Brown.

On 19 May the first flight of medium-range feeder liner, the Cunliffe-Owen Concordia Y-0222, was made from Eastleigh by A. Corbin. Designed to take up to 12 passengers and a crew of two on two 550 hp Alvis Leonides engines, its maiden flight was made shortly after that of the six-passenger Percival Merganser from Luton

E.J.R. and Stanley Orton Bradshaw flew to the official resurrection of the Leicestershire Aero Club at Ratcliffe in D.H. 87B Hornet Moth G-ADNB on 1 June on behalf of *The Aeroplane*, their illustrated report being published in the 13 June issue. Highlight of the re-opening was a succession of beat-ups by a No. 605 Squadron Mosquito N.F.36 that took off from an all too short field and diced with hoards of light aircraft.

Another great hope for the British light aircraft industry, the twin-boomed, twin-engine Portsmouth Aviation Aerocar G-AGTG, made its maiden flight on

18 June from Portsmouth in the hands of Major F. L. Luxmore. Despite hundreds of orders and plans to produce the aircraft in India 'TG was the sole example built.

On 21 May E.J.R. drove to Burnaston, Derby, to attend the International Air Rally, one of the most popular immediate post-war meetings of the decade. A national transport strike meant that of the 20,000 crowd anticipated only 12,000 turned up. Fire during the night of 22 June depleted severely the fleet of the Herts and Essex Aero Club at Broxbourne, destroying two hangars and ten aircraft. J. 'Mutt' Summers made the first flight of Vickers Valetta VL249 from Brooklands on 30 June. A military version of the Viking, the Valetta C. Mk 1 was described as 'five aeroplanes in one': troop carrier, ambulance, freighter, glider tug and parachute transport.

First flight of prototype Airspeed A.S. 57 Ambassador G-AGUA was made from Christchurch by chief test pilot George Errington on 10 July. On the 16th Geoffrey Tyson, chief test pilot for Saunders-Roe, made the first take-off of SR.A/1 TG263, the world's first jet-propelled flying boat, from the Solent.

Such was the heightened interest in aviation generally that public enclosures were opened at Northolt Airport on 26 July with accommodation for 3,000 visitors at 3*d* a time and space for 150 cars at 1*s* each. For those who wanted a taste of flying the misleadingly titled Congo Air Charter advertised pleasure flights over London in Airspeed Consuls at 17*s* 6*d* for 15 minutes and 28*s* for 30 minutes.

During August it was announced that Permits to Fly would be granted to ultra-light aeroplanes constructed by amateurs to approved designs. A normal Certificate of Airworthiness would not be required, provided such aeroplanes were not made available for sale to the general public.

On 2 August British South American Airways Corporation's (BSAAC) Avro Lancastrian G-AGWH *Star Dust* disappeared in the Argentinean Andes during a flight from Buenos Aires to Santiago, Chile. In 1998 parts of the wreckage were discovered and it was concluded that 'WG had flown into Mount Tupungato precipitating an avalanche and becoming buried under snow, where it remained until emerging in a glacier more than 50 years later.

Ken Waller made the first flight of Miles M.71 Merchantman G-AILJ from Woodley on 7 September and on the following day P. Stanbury did likewise with the Newbury A.P. 4 Eon G-AKBC from Welford, Berkshire.

On 9 August E.J.R. attended the International Air Rally and Air Races at Southend, coinciding with the official opening of the municipal aerodrome. The highlight was an aerobatic demonstration by a formation of No. 54 Squadron D.H. 100 Vampires in front of a 10,000 strong crowd. During the morning E.J.R. had a 20-minute flight, costing £28, with Rex Steadman in Chrislea Ace G-AHLG, from which he took aerial photographs of the event.

During early August E.J.R. and family, which had grown to five by this time, holidayed in Wimborne, close to Poole Harbour and Hurn Airport. That provided the opportunity to photograph flying boats at one and Avro Yorks on crew training at the other.

Starting 18 August what was claimed to be the first helicopter mail service in Britain was opened. Two RAF Sikorsky Hoverfly Is flew daily from Aberdeen Dyce with the King's mail to Balmoral Castle where the Royal family was in residence.

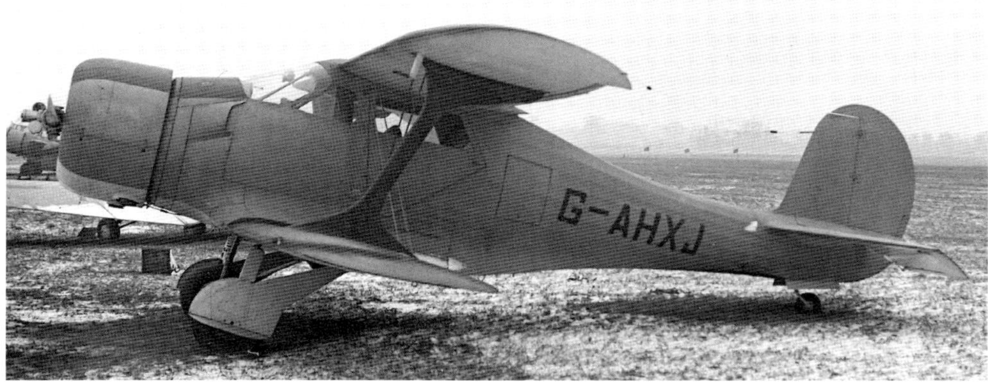

Beech D-17S Traveller G-AHXJ was built in 1944 and supplied to the US Navy as 42-3674 before being shipped to the UK and assigned to the Royal Navy as FT465. It flew with No. 781 Sqn and later with No. 701 Squadron at Heston. Once demobbed it was put back in civil guise by Airwork Ltd and registered as 'XJ in February 1947 and sold to Aero Industries Ltd at Heston, to be flown by Frank ten Bos. On 6 June, when taking-off from Ypenburg, Netherlands, 'XJ collided with D.H. 82A Tiger Moth PH-UAX, despite being given ATC clearance, and was destroyed.

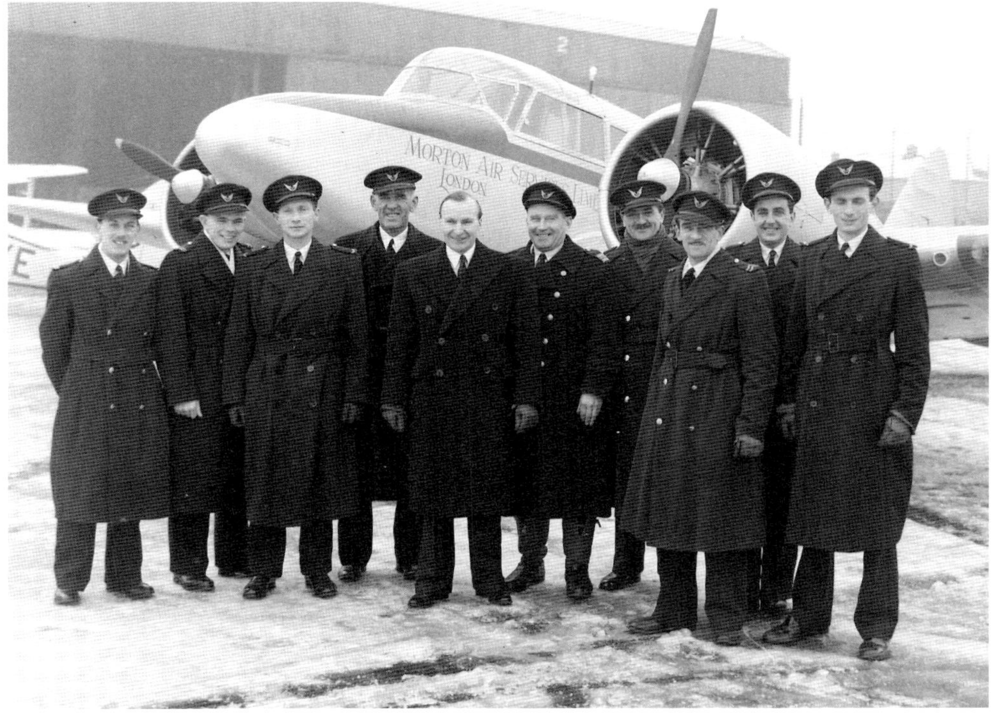

A row of cheerful faces in the snow at Croydon on 15 February as a line-up of Morton Air Services flying crew pose for E.J.R.'s camera. Hatless and in the centre stands 41 year-old managing director T. W. 'Sammy' Morton who, before setting up the charter company in 1945, was chief pilot for London Aircraft Production, testing Halifaxes at Leavesden, often accompanied by E.J.R.—see chapter 1.

The first flight of Miles M.68 G-AJJM took place from Woodley on 22 August, flown by George Miles. On the following day E.J.R. had flights in Short Sunderlands G-AHYY and G-AHZD from Poole to Hythe and return. The 45-minute return trip from Hythe with Capt. McKenzie in 'ZD took in Bournemouth, Brockenhurst, the Needles and Swanage. The author possesses 16 mm film taken by E.J.R. from both aircraft.

Continuing a bad year for A. V. Roe, Tudor II G-AGSU crashed on take-off from Woodford on 23 August killing chief designer, Roy Chadwick, S. A. 'Bill' Thorn, the pilot and two other crew members. Cause of the accident was the reversed assembly of the aileron controls. The day before the accident a new control column had been fitted to the aircraft.

E.J.R. visited Lympne for the Folkestone Aero Trophy on 30–31 August and was flown around the course (Lympne–Capel–Hythe–Lympne) by J. B. 'Tommy' Thompson in Percival Proctor G-AIYH with A.J.J. also as a passenger. Some 120 aircraft were present and the coveted trophy won by one of the slowest competitors, Paul Godfrey's B.A. Swallow G-AELG, averaging 100 mph. At the other end of the speed scale, the Lympne High Speed Handicap race was won by Peter Twiss in Fairey Firefly IV VG979 at 305 mph, three times that of the Swallow.

Two new aircraft took to the skies on 2 September. From Radlett H. G. Hazelden carried out the maiden flight of the second prototype Handley Page Hermes G-AGUB, the first having crashed on its initial flight in December 1945. Further south, at Boscombe Down, Bill Humble made a successful first flight of the Hawker P.1040 VP401 prototype, forerunner of the Sea Hawk. Further flight trials were carried out at Farnborough a few days later.

The Eighth SBAC Show was held at Radlett on 9–12 September and E.J.R was there with his camera. The general public though was not admitted because of the anticipated difficulties of traffic control caused by thousands of people converging at one time on a small, rural area. Instead, 3,000 invited guests from 50 countries were able to examine 72 aircraft in the static park. Highlights of the show were the Westland Wyvern, Handley Page Hermes II, three General Aircraft flying wings and jet aircraft such as the Supermarine Attacker, the D.H. 108 and a couple of Vampires.

The last scheduled service was flown from Croydon on 1 November by D.H. 89A Dragon Rapide G-AGIF, operating the BEA service to Guernsey. The airport then closed to scheduled air services. At Yeovil, BEA's Experimental Helicopter Unit began operating trial mail flights (with dummy mail loads) with three Sikorsky S-51s and a Bell 47B under the command of autogiro/helicopter maestro Wg Cdr R. A. C. Brie.

At Boscombe Down another futuristic shape took to the air on 13 November in the form of the Armstrong Whitworth A.W.52 TS363, flown by Sqn Ldr E. G. Franklin. Further trials were conducted from Armstrong Whitworth's Bitteswell aerodrome and Franklin appointed the company's chief test pilot the following month.

The year ended with the first tethered flight of Fairey Gyrodyne G-AIKF by Basil Arkell at Fairey Aviation's new premises at White Waltham on 7 December, the move from Heston almost completed.

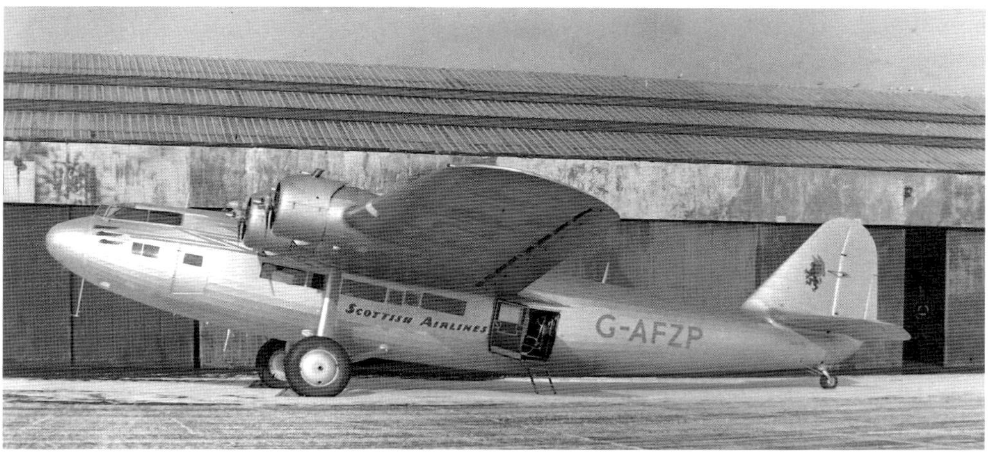

Four Fokker F.XXII 22-passenger airliners were built at Schiphol for KLM in 1934 of which two became British civil registered aircraft in 1939—PH-AJR (later G-AFXR) and PH-AJP (G-AFZP). 'ZP went to Scottish Aviation Ltd as a navigational trainer before impressment into the RAF as HM160 in October 1941. During service with No. 24 Communications Squadron the F.XXII suffered an engine fire during take-off, was taken off charge and later overhauled completely by Scottish Aviation. It flew again in October 1946 and is seen at Prestwick on 22 February 1947 in Scottish Airlines livery. Re-engined with 600 hp Pratt & Whitney Wasp Rs, it was used on the Prestwick-Belfast route and was withdrawn from use in 1952. This fine old lady was broken up and burnt at Prestwick in July 1952

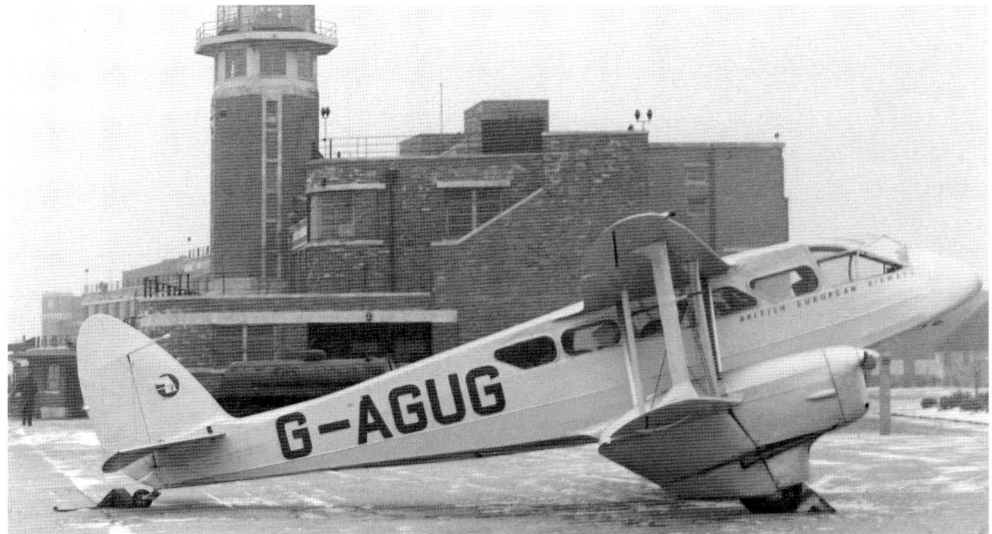

Parked in front of the unmistakeable edifice that is the control tower of Liverpool's Speke Airport (re-named John Lennon International 2002—why not Ken Dodd International?) on 21 February is BEA D.H. 89A Dragon Rapide G-AGUG with a BEA Junkers 52 lurking in the background. 'UG began life as RAF D.H.89B Dominie NR783, built by Brush Coachworks Ltd, Loughborough, in 1945. It was soon acquired by the Ministry of Civil Aviation and registered in November that year. In 1953 the Rapide was sold to Pakistan as AP-AGL, returned to the UK in 1956, only to leave again in January 1963 for Dakar, French West Africa, to become F-OCAG.

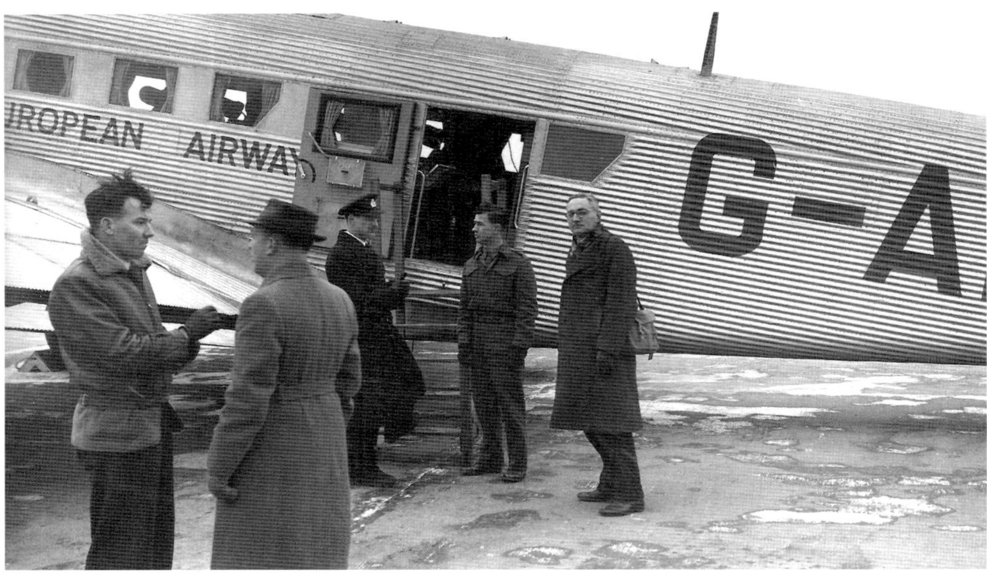

Passengers waiting in the bitter cold to board BEA Junkers 52/3m G-AHOG at Croydon for a flight to Nutts Corner, Belfast, via Speke, on 21 February 1947. Standing at extreme right is aviation author A. J. Jackson. The Ju 52, flown by Capt. Moynihan, flew blind after leaving Croydon on a course of 340 degrees at a steady 130 mph, before letting down for Speke between Nantwich and Frodsham, to land there one hour 25 minutes later.

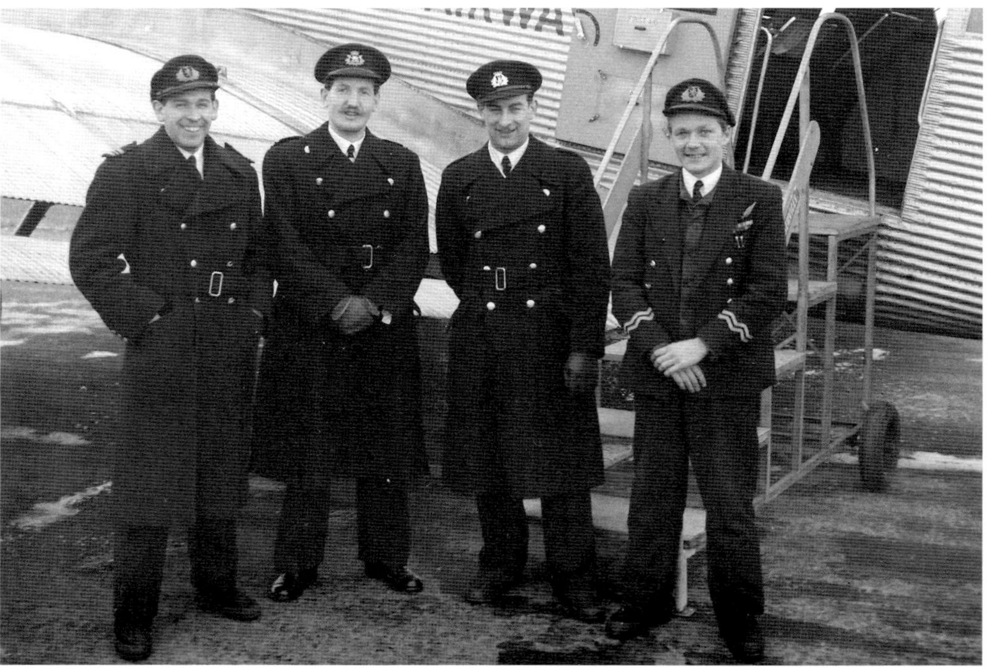

Capt. Moynihan and crew stand at the passenger entrance to Junkers Ju52/3m G-AHOG at Croydon on 21 February. What must they have thought when they first learnt they were to fly German-built aircraft on British domestic routes?

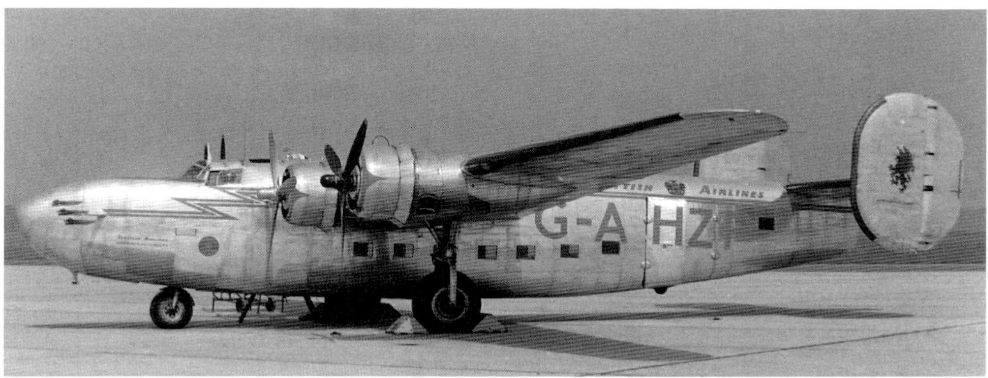

It may come as a surprise that no fewer than 27 Consolidated Liberators were allocated British registry during and in the immediate post-war period. Many were acquired by BOAC though operated in RAF markings and camouflage for use on the Atlantic Ferry. Consolidated Liberator II G-AHZP, seen at Prestwick on 22 February, formerly RAF aircraft AL516 (other sources say AL510), took up civil registry in August 1946 and was put into service by Scottish Airlines after being civilianised by Scottish Aviation Ltd. This included installation of seven rectangular windows on each side of the fuselage and seats for 30 passengers. 'ZP was lost in a crash at Speke, Liverpool, on 13 October 1948 whilst flying the 'milk run'. The three crew members escaping unhurt. During 1947–48 there was a shortage of milk in parts of England but plenty available in Northern Ireland. Scottish Aviation Liberators and Dakotas were used to ferry ten-gallon milk churns from Belfast to Liverpool.

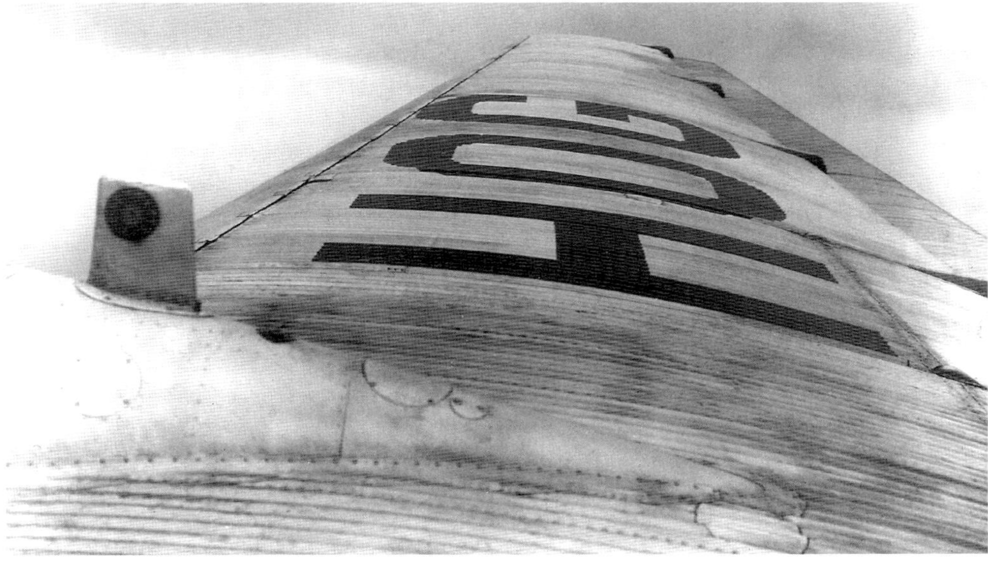

This was the view from G-AHOG on the Speke to Nutts Corner second leg. Capt. Moynihan kept the Junkers at 2,000–3,000 ft the entire way, flying in and out of snow showers and landing at Nutts Corner one hour 15 minutes later. The first Ju 52/3m Jupiter class service to Nutts Corner was flown on 18 November 1946. By the end of 1947 Dakotas replaced the Ju 52s, some of which were abandoned at Ringway and the rest of the fleet scrapped at Warrington in 1948.

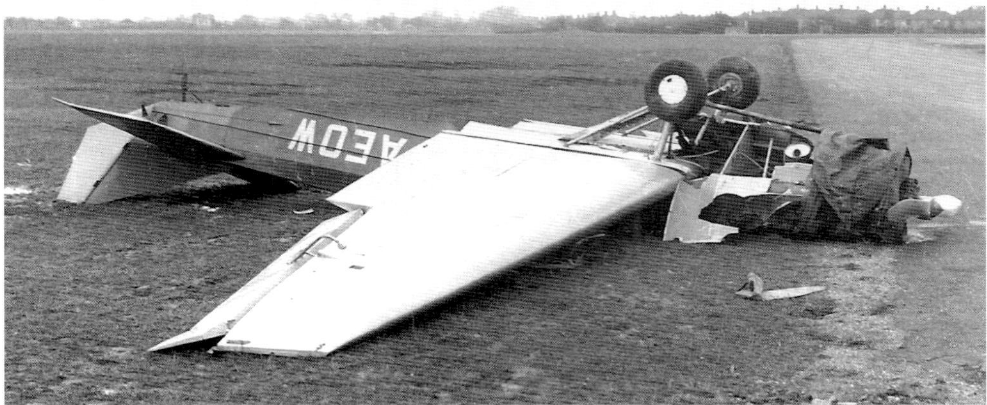

A victim of a gale that hit Heston in March was B.A. Swallow 2 G-AEOW belonging to A. R. 'Tiny' Pilgrim and normally kept at Elstree. Registered in November 1936, 'OW was on the strength of the London Air Park Flying Club at Hanworth until purchased by Pilgrim in September 1939. Stored during the war and restored to the register to the same owner in April 1946, 'OW was powered by a 90 hp Pobjoy Cataract III radial engine, giving the 42-foot-span Swallow a cruising speed of 90 mph—on a good day!.

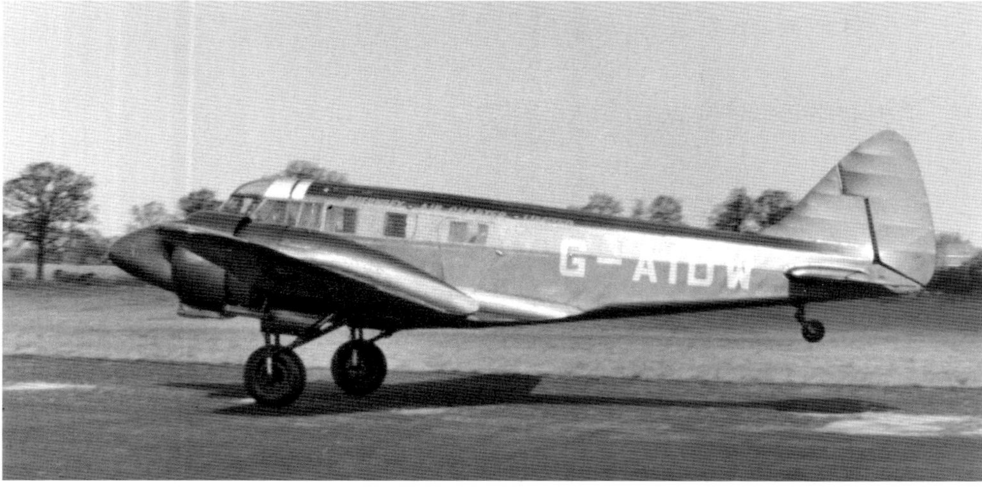

With tail up, Airspeed A.S. 65 Consul G-AIDW of Guernsey Air Charter Ltd takes-off from its Elstree base on 3 March. Formerly RAF Oxford HN783, the aircraft was delivered to No. 8 Anti-Aircraft Co-operation Unit at Pengam Moors in July 1943. Stints at several advance flying units followed before the Oxford was sold back to Airspeed in May 1946 for conversion to civilian Consul status and being acquired by Atlas Aviation at Elstree. In November 1947 'DZ passed to Dexford Motors Ltd at Southend and was scrapped there in September 1951.

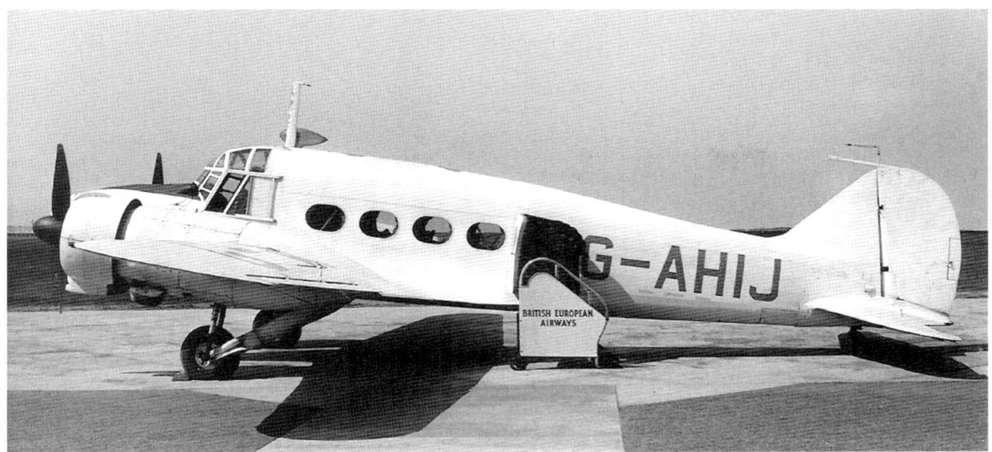

Seen at Jersey Airport awaiting passengers in April is BEA Avro 19 Anson G-AHIJ. First registered in July 1946, 'IJ was delivered to Railway Air Services although it flew in BEA livery until acquired by the Ministry of Civil Aviation's Civil Aviation Flying Unit in May 1948. In November 1951 it was sold to the Sperry Gyroscope Company at Cranfield and then exported to Pakistan in December 1952, to become AP-AGA. It was operated for several years on behalf of the Government of East Pakistan at Dacca until damaged in a storm there in March 1955.

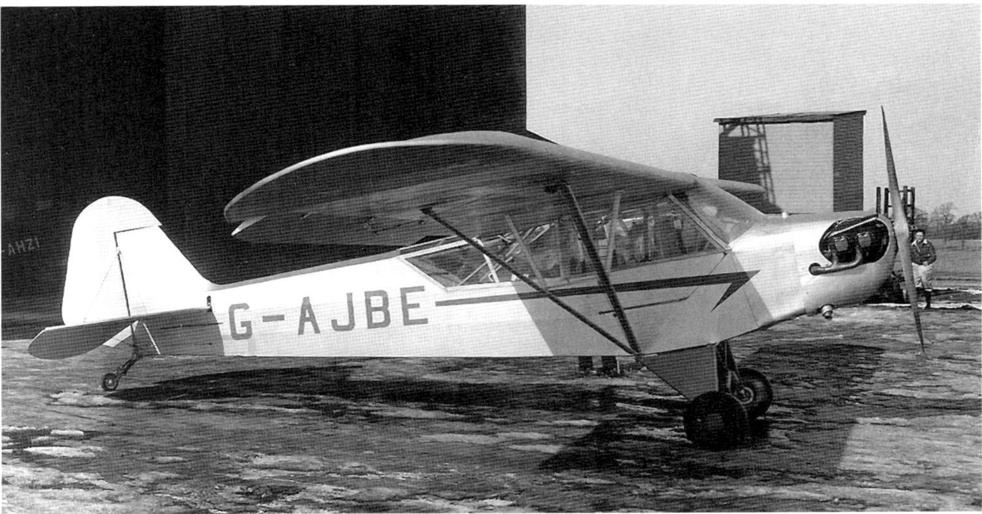

Many hundreds of Piper Cubs have been registered in the UK since Taylor Cub J-2 G-AEIK was shipped to UK agent A. J. Walter in 1936, the first UK Piper Cub proper being G-AFFH, imported in 1938. Piper L-4H Cub G-AJBE with extended rear glazing is seen at Elstree on 3 March. Shortly afterwards the 'BE registration was applied to a Halifax and the Cub re-registered as G-AKNC. After being exported to Finland, where it became OH-CPC, it was lost in a bizarre crash in January 1952 while landing at Helsinki-Malma. Noticing that the Cub was approaching at too low an airspeed, air traffic control fired a red warning flare causing the pilot to lose control while taking avoiding action. He was killed in the ensuing crash!

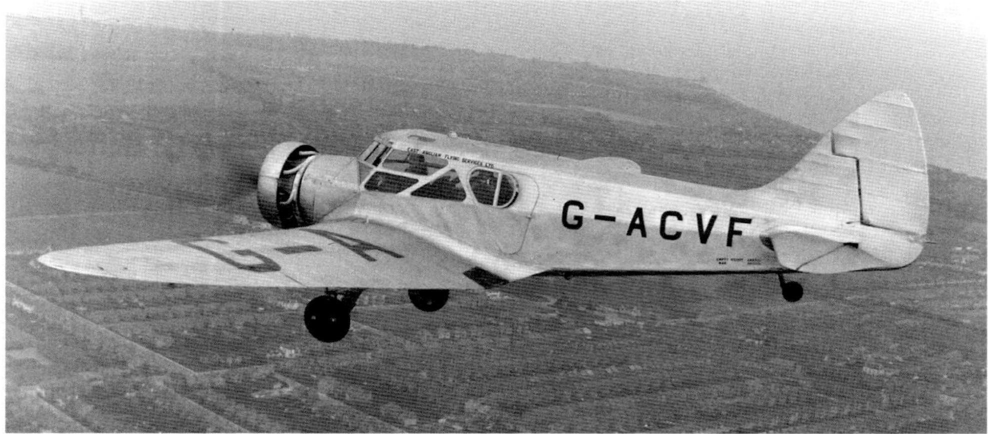

Pictured over Southend-on-Sea is East Anglian Flying Services (EAFS) Airspeed A.S. 5 Courier G-ACVF flown by Sqn Ldr R. J. 'Jack' Jones, the company's proprietor. Jones started EAFS in 1946 with two D.H. 80A Puss Moths and the Courier, all purchased at the famous RAF Kemble sale of impressed light aircraft in January 1946. His charter company was one of the first residents at Southend Airport when it opened officially in January 1947. Later, EAFS became Channel Airways, still under Jones' ownership. 'VF was built in 1936, owned first by North Eastern Airways until impressed into the RAF as X9437 in April 1940, and to begin with used by the Air Transport Auxiliary (ATA) at Hawarden. Subsequently flown as a communications aircraft by Boulton & Paul, the Courier spent much of the war at various maintenance units until it turned up for sale at RAF Kemble. After purchase by Jones 'VF was used for pleasure flying until expiry of its C of A in December 1947, after which it was withdrawn from use at Southend.

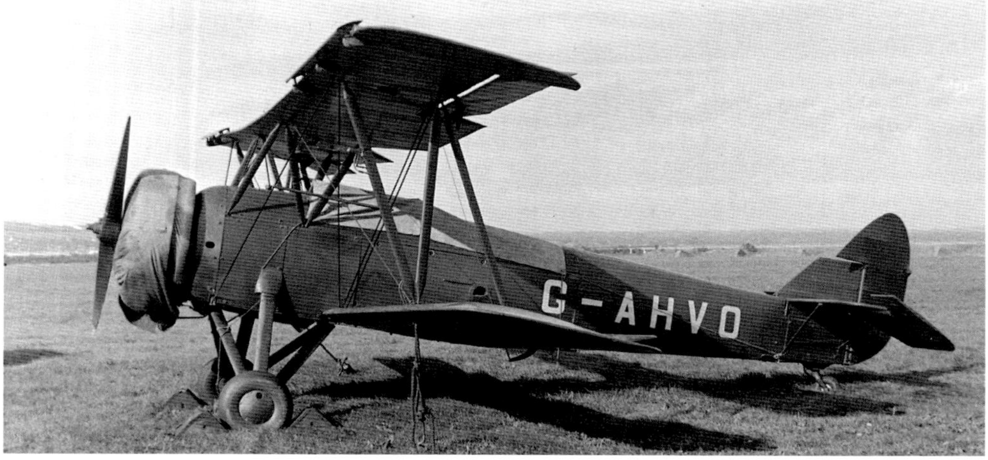

Pictured at Portsmouth on 3 May is Avro 626 Prefect G-AHVO belonging to Southern Aircraft (Gatwick) Ltd. Built as K5066 for the RAF in 1935 and delivered to the School of Navigation, the Prefect led a fairly sedentary life, mostly in storage at various maintenance units. Its only excitement occurred in March 1943 when it was hit by a Miles Magister while parked at Staverton. In May 1946 the Prefect was acquired by Southern Aircraft but sold on to L. E. Gisborne the same year and kept at Denham. When bought by A. G. Harding in September 1948 'VO was kept at Hastings, where it was scrapped in 1950.

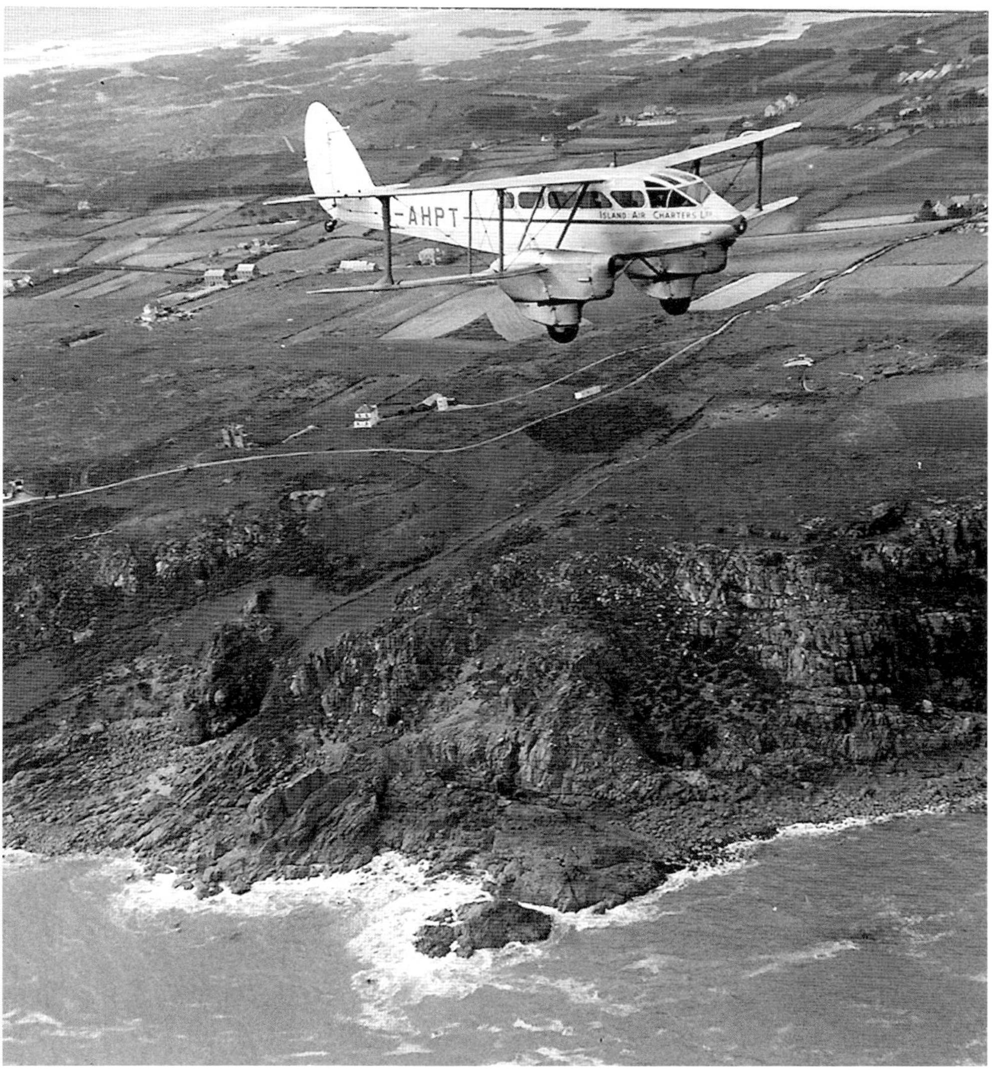

Island Air Charter's D.H.89A Dragon Rapide G-AHPT over Jersey on 22 April bound for Croydon, photographed from Percival Proctor I G-AHVD. 'PT started life as D.H. 89B Dominie I R9550 in 1940. Following a spell with the ATA it passed to the RAE and finally to RAF Hendon, presumably engaged on communications duties, before being sold to Field Consolidated Aircraft Services, Croydon. The Rapide was acquired by Island Air Charters Ltd in August 1946 and after several more ownerships went to Don Everall (Aviation) Ltd at Elmdon. During 1959 it was used by Tarmac Ltd to fly executives to Elstree, a mile or two from where the company was constructing the southern half of the M1 motorway. On 7 July 1959 Capt. Eric 'Tubby' Ashton took off from Elstree with one passenger to land on the adjacent and not yet open M10 at Leverstock Green, near St Albans, but struck a truck, the Rapide crashing, and bursting into flames. Miraculously, Ashton escaped via an impossibly small cockpit window; his passenger perished. After the accident Ashton told the author that he could not believe he had got out through such a small aperture. The author saw 'PT depart on the fateful flight and sold a photograph taken immediately before take-off to one of the London evening newspapers.

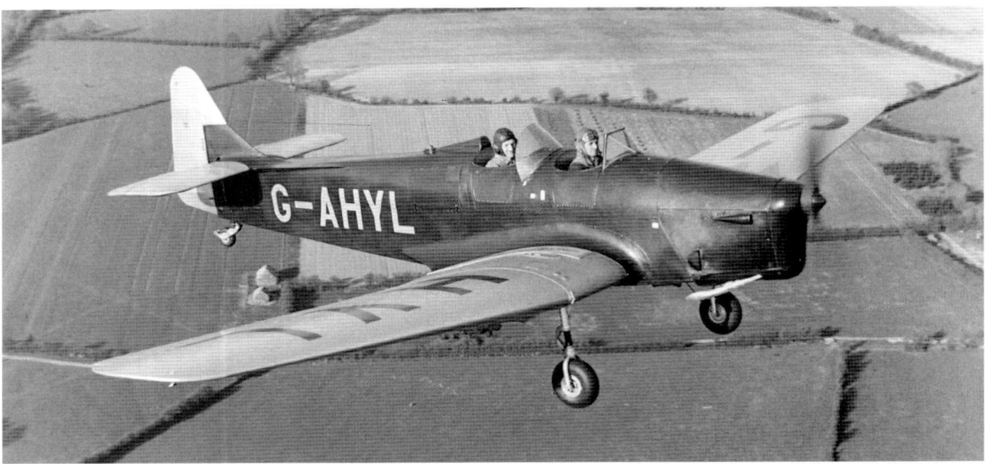

Former ATA pilot David Cotter flying the Fairey Flying Club's Miles M. 14 Hawk Trainer 3 G-AHYL near White Waltham on 26 April. 'YL was built in 1940 as T9834 for the RAF and was delivered to the station flight at RAF Coltishall followed by spells at various flying training schools before ending up at No. 6 (Observers) Advanced Flying Unit at Staverton. The 'Maggie' was sold in May 1946 and converted at Ringway for the Fairey Flying Club. During the 1950s it was owned by Derby Aviation Ltd and resided at Elstree, during which time it was flown in the 1957 King's Cup air race by CFI W. H. 'Bill' Bailey. The 'Maggies' were made redundant in 1958 with the arrival of the school's first D.H.C.1 Chipmunks. 'YL was bought by local high class butcher Sid Aarons and doped in an attractive yellow and black paint scheme. One day, c. 1960, the over-exuberant Sid, who liked low flying, hit a five-bar gate, 'YL afterwards languishing disgraced behind the main hangar.

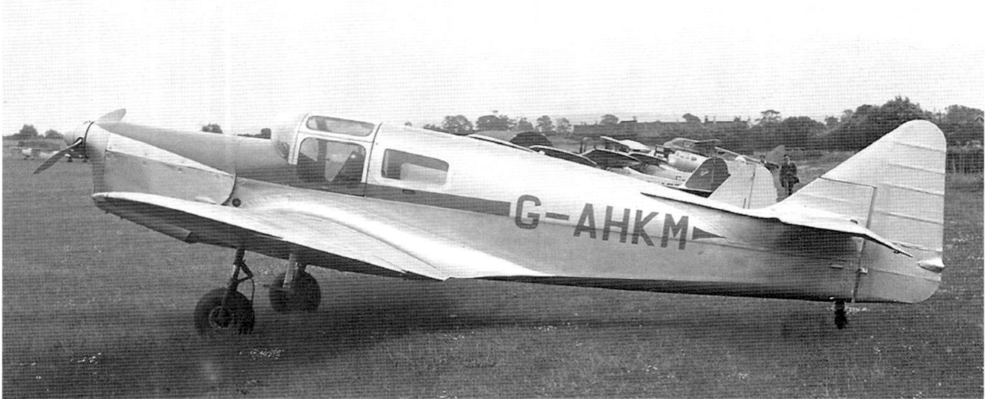

The unsuccessful Miles M. 16 Mentor was designed as a three-seat RAF trainer for a variety of roles, failing to reach the required standards and instead relegated to communications duties. Derived from the Miles M. 7 Nighthawk, the prototype was first flown in January 1938 and the RAF order for 45 fulfilled by June 1939. L4420 was delivered to the station flight at Hucknall in January 1939 and appeared at the sale of surplus light aircraft at RAF Kemble in July 1945, becoming G-AHKM in April the following year, the only Mentor to take up British registration. It came eighth in the 1949 King's Cup air race held at Elmdon but was lost in a fatal crash at Clayhidden, Devon, on 1 April 1950 in poor visibility. It is seen at the International Air Rally held at Burnaston, Derby on 21 June.

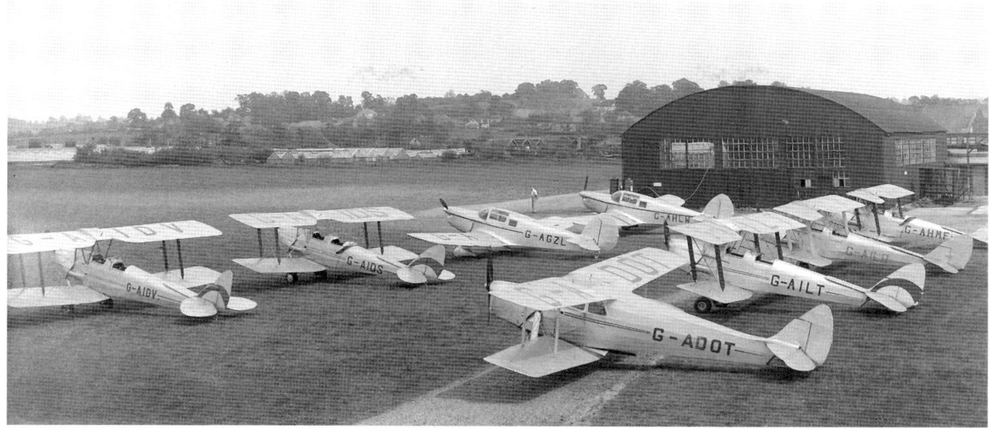

Most club and private aircraft during the first years of peace were demobbed war-surplus trainers and this photograph could have been taken at any one of dozens of flying clubs. Broxbourne was the home of the Herts & Essex Aeroplane Club (1946) Ltd and most of its fleet of aircraft, consisting of D.H. 82A Tiger Moths, Percival Proctor Is and a D.H. 87A Hornet Moth, were lined up for the benefit of E.J.R.'s camera on 17 May.

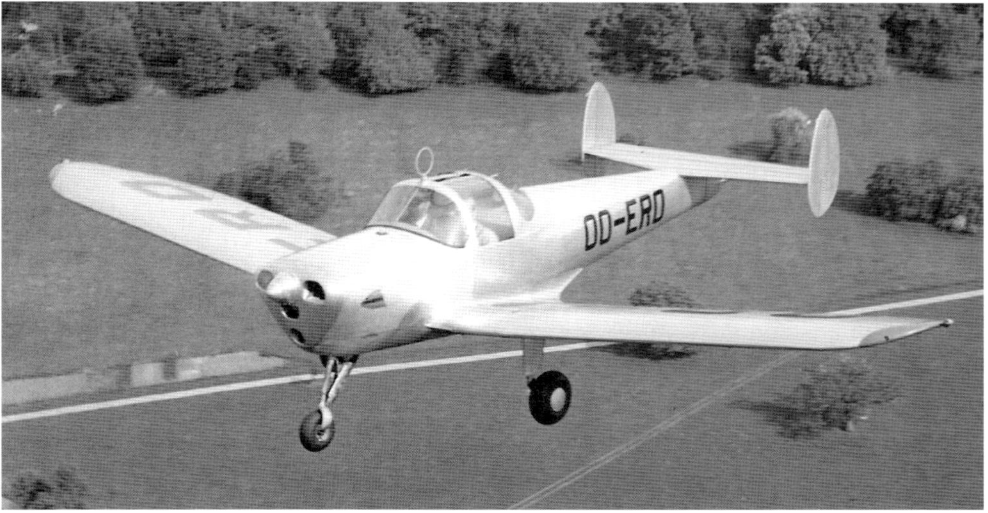

The arrival in the UK early in 1947 of Erco 414-C Ercoupe OO-ERO from Belgium caused much interest and diversity of opinion among pilots. First flown in 1937, its simple car-like handling made it popular with trainee pilots. A control wheel operated the ailerons, rudder and elevators and the aircraft could not be spun, side-slipped or barrel- rolled. Although welcomed by the inexperienced, its limited capabilities to kill the driver were frowned upon by seasoned pilots. Perhaps Stanley Bradshaw summed up the situation when he wrote in *The Lightplane*: '*I find it practically impossible to fault…On the other hand, very few people could not be taught to fly the Ercoupe, and any pilot of normal experience could go straight to it. Possibly no pilot taught exclusively on the Ercoupe could safely fly any normal aeroplane.*' OO-ERO is seen in the vicinity of White Waltham on 11 May flown by the Belgian export sales manager, Julian Zenitz. The same day, E.J.R. had a ride in the Ercoupe when being photographed in colour by Charles E. Brown. 'RO was damaged beyond repair at Bienne, Switzerland on 6 July 1951.

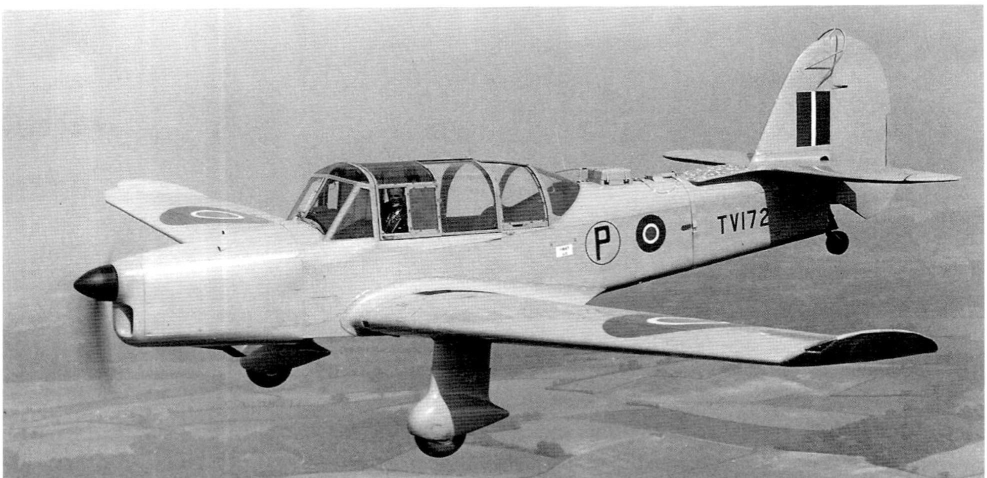

The RAF's standard basic trainer from 1948-53 was the Percival Prentice, superseding the Tiger Moth and itself succeeded by the piston Provost. It was also the Service's first basic trainer with side-by-side seating for instructor and pupil. TV163, the prototype Prentice, first flew on 31 March, but was found to be short of adequate rudder control; later prototypes and production aircraft had turned up wing-tips. The all-yellow TV172, seen here not far from its Luton birthplace on 16 May flown by Percival test pilot Capt. Leonard Turnell Carruthers, was the fourth prototype and incorporated the aforementioned modifications. The 46-foot span Prentice was powered by a 251 hp D.H. Gipsy Queen 32 and cruised at 136 mph. When retired by the RAF 250 were released for the civil market, so many being herded together at Stansted and Southend they were probably marked on the Ordnance Survey maps of the period! Only about 30 were issued with Certificates of Airworthiness, the rest scrapped.

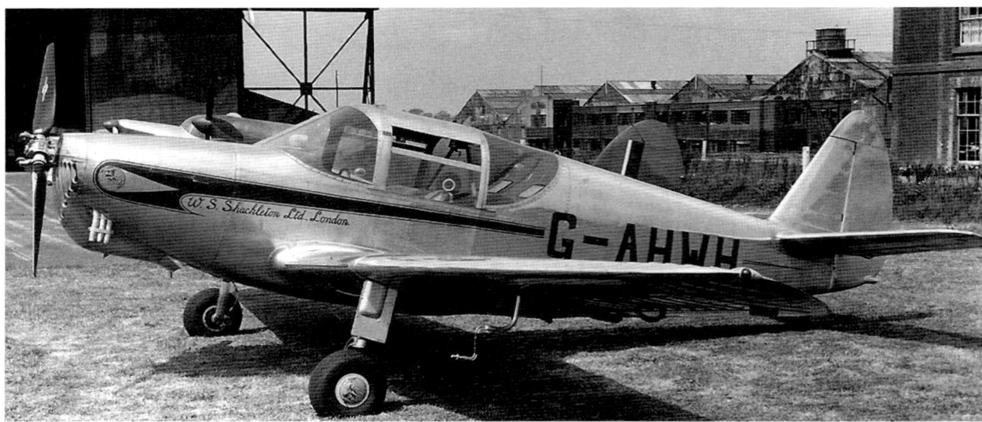

One of the new aircraft to catch the eye of the light plane enthusiast at the meeting of the Informal Light Aircraft Committee at White Waltham in January 1947 was the all-metal petite American Globe Swift, built at Dallas, Texas in 1946. G-AHUU arrived at the show with a beat up by Peter Clifford, chief pilot of Hellewells Ltd of Walsall. Plans for Hellewells to licence-build the Swift came to nothing, but four examples appeared on the civil register, the second of which was G-AHWH, seen at Luton on 16 May 1947. This neat little two-seater was powered by a 125 hp Continental C-152-2 engine and registered in March 1947. It was withdrawn from use at Wombleton in June 1961.

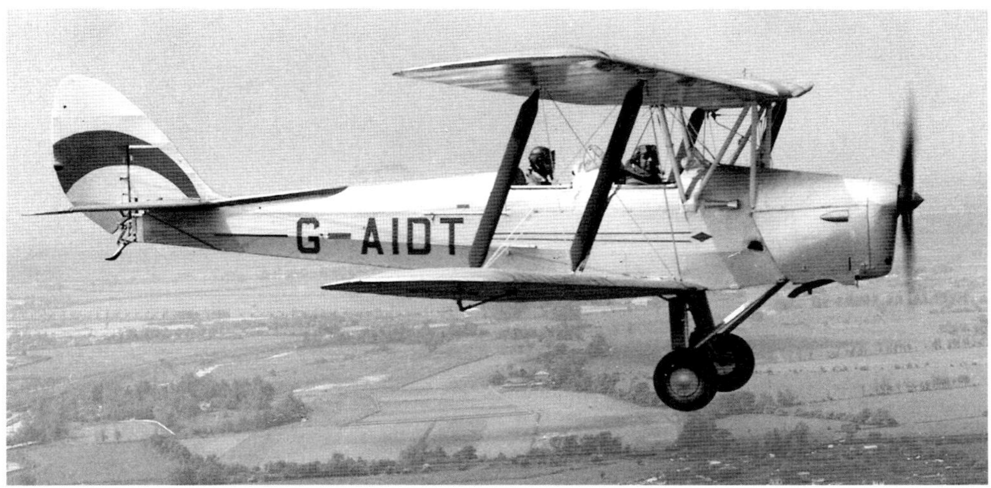

Herts & Essex Aeroplane Club's D.H. 82A Tiger Moth G-AIDT, airborne near Broxbourne on 17 May 1947, photographed from Percival Proctor I G-AHLW flown by Herts & Essex instructor Dennis Cather. Built for the RAF as T6302 and one of a batch of 2,000 Tiger Moths produced by Morris Motors at Cowley during 1940–41, it was delivered to the signals flight at Newton and served with Nos 17 EFTS at North Luffenham and No. 15 EFTS at Redhill before being demobbed in August 1946. In October 1957 'DT was sold in Germany to become D-EJOM.

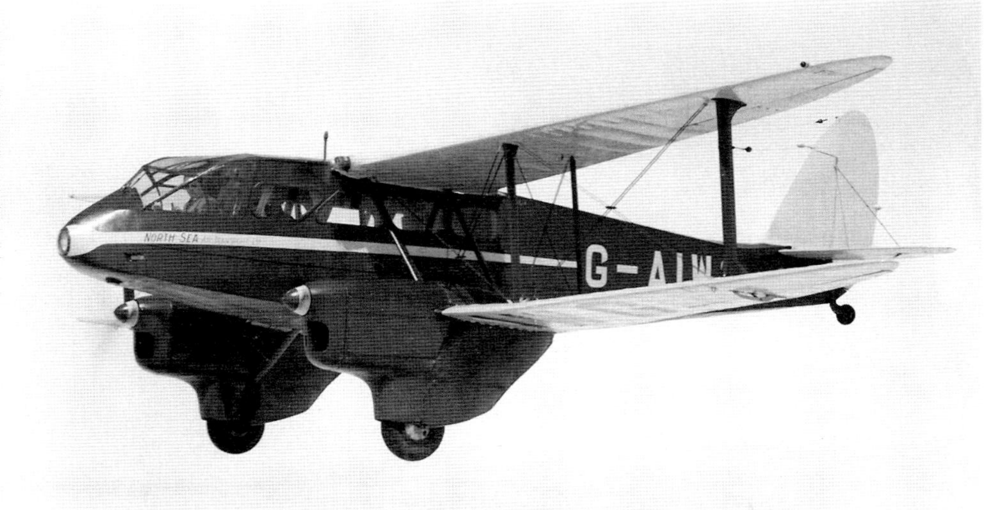

Formed as a subsidiary of Blackburn Aircraft in 1945, North Sea Air Transport (NSAT) Ltd operated a fleet of five maroon and cream D.H.89A Dragon Rapides, one of them G-AIWG, seen flying from Hanworth Air Park on 20 May. Built as D.H. 89B Dominie X7324 in 1940 and delivered to the ATA, it was damaged in January 1943 when taxiing into an Anson. After repair it ended its Service career with No. 24 Metropolitan Communications Squadron at Hendon before coming up for sale at RAF Kemble. Purchased by NSAT in November 1946 'WG was engaged mostly in flying holidaymakers to the Channel Islands. It was sold in February 1950, migrating the same month to Australia to become VH-AIK. In September 1951 the Rapide was written-off when it caught fire while starting up at Turkey Creek, Western Australia.

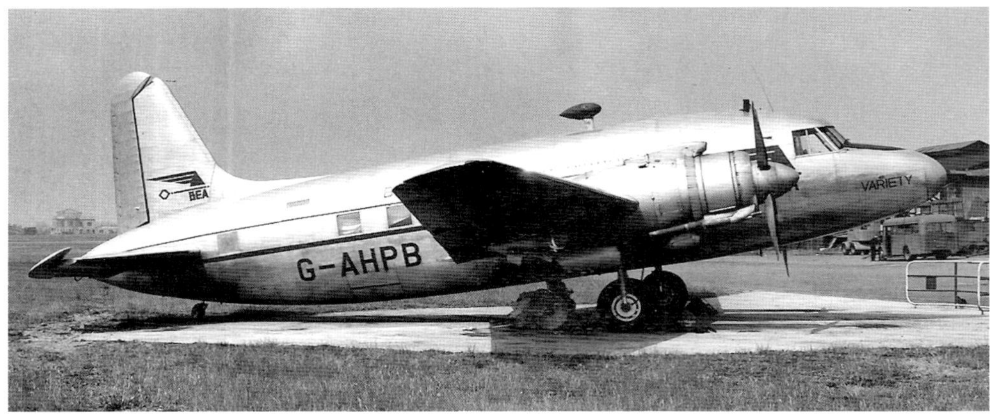

BEA Vickers Viking 1A G-AHPB *Variety* at Northolt on 31 May. Following the first flight of the prototype Viking on 22 June 1945, BOAC ordered 19 Type 498 Vikings for European services, to be flown by newly-formed sister corporation BEA, deliveries beginning in April 1946. The corporation later ordered Type 614 Viking 1As, of which 'PB was one, remaining in service until sold to Tradair, later passing to Autair. Following withdrawal from use in 1968 the Viking was displayed in the Technorama Museum at Winterthur, Switzerland and later as D-BABY at Dusseldorf.

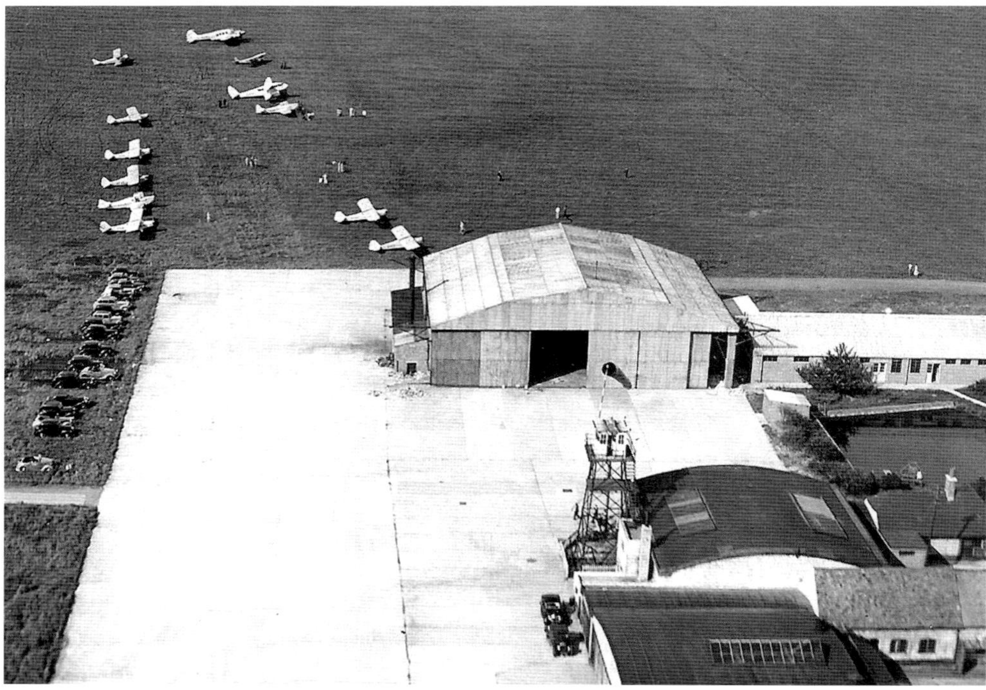

This aerial view of Ratcliffe aerodrome was taken from D.H. 87B Hornet Moth G-ADNB on 1 June on the occasion of the opening of Leicester Aero Club. Remembered as being the happiest of all ATA Ferry Pools (No. 6), the private aerodrome of Sir Lindsay Everard JP had been in use since September 1930. Highlights of the Leicester Aero Club's opening were repeated beat-ups by a No. 605 Squadron D.H. 98 Mosquito N.F.36 and some aerial cavorting by a crimson Auster, courtesy of Auster Aircraft Ltd.

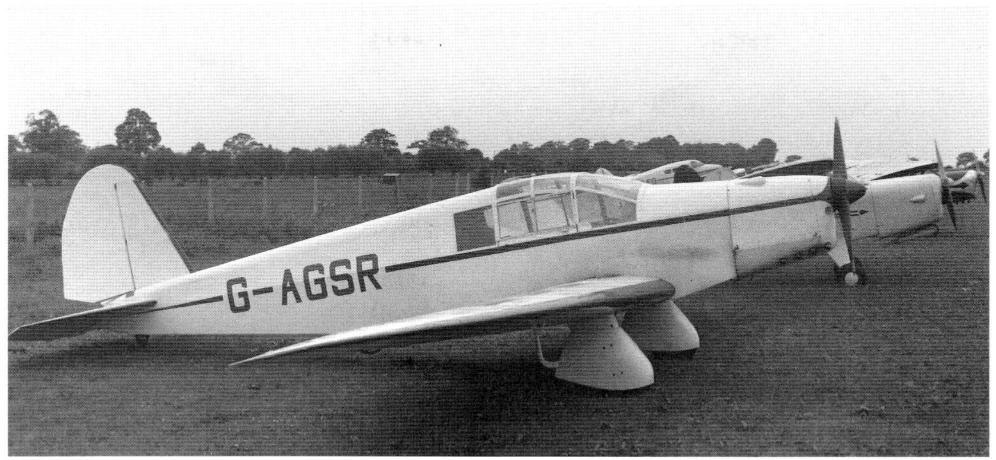

Looking like the product of an unnatural liaison between a Percival Gull and a BA Eagle, the sole British registered Czechoslovakian Benes Mraz Be.550 Bibi, G-AGSR, was built in 1937 and imported to the UK as OK-BET in 1938. Powered by a 62 hp Walter Mikron II and stored during the war, it received a C of A in May 1947 and was based at Heston. It is seen at Burnaston, Derby, on the occasion of the International Air Rally on 21 June, attended by 140 visiting aircraft. The Bibi was destroyed and its owner killed when crashing at White Waltham on 25 October, a victim of crossed controls.

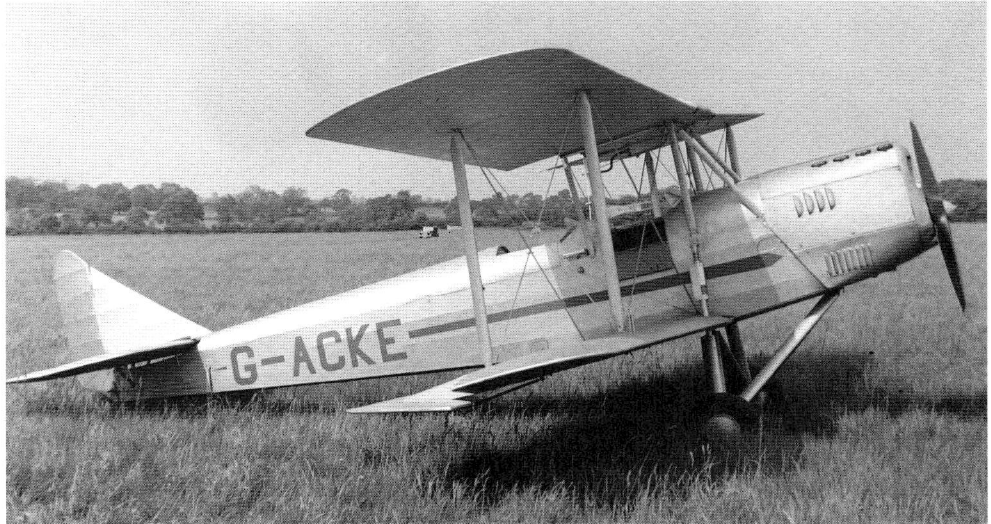

One of the visitors at Ratcliffe at the opening of the Leicester Aero Club on 1 June was Avro 616 Avian IVM G-ACKE, built in 1930 and exported to Australia to become VH-UOB with Australian National Airways. It returned to the UK in 1933 and at the time it appeared at Ratcliffe was owned by Ernest Morton. On 26 July 1950 'KE collided with D.H. 82A Tiger Moth G-AHKZ at Baginton, Coventry and was destroyed, though parts of its anatomy went into keeping Avian G-ABEE alive.

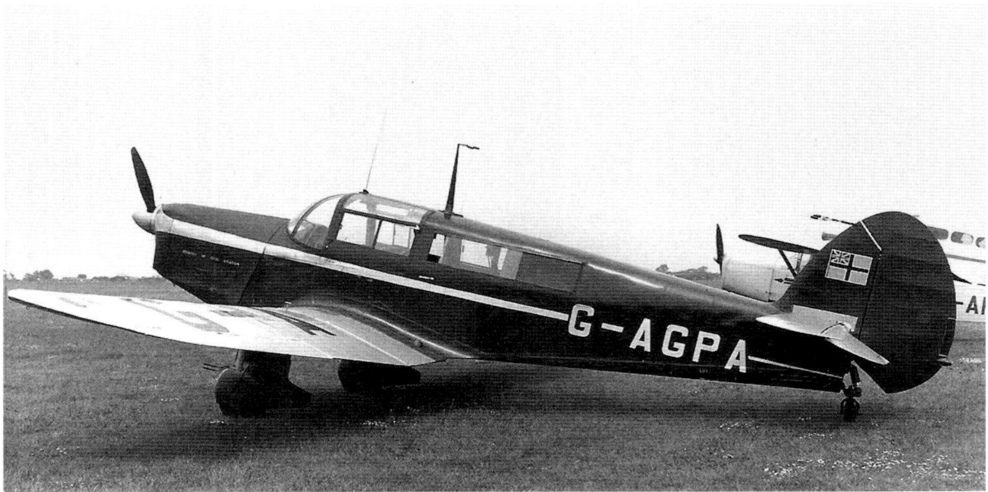

Built as Percival Proctor 4 RM161 for the RAF in 1944, this aircraft passed to the Ministry of Civil Aviation in June 1945 and was converted at Luton for radio calibration duties, based at Gatwick. It is seen here at Burnaston, Derby, on 21 June. On 4 August 1947 'PA was damaged beyond repair at Plympton St Mary, Devon.

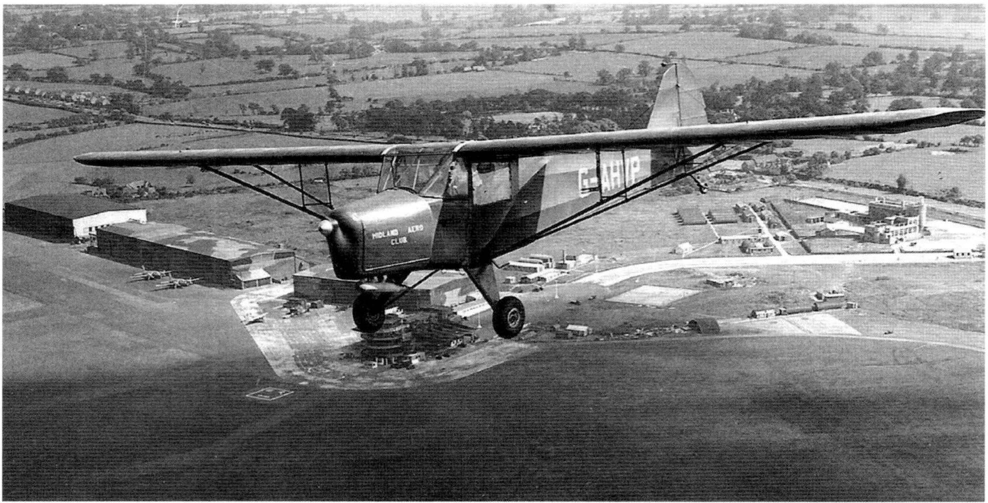

Taylorcraft Plus D G-AHVP, nicely positioned above its Elmdon Airport, Birmingham, base on 26 June. Built as LB276 for the RAF by Taylorcraft Aeroplanes at Rearsby in 1942, it served with No. 651 Squadron and was struck off charge in Malta in February 1944. 'VP was first registered in August 1946 to the Midland Aero Club but was destroyed and both occupants killed in a landing accident at Elmdon in April 1951.

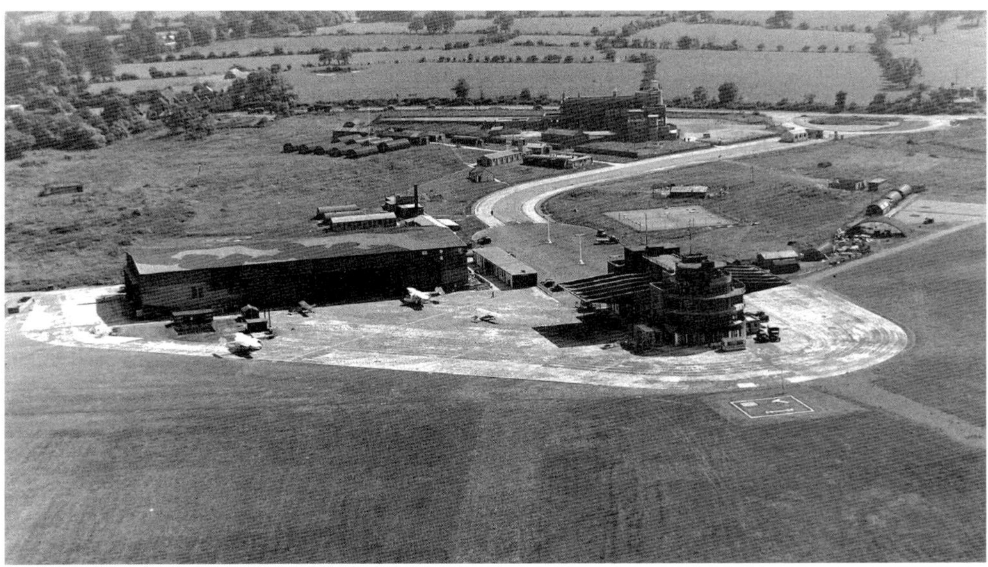

The Duchess of Kent opened Birmingham's Elmdon Airport officially on 8 July 1939 although it had been operational since May, only to be requisitioned by the RAF on the outbreak of war. This aerial photograph was taken on 26 June 1947 from the Midland Aero Club's Taylorcraft Plus D G-AHVR. Note the camouflaged hangars and airport buildings and the lack of aircraft, barring two Miles Aerovans and a Taylorcraft Plus D.

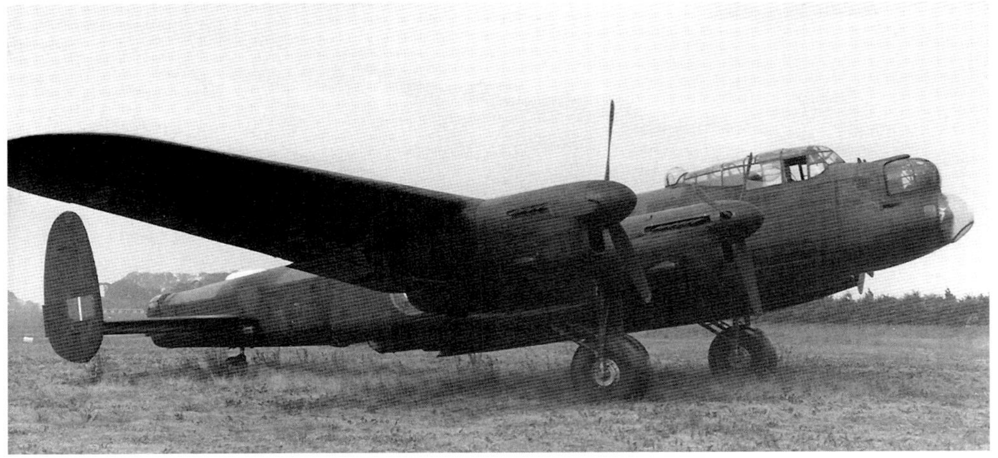

BEA once owned Avro Lancaster I PP741, complete with turrets (but lacking guns) and still in war paint that arrived at White Waltham in June 1947. After receiving the temporary markings G-AJWM and named *Alitalia-Roma*, the Lancaster flew to Italy in November 1947 where it was used for training Alitalia crews on newly-acquired Avro Lancastrians. Here it is seen at White Waltham on 26 June with its special double curvature bomb doors open. Built at Castle Bromwich by Vickers-Armstrongs, this Lancaster was first flown in June 1945.

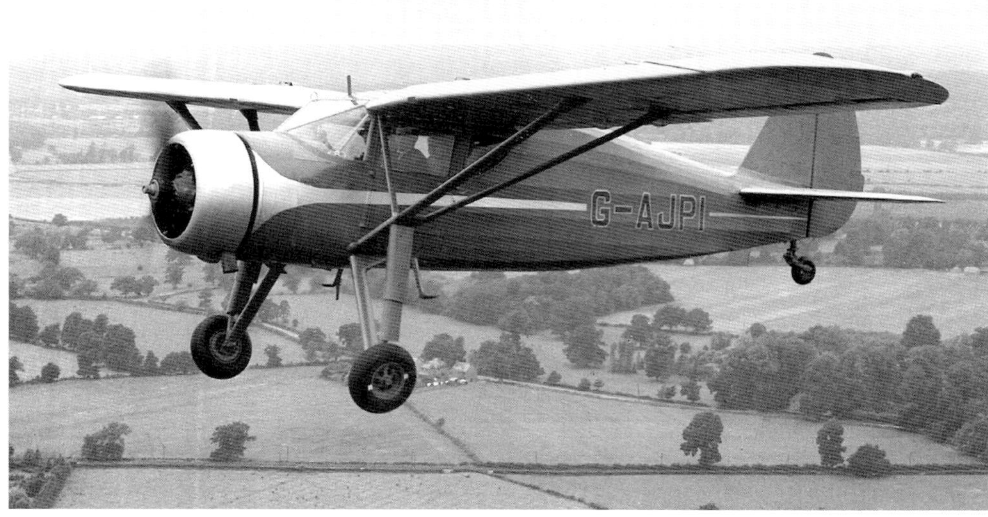

Former ATA pilot David Cotter flying dark blue Fairchild 24W-41A Argus 2 G-AJPI from White Waltham on 3 July during an air-to-air sortie photographing Joan Nayler in her D.H. 80 Puss Moth G-ABYP. Powered by the 165 hp Warner Scarab radial engine, many Fairchild 24s were supplied to the RAF during the Second World War under Lend-Lease, the type used mostly as a taxi and communications aircraft by the ATA. Formerly HB614, this 1943 Argus was one of more than 50 surplus examples of the type that acquired civil registrations post-war. At the time of writing 'PI was still airworthy, aged 70.

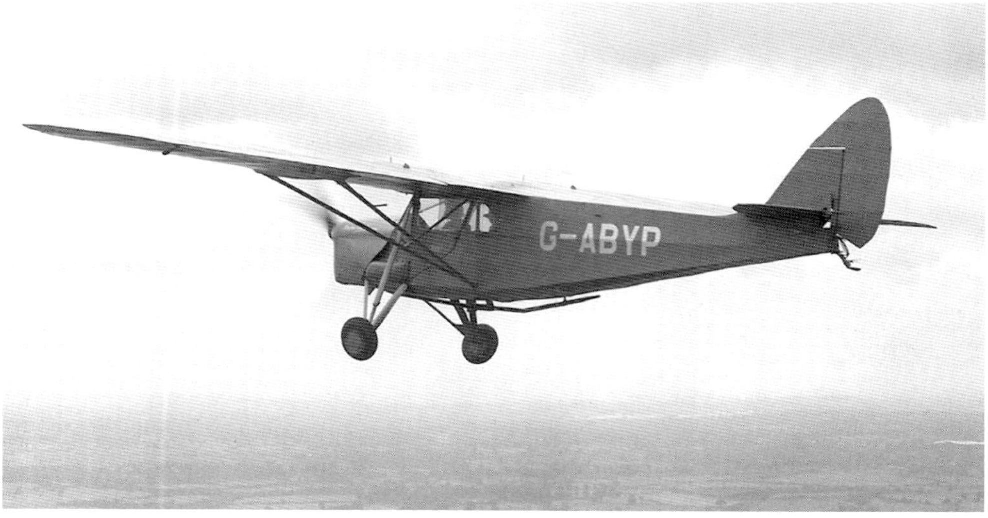

Former ATA 1st Officer Joan E. Nayler (later Russell) flying her Nayler Air Services D.H. 80A Puss Moth G-ABYP *Widget* from Eaton Bray on 3 July, photographed from Fairchild 24W-41A Argus G-AJPI flown by former ATA colleague David Cotter. Registered in August 1932, 'YP was impressed into RAF service as BK870 and operated by No. 1 Ferry Pool ATA. It later passed to the communications flight at Wick before being restored to the register in July 1946. Having been acquired by Miss Nayler, it was destroyed at Eaton Bray where it crashed and caught fire a year later on 31 August 1947—see right.

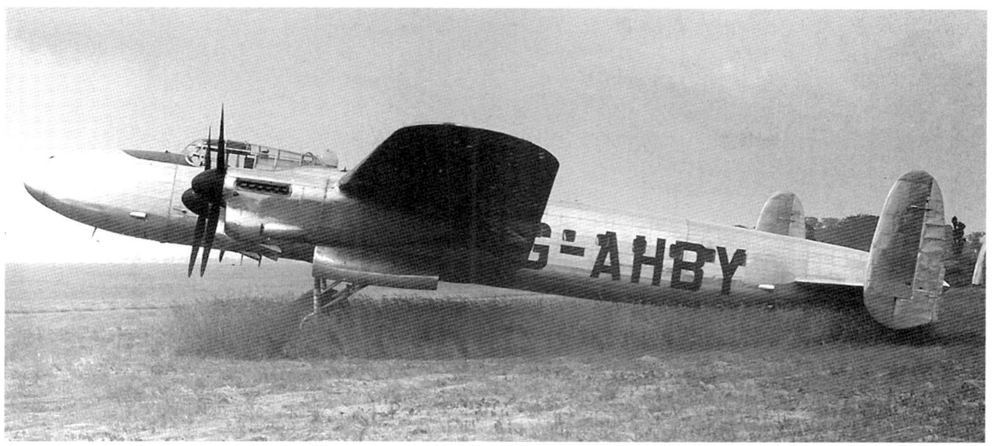

Pictured at White Waltham on 28 June is Avro 691 Lancastrian 3 G-AHBY, sold by BEA to Italian airline Alitalia. It sat at the airfield for a while, as can be seen by the jungle of long grass on which it is parked, but was delivered finally to Italy to become I-AHBY and named *Libeccio* (a westerly wind that blows in Corsica) in November. The Alitalia fleet of nine-passenger Lancastrians operated a weekly Rome-Montevideo South Atlantic service which began in June 1948.

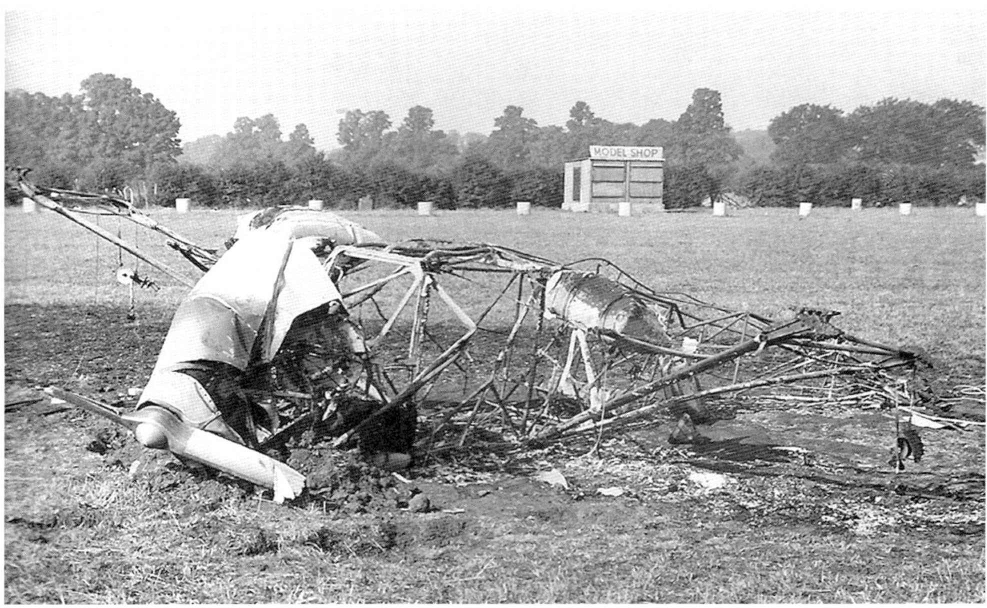

Joan Nayler and her female passenger managed to escape from the burning Puss Moth totally unscathed after it crashed and caught fire whilst landing at Eaton Bray on 31 August 1947.

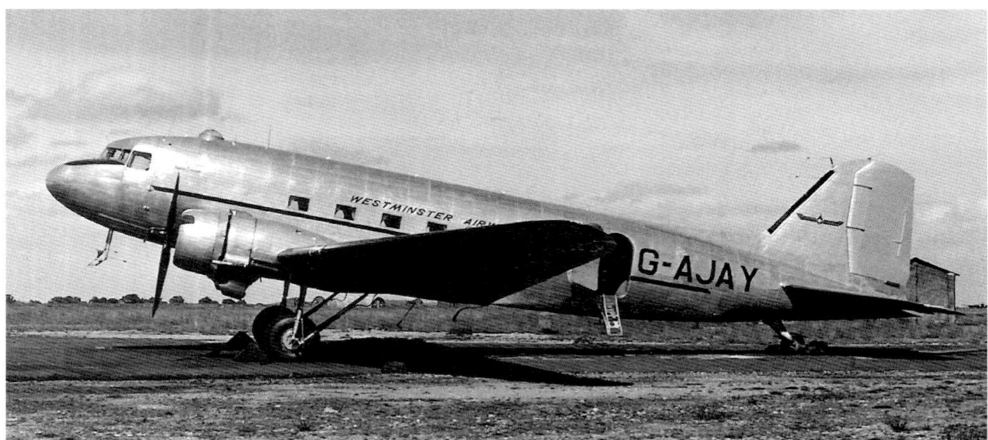

Douglas C-47 Dakota 3 G-AJAY, formerly KG616 with the RAF, was registered in May 1947 to Westminster Airways, formed by a group of Members of Parliament in June 1946. 'AY and the company's two other Dakotas operated in India and throughout Europe, taking part in the Berlin Airlift during 1948. They were based at Blackbushe, where 'AY was photographed on 20 July. In June 1950 it was sold to Spain as EC-AET.

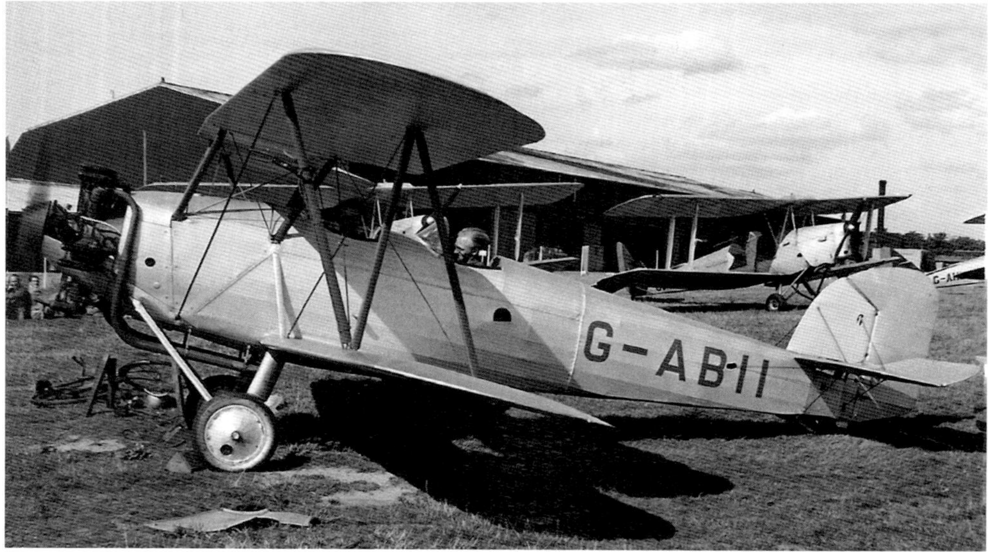

Although most Hawker Tomtits were built as trainers for the RAF and many sold later on the civil market, five were registered to civil owners from the outset. G-ABII was used by the manufacturer until acquired by Gloster Aircraft Ltd in 1943 as a camouflaged company hack. After the war it was kept at Fairoaks by R. C. Cox and later E. Williams, where it is pictured with engine running on 20 July. In April the following year 'II was badly damaged at Somerton aerodrome, Cowes, Isle of Wight, leaving Tomtit G-AFTA as the sole airworthy survivor of the breed and still flying from Old Warden in the care of the Shuttleworth Collection.

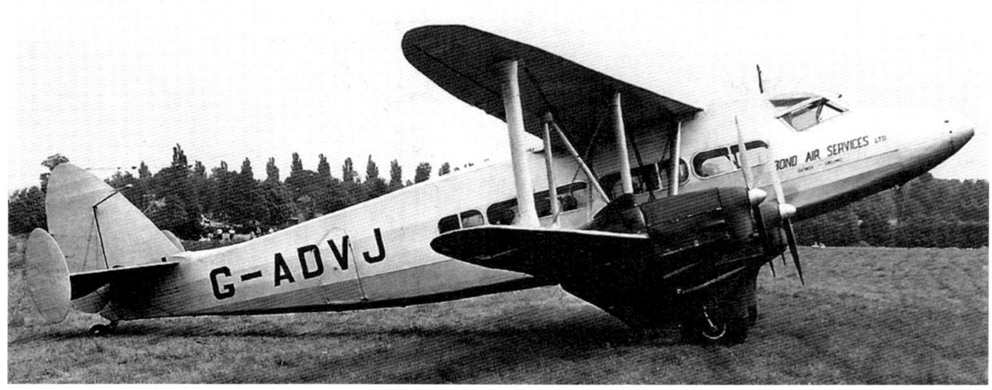

Of the 60 or so D.H. 86s built at least nine were still airworthy after the war, including G-ADVJ, seen at Elstree on 27 July. First owned, albeit briefly, by Blackpool and West Coast Air Services Ltd from mid-1936 and named *Ronaldsway*, it operated the Isle of Man ferry service until passing to Aer Lingus in September that year, to be registered EI-ABK and named *Eire*. It was restored to the UK register in October 1946 and operated by Bond Air Services Ltd, joining sister ship G-ADUH on charter work from Gatwick. Later 'VJ went to Gulf Aviation Ltd in Bahrein where it deteriorated and lay derelict in the early 1950s.

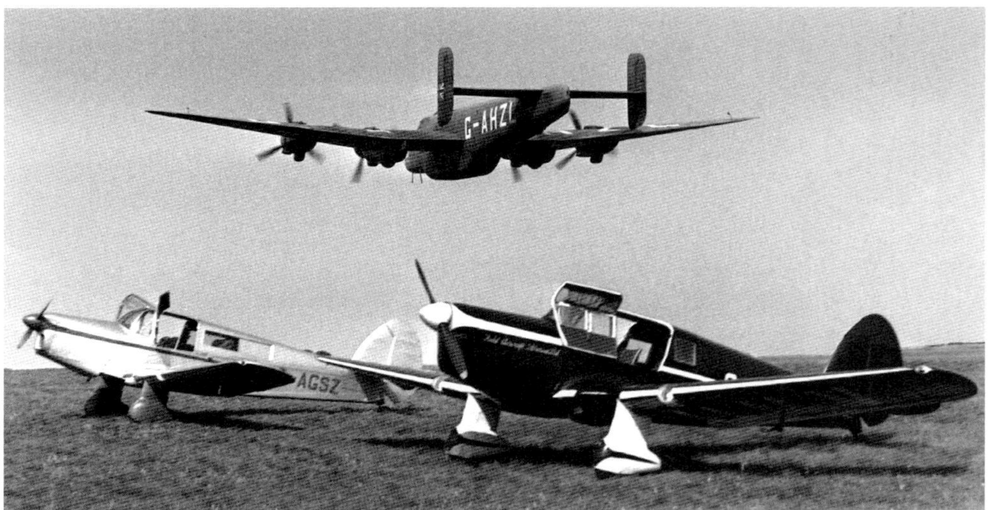

LAMS's Handley Page H.P. 70 C.Mk8 Halifax G-AHZI *Port of Oslo* during one of several beat ups of Elstree aerodrome at the air display of 27 August. During the demonstration the commentator, LAMS managing director Dr Graham Humby, commented upon the aircraft's 'lousy' performance. After the collapse of LAMS in mid-1948 'ZI lay neglected at the company's Stansted base before being dismantled there in June the following year.

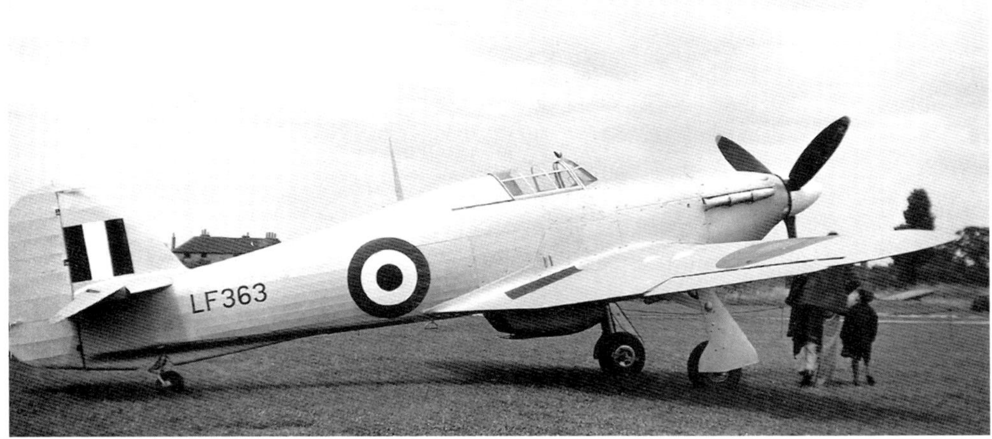

Miles Aircraft Ltd held its third 'At Home' at Woodley aerodrome on 20 July. One non-Miles product present was Hawker Hurricane IIC LF363. One of a batch of 2,005 Hurricane IIs and IVs delivered to the RAF between May 1943 and March 1944 from Hawker Langley, LF363 served with several squadrons and operational training units before passing to the Historic Aircraft Flight, which became the Battle of Britain Memorial Flight in 1957. On 11 September 1991 the Hurricane crashed and caught fire at RAF Wittering following engine failure, fortunately without serious injury to the pilot. Following a seven-year rebuild by Historic Flying Ltd LF363 remains airworthy with the BBMF as Hurricane YB-W of No. 17 Squadron.

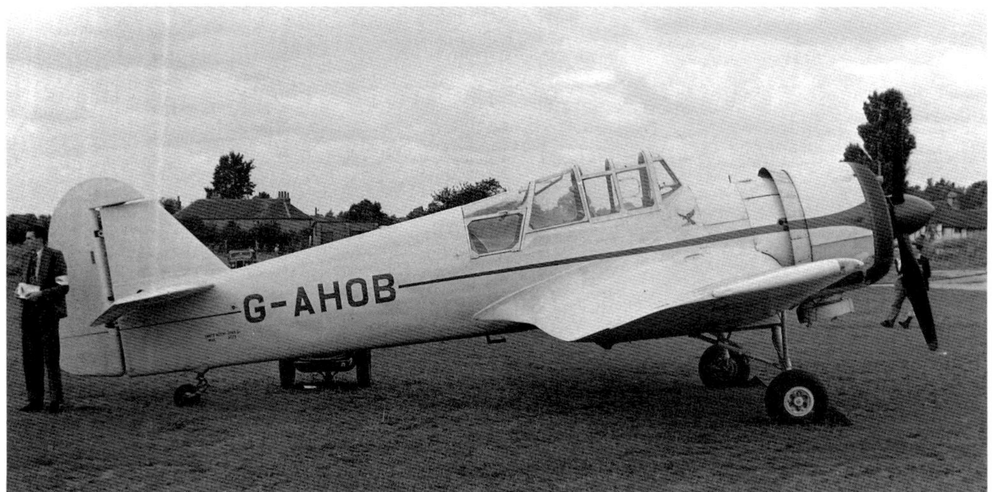

Although Miles M.19 Master 2 G-AHOB was one of three examples of this advanced military trainer to appear on the British civil register it was the only one to be converted to civil guise and given a C of A. Registered in May 1946 and powered by a 870 hp Bristol Mercury 20 radial engine, 'OB was used as a company demonstrator until scrapped in 1950 and is seen at the 20 July 'At Home'. The two other Masters, G-AIZM and G-AIZN, remained unconverted and were broken up for spares.

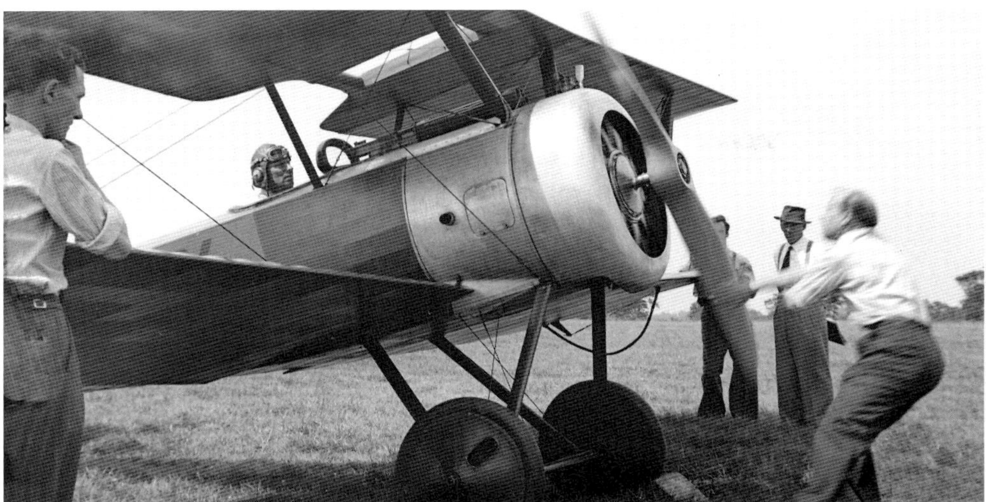

A photograph of the Shuttleworth Collection's Sopwith Pup G-EBKY being readied for flight at Elstree on 27 August by L. A. Jackson, in shirt sleeves, and Gp Capt. Allen H. Wheeler, with flying helmet, who delighted the crowd with snappy loops. 'KY began life in 1925 as a two-seat Sopwith Dove and was flown by D. L. Hollis-Williams and later by C. H. Lowe-Wylde, designer of the BAC Drone. In 1936 it was acquired by Richard Shuttleworth and Warden Aviation Ltd, converted into a Pup and painted in First World War camouflage. The Pup remains airworthy and still operates from Old Warden, Bedfordshire.

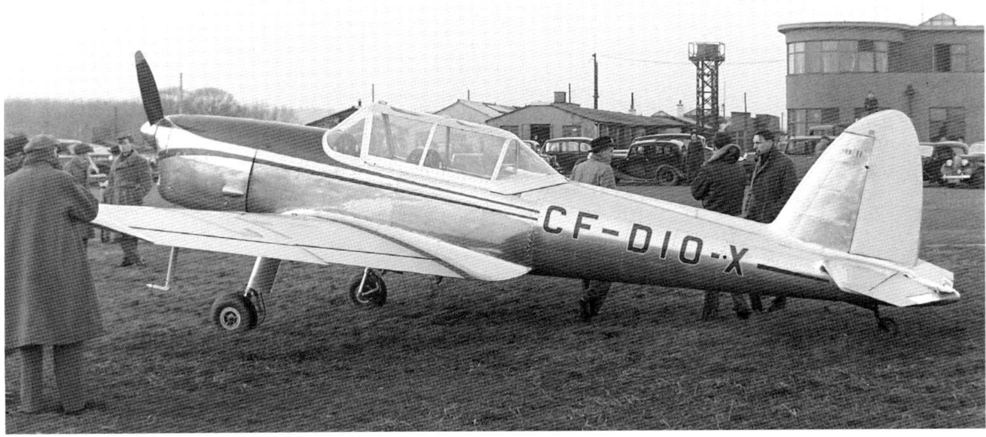

One of the stars of the show at the Informal Light Aeroplane Committee's meeting held at White Waltham on 18 January 1947 was prototype D.H.C.1 Chipmunk CF-DIO-X, displayed for the first time in the UK. Built by de Havilland Aircraft of Canada Ltd, it was first flown at Toronto on 22 May 1946 by chief production pilot W.P.I. 'Pat' Fillingham. The prototype was powered originally by a 130 hp D.H. Gipsy Major 1C though production aircraft were fitted with the 145 hp Gipsy Major 10. Two further Chipmunks were shipped to the UK, becoming G-AJVD and G-AKDN, and after evaluation at Boscombe Down the type was adopted as the standard RAF trainer, more than 1,000 being built at Hatfield and Chester. The prototype was registered G-AKEV in March 1948 and withdrawn from use at Panshanger in January 1951. What a shame that this historic aircraft was not preserved.

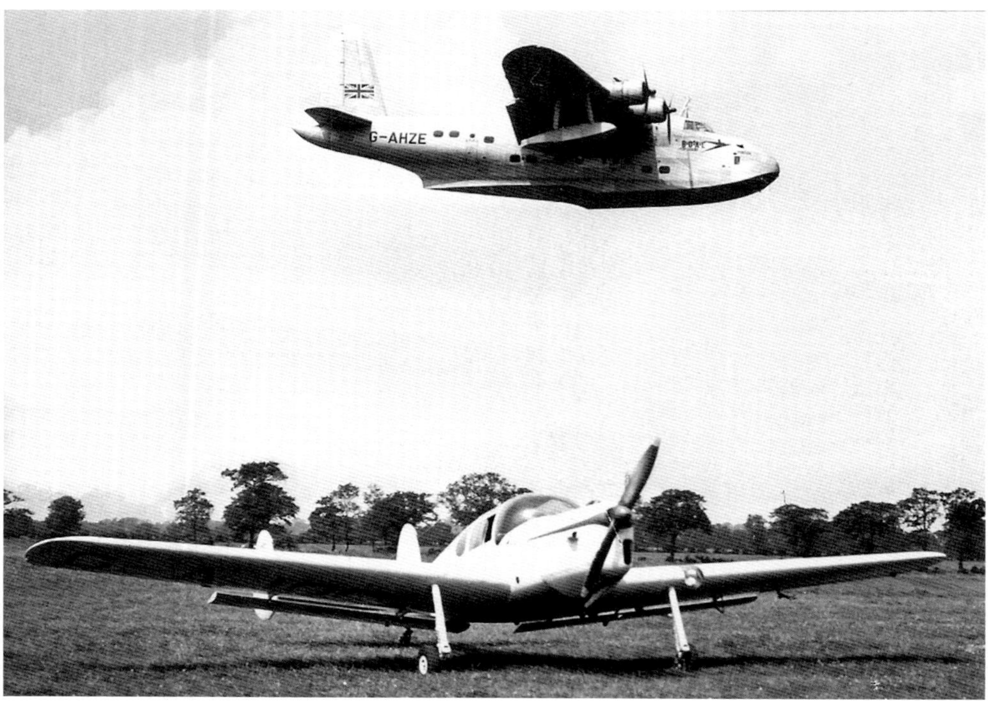

Also pictured making a low run across Elstree aerodrome on 27 July is BOAC Short S.25 Sandringham 5 G-AHZE *Portsea*. Built in 1944 as Sunderland III ML818 for the RAF, it was converted to a GR.V before being sold in May 1946 and civilianised to Sandringhan 5 configuration. Powered by four 1,200 hp Pratt & Whitney Twin Wasp radial engines, the nine Sandringham 5s that formed BOAC's Plymouth Class were fitted out to carry 22 day or 16 night passengers. 'ZE was scrapped at Hamworthy, Poole Harbour, in March 1959.

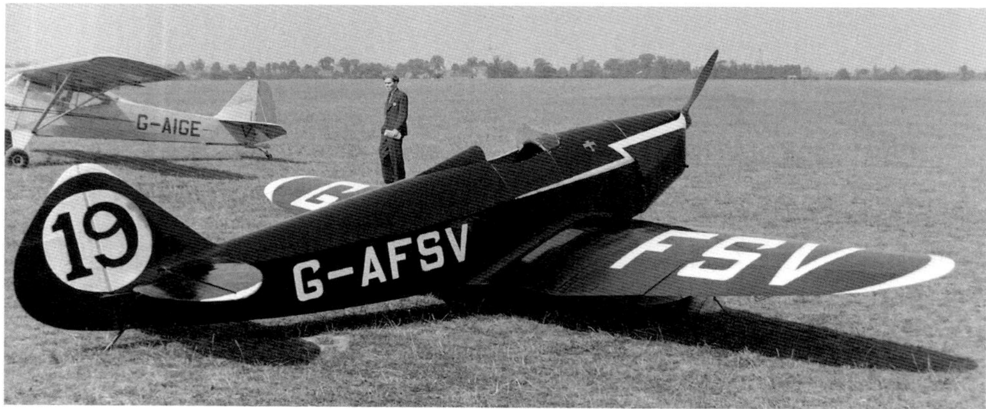

The Train-engined Chilton D.W.1 G-AFSV taking part in the Southend Cup on 9 August flown by former Chilton test pilot Ranald Porteous. A few days later he broke the 100km international closed circuit record at Lympne, recording an average speed of 124.5 mph. First flown by the Hon Andrew Dalrymple in July 1939, 'SV was re-engined with a 62 hp Walter Mikron 2 engine and later sported a bubble cockpit canopy. In recent years the D.W.1 has been restored to its original Train-engined form by Roy Nerou.

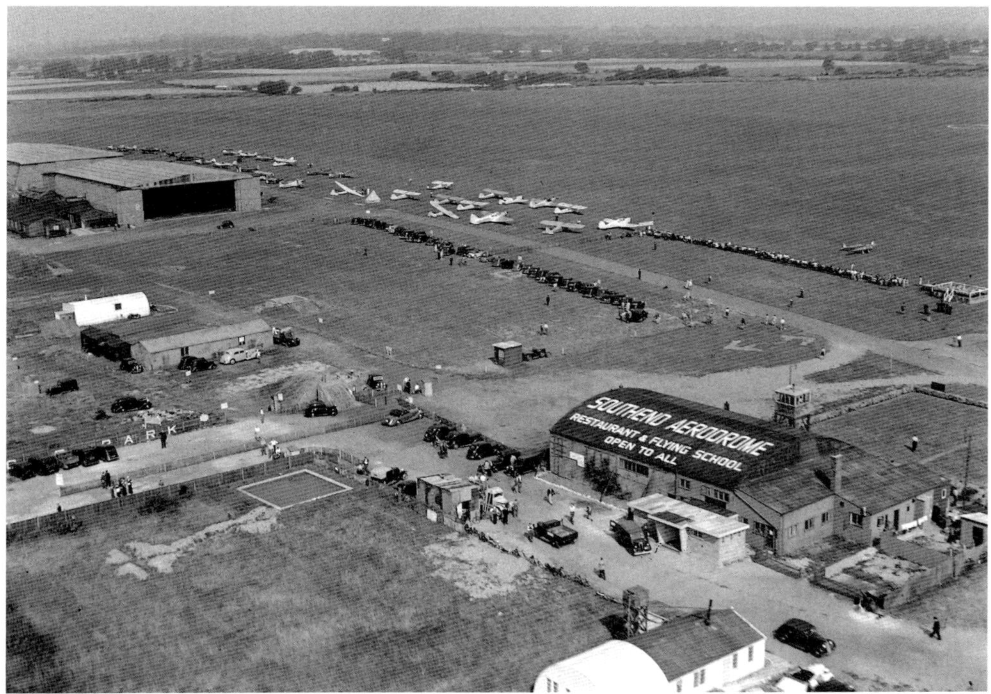

Southend-on-Sea (Rochford) photographed on 9 August from Chrislea Ace G-AHLG flown by Rex Steadman. The occasion was the first International Rally and Race during which heats for the Southend Cup were flown over three laps totalling 60 miles. During the afternoon official opening of the airfield took place, to the accompaniment of aerial antics by nine Supermarine Spitfire IXs and nine Gloster Meteors.

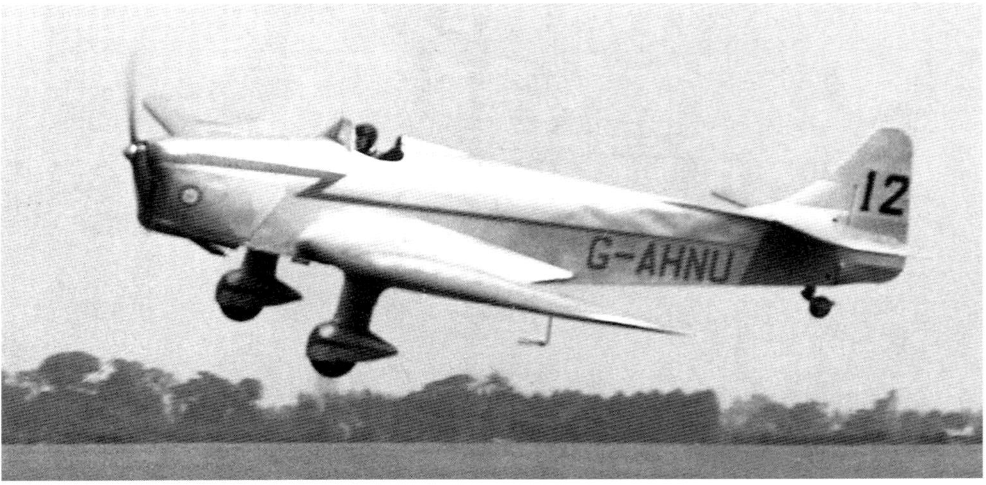

Ron Paine winning the Southend Cup on 9 August in the Wolverhampton Flying School's Miles Hawk Trainer G-AHNU, with rear cockpit faired over for the occasion. 'NU was lost in a crash near Sandbach, Cheshire, in February 1951.

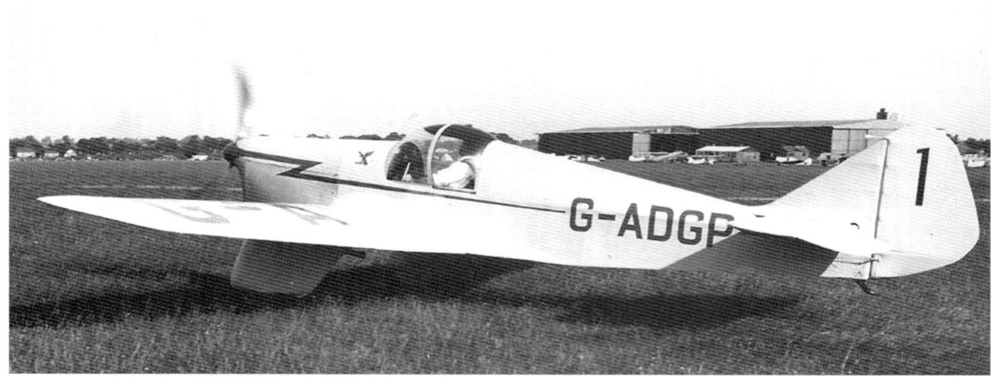

Former Miles test pilot Tommy Rose lifts the tail of Hawk Speed Six G-ADGP whilst taking part in the Southend Cup race at Southend-on-Sea on 9 August. Rose recorded the fastest time for the race, 178 mph, but the winner was Miles Hawk Trainer G-AHNU, flown by Ron Paine. Registered in June 1936, 'GP had a chequered career as a racer, appearing in a variety of guises with and without cockpit glazing. It is flown currently in its original open cockpit configuration and is one of too few Miles types still airworthy.

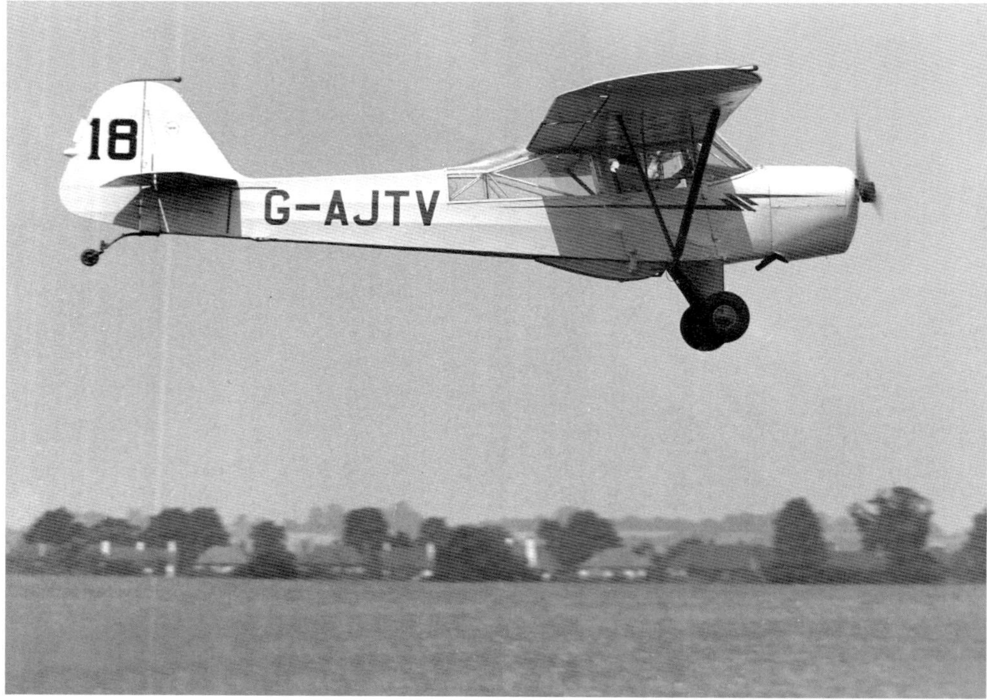

Auster 5 G-AJTV taking part in the Southend Cup race on 9 August. Supplied to the RAF as TJ367, 'TV was registered in July 1947 and sold in Turkey in April 1952 where it became TC-URER, later TC-URE.

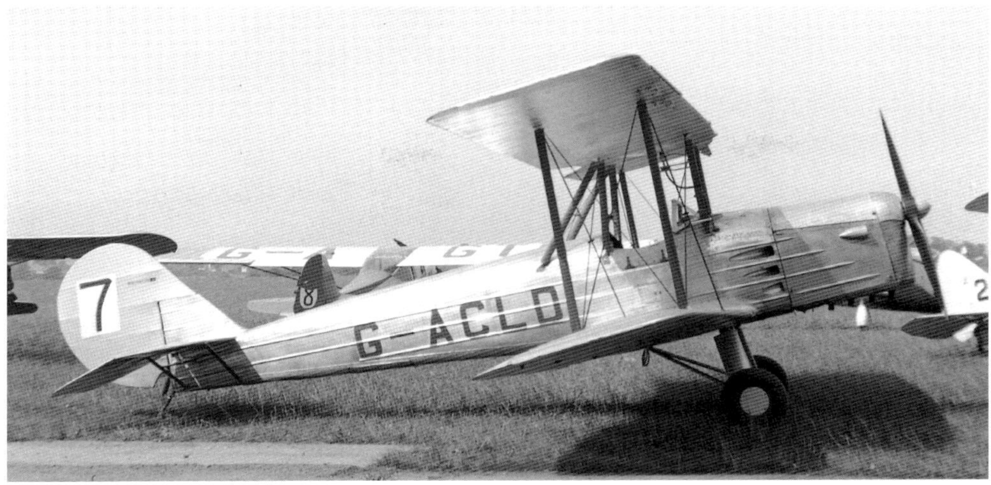

Only two examples of the all-metal Blackburn B-2 side-by-side trainer survived the Second World War, G-ACLD and G-AEBJ. The former was built at Brough in 1934 and delivered to the North Sea Aerial & General Transport Company Ltd. In December 1936 'LD returned to the makers and remained at Brough until after the war when it was re-engined with a Cirrus Hermes Major III during renewal of its C of A in July 1946. The B-2 was raced extensively and is seen about to take part in the Southend Cup on 9 August, the oldest aircraft competing. Whilst performing at an air at display at Clifton airfield, York, in June 1951 Blackburn test pilot H. Radcliffe was badly injured, crashing after stalling the old B-2 off a very low-level turn.

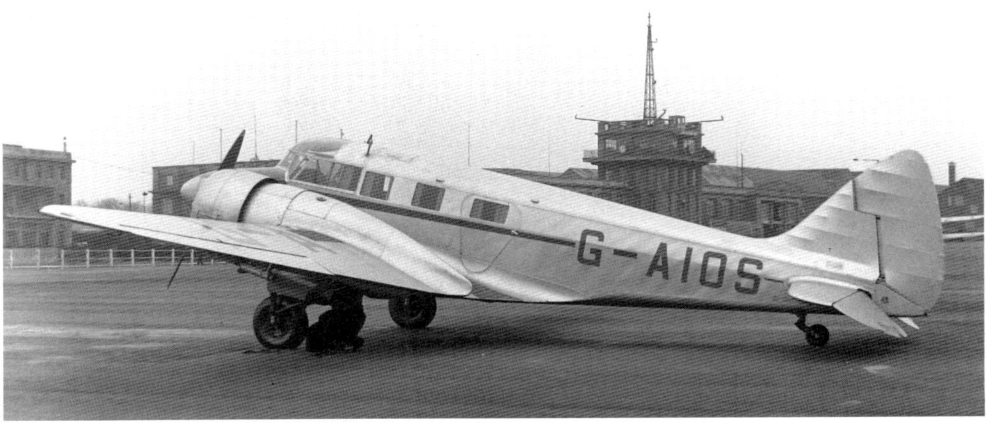

Morton Air Services Airspeed A. S. 65 Consul G-AIOS, seen at Croydon on 15 August, was used for crew training. Built as an Oxford I for the RAF and delivered as PK265 in early 1945, the aircraft was sold in October the following year and converted to a Consul for commercial use; standard versions accommodated five passengers. Conversion involved adding two extra passenger windows and a new aluminium nose section. During the early 1960s 'OS was used as a film extra until scrapped in 1969.

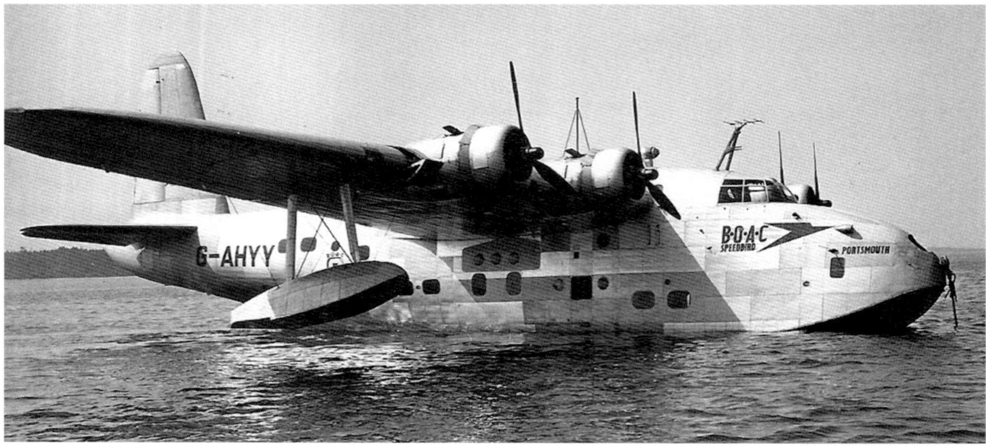

During summer holidays, taken invariably at his mother's home in Wimborne, Dorset, E.J.R. would take the family on boat trips around nearby Poole Harbour. There was always an ulterior motive. He would tip the skipper a couple of shillings to take the boat via any flying boats moored in the harbour, much to the amusement of the other passengers. This Short S. 25 Sandringham was one of many photographed in this manner during August 1947. G-AHYY *Portsmouth* was built as Sunderland III ML838 in late 1943 and sold to BOAC in April 1946 to become the first of nine Plymouth Class Sandringham 5s. Powered by four 1,200 hp Pratt & Whitney Twin Wasps, each carried 22 day or 16 night passengers. 'YY soldiered on until scrapped at Hamworthy, Poole, in March 1959.

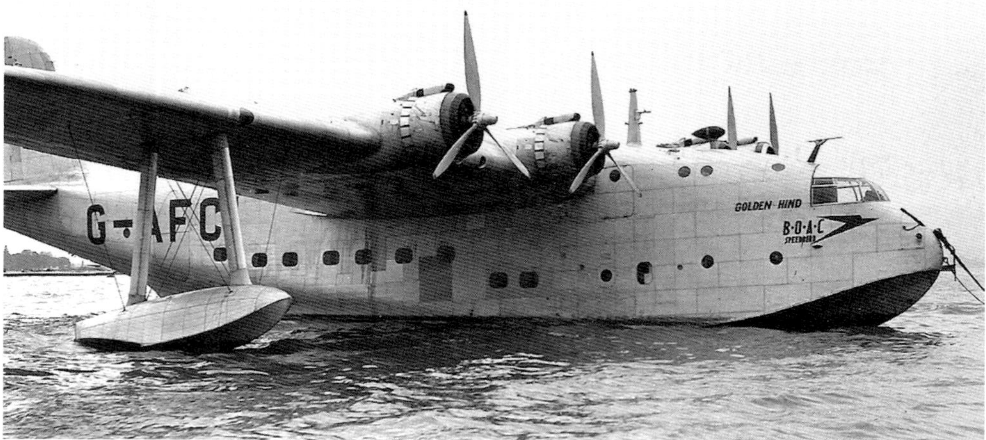

First flown in July 1939, Short S.26 G Class flying boat G-AFCI *Golden Hind* was ordered by Imperial Airways Ltd for non-stop mail services across the Atlantic, but the war intervened. Larger than the S.23 Empire Boats, three S.26s entered RAF service with No. 119 Squadron for long range reconnaissance work, for which guns and additional modifications were added. 'CI and sister ship G-AFCK were then acquired by BOAC in 1940, stripped of all military gear, fitted-out to accommodate 40 passengers and used on the airline's long range routes from Lisbon to Africa. Post-war 'CI was used for a while on BOAC's Poole–Cairo service and is seen at Hythe in August 1947, a few weeks before retirement. Buchan Marine Services Ltd acquired her for planned use on tourist flights, but instead the 'boat was sold to a private owner, sinking at Hart Ferry on the River Swale in May 1954 during a gale.

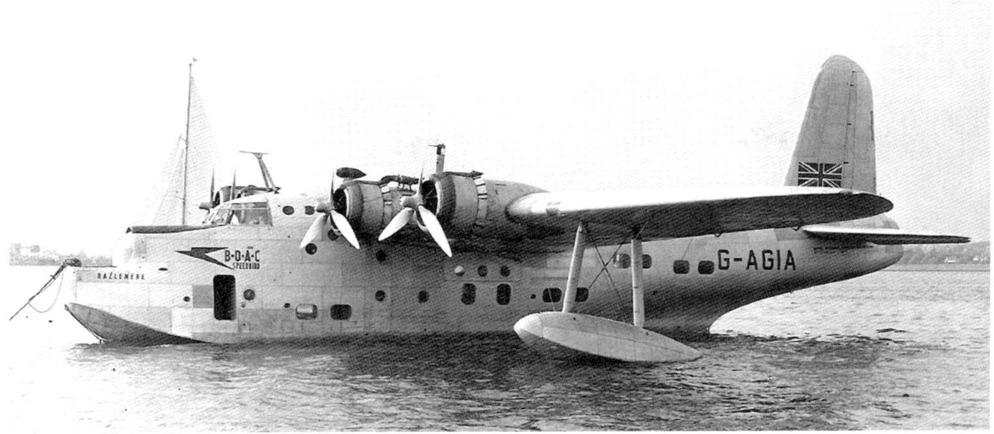

BOAC's Short S.25 Sunderland III G-AGIA *Haslemere* moored in Poole Harbour in August 1947. Flown initially as ML728/OQZA and used on joint BOAC and RAF Transport Command routes in 1942, this and other Sunderland IIIs were stripped of all armament, gun turrets being replaced with retractable bulbous fairings. Additional bench-type seats were added for services between Poole and West Africa. After the war these Sunderlands were converted by BOAC at Hythe to Hythe Class 'boats. Re-engined with Bristol Pegasus 38 engines and provided with proper seating and/or night berths, they were used on pre-war Empire routes. Hamble-based Aquila Airways Ltd became 'IA's new operator in July 1948 before its dismantling for spares in July 1952.

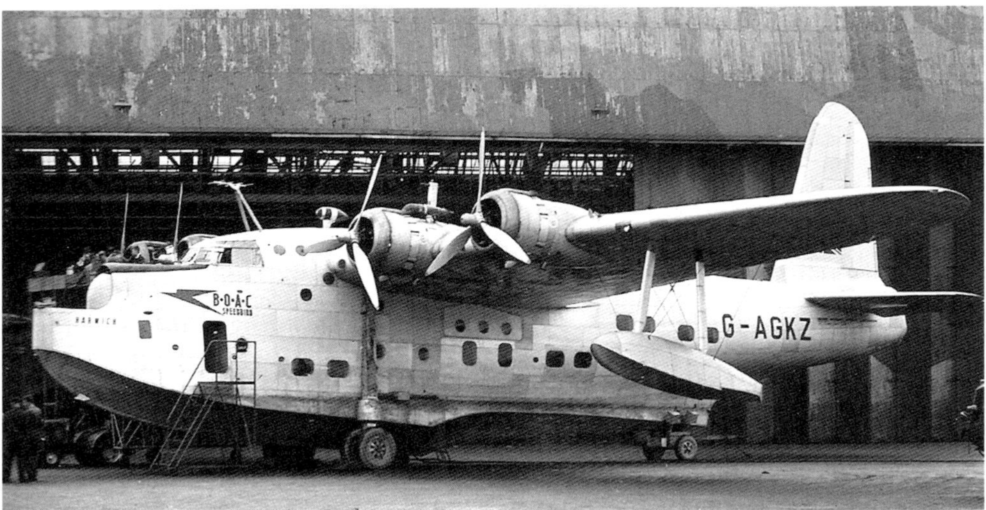

Only when out of water could one appreciate the huge bulk of the Short Sunderland. Hythe Class S. 25 Sunderland III G-AGKZ *Harwich* stands on the hard at BOAC's Hythe maintenance base on 23 August, the same day that E.J.R had a ride in Sandringham 5 (see below) G-AHYY from Hythe to Poole Harbour, returning in Sandringam 5 G-AHZD. Formerly ML790/OQZH and delivered new to BOAC in August 1944 with other Sunderland IIIs, 'KZ operated joint RAF Transport Command/BOAC services devoid of the usual armament and equipped to carry 24 day or 16 night passengers. It was scrapped at Hythe in May 1949.

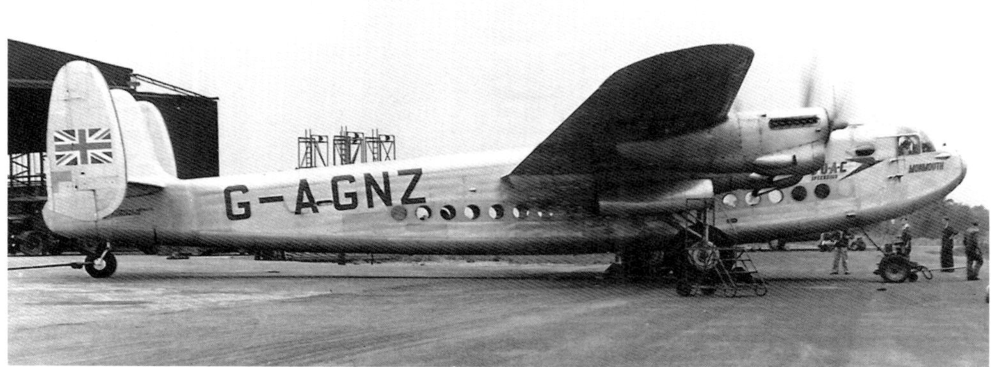

Built by A. V. Roe and Company Ltd at Newton Heath, Manchester, York TS802 was first flown in August 1945 and operated joint BOAC/RAF services. Taking up the civil registration G-AGNZ in June 1946, it then flew M-Class passenger/sleeper services for BOAC, for which it bore the name *Monmouth*. 'NZ is seen at Hurn on 17 August undergoing test running of its four 1,620 hp Rolls-Royce Merlin engines. Earlier that year it was seconded briefly to South African Airways as ZS-BRB, returning to BOAC and remaining with the corporation until sold to Eagle Aviation Ltd in October 1949. On 24 August 1952 the York suffered an engine fire taking off from Gatow, Berlin, crashing into a nearby field.

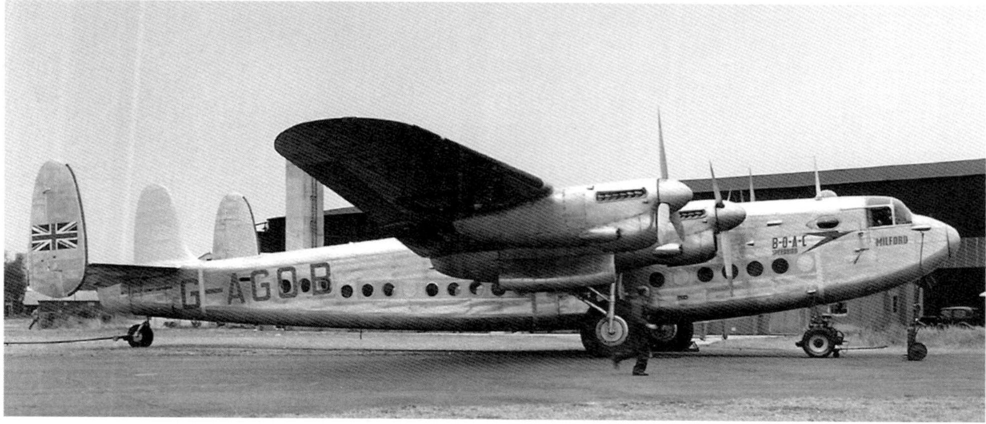

Also photographed at Hurn on 17 August whilst engaged on crew training is Avro 685 York G-AGOB *Milford*. Built as TS804 for the RAF, it had a similar career pattern to G-AGNZ. After five years with BOAC the York passed to the Lancashire Aircraft Corporation in June 1951 and was used on trooping duties under the new guise of WW501. In March 1955 'OB was acquired by Skyways Ltd and flew more trooping flights until withdrawn from use in February 1962, ending its days at Stansted.

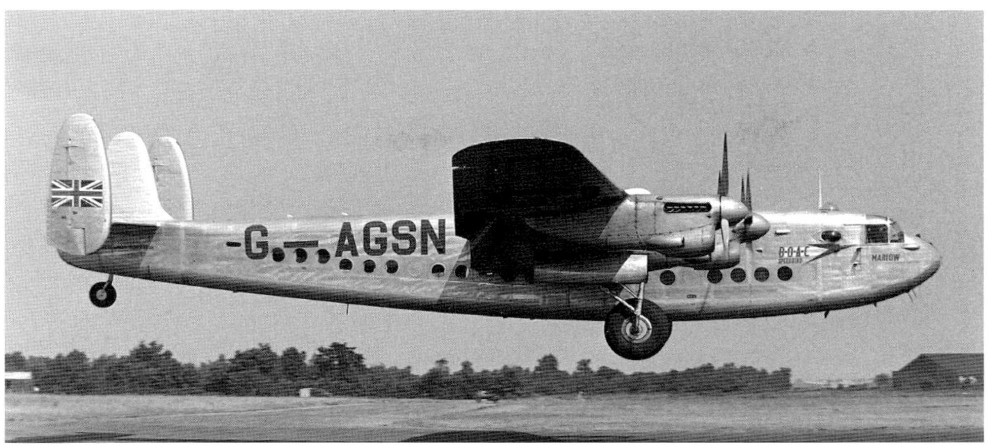

As a five year-old the author used to accompany his father (E.J.R.) to Hurn, Bournemouth, to stand at the end of the runway watching BOAC Avro 685 Yorks flying circuits and bumps during crew training—sounds and sights never to be forgotten. Here York G-AGSN whistles past, Merlin engines crackling as they are throttled back only feet from touch down. 'SN, delivered originally as TS811 to the RAF was registered to BOAC in November 1946 and named *Marlow*. In 1951 it passed to the Lancashire Aircraft Corporation and was based at Squires Gate, Blackpool. In 1952 the York was re-militarised as WW578 and used for trooping flights before being scrapped at Stansted in 1952.

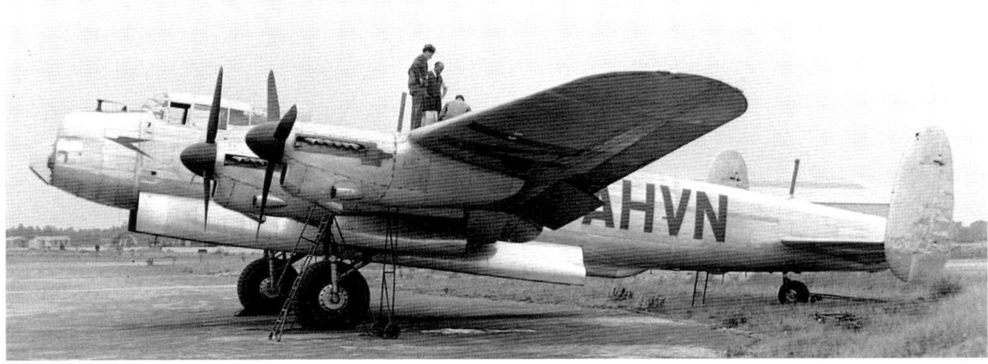

Built at Castle Bromwich by Vickers-Armstrongs and first flown in June 1945, Avro Lancaster PP744 was sold in July 1947 and registered G-AGUN, but later civilianised and re-registered G-AHVN. It was acquired by the BOAC Development Flight and based at Hurn where it is seen with bomb doors open on 17 August. The Lancaster was later converted into a tanker and during 1948 operated with Flight Refuelling Ltd until scrapped at the company's Tarrant Rushton, Dorset, base in January 1950.

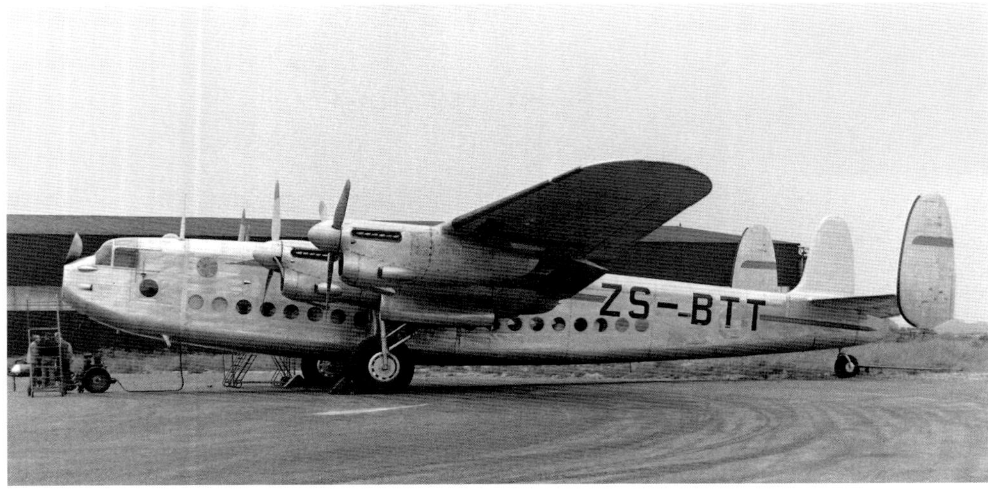

Avro York TS795 was acquired by BOAC in 1945, became G-AGNS and was named *Melville*. In April 1947 it was loaned to South African Airways as ZS-BTT and is pictured at Hurn on 17 August being made ready for service. During 1948-9 the York passed to British South American Airways Corporation and was re-named *Star Glory*. At the end of 1949 it returned to BOAC and was re-named once again, this time *Pacific Trader*. Two years later it took up the RAF serial WW466 for trooping duties, but was damaged beyond repair while taking off from Idris, Libya, in April 1956.

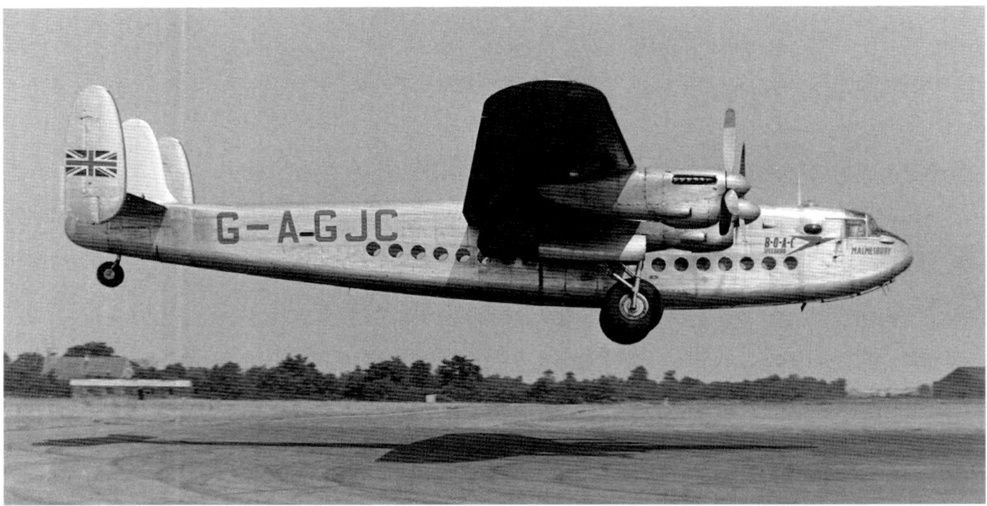

A fine shot of BOAC Avro 685 York G-AGJC *Marlow* about to touch down at Hurn, Bournemouth, on 17 August during a crew training flight. Delivered to the RAF as MW113 in 1944, this York was assigned almost immediately to BOAC and configured to carry 12 passengers in a rear cabin and freight in the forward compartment on the UK–Cairo route in 1944. In 1951 the York was on trooping duties as WW504, spending the last few years of its life with Skyways Ltd before being withdrawn from use at Stansted in January 1958.

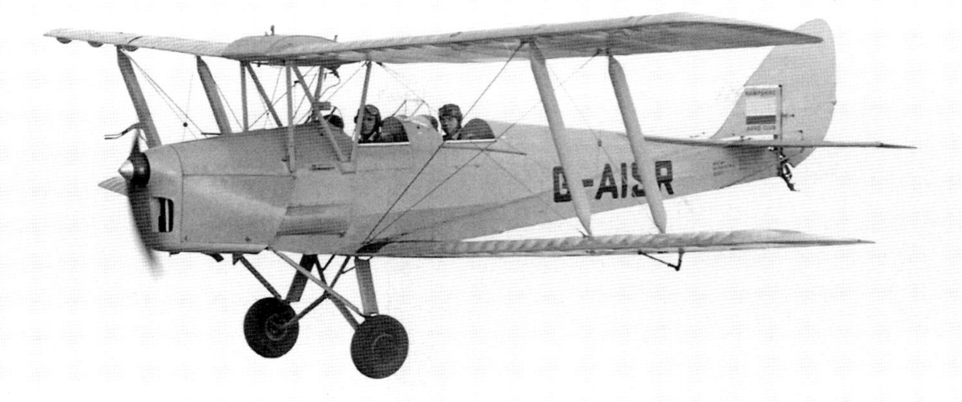

Caught loitering near its Eastleigh base on 24 August is D.H. 82A Tiger Moth G-AISR of the Hampshire Aero Club. Formerly T6068 with the RAF before becoming 'SR in April 1947, the Tiger was sold in Italy in February 1965 where it became I-GIVI. It was lost in a crash at Lucca–Tassignamo in June 1974.

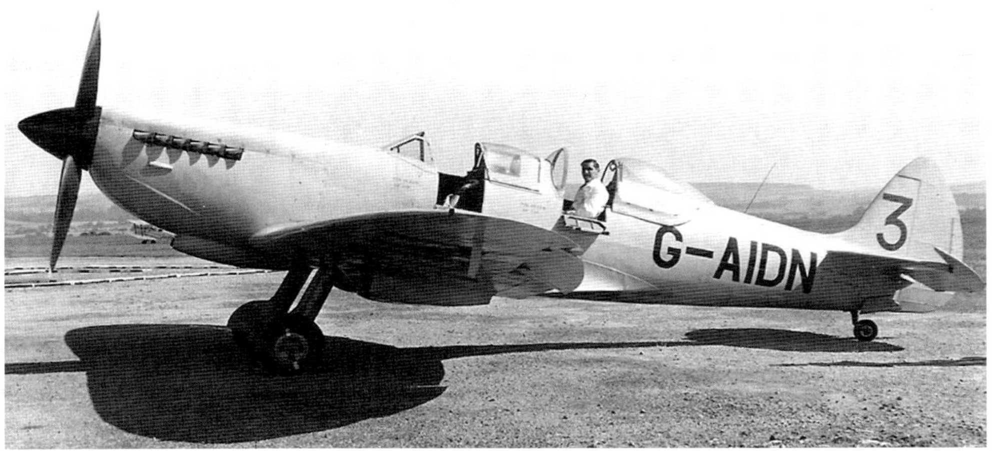

A competitor in the Lympne High-speed Handicap race at Lympne during the weekend of 30–31 August was all-yellow Supermarine Type 502 Spitfire T.8 G-AIDN. Built in 1944 as single-seat Mk VIII fighter MT818, it was converted by Vickers-Supermarine at Chilbolton in 1946 to become the first two-seat Spitfire trainer, carrying the Class B marks N-32 before civil registration. Flown as the manufacturer's demonstrator until 1952, it was stored at Chilbolton until acquired by the Hampshire Aeroplane Club in 1956. John Fairey and Tim Davies co-owned 'DN for several years from 1963 until it was sold to M. S. Bayliss. After suffering major damage in a landing accident at Baginton, Coventry, in 1978 'DN spent several years in the USA and was restored to airworthy condition in 1986 as N58JE. The Spitfire returned to the UK in 2007 and restored to the British civil register with its original registration.

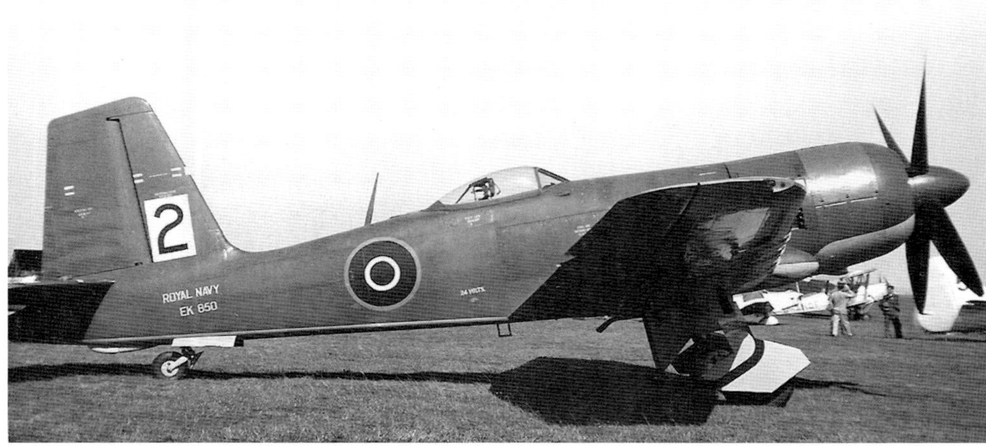

The Blackburn Firebrand T.F.V entered for the High-speed Handicap Race at Lympne during 30-31 August was EK850, rolled out at Brough in March. Powered by a massive 2,520 hp Bristol Centaurus, the Firebrand, flown by Gp Capt. Flood, completed the 100 km course at an average speed of 311 mph, coming second to John Cunningham flying a D.H. 100 Vampire I.

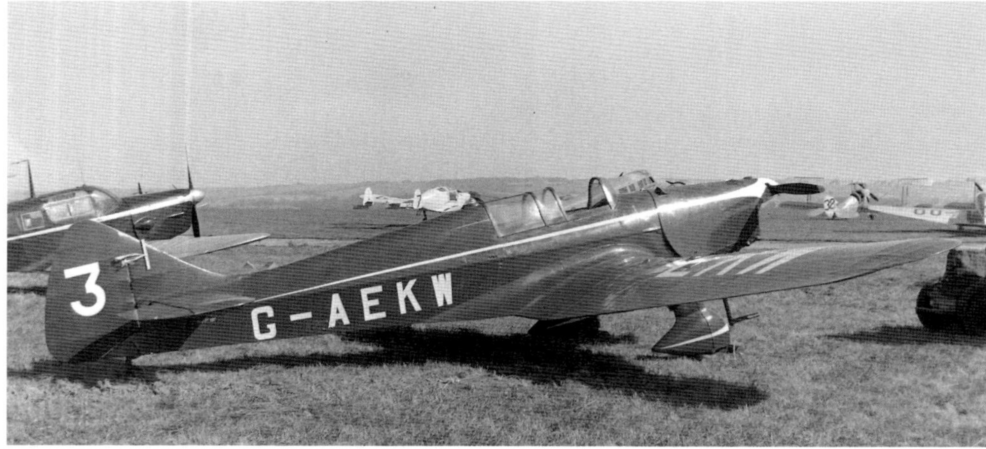

It was a tremendous coup for Miles Aircraft to receive an order for a special aircraft from Atlantic crossing hero Charles Lindbergh. M. 12 Mohawk G-AEKW, first registered U8, was built at Woodley during 1936 and flown on 22 August. After the C of A was issued in January 1937 the Mohawk was delivered to Lindbergh the following month. Impressed as HM503 in October 1941, 'KW did little other than spend time at maintenance units until restored to the register to Southern Aircraft (Gatwick) Ltd in May 1946. The aircraft was raced on a number of occasions and is seen at the Lympne Air Races on 31 August when flown by Wg Cdr Earle. The early 1950s were spent in Spain, but following a forced landing the damaged airframe was put into store until discovered in Seville in 1973. It was purchased by American Louis Casey, shipped to Washington and after being shunted around the remains were returned to the UK. Rebuilt by SkySport Engineering, the Mohawk is on exhibition at the RAF Museum, Hendon.

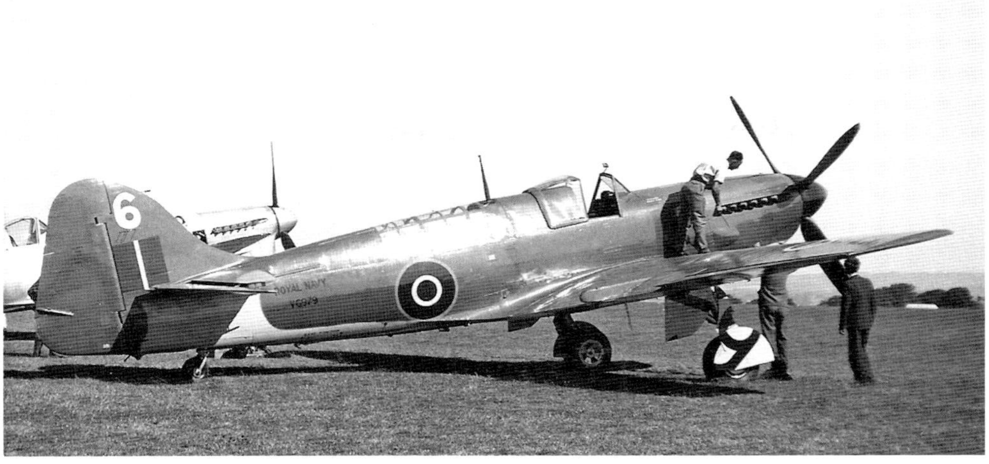

The mount of Fairey Aviation chief test pilot Peter Twiss for the High-speed Handicap Race at Lympne was Royal Navy Firefly IV VG979 in which he won the event, averaging 305 mph. The Mk IV Firefly was powered by a 2,250 hp Rolls-Royce Griffon with a two-stage supercharger driving a four-blade propeller.

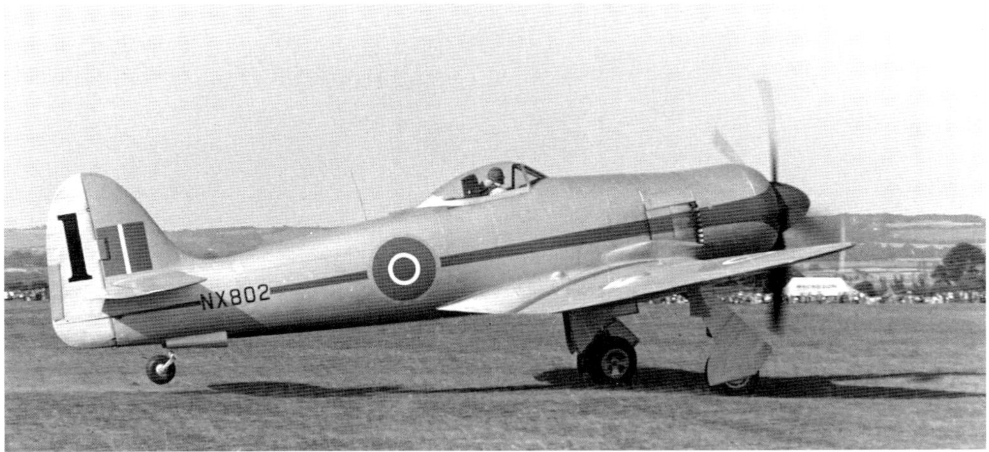

Bill Humble about to get airborne in Hawker Fury I NX802 at the start of the Lympne High-speed Handicap Race during the weekend of 30–31 August. Although he recorded an average speed of 358 mph he was placed second to last over the 100 km closed-circuit course, winner John Cunningham setting a world record speed for the course of 496 mph in a D.H. Vampire I. What would one give to see such a race today? The author has a short 16mm film of the event taken by E.J.R.

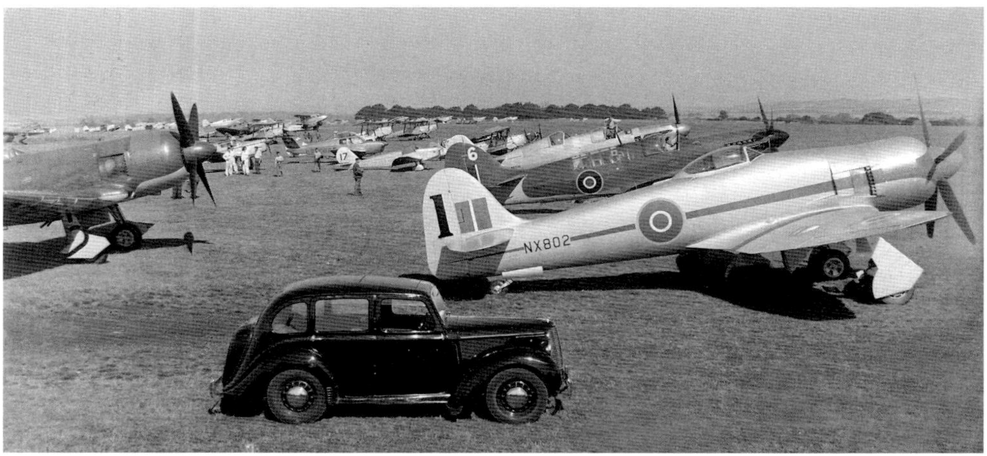

A panoramic view of some of the race competitors at Lympne on the occasion of the two-day International Air Races held in perfect heatwave weather during the weekend of 30-31 August. More than 80 visiting aircraft flew in, but the races were scarcely international as only one foreign registered aircraft took part - Beechcraft Bonanza HB-EBF. Dominating the foreground (apart from the car, which did not compete in the race), is Hawker Fury I NX802 flown by company test pilot Bill Humble. Other high speed competitors were John Cunningham (D.H. Vampire I), Peter Twiss (Fairey Firefly IV), Gp Capt. Slade (Fairey Firefly trainer), Sqn Ldr C. Morgan (Supermarine Spitfire trainer) and Gp Capt. C. J. P. Flood (Blackburn Firebrand T.F.V.)

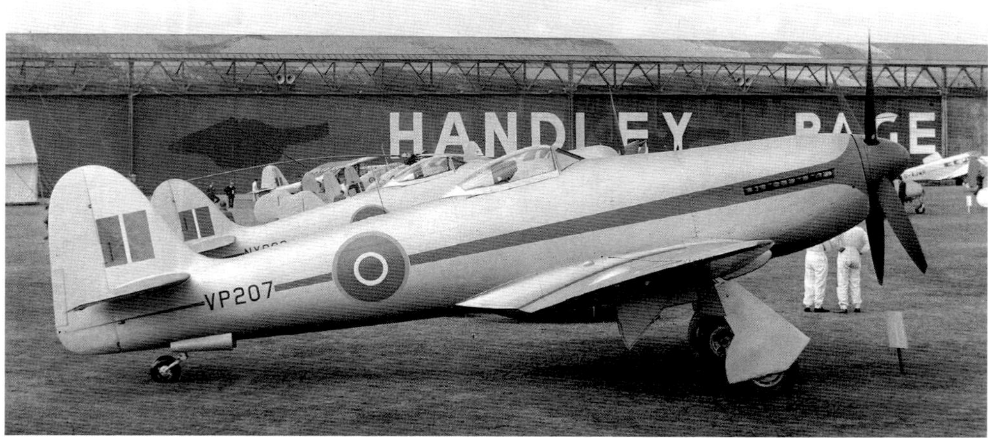

Four prototypes for a smaller and lighter version of the Hawker Tempest, the Fury, were produced and the first to fly was NX798, powered by a Bristol Centaurus XII. The fourth prototype, VP207, built from spare components in 1947 to test the Sabre VII engine and the fighter's suitability for export to countries that could not afford the new generation of jet fighters, is seen at the SBAC show at Radlett. The Sabre-powered Fury came to nought, though it was probably one of the fastest-ever piston-engine fighters, achieving a speed of 485 m.p.h. at 18,500 ft on its 3,055 horses.

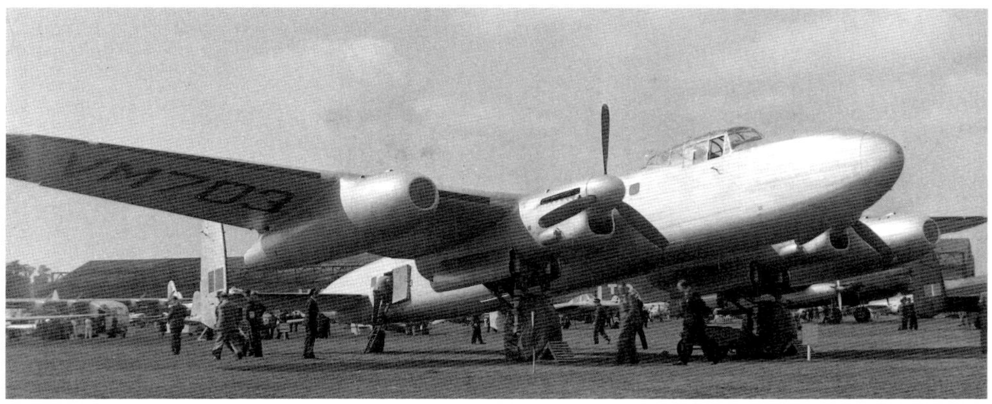

The second half of the 1940s were exciting years for jet and turboprop development, leading to a number of four-engine bombers being adapted for use as flying test beds for trialling turbine engines for eventual use in both civil and military aircraft. One such was Avro Lancastrian C.2 VM703, built in 1945 and fitted with two de Havilland Ghosts in each outer nacelle. Developed from the earlier Goblin, the 5,000 lb Ghost had a single stage centrifugal flow compressor and a single stage turbine compressor drive. VM703 was first flown in this form from Hatfield on 24 July 1947 by John Cunningham, appearing at the SBAC show at Radlett in September. VM703 later carried out rocket assisted take-off tests at Hatfield and was finally struck off RAF charge in June 1950.

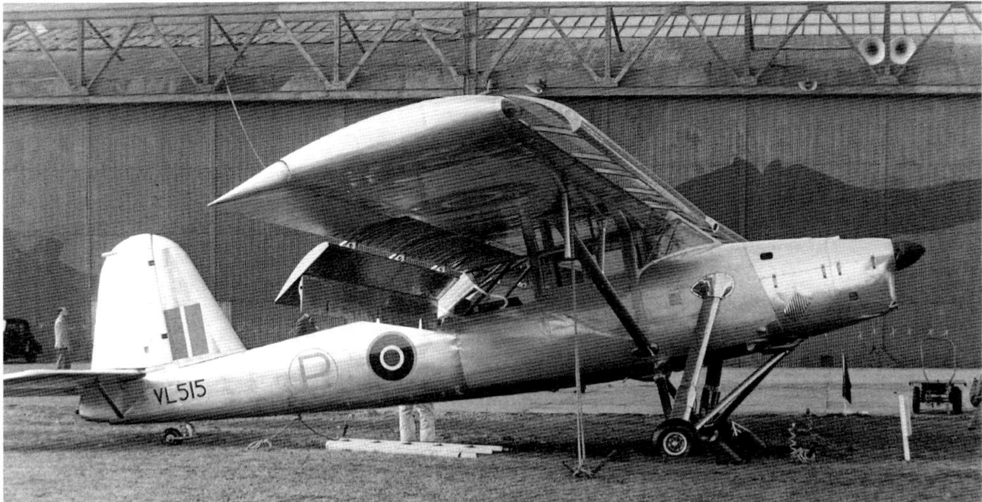

The Prestwick A.4/45 was Scottish Aviation's answer to an Air Ministry requirement for a communications aircraft capable of operating into, and out of, confined areas. Seen at the SBAC show at Radlett in September is VL515, the prototype, powered by a 240 hp D.H. Gipsy Queen 32 engine. In the absence of a military contract Scottish Aviation set its sights on the civil market and to this end the prototype was modified to accommodate four passengers and re-engined with a 520 hp Alvis Leonides. Registered G-AKBF, the Mk 2 was demonstrated at the 1950–53 SBAC shows and attracted customers for both civil and military versions. 'BF was converted to a Pioneer C.C. 1, serialled XE512 and assigned to No. 267 Squadron in Malaya before being struck off charge in August 1966.

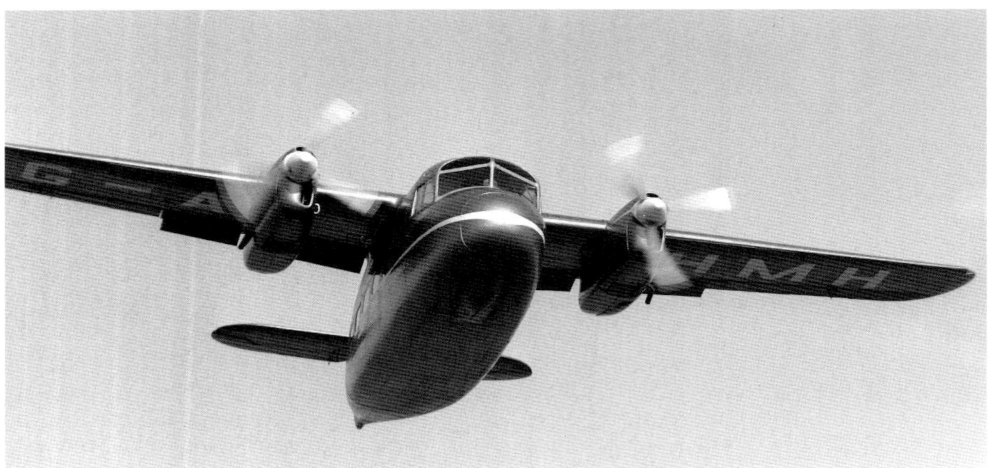

The Percival P. 48 Merganser, now registered G-AHMH and painted in metallic royal blue with cream lettering, makes a low pass over the SBAC show at Radlett on 7 September, looking for all the world like a Gipsy Queen-engined Percival Prince, for which it provided much useful data. The Merganser was not put into production because of non-availability of the D.H. Gipsy Queen 51 and so was scrapped in 1948, the fuselage becoming a hen-house!

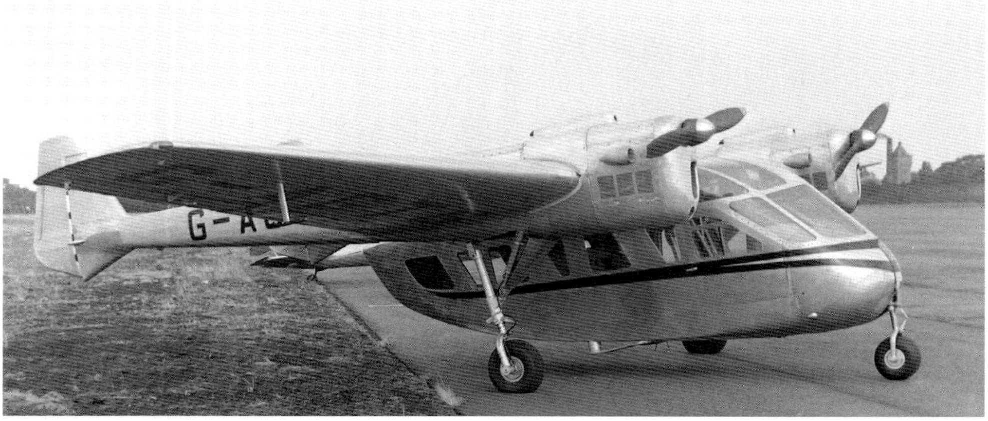

The neat, one-off, Aerocar Major G-AGTG, built by Portsmouth Aviation Ltd, was first flown on 18 June 1947 by F. L. Luxmoore the firm's managing director. Powered by two 155 hp Blackburn Cirrus Major IIIs, the Aerocar was found to be very overweight. It was designed to carry five passengers in a pod-type fuselage and featured a retractable undercarriage. 'TG was flown at the SBAC Show at Radlett in 1947 and a model Aerocar fitted with floats was on view in the static exhibition. The Aerocar appeared again at the 1948 SBAC show at Farnborough and although, according to *Flight* magazine, orders amounted to a reported 288, a shortage of steel and government restrictions on bank finance, made production impossible. Plans to produce the Aerocar in India were stillborn even though the components for a second Aerocar had been shipped there. Efforts to interest Blackburn & General Aircraft did not proceed far because the company was already over-committed with other ventures. Thus, production was abandoned and 'TG scrapped in 1950.

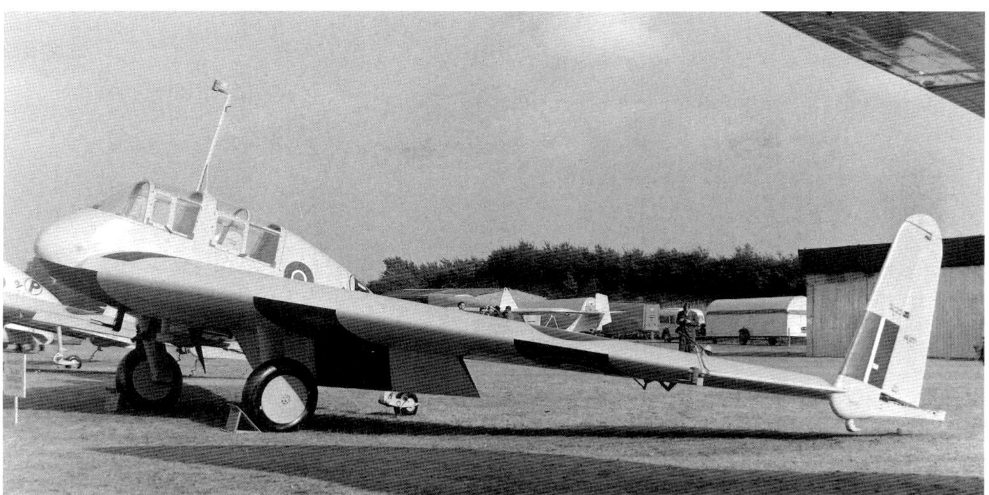

Three examples of General Aircraft's series of tailless experimental gliders were on show at the eighth annual SBAC show at Radlett, 9-14 September, namely G.A.L. 56/Med V TS507, G.A.L. 56/Max V TS513B and G.A.L. 56/Med U TS510D; the 'V' and 'U' designations referred to the wing shapes. Dogged by stalling problems, testing of the concept was terminated after TS507, seen at the Radlett show, crashed, killing Robert Kronfeld.

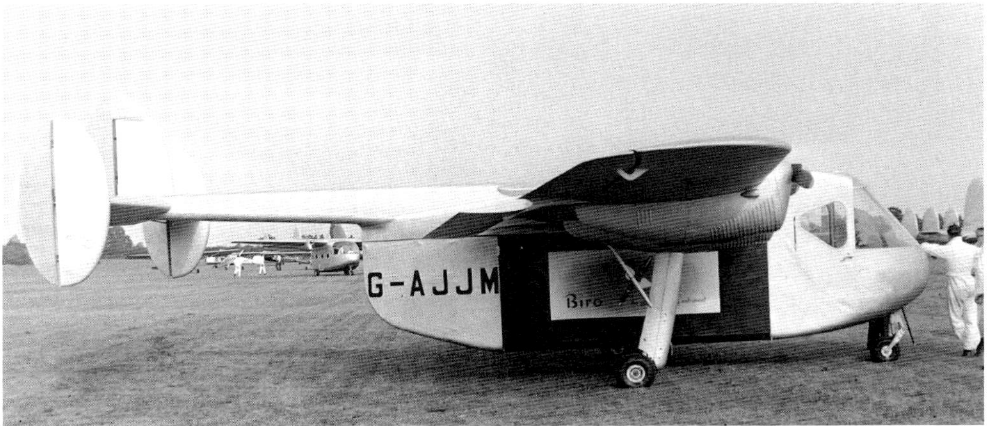

The sole Miles M.68, G-AJJM, one of six Miles types present, only just made it in time for the 1947 SBAC show at Radlett, designer George Miles having made its first flight from Woodley only a few days before. Utilizing the same 50 ft span wing as the Aerovan, the all-wood M.68 was powered by four 90 hp Blackburn Cirrus Minor engines and had an ingenious detachable freight box, doubling as a roadable transporter. Capable of carrying a one ton load, the container could be unhitched from the aircraft in 100 seconds and gave rise to the unofficial name 'Boxcar' for the aircraft. The M.68 could be flown with and without the freight box and attracted great interest at the show. Sadly, the vision of hundreds of Boxcars delivering freight around the country like an aerial arm of Pickfords never materialised. The wonderfully innovative and productive Miles firm went bust soon afterwards and the promising M.68 was scrapped in 1948.

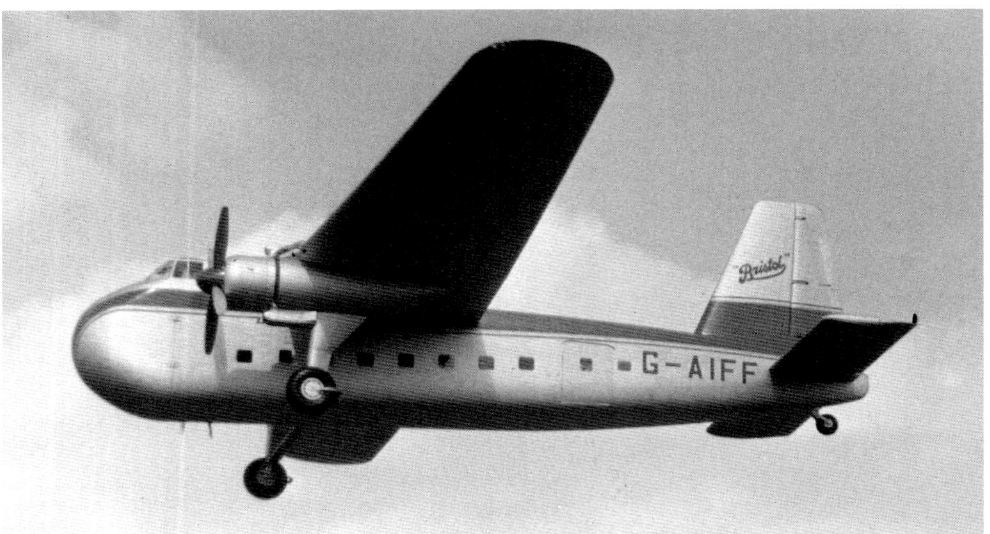

Another ingenious load carrier at the Radlett SBAC show was the prototype Bristol Freighter XI, G-AIFF, with increased wing span and powered by two 1,675 hp Bristol Hercules 632 engines. 'FF went on to be developed into the prototype Mk 21 in 1948 and when in 1949 it was fitted with more powerful Hercules engines driving 14 ft propellers and strengthened to carry a maximum permissible weight of 40,000 lb, became the prototype Mk 31. Throughout its life 'FF was retained by Bristol Aircraft but lost off Portland, Dorset, on 6 May 1949 on test from Filton. During single engine climbs the fin detached and the Freighter crashed into the sea, killing all seven occupants.

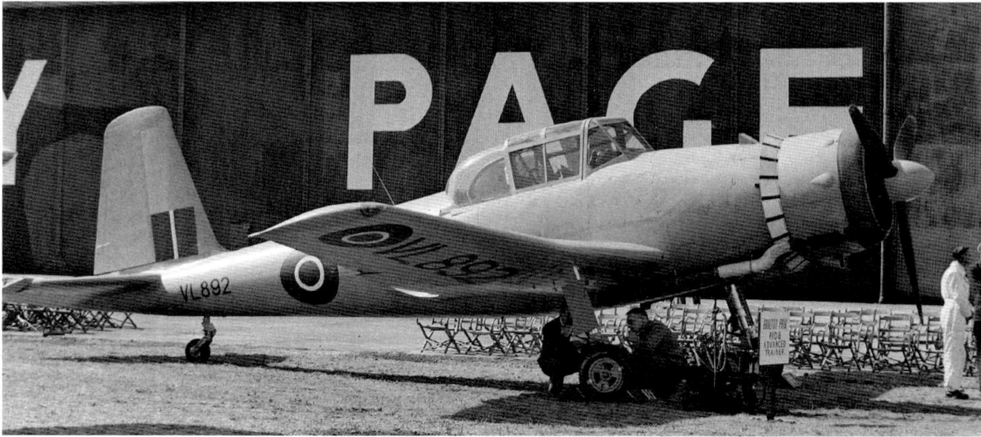

While production versions of the Boulton Paul Balliol had the Rolls-Royce Merlin 35 engine, one prototype, VL892, was powered temporarily by an 820 hp Bristol Mercury 30 radial engine, somewhat spoiling the lines of this advanced trainer for which the Air Ministry initially specified three seats. It was on view at the SBAC show at Radlett in September. The aesthetics of VL892 were improved slightly when later re-engined with an Armstrong Siddeley Mamba, but the Air Ministry did not proceed with the idea of a turboprop three-seat trainer, the two-seat Merlin-powered Balliol winning the day.

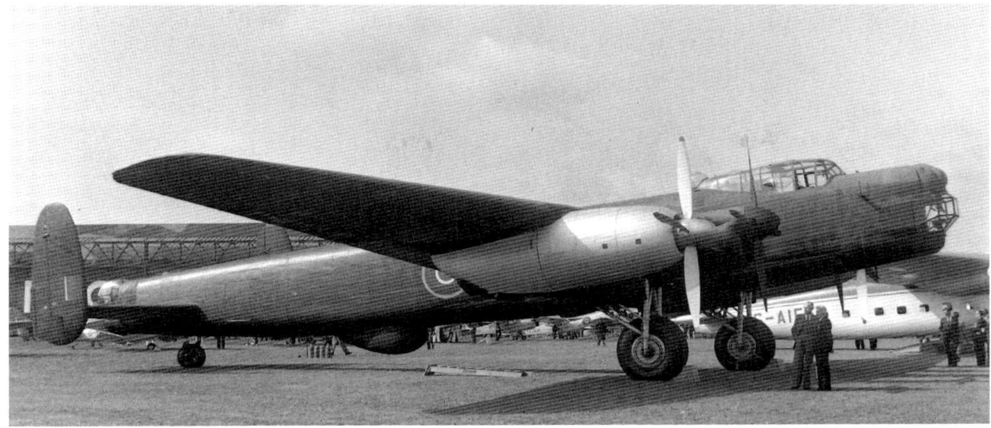

Another flying test bed pictured at the Radlett SBAC show on 7 September was Avro Lincoln II RA716G, fitted with two 2,400 hp Bristol Theseus turboprops in the outer nacelles. First flown from Filton by A. J. 'Bill' Pegg on 17 February, the Lincoln later flew with two Rolls-Royce Avons turbojets, also in the outboard nacelles, before ending up at Aldergrove in April 1957.

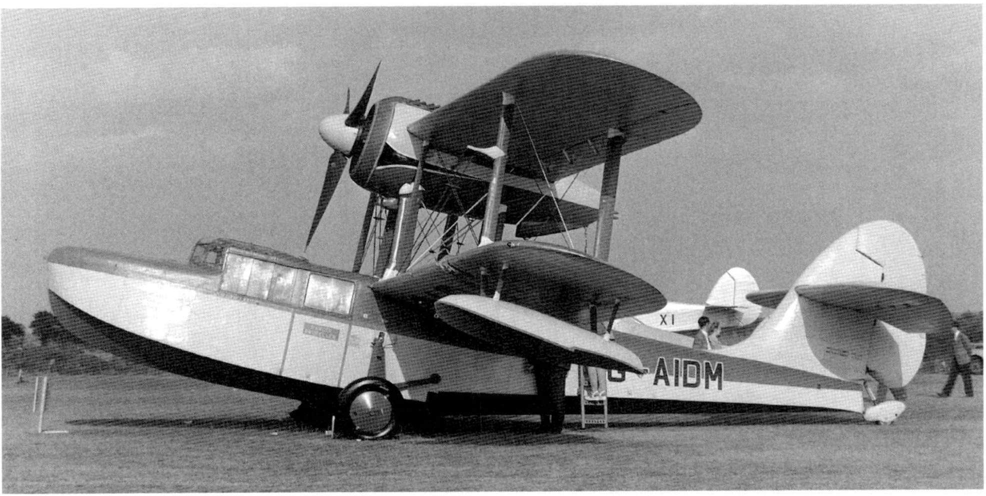

A fish out of water. Vickers-Supermarine Type 309 Sea Otter G-AIDM attracted much attention at the SBAC show at Radlett. Furnished as a four-seat commercial amphibian, the Sea Otter was developed from the legendary Walrus but was larger, had a longer range and was powered by a tractor 855 hp Bristol Mercury 30 radial engine, the propeller tips missing the cabin roof and entry door by inches! Although 24 Sea Otters were earmarked for civil conversion only a handful progressed beyond the scrap man's torch. Some were sold to foreign air arms, such as the Dutch Navy, others were earmarked for use by British South American Airways Corporation, but got no further than Langley where they were soon scrapped. 'DM, the resplendent demonstrator, was the exception; it was converted to the order of the Royal Dutch Shell Group and shipped to Venezuela for geological survey work in the swamp areas around Lake Maracaibo in November 1947.

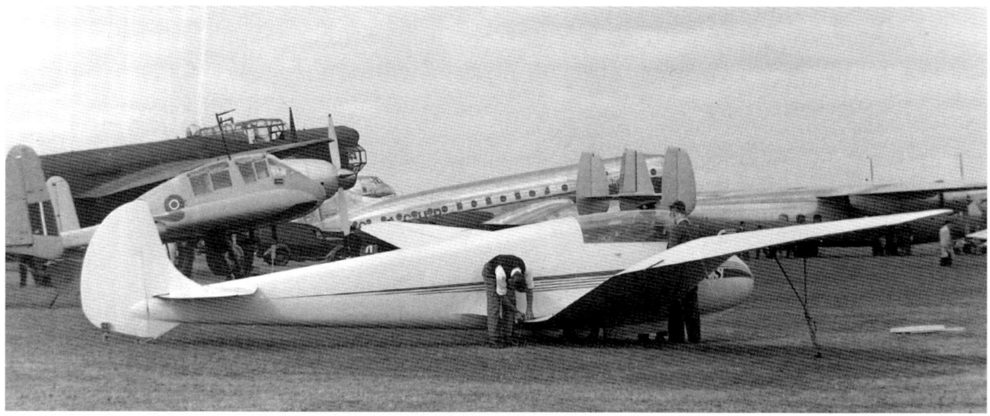

The last aircraft designed, built and flown from Short Brothers' Rochester works was the two-seat Nimbus wooden sailplane. The gull-winged craft was first flown there in December 1946, making its first winch-launch the following month. Leading lights in the gliding fraternity were so impressed that Short Brothers considered putting the Nimbus into limited production and the 62 ft span glider was exhibited at the SBAC show at Radlett in September. Sadly, there were insufficient orders and the sole example ended up at the Ulster Folk & Transport Museum in Cultra, Holywood, near Belfast.

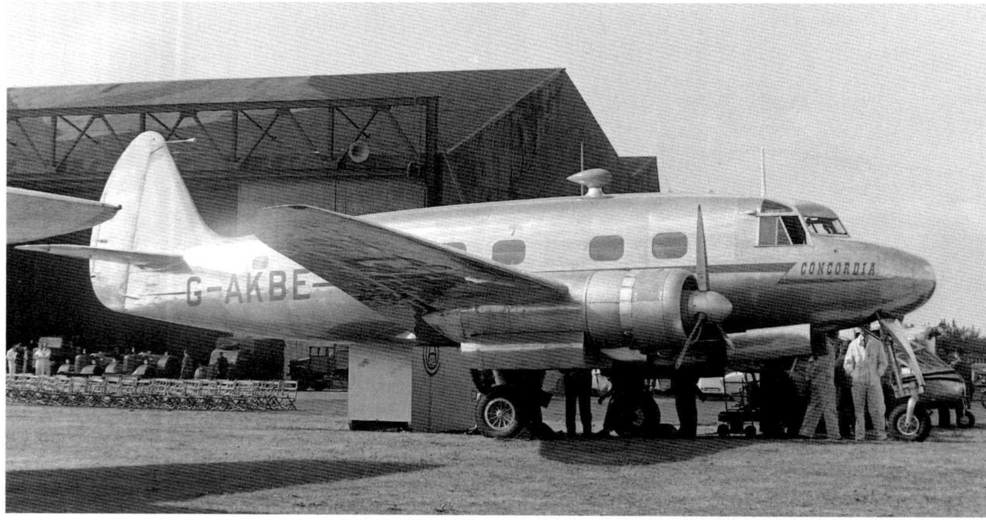

The first prototype of the 10-seat Cunliffe-Owen Concordia, Y-0222, built at Eastleigh, was first flown in May 1947 and was quickly followed by G-AKBE, seen here at the Radlett SBAC Show in September. Powered by two 550 hp Alvis Leonides, the Concordia had a maximum speed of 216 mph and cruised at 160 mph. The second Concordia had a 5 inch extension to the forward fuselage to position the pilot forward of the airscrews and there were plans to produce freighter and ambulance versions in addition to a deluxe passenger aircraft. A batch of six aircraft was under production, including two for BEA, but despite an extensive European tour, sales were poor and work ceased in November that year.

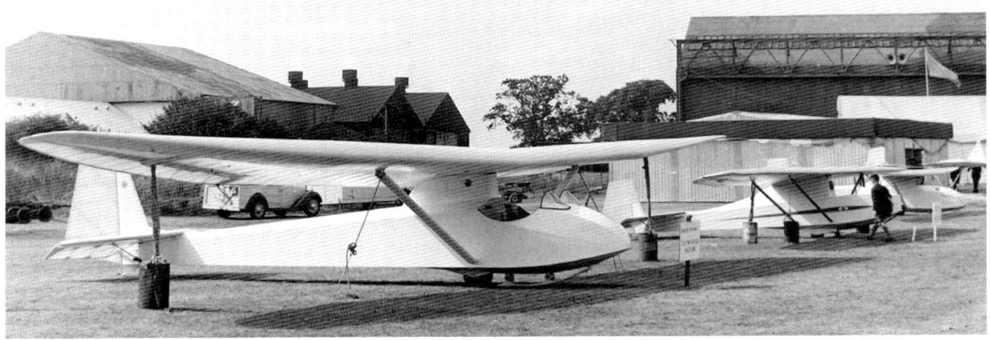

Slingsby Aircraft Ltd exhibited four glider types at the SBAC show at Radlett, including the two-seat, side-by-side, Type 21, seen nearest the camera. The 54 ft span Type 21B was designed for use by the Air Training Corps (ATC) as the Sedburgh TX and first flew in December 1947. In 1948 the list price was £780. Ultimately, around 220 21Bs were produced, of which a third went to the ATC.

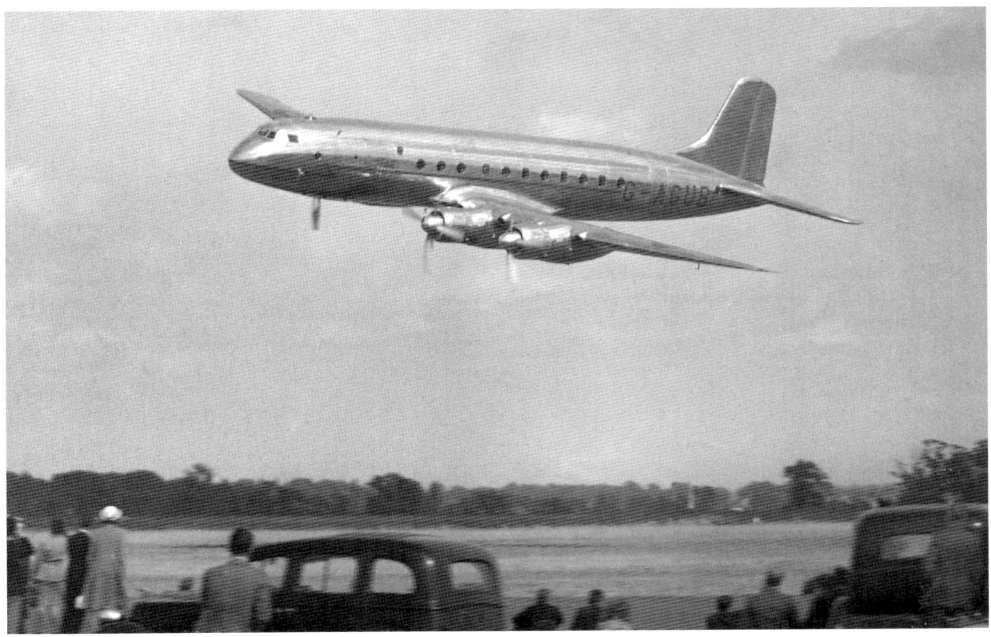

Following the disastrous crash of prototype H.P. 68 Hermes G-AGSS at Radlett on 3 December 1945 the second prototype, H.P. 74 Hermes 2 G-AGUB, was flown on 2 September, just days before being demonstrated at the 1947 SBAC show by chief test pilot, H. G. Hazelden. With a 15 ft extension to the front fuselage, the pressurized Mk 2 accommodated 50 passengers and led to the production of 25 H.P. 81 Hermes 4s and two H.P. 82 Hermes 5s with tricycle undercarriages. After a period with the Ministry of Supply 'UB took up the RAF serial VX234 in 1953 and was assigned to RRE Defford before being scrapped eventually at Pershore in 1969.

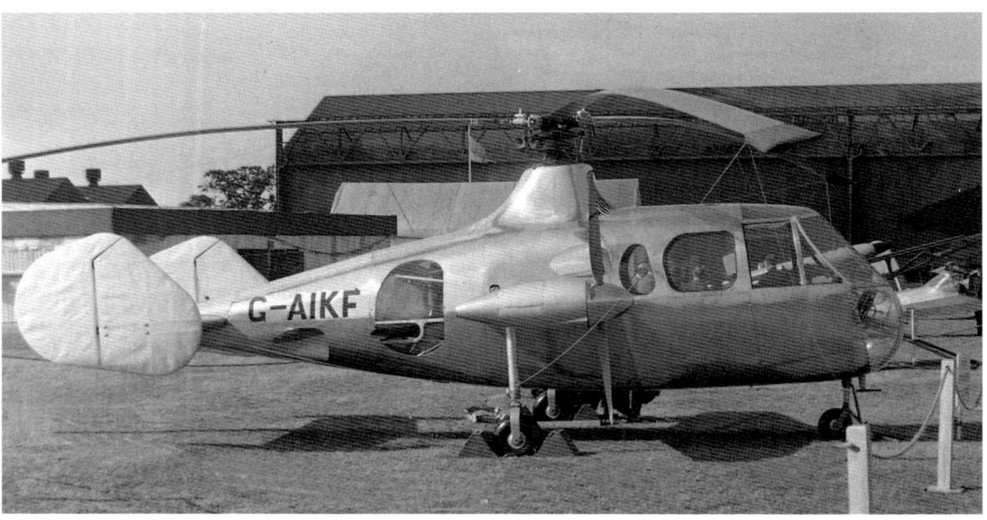

A non-flier at the 1947 SBAC show at Radlett was four-seat Fairey Gyrodyne G-AIKF, powered by a 505 hp Alvis Leonides that drove the main rotor and a propeller on the starboard stub-wing, providing forward thrust as well as counteracting rotor torque. The rudders were added so that directional control could be sustained in the event of engine failure and subsequent autorotative descents. Built at Hayes, first tentative hops were made by helicopter supremo Basil Arkell from 7 December that year at Heston and later, on 28 June 1948, the same pilot raised the international helicopter 3 km closed circuit record to 124 mph. During preparations for another record attempt on 17 April 1949 'KF suffered rotor head fatigue failure and crashed at Ufton, Reading, killing Fairey's chief test pilot, F. H. Dixon and flight observer Derek Garroway. E.J.R. flew as 'observer' on many Fairey Albacore test flights with Dixon during the war.

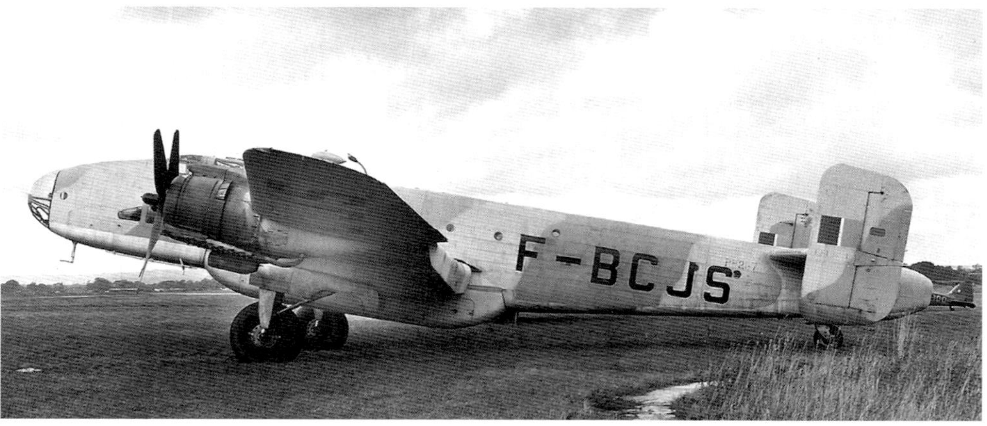

Airfields in the late 1940s were full of surprises. Captured at Gatwick on 20 September is a French registered and camouflaged Halifax C. Mk 8. Just visible is the aircraft's RAF serial number, PP287. Assembled at Radlett in 1945, this Halifax was registered G-AGPC in October 1947 to Anglo French Distributors Ltd at Gatwick and sold immediately to Aero Cargo, Lyons, becoming F- BCJS. It crashed at Lyons on 1 December the following year while taking off in fog, three of the eight occupants perishing.

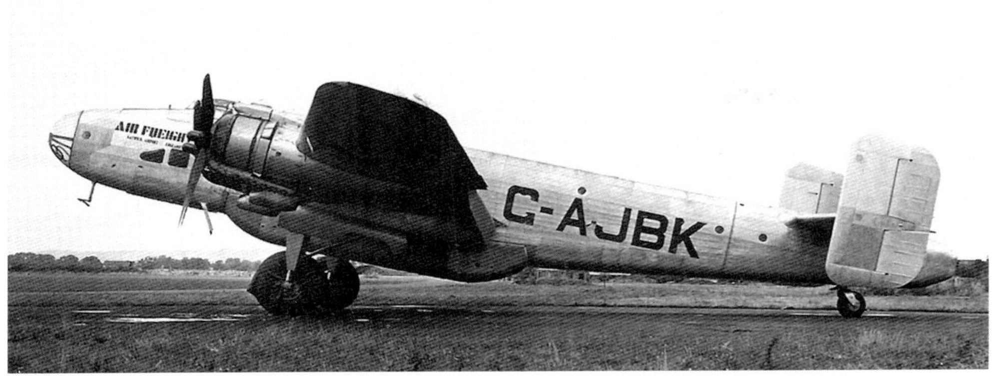

Yet another H.P. 70 Halifax C. Mk 8 photographed at Gatwick on 20 September was Air Freight Ltd's G-AJBK, formerly PP264 and registered in July 1947. It was soon sold in France as F-BCJZ but came to grief landing at Le Bourget, Paris, on 17 December that year killing the crew of three.

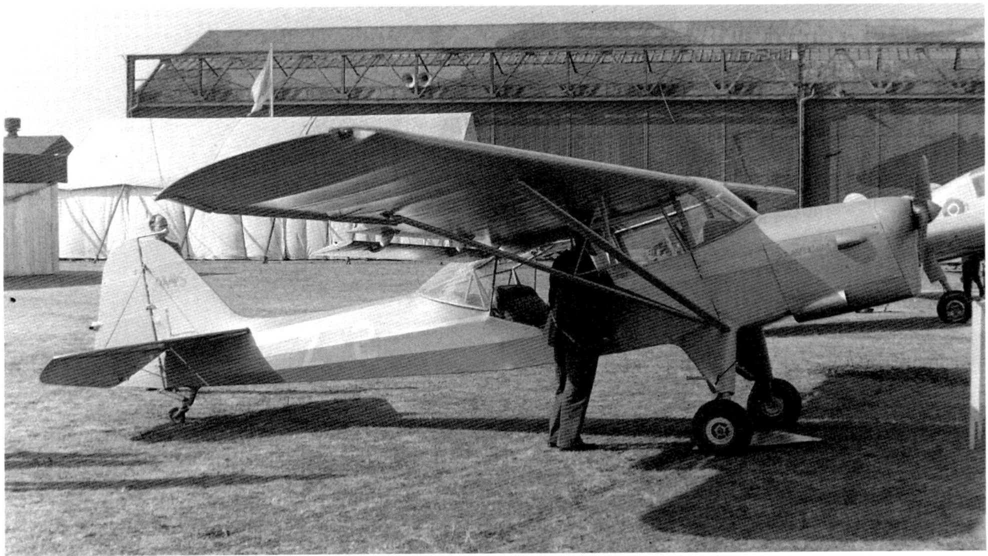

Resembling a half-starved Auster Autocrat, Auster Model P Avis Z-2, later G-AJXW, was an attempt to produce a four-door, four-seater as a follow-up to the successful J/1 Autocrat. Based on an Auster Mk 6 airframe, the rear fuselage enlarged to accommodate two people, the Avis featured auxiliary aerofoil flaps and telescopic undercarriage legs. Auster test pilot George Snarey demonstrated Z-2 at the Radlett SBAC show in September and appeared again the following year, but it was not a success and dismantled at Rearsby in 1949. A brighter future beckoned for the two-door, four-seat Auster J/5B Autocar, first flown in August 1949.

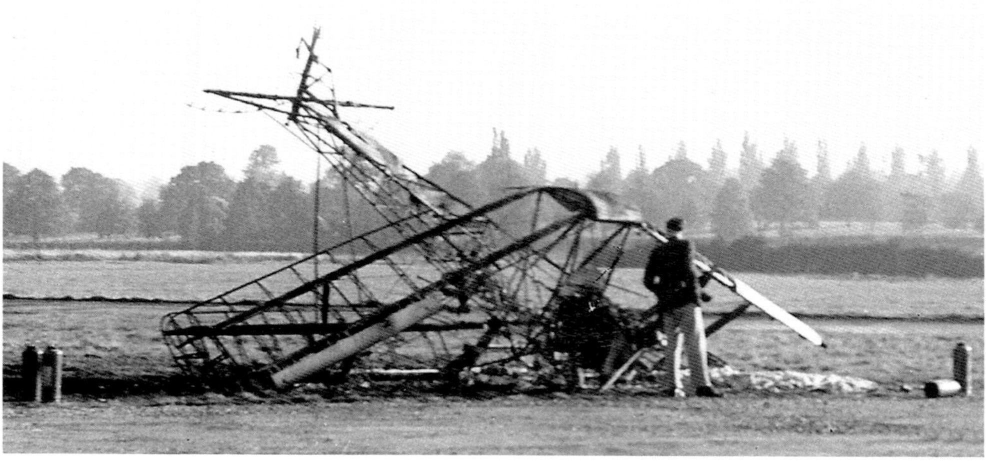

This was the scene that greeted visitors to Elstree aerodrome on 15 September. Phyllis Mairet and her instructor were preparing for a flight in D.H. 82A Tiger Moth G-AJHN, operated by London Aero & Motor Services (LAMS), when it caught fire during starting. Though the pilot escaped injury his pupil, who was sitting in the aeroplane, suffered burns and shock. Built by Morris Motors at Cowley for the RAF as DE734, it was delivered to No. 277 Squadron at Stapleford Tawney, Essex, before passing to No. 308 Squadron at Squires Gate, Blackpool. It was sold in September 1946 and registered 'HN in May 1947.

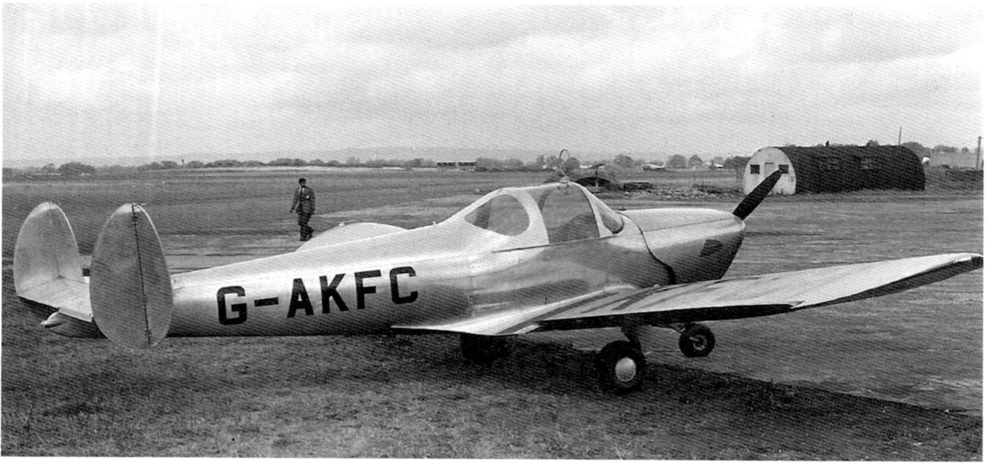

The first Ercoupe 415 to be registered in the UK was G-AKFC, formerly NC7465H in the USA and then OO-ERU when imported into Belgium and registered to Intercontinental Aeronautics in August 1947. The same month it was delivered to the Ministry of Supply for evaluation at Boscombe Down as VX147. Former ATA pilot Lettice Curtiss raced 'FC in the 1949 Grosvenor Trophy Race at Elmdon and averaged 112.5 mph. In February 1952 'FC was restored to the register and acquired by Aviation Traders before joining the Blackpool & Fylde Aero Club Ltd. Its final owner was Norman Brook. On 13 August 1967 'FC crashed at Halfpenny Green after hitting a tree on the approach; the pilot was hurt only slightly.

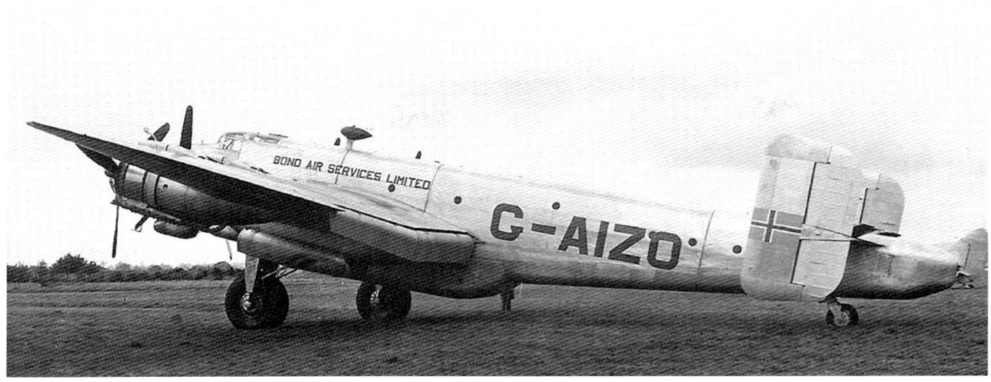

Also parked at Gatwick on 20 September was Halifax C. Mk 8 G-AIZO. Assembled as PP293 at Radlett in late 1945, it was sold to Gatwick-based Union Air Services Ltd in August 1947. Within a few weeks the company took over Bond Air Services Ltd and 'ZO was repainted accordingly. During the evening of 23 May 1948, when inbound from Valencia with a load of apricots and minutes from landing at RAF Bovingdon in filthy weather, 'ZO … turn to pp. 154 to find out how the flight ended.

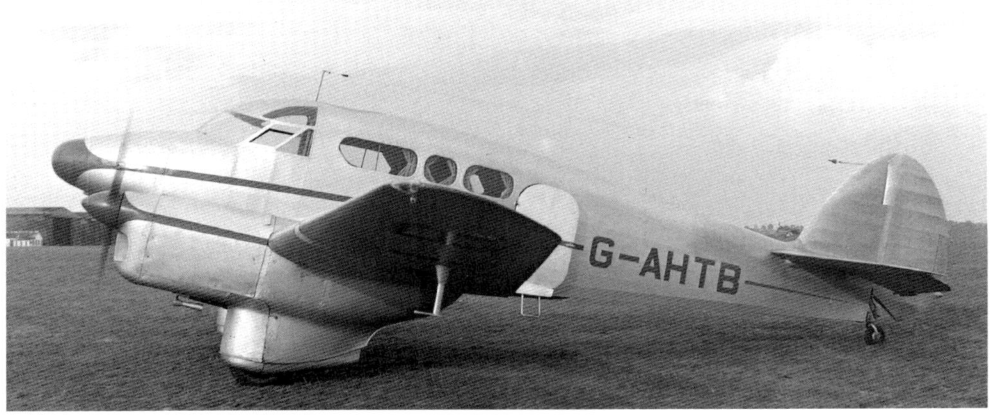

The Percival Q.6 was a bold departure from the standard six to ten-seat passenger biplanes of the pre-war years. Built at Luton in 1937, prototype G-AEYE first flew in September, production beginning the following year. The all-wood, low-wing monoplane was powered by two 205 hp D.H. Gipsy Six Series II engines and carried five or six passengers at a cruising speed of 175 mph. Versions with retractable undercarriages were around 10 mph faster. Including the prototype, 27 Q-6s were built and nearly all but exported aircraft were used at some time by the RAF during the war. The Air Ministry ordered seven Q-6s, known in the Service as the Petrel, and civil examples were impressed, mostly for communications duties. G-AHTB, seen at Luton on 17 September, was delivered new to the RAF as P5634 and served as a communications aircraft at RAF Northolt, Benson, Halton and back to Hendon. After it was sold in May 1946 this Q.6 was purchased by the London and Oxford Steel Company Ltd and based at Weston-super-Mare. On 2 November it was damaged in a landing accident at Almaza, Cairo and was acquired by Egyptian Transair Services and registered SU-AEQ, but was damaged again whilst landing at Hurghada in March 1955.

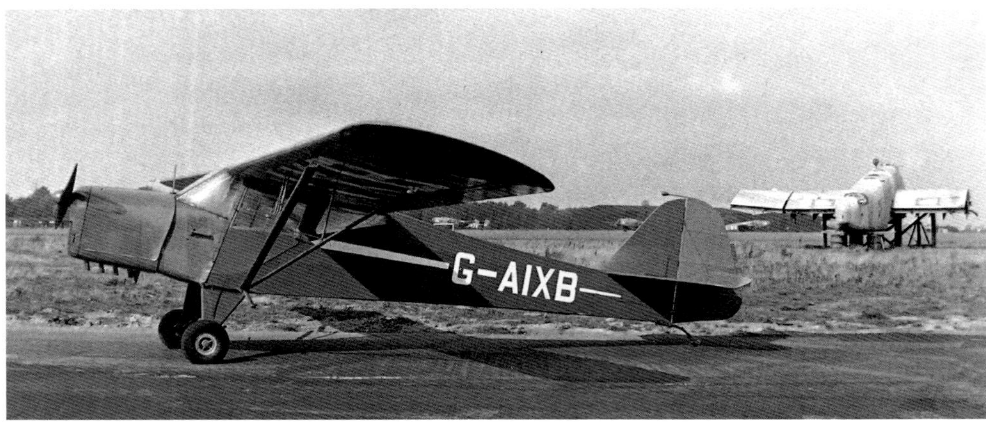

Taylorcraft Plus D G-AIXB at Stansted Mountfitchet (as it was known originally), on 11 October. 1947. At the time Stansted was inundated with former RAF Halifaxes awaiting uncertain fates and was also the base for the Halifax fleet of London Motor & Aero Services. 'XB, formerly LB378 of the RAF, was registered in July 1947 to the United Services Flying Club at Elstree and flown often by E.J.R. In February 1956 it was sold in Southern Rhodesia and became VP-YNM and then ZS-DVV.

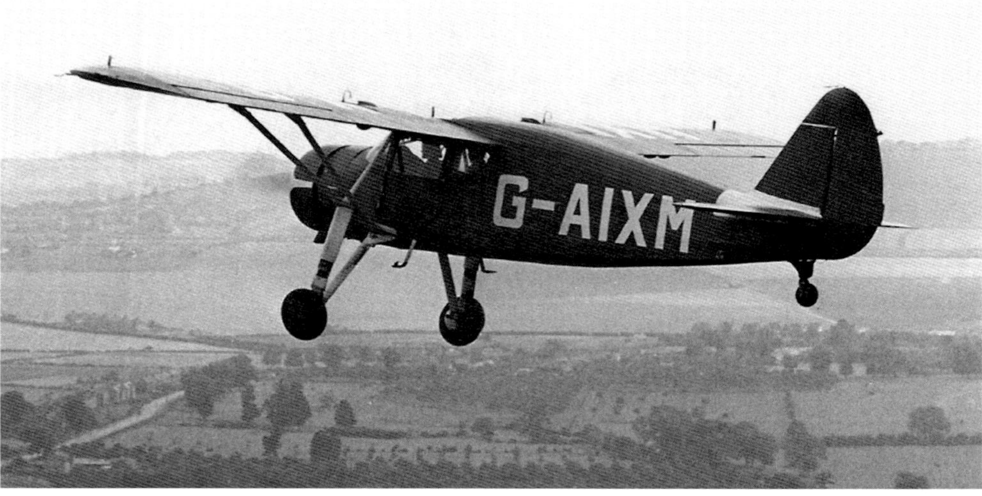

Less than a month after her narrow escape at Eaton Bray on 31 August Joan Nayler is pictured flying passengers from there in crimson Fairchild Argus G-AIXM during an air display on 21 September. Shipped from the USA under Lend-Lease as Fairchild UC-61A Forwarder 43-14892, it became Argus II HB619 and was used as an air taxi by the ATA for part of the war. The Argus transferred to the civil register in December 1946, was owned for a time by Noreen Dimpfl and based at Denham. In 1952 it migrated to Australia to become VH-BLB, passing through various hands until rebuilt in 1981. In 2000 'LB was purchased by Australian children's author Prue Mason and her airline pilot husband Kerry. They named her Argus *Belle* and continue to receive huge enjoyment flying her round Australia.

4

Mostly Wolves in Sheep's Clothing (1948)

Passed by Hurn this afternoon and watched Lancastrian
G-AGME doing crosswind landings...

Letter from E. J. Riding to A. J. Jackson in 1948.

The editorial in the 2 January edition of *The Aeroplane* recorded that a number of people had been discussing speculatively the possibility of a merger of BOAC, BEA and British South American Airways (BSAA) with ex-RAF Pathfinder supremo and BSAA chief, Air Vice-Marshal Donald Bennett, to run all three.

A survey of charter companies in Europe, particularly in Great Britain and in France, showed that aircraft operated by them were, in the main, converted bombers and pre-war designs. *The Aeroplane* reported:

> For example, in the heavier class there are 45 Haltons, 37 Dakotas and a number of Lancastrians, Yorks and DC-4s owned by the British companies, in addition to Haltons and DC-4s, owned by French companies... these clearly cannot go on running for ever—although no one, so far as we know, has dared to prophecy what the life of this type of aeroplane might be. In particular, the Junkers 52 must be very uneconomic compared with present day aircraft, since the design is over 17 years old. What is going to replace them?

BEA's first year of operation ended with a loss of more than £2 million. BOAC lost £8 million in 1947, working out at a deficit of more than £20,000 a day, '... more than most people earn over the best paid years of their life,' commented *The Aeroplane*. It was suggested that money would have been saved by paying every one of BOAC's 130,000 passengers £50 not to go by air! Running three Lancastrian services each week involved well over £1 million of subsidy alone. BSAA made a small profit for 1946–47.

The year's notable maiden flights began with one from water when the first British post-war amphibian, Short Sealand G-AIVX, was flown by H. L. Piper on 22 January from Belfast Lough.

Another blight on the safety record of Britain's airlines, and damaging to the reputation of the Avro Tudor besides, was the disappearance of BSAA's Tudor IV G-AHNP *Star Tiger* on the night of 29–30 January during a flight from Santa Maria, Azores, to Bermuda. Coincidentally, it was announced that an order for 16 Tudor Is and another 50 Tudor IIs had been put in hand for BOAC, via the Ministry of Supply. The outlay for these aircraft was estimated to be about the same as the Corporation's loss for 1946–47, but the deliveries were never made. The Tudor was grounded in February 'as a measure of prudence' pending investigation into *Star Tiger*'s disappearance (never resolved) and not lifted until December. Meanwhile, Air Vice-Marshal Bennett, BSAA's chief executive, had his appointment terminated on 9 February as a result of disagreement with the BSAA board. More first flights followed late winter/early spring. That of Chrislea C.H.3 Super Ace G-AKFD, with its odd-ball flight control system, took place at Exeter on 15 February, flown by Rex Stedman.

On 9 March Sqn Ldr W. A. 'Bill' Waterton made the first flight of Gloster E.1/44 TX145 from Boscombe Down, unkindly and unofficially nicknamed the 'Gormless'. The first prototype, SM809, had been damaged during transit to Boscombe Down by road. Ten days later, Waterton made the first flight of Meteor T.7 two-seat trainer G-AKPK from Brockworth.

Another test pilot, de Havilland's John Cunningham, established a new world height record of 59,446 ft on 23 March in D.H. 100 Vampire TG278 flying from Hatfield. The specially-modified aircraft had a wing span increased by eight feet, a strengthened cockpit hood and, instead of the usual Goblin engine, was a test bed for the de Havilland Ghost turbojet

First flight of the Mamba turboprop-powered version of the Boulton Paul Balliol, VL917, from Pendeford, Wolverhampton, on 24 March ended in disaster. On final approach the propeller 'disked' producing an air brake-type effect, the Balliol hit the aerodrome boundary and was wrecked. Although badly injured, pilot Lindsay Neale recovered to resume test flying, only to lose his life in Balliol VW897 on 3 February the following year.

E.J.R. added D.H.C.1 Chipmunk G-AJVD to his list of types on 25 March, flown by test pilot R.L.C. Blythe, whom he had accompanied on Mosquito test flights during the war years. Afterwards he took air-to-air photographs of 'JVD from Tiger Moth G-AHXC, flown by Dennis Cather from Panshanger.

Losses incurred by BOAC, BEA and BSAA for the financial year to 31 March made for depressing reading. They were £7,091,439; £3,573,989 and £421,481 respectively. In all three instances root cause for the poor figures was attributed to the use of unsuitable and uneconomic aircraft, multiplicity of aircraft types and consequent high maintenance and operating costs. Currency restrictions and unsettled world conditions were also said to be a factor.

BEA's gloom deepened when Vickers Viking G-AIVP *Vimy* lost a wing after colliding with a Soviet Yak-3 fighter while approaching Gatow, West Berlin, on 5 April.

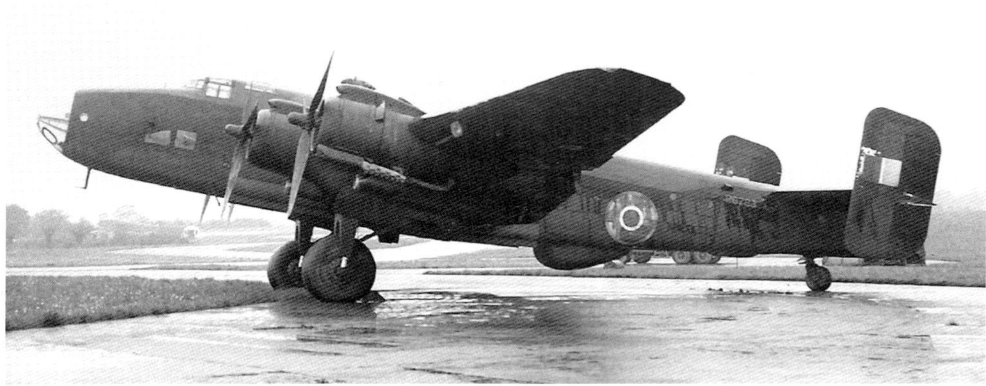

Another Halifax B. Mk 6 seen at Stansted on 1 May was RG783, also built by English Electric at Preston in 1943 and acquired by LAMS in 1947 as G-AKLI. It too ended up with the Pakistan Air Force together with five other Mk 6s and was probably transferred to long-term storage in 1954 before being scrapped.

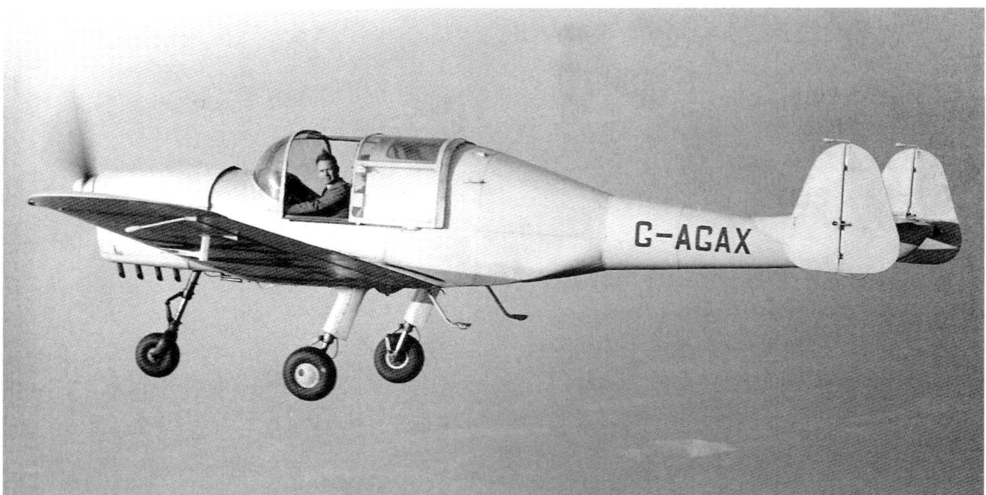

General Aircraft G.A.L. 42 Cygnet II G-AGAX formates on Auster J/1 Autocrat G-AHCK over Redhill on 25 April. The first Cygnet, G-AEMA, was built in 1936 by C.W. Aircraft as a tail dragger with a raked windscreen, flying in May 1937. Since no orders were received the design was sold to General Aircraft which improved it by switching to a tricycle undercarriage and adding twin fins and rudders. This led to prototype G.A.L. 42 Cygnet II G-AFVR and a short production run of about a dozen aircraft. 'AX was completed in 1944 and remained with General Aircraft until sold to R. C. Cox and based at Fairoaks from early 1948. That's probably him flying the aircraft with the cockpit hood slid back for a better view of the Autocraft camera aircraft. After several more owners 'AX crashed near Barnsley on 4 April 1955.

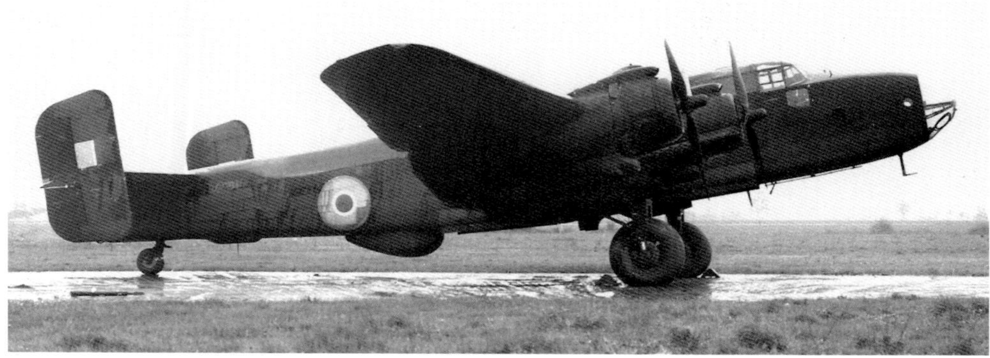

Dozens of wartime Halifaxes earmarked for civil conversion littered airfields all over the country in the early post-war years, most never progressing further than the scrap man's torch. Here Halifax H.P. 61 B. Mk 6 RG781 awaits its fate at Stansted on 1 May. Built by English Electric at Preston in 1943, it was registered G-AKLJ in November 1947 to London Aero & Motor Services Ltd (LAMS) and delivered to Stansted shortly before this photograph was taken. In October the following year 'LJ was sold to the Pakistan Air Force.

All ten passengers and four crew were killed in the crash, together with the pilot of the Yak. The British Government sent a note of protest to the Soviet Government declaring that the accident was the result of the Yak pilot's neglect and dangerous conduct and claiming compensation. The Soviet's rejected the note, making counter-claims. The day following, 6 April, was more momentous, J. 'Mutt' Summers making the first flight of the experimental Vickers Type 618 Nene Viking G-AJPH at Wisley, the world's first pure jet transport to fly.

E.J.R. had a busy flying day on 6 May. In the morning he and Stanley Orton Bradshaw S.O.B. left Denham in Miles M.14 Magister G-AJGM, landing at Chalgrove, the Martin-Baker airfield. There, on behalf of *The Light Plane*, they flew handling trials in Hawker Tomtit G-AFTA, including two stall turns and a spin from 2,000 ft. Leaving Chalgrove in the 'Maggie' for Thruxton, here they received a handling demonstration of Chrislea Ace G-AKFD with Rex Steadman. E.J.R. took air-to-air photographs of the Ace during the flight back to Denham. Near Bovingdon the 'Maggie' suffered fuel starvation, but managed to limp home.

During the first days of May E.J.R. photographed dozens of civil-marked Handley Page Halifaxes at Stansted Mountfitchett, Thame and Bovingdon. On a visit to Heathrow on 8 May he came across the Consolidated Liberator G-AHYG.

Another of 1948's first flights was that of Percival Prince G-23-1/G-ALCM on 13 May from Luton and made by Wg Cdr H. P. Powell.

On 1 June BEA and the GPO began an experimental helicopter mail service in East Anglia. Using Peterborough as the base, calls were made at King's Lynn, Wells-next-the-Sea, Sherringham, Cromer, Norwich, Thetford, Diss, Harleston and Great Yarmouth. E.J.R. was to come across one of the S-51s whilst flying in the Apethorpe area on 27 May during a visit to Farmer W. Tompkins—*see* accompanying photograph.

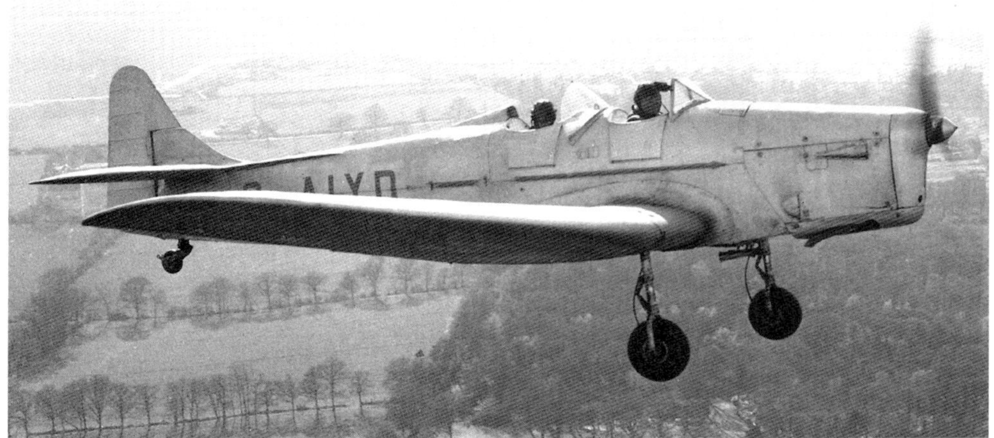

C. A. Nepean Bishop edges Miles M.14A Hawk Trainer Mk 3 G-AIYD nearer to Auster J.1 Autocrat G-AHCK flown by Alec Lumsden over Redhill on 11 April. Built in 1941 at Woodley as Miles M.14 Magister T9915 for the RAF, the aircraft was delivered to No. 232 Squadron at Stoney Cross before passing to No. 5 Flying Instructors School at Scone, Scotland. Demobbed in June 1946 and with the designation Hawk Trainer Mk 3, it was registered in May 1947 to the Redhill Flying Club and destroyed at Redhill on 29 November 1953.

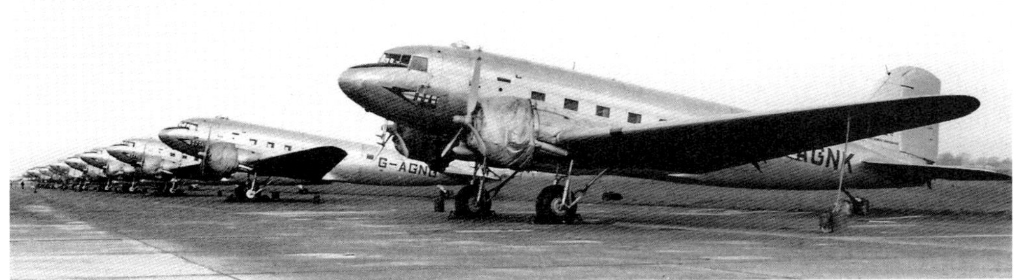

Above: This line-up of BOAC Douglas C-47B Dakota 4s with engines covered was taken at Heathrow on 8 May. Nearest the camera is G-AGNK, formerly KK206 with the RAF and registered in March 1945. Named *Edward Mannock* after the First World War RFC ace, 'NK was transferred to the newly-formed BEA Pionair fleet, finally being scrapped for spares at Southend in 1964.

Below: London Aero & Motor Services (LAMS) blue and white H.P. 70 Halifax C. Mk 8 G-AIWN *Port of Darwin* at Stansted, the company's initial base, on 8 May. Built for the RAF as PP235 at Radlett in 1945, it was registered to LAMS in May 1947. Two years later it transferred to Payloads Ltd, an associate company of LAMS, before going to Bond Air Services Ltd at Gatwick in May 1949. The Halifax was withdrawn from use in 1950.

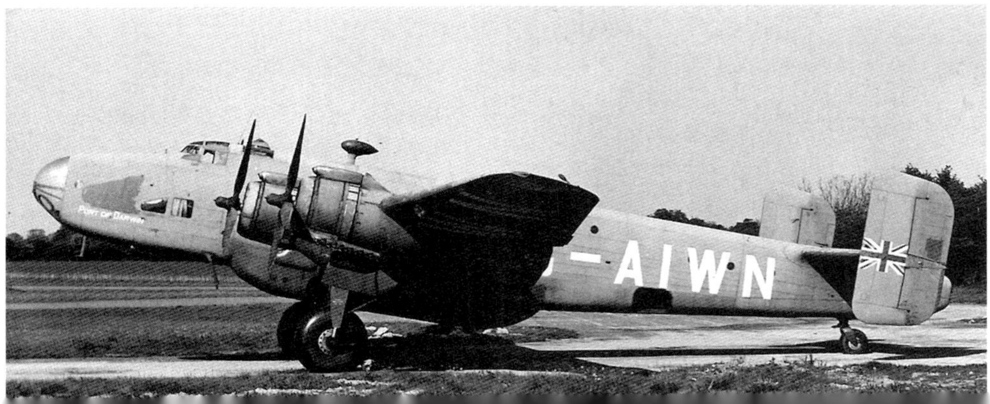

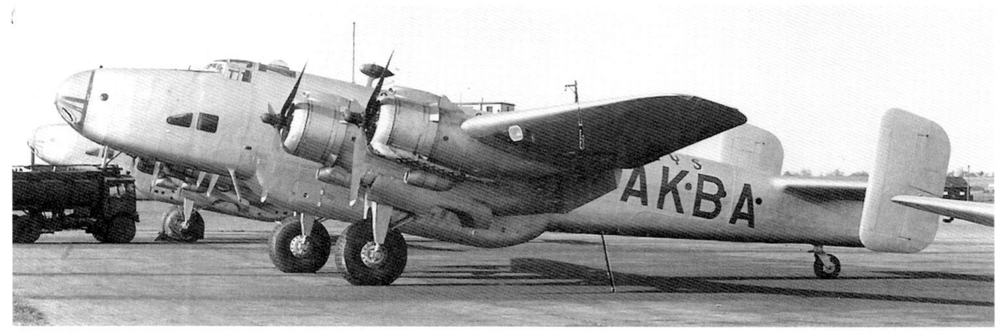

RAF Bovingdon, near Hemel Hempstead, Hertfordshire, was another haunt for civil registered Halifaxes. Seen there on 8 May is Alpha Airways (Pty) Ltd's Halifax C. Mk 8 G-AKBA. Assembled at Radlett in 1945 as PP219, the brand new aircraft passed to Airtech Ltd at Thame for conversion to commercial use and leased to Alpha Airways. Less than three weeks after this photograph was taken 'BA crashed, killing the five occupants, after suffering engine failure when taking off from Albacete, Spain, for Haddenham, Oxfordshire, with a full cargo load.

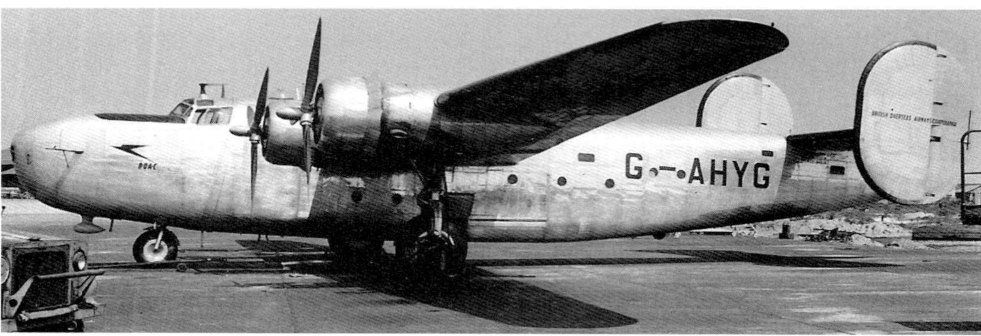

In 1946 several former RAF Consolidated Liberators were converted at Montreal for BOAC's Heathrow–Prestwick–Montreal freighting service, among them G-AHYG, seen at Heathrow on 8 May. Originally AL603 with the RAF, this Liberator II had been assigned to No. 1445 Ferry Training Flight at Lyneham before going to Nos 160 and 159 Squadrons at Leuchars and Molesworth respectively. In August 1942 AL603 was acquired by BOAC and in April 1951 sold in France to become F-BFGK.

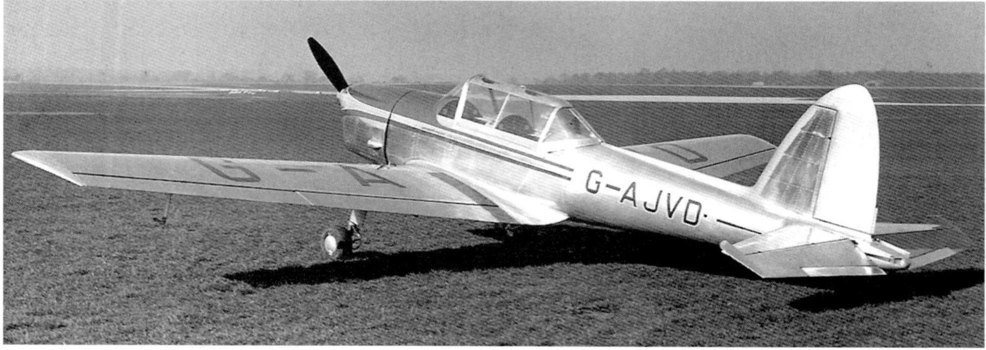

Gleaming in the March sunlight at Hatfield on 25 March 1948 is D.H.C.1 Chipmunk G-AJVD, the tenth example built, shipped from de Havilland Aircraft of Canada Ltd and registered in July 1947. After installation of a British radio and a D.H. Gipsy Major 10 Engine 'VD was evaluated by A%AEE Boscombe Down. Subsequently the type was adopted as the RAF's standard trainer and designated Chipmunk T. Mk 10. 'VD spent several years with the London Aeroplane Club at Panshanger and was re-registered G-ARFW in March 1960 to incorporate the new owner's initials. On 20 June 1966 the aircraft was damaged beyond repair at Cherbourg, France.

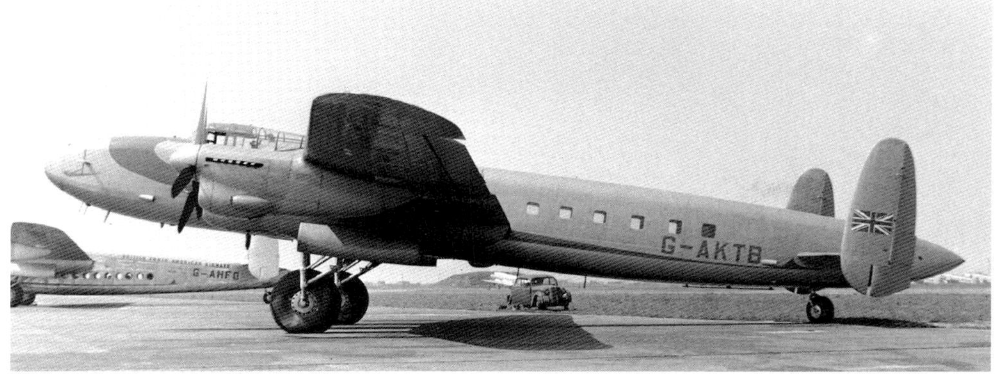

Built during the winter of 1945–46, Avro 691 Lancastrian C.2 VM738 was assigned to RAF Full Sutton, near Stamford Bridge, probably to No. 231 Squadron. In February 1948 it was sold to British South American Airways, registered G-AKTB and named *Star Glory*. This picture taken at Heathrow on 8 May has E.J.R.'s Ford car visible in the background. When Flight Refuelling Ltd acquired 'TB in early 1949 it was equipped with a 2,500 gallon tank for carrying petrol or oil and used on the Berlin Airlift. The Lancastrian was withdrawn from use in May 1951 and probably scrapped at Tarrant Rushton.

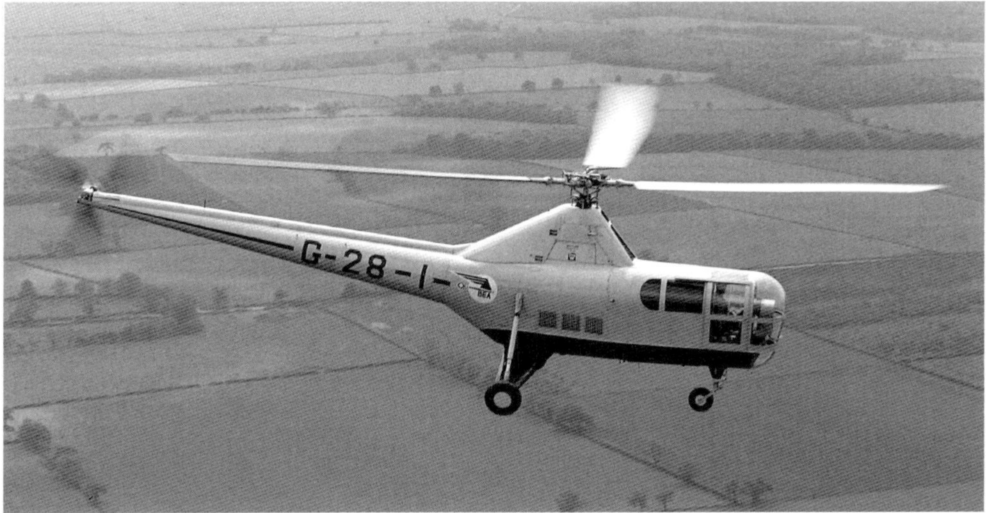

The 12 June 1948 issue of the much-read *Aeroplane Spotter* published the following letter from E.J.R. with the photograph reproduced here: 'I enclose a photograph of a Westland Sikorsky S-51 (G-28-1) which I took on the afternoon of May 27. Whilst 'lingering' in the vicinity of Horsey Toll I saw this contraption come up from Peterborough aerodrome and proceed in a northerly direction, whereupon chase was given and much to the pilot's amusement, his (or his machine's) likeness recorded for posterity. Now, as you will agree, there's nothing new in a mere S-51, but take a look at those markings! Does this presage the advent of motorcar index numbers and the consequent abolition of our hobby, or is it merely a new form of identification?' The reply from editor Charles Cain began: 'We are surprised that such an old hand at the civil aircraft registration game as E. J. Riding should have been unaware of this new system of markings for British experimental aircraft'… etc., etc. E.J.R. was flying from Apethorpe to Sywell in Auster J/1 G-AHAT when he came across the S-51. Six were imported from the USA in 1947, one of which was G-28-1, first flown in August 1947 from Yeovil. It was subsequently registered G-AJOR, named *Sir Owen* and flew trial mail flights for a BEA experimental helicopter service from Peterborough Westwood to towns in Norfolk—a kind of aerial postman. In June 1967 'OR was sold in Canada and became CF-JTP.

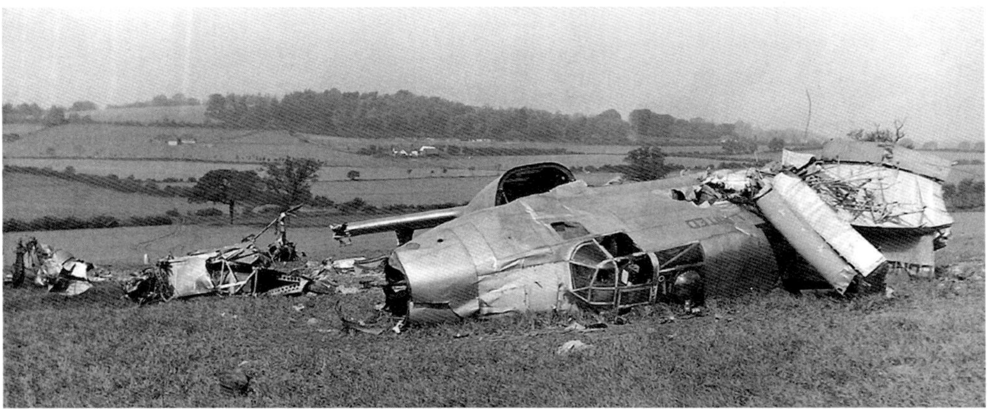

More pictures of Halifax G-AIZO as a sequel to that on p. 145 During the evening of 23 May 'ZO was inbound to RAF Bovingdon from Valencia in filthy weather with a load of apricots. Just minutes from landing the pilot lost control, the aircraft hitting the ground in level flight on full power in open countryside near Berkhamsted. Fortunately, it broke into component parts, as Halifaxes tended to do, and amazingly all five crew survived. The area probably stank of rotting apricots for weeks afterwards!

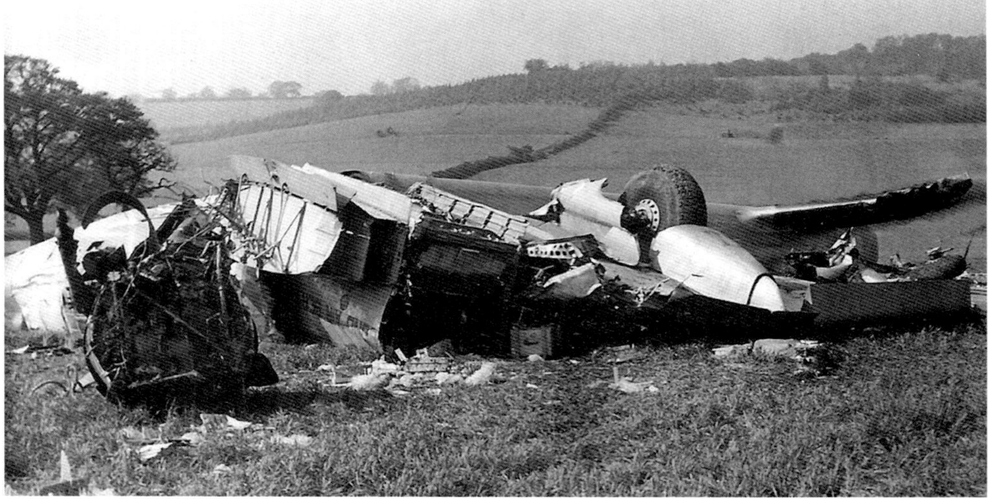

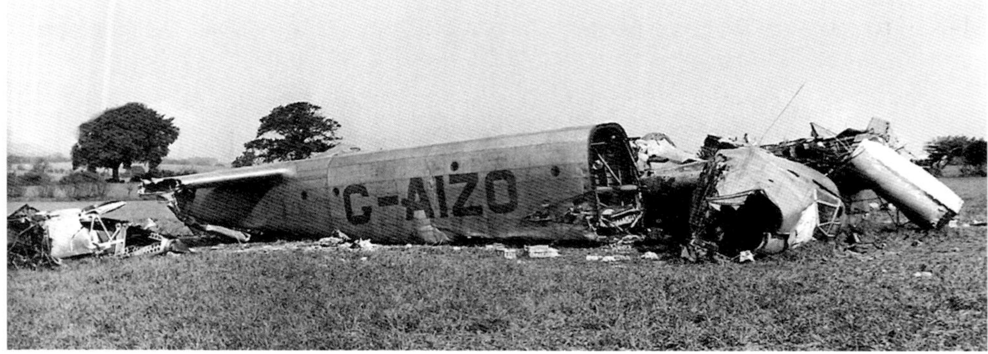

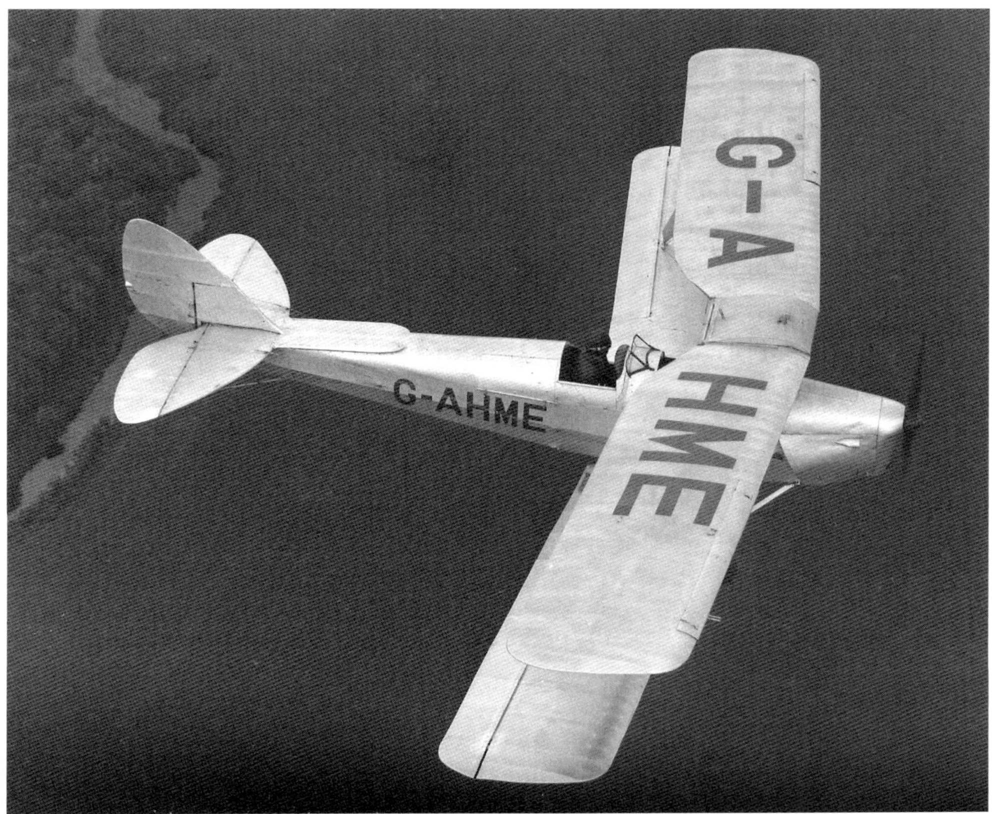

Earlier on the same day as the interception of the S-51, E.J.R. came across Farmer Bill Tomkins flying his D.H. 82A Tiger Moth G-AHME. Famous for once owning civil Gloster Gamecock G-ADIN during 1935–36, he also used Miles Aerovan G-AILF for the aerial sowing of 20 acres of rain-sodden land with wheat. Sadly Farmer Bill died in a road accident in 1967; his aviation exploits would make an entertaining and hilarious book. His Tiger Moth, formerly T7790 with the RAF, was retired at Apethorpe in September 1956. Bill was a marvellous exponent of the Tiger and the author has cine film showing him flying heart-in-mouth circuits around his house, taking-off and landing in less than a minute.

First flight of Avro 701 Athena VM125 took place from Woodford on 12 June, flown by J. H. Orrell. The Athena was a rival to the Boulton Paul Balliol (flown in March) to meet an RAF requirement for an advanced trainer and, like the Balliol, had a Mamba turboprop.

Come 21–30 June, the Riding family were once again holidaying in Dorset and, as was his custom, E.J.R. visited Christchurch, Eastleigh, Poole Harbour, Hythe and Hurn, the author standing with him at the end of Hurn's runway as crew training BOAC Yorks flew circuits and bumps. E.J.R. wrote in a letter to A.J.J:

Passed by Hurn this afternoon and watched Lancastrian G-AGME doing crosswind landings, eventually taking up a favourable position at the end of N–S runway. I screwed in the telephoto lens and popped him a la 'AGJC and 'AGSN—I hope!

'Operation Plainfare' the British contribution to the Berlin Airlift, began on 26 June using RAF aircraft. Civil aircraft joined in from 28 July.

A very sad day for aircraft spotters occurred on 10 July as Temple Press published the last of 217 issues of *The Aeroplane Spotter*. It first appeared as a weekly on 2 January 1941, priced 3*d*, consisted of eight pages only and was edited by Peter Masefield. He went on to become a towering figure in British civil aviation, running among others BEA, Bristol Aircraft, the British Airports Authority and Beagle Aircraft. Interestingly, the final photograph published by the *Spotter* on the penultimate page of the last issue was E.J.R.'s photograph of coupe Miles M.14 Hawk G-AKRW.

On 16 July J. 'Mutt' Summers and G. R. Bryce made the first flight from Wisley of prototype Vickers Viscount G-AHRF, the world's first turboprop transport. Originally named Viceroy, the name was changed to Viscount following Indian independence and partition in 1947. Political correctness was around even then, it seems.

Another Vickers product, Nene Viking G-AJPH, dashed from Heathrow to Villacoublay, near Paris, in 34 minutes, returning the same day in 36.5 minutes, on 24 July.

For two days E.J.R. was busy with an air display he was arranging at Eaton Bray, the home of Harborough Publications. On 31 July he and Joan Nayler, future wife of Harborough boss Douglas A. Russell, flew back and forth between Elstree, White Waltham and Eaton Bray in Auster Autocrat G-AGXT, making time for a few beat ups of nearby Slapton to drum up business for the show. A full flying programme had been arranged at Eaton Bray for the following day, during which Joan Nayler flew pleasure trips. The weather clamped at the end of the afternoon and E.J.R. and Joan Nayler were forced to navigate back to Elstree via 'Bradshaw'.

On 26 August E.J.R. and Stanley Bradshaw left Elstree in Autocrat G-AGXJ for White Waltham to take air-to-air photographs of Fairey chief test pilot, Peter Twiss, flying Fairey Junior OO-TIT. Two days later, this time with A.J.J., E.J.R. flew in D.H.82A G-AINY from Southend to attend the Lympne International Meeting. Highlights were a neat drill demonstration from Spitfires of 615 Squadron and the customary Lympne High-speed Handicap. Competitors were a Fairey Firefly 4 (J. O. Matthews), Supermarine Spitfire II (Lettice Curtis), Spitfire Trainer (L. R. Colquhoun), Spitfire 24 (W. J. G. Morgan), Hawker Sea Fury (T. S. Wade) and two D.H. 100 Vampires (John Derry and John Cunningham). The winner was Colquhoun in Spitfire Trainer G-AIDN who averaged 326 mph. Fastest time was 472 mph put up by Cunningham.

First flight of Hawker N.7/46 Sea Hawk VP413 took place on 3 September. Six days later John Derry exceeded the speed of sound in D.H. 108 VW120 while diving from 40,000 ft.

E.J.R. visited the Isle of Man during 5–8 September, arriving at Ronaldsway from Ringway in BEA Dakota G-AGYX on a scheduled service, piloted by Capt. McEwen. On his return E.J.R. wrote to A.J.J.:

This Wed pm found me once more at Ronaldsway, idly passing lengths of gelatine [film] behind my Fox's Glacier Mint [camera lens] until G-AJIB (Dakota) was drawn up and 21 persons, including yours truly, embarked. We got into Ringway at 5.10 pm, and finding the Ford still intact (I half expected to find it jacked up on four bricks with the battery gone), took on fuel and oil and prepared to journey southwards thro' the night. Although it came on to rain in the Potteries I had an uneventful run, getting home at midnight.

I went to Farnborough the following am and again on Friday and think I have covered things to everybody's satisfaction [*Aeromodeller*].

The 9th Annual Exhibition and Flying Display of the Society of British Aircraft Constructors, to give its full title, was held during 7–12 September. The first day was marred by poor weather but improved thereafter. *The Aeroplane* reported that the show would be remembered for the interest in the aircraft parks rather than the static exhibition. Air show highlights included Geoffrey Tyson's startling inverted flying of the bulky Saro S.R.A. 1 fighter flying boat at 200 ft across the airfield, the curiosity of the A.W. 52 Derwent-powered flying wing and the low passes of a BOAC Short Solent. *The Aeroplane* summed up the flying thus:

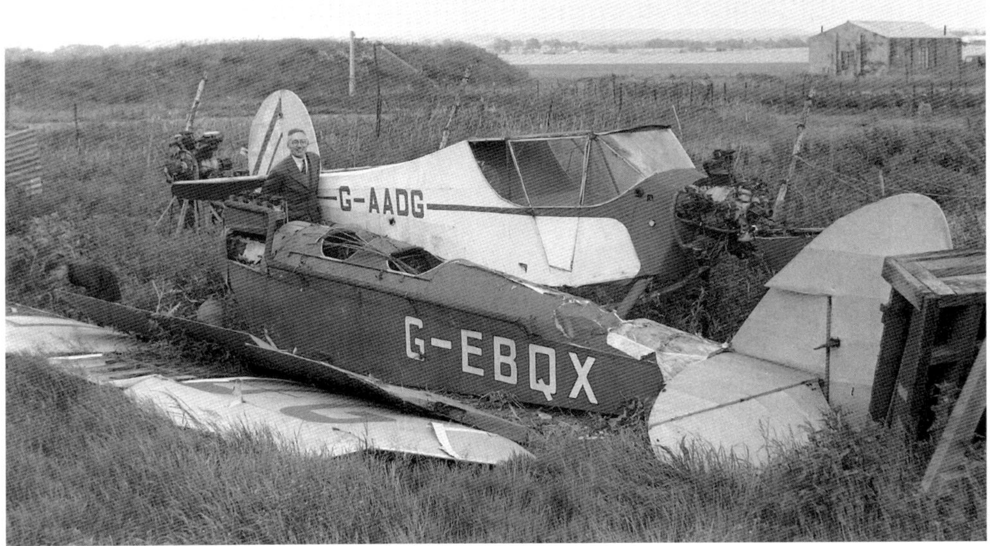

Can you imagine seeing a sight like this at Gatwick Airport today? A.J. Jackson is seen doing a strong man act with the back end of Monocoupe 70 G-AADG at the Gatwick dump on 5 June. 'DG entered the UK in December 1928, was re-engined with an 80 hp Armstrong Siddeley Genet II and ended its flying days at Maylands, Essex. Though stored throughout the war, it was broken up at Gatwick shortly after this photograph was taken. Next to the Monocoupe is the sad spectre of dead D.H. 60 Cirrus Moth G-EBQX, last flown in 1937 and destined to be scrapped at Beddington, Surrey, although it looked to be on its last legs at Gatwick. Midway up at the left-hand edge of the photograph you can just spot the author, aged six, inspecting one of the Moth's wings. Interestingly, both aircraft still have engines intact.

Those who went to the show must, above all, have been impressed by the way the turbine engine is gradually becoming an accepted part of British aviation. The jets, which a few years ago, would turn every head as soon as a compressor started shrieking, are now part of the occupational noises of the SBAC display.

On 23 September E.J.R. flew into Welford, near Newbury, to take air-to-air shots of duck egg blue Newbury Eon G-AKBC and to make a 10-minute sampling flight. He noted that the Eon's maximum speed was 136 mph, cruising speed 116 mph and the stall took place at 48 mph. The Eon became the subject of E.J.R.'s *Aircraft Described* series in the November 1948 issue of *Aeromodeller*.

More notable first flights took place as 1948 drew to a close. That of Westland-built Dragonfly (Sikorsky S-51) G-AKTW was at Yeovil on 5 October, flown by Alan Bristow. On 19 November Hawker P.1052 VX272, in effect a swept wing Sea Hawk, was flown from Boscombe Down by Sqn Ldr T. S. Wade.

On 7 December the first flight of Cierva W.11 Air Horse VZ724 was made from Eastleigh by H. A. Marsh—brave man! The Air Horse had been seen in public for the first time as a static exhibit at the SBAC show in September. Powered by a single Rolls-Royce Merlin 24 engine powering three 47-ft rotors on outriggers and rotating in the same direction, the W.11 had the distinction of being the world's largest helicopter undergoing flight tests at the time. Quirkily, the tail unit was attached to the large loading doors at the rear end of the fuselage.

Finally, on 29 December Mike Lithgow got Supermarine Type 510 Swift prototype VV106 airborne from Boscombe Down.

And by the year end E.J.R. had added another 38 flying hours to his flying log book.

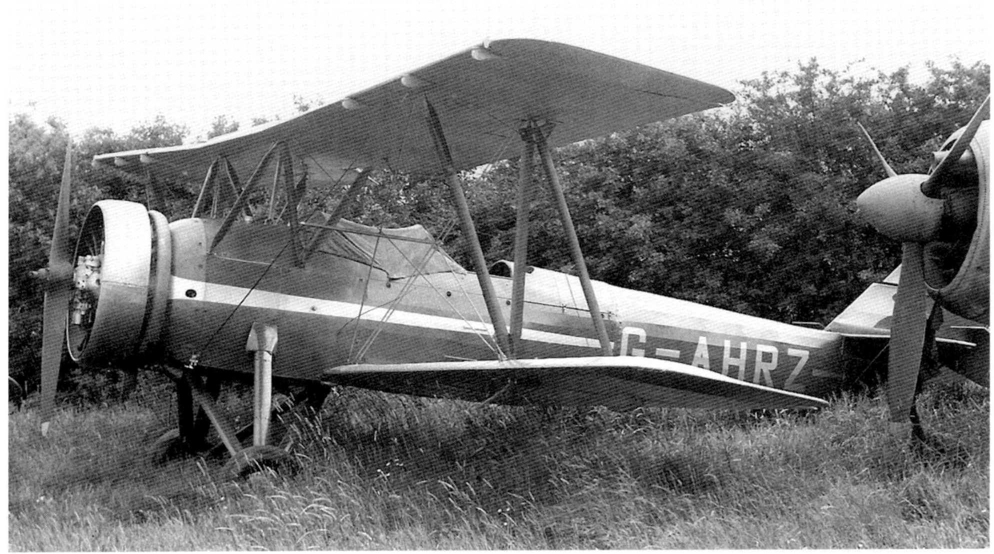

Avro 626 Prefect K5069 was built in 1935, serving with No. 48 Squadron at RAF Bicester, and then with the practice flight at RAF Henlow before being shuttled from one MU to another. In May 1946 the Prefect was sold to Southern Aircraft, becoming G-AHRZ. It is seen at Gatwick on 5 June shortly before it was scrapped.

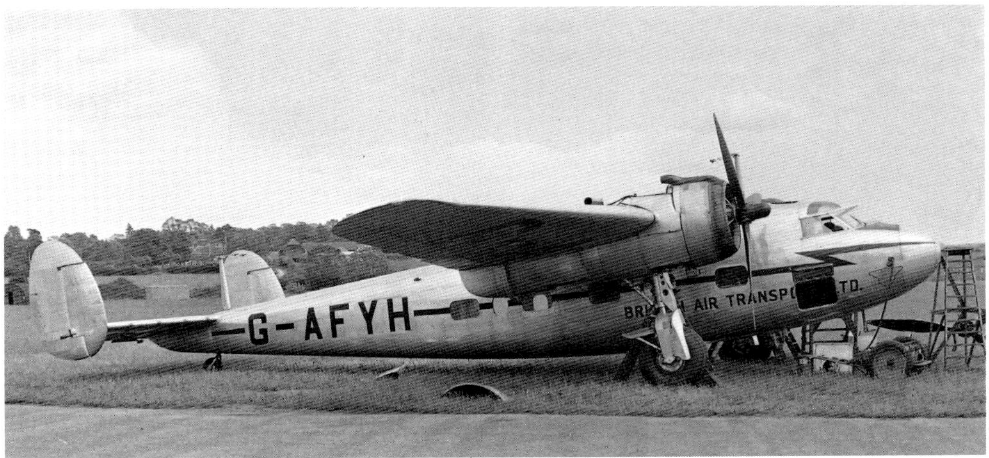

The D.H. 95 Flamingo was the creation of R. E. Bishop, designer of the D.H. 98 Mosquito, and was de Havilland's first all-metal, stressed skin aircraft. Powered by two 890 or 930 hp Bristol Perseus engines, it carried 12 or 17 passengers. Prototype G-AFUE was first flown from Hatfield on 28 December 1938. As well as BOAC, the RAF ordered several for use by No. 24 Communications Squadron at RAF Hendon. Twenty were built at Hatfield during 1938–41. G-AFYH was first flown in November 1940, delivered to No. 782 Squadron at Donibristle as BT312 and named *Merlin VI*. After the war it was restored to the register by Southern Aircraft Ltd and acquired by British Air Transport Ltd for charter work based at Redhill, where it was photographed on 5 June. Instead, though, it languished as a hangar queen until pushed outside and broken up in May 1954.

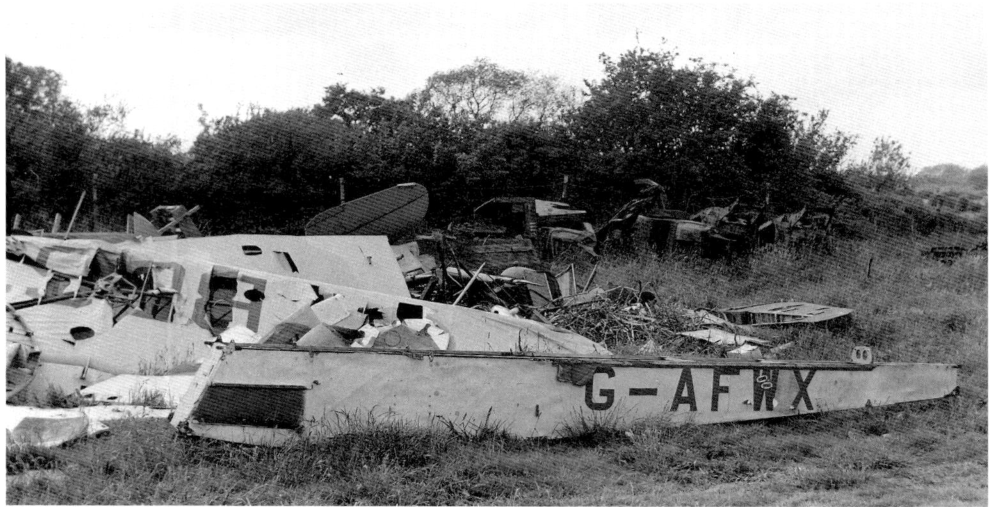

Another piece of history lying festering at the Gatwick dump on 5 June was G-AFWX, once a pristine D.H. 60GIII Moth. Built in 1933 and registered EI-AAU when resident in Ireland, it returned to the UK for service with Southern Aircraft Ltd at Gatwick.

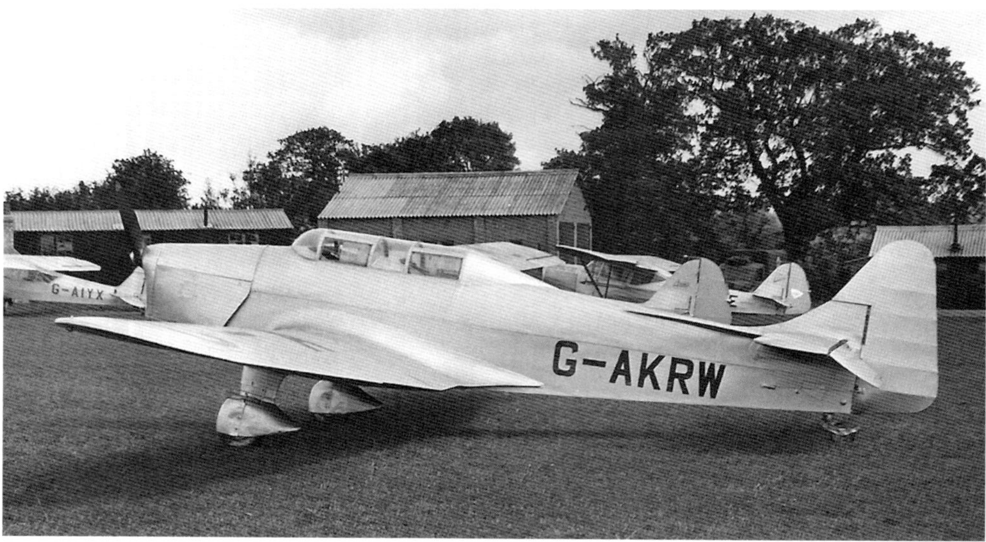

Only a handful of Miles M.14A Hawks were modified with enclosed cockpits, one of which was G-AKRW, seen at Panshanger on 6 June. Built as Magister N3890 for the RAF and assigned to various elementary flying schools, it was sold to Short Bros in 1948 and flown by the Rochester Flying Club. It is believed that it acquired the hood in 1944, courtesy of the makers. Whilst landing at Sherburn-in-Elmet in July 1950 'RW was damaged when the undercarriage collapsed, and in July 1953 was declared a write-off following engine failure when landing at Hawkhurst, Kent. Its mortal remains were taken to Rochester and burnt that November.

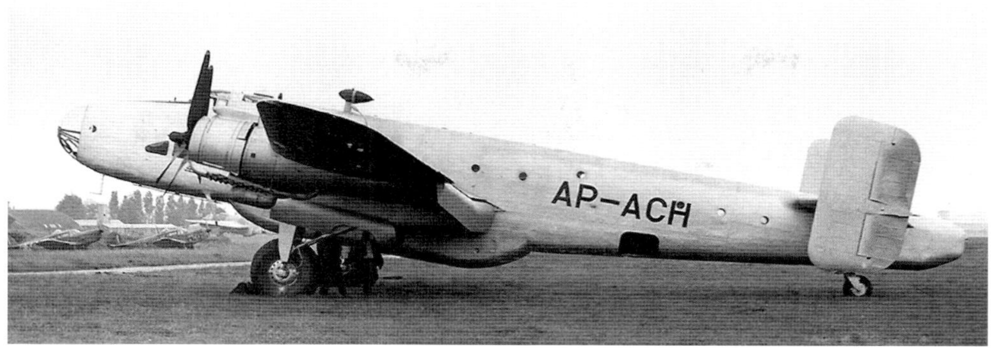

Handley Page H.P. 70 Halifax C. Mk 8 PP279 was assembled at Radlett in 1945 and sold in May. In April 1947 the Halifax was registered G-AJNU to Payloads Ltd, an associate company of LAMS that carried out charter work from Croydon and later Stansted. Most of the Halifaxes acquired were converted into civilian freighters and sold abroad, including 'NU which became AP-ACH of Pakistan Airways in May 1948. Here it is awaiting collection at Thame on 11 June after overhaul by Air Tech Ltd. In October that year the Halifax was acquired by the Royal Pakistan Air Force and used as an instructional airframe.

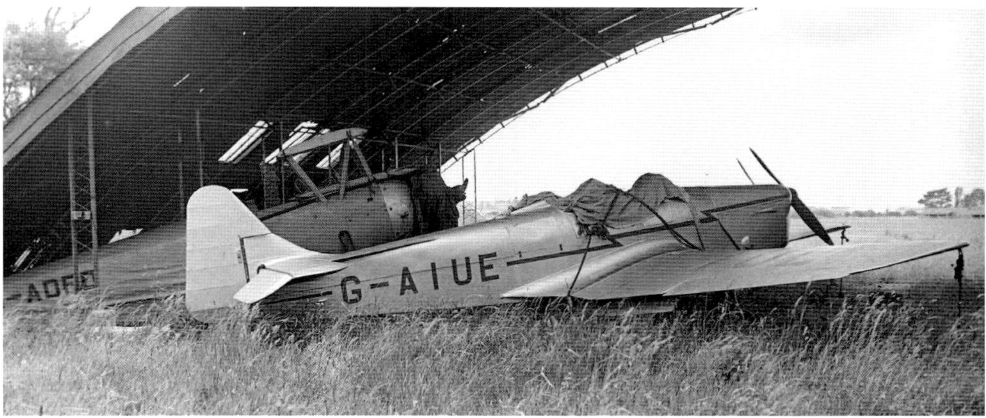

In the immediate post war years there were many blister hangars, designed by famed architect Graham R. Dawbarn, scattered all around the country and invariably giving temporary cover to tired aeroplanes surviving long after their useful lives had ended. Christchurch was no exception. In the foreground is Miles M. 14A Hawk Trainer G-AIUE, cockpits protected from the weather and still equipped with wartime rear cockpit blind flying hood. Built in 1939 as N3962 and delivered to No. 44 ERFTS at Elmdon in May, this 'Maggie' was reportedly converted to a light bomber by the makers and shuttled between various MUs and flying training schools. After the war it was acquired by T. C. Sparrow and kept at Christchurch, where it was photographed on 21 June. In 1950 the unforgettable Doug Bianchi prepared 'UE for the 1950 King's Cup air race, adding a few extra mph by fairing over the front cockpit. Subsequently, 'UE passed through many ownerships, eventually settling with the aptly named Magister Aero Club at Ipswich, in whose ownership it crashed while taking off from Seething, Norfolk, on 11 October 1962. Lurking in the background are the remains of Avro 643 Cadet G-ADFD, late of the Bristol & Wessex Aeroplane Club. In 1950 'FD was donated to the nearby Wimborne ATC Squadron, but scrapped in 1961.

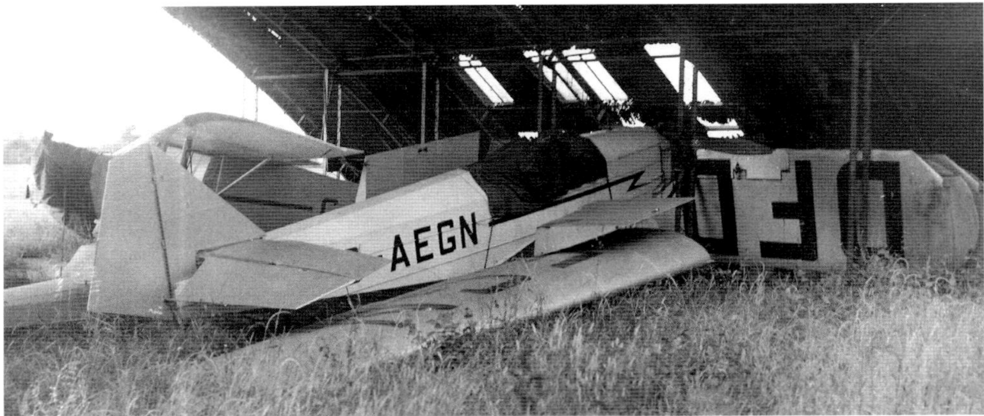

Also seen in the hangar is dismantled Pobjoy-engined B.A. Swallow 2 G-AEGN. Built in 1936 and delivered to the Liverpool & District Aero Club at Hooton Park, 'GN moved south to the Bristol & Wessex Aero Club at Whitchurch, Bristol, shortly before the war. Post-war the Swallow was acquired by Sparrow and eventually scrapped at Christchurch in 1950. This photograph also reveals the wings of Avro 643 Cadet G-ADFD.

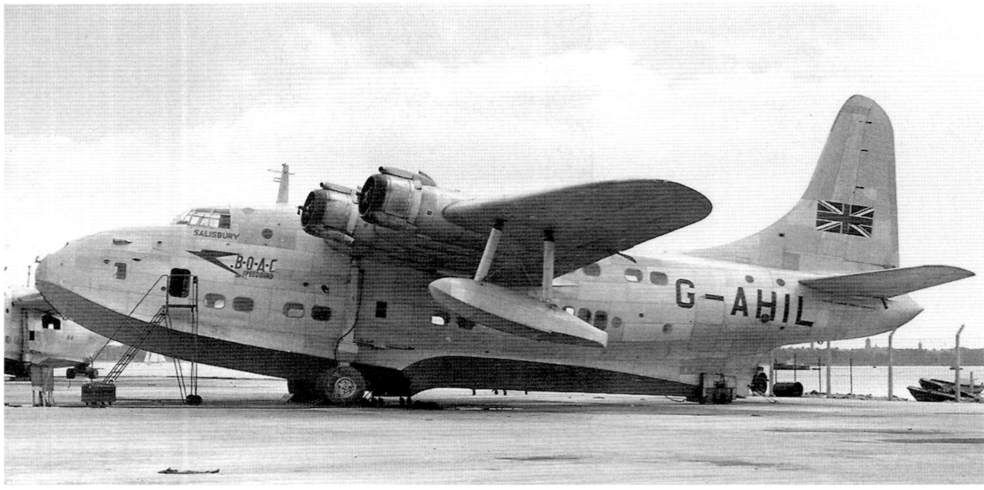

This quartet of Short Hythe and Solent flying boats was photographed at Hythe in June and July. *Above*, standing on the hard on 3 July minus its propellers is BOAC's Short S. 45 Solent 2 G-AHIL *Salisbury*, launched and flown by Geoffrey Tyson at Rochester on 11 November 1946. Designed to carry 34 day passengers and seven crew members in two-deck luxury, complete with dining room and cocktail bar, Solent 2s and 3s were powered by four 1,690 hp Bristol Hercules 637 radial engines. In 1950 'IL was upgraded to Solent 3 standard, the all-up weight increasing by 600 lb to 78,600 lb, but was withdrawn from use in September the following year and scrapped at Hamworthy, Poole in 1954.

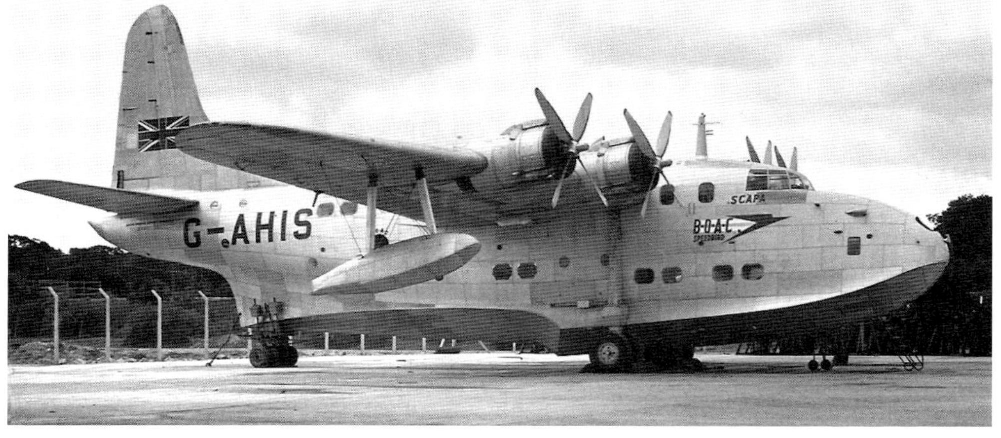

Another Solent 2, G-AHIS, seen on 3 July, was christened *Scapa* by BOAC. After conversion to Solent 3 status in 1950 it was renamed *City of York*. Withdrawn from use in September the following year, 'IS was flown to Belfast where it was scrapped in 1952.

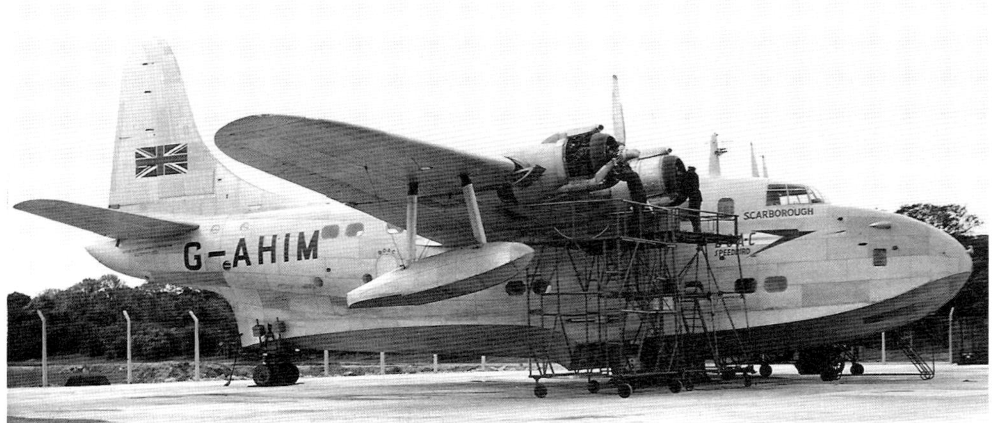

Above: BOAC Short Solent 2 G-AHIM *Scarborough* undergoing engine checks on the Hythe hard on 23 June. A few weeks later it made a fleeting appearance at the 1948 SBAC Show at Farnborough in September. Fitted out identically to G-AHIL, it was withdrawn from service in June 1950 and flown to Belfast where it was scrapped in 1952.

Below: BOAC Short S.25 Sunderland 3 G-AGEW *Hanwell* on the Hythe hard on 23 June. Formerly JM665/OQ-ZW, at one time it was operated jointly by the RAF and BOAC. Stripped of armament and military equipment and fitted hastily with austerity bench-and-mattress seating, six Sunderland 3s, among them 'EW which had been registered in March 1943, were used on the Poole–West Africa priority passenger and mail service. Shortly after this photograph was taken 'EW lost a float and overturned when taking off from Sourabaya, Java, in September 1948.

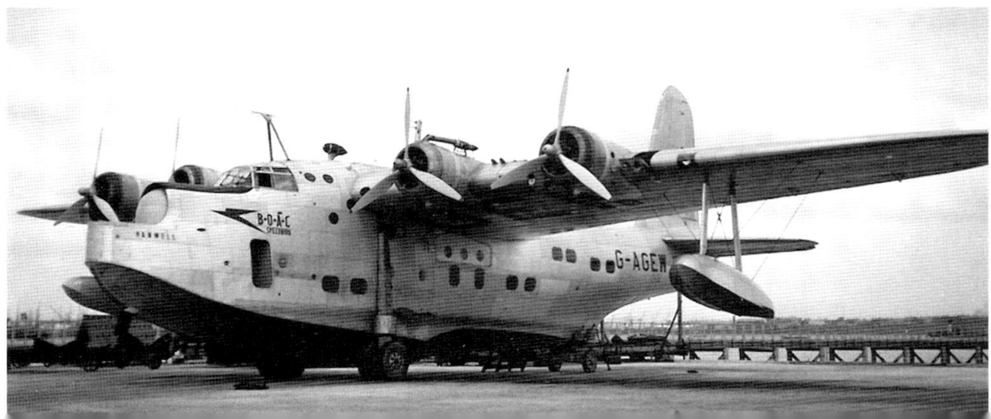

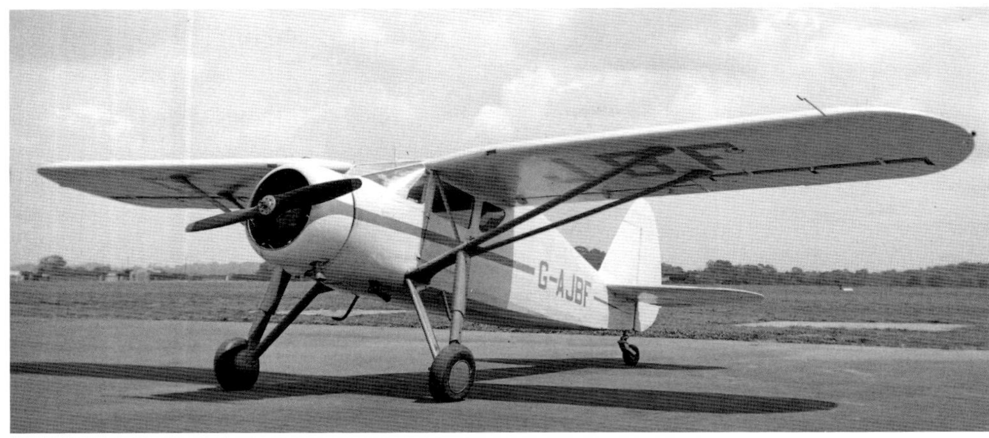

Fairchild 24W Argus G-AJBF at Eastleigh on 23 June. Shipped from the USA to the UK under Lend-Lease in 1944, it became Argus II HB632 and was used by the ATA as a taxi aircraft. Post-war, 'BF was operated by Thorne Aviation and based at Squires Gate, Blackpool, until sold to Finland in November 1951 as OH-FCH.

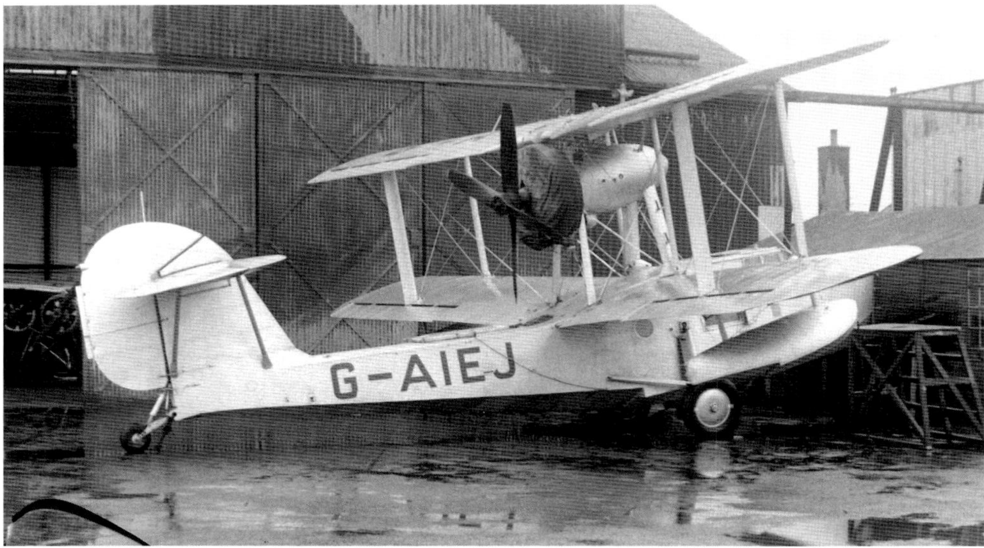

Eighteen Vickers-Supermarine Walrus amphibians were earmarked for British registry during 1946–50, of which a third never flew again. Wooden-hulled Walrus II G-AIEJ, powered by a 775 hp Bristol Pegasus VI, was built by Saunders-Roe at East Cowes in 1943 for the Admiralty as HD903, but was transferred to the RAF in January 1945. After spending most of its time at various MUs, the Walrus was sold and registered G-AIEJ to Western Airways in April 1946, based at Western-super-Mare. It was used for occasional film work and is seen at Weston on 4 July where it was eventually scrapped in December 1948.

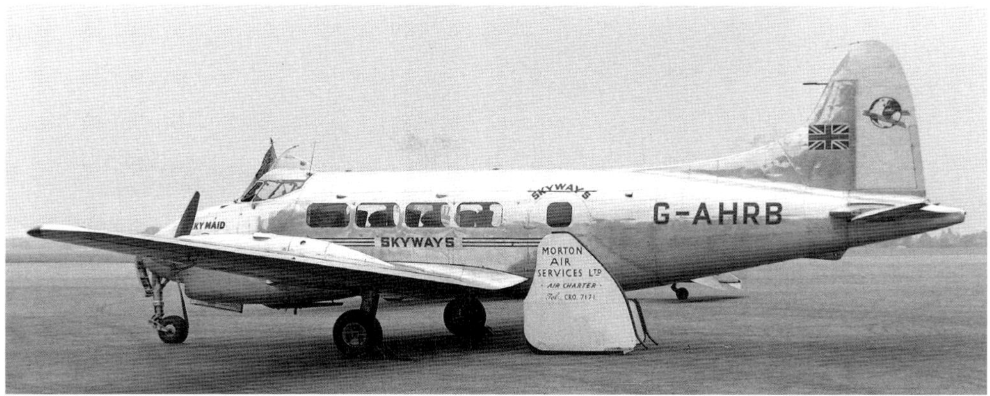

Seen at Croydon on 10 July is the much-travelled fifth production D.H. 104 Dove G-AHRB, first registered in October 1946, sold to Skyways Ltd and named *Sky Maid*. During 1949-50 'RB was in India on charter to the United Kingdom High Commission before being sold to West African Airways Corporation as VR-NAJ and based at Lagos, Nigeria. Restored to the UK register in March 1957, it was soon off on its travels again, arriving in the Cape Verde Islands at the end of the year where it became CR-CAD. Operated by Aero Club de Cabo, the Dove came to grief on 7 September 1961 when the undercarriage collapsed on landing.

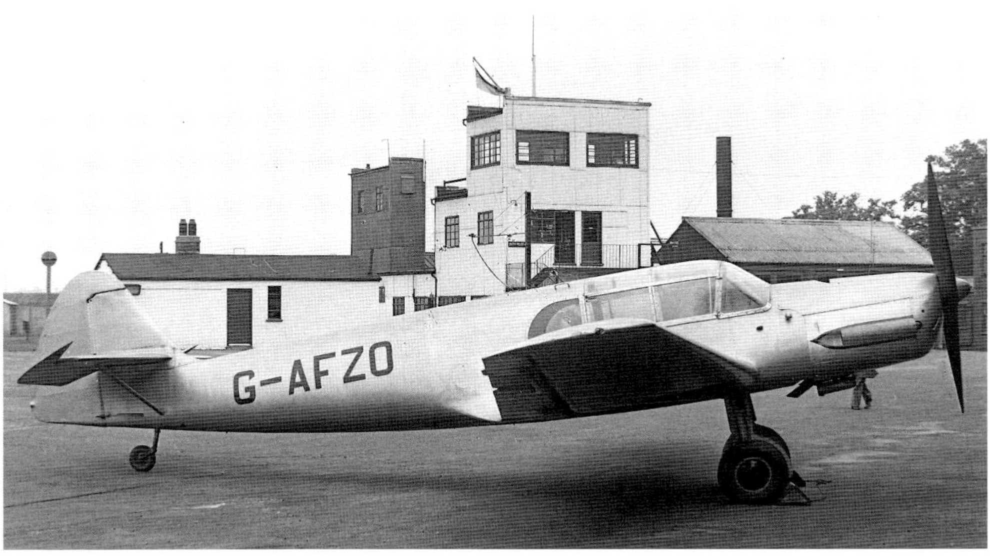

Not many genuine products of the German Messerschmitt company have appeared on the British civil register, but one example was Bf 108-1 Taifun G-AFZO, pictured at Fairoaks on 10 July. 'ZO was imported into the UK in 1939 as D-IDBT and was operated by H. J. Aldington of A.F.N Ltd (makers of Frazer Nash cars) before it was impressed in September 1941 and was marked ES995, a serial number already allocated to a Wellington Ic. It flitted between RAF Northolt and RAF Andover station flights painted in a high gloss blue paint scheme. After the war it was re-registered in September 1946 to Aldington, but in April 1950 it was flown to Switzerland where it became HB-ESL. After various changes of ownership there and elsewhere it is currently owned and flown by the Messerschmitt Foundation registered D-ESBH.

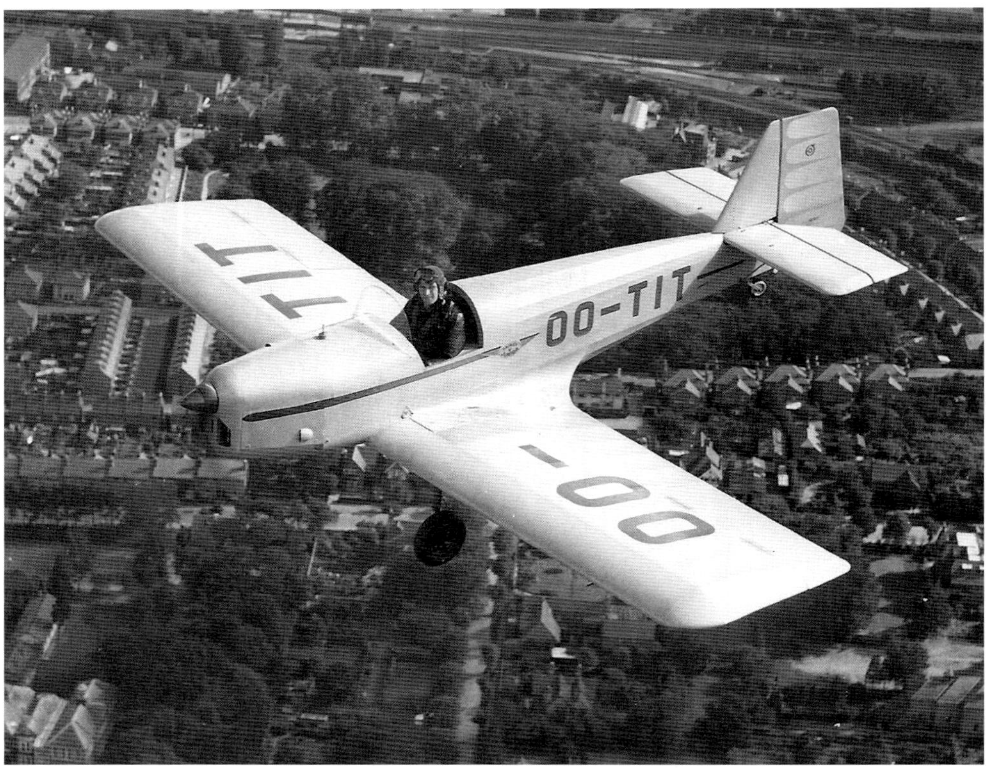

Fairey Aviation's chief test pilot, Peter Twiss (1921–2011), positions Fairey Junior OO-TIT for E. J. Riding's camera over Berkshire on 26 August. Based at White Waltham, this was the second Junior to be built by Fairey Aviation's Belgian subsidiary, Avions Fairey S.A. at Gosselies. It was badly damaged following a heavy landing shortly after this photograph was taken. A second example, OO-ULA, was acquired by Fairey Aviation and registered G-AMVP in March 1953. The little ultra-light did not catch on and no further examples were completed.

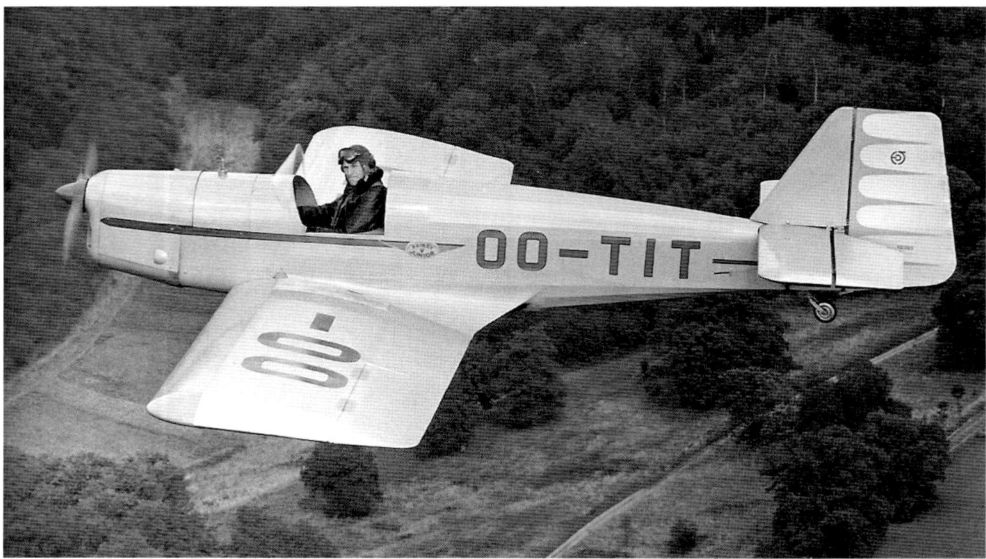

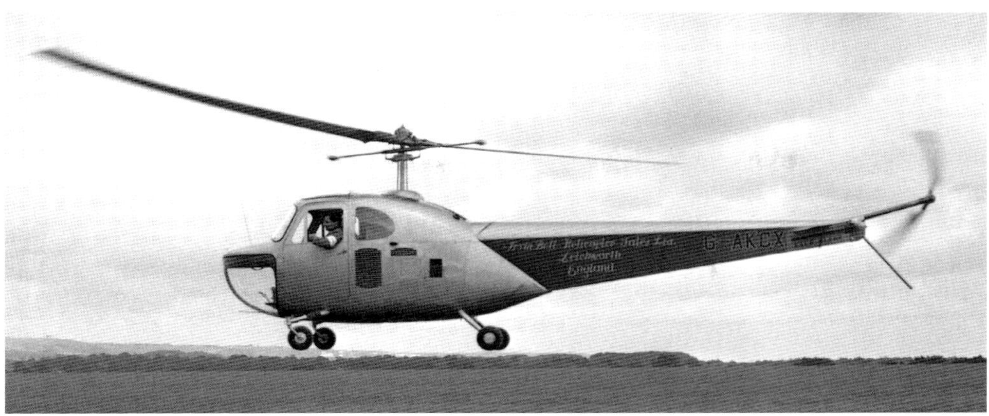

At the end of September 1947 this two-seat Bell Model 47B was flown across the Channel by Capt. A. B. Youell of Irvin-Bell Helicopter Sales Ltd on the first stage of a European sales demonstration tour. This was believed to be the first Channel flight made by a helicopter. G-AKCX, formerly NC1296, is seen loitering at Lympne on 28 August whilst attending the Folkestone Aero Trophy meeting. Imported into the UK in 1947, 'CX was damaged beyond repair at Heathfield, near Prestwick, in February 1949.

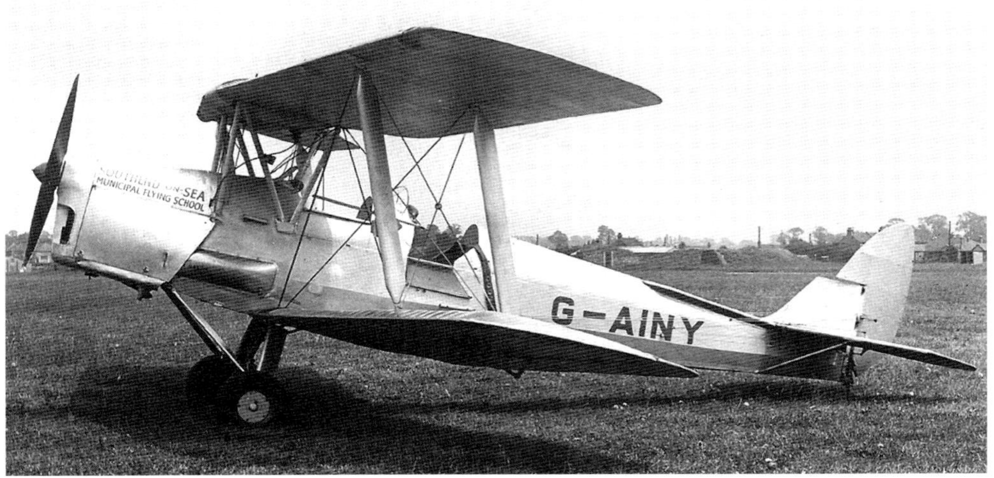

D.H. 82A Tiger Moth G-AINY at Southend on 25 August prior to being flown to the Lympne International Air Races by A. J. Jackson with E.J.R. as passenger. 'NY belonged to Southend-on-Sea Municipal Airport at the time and was sold in New Zealand as ZK-AYC in February 1952.

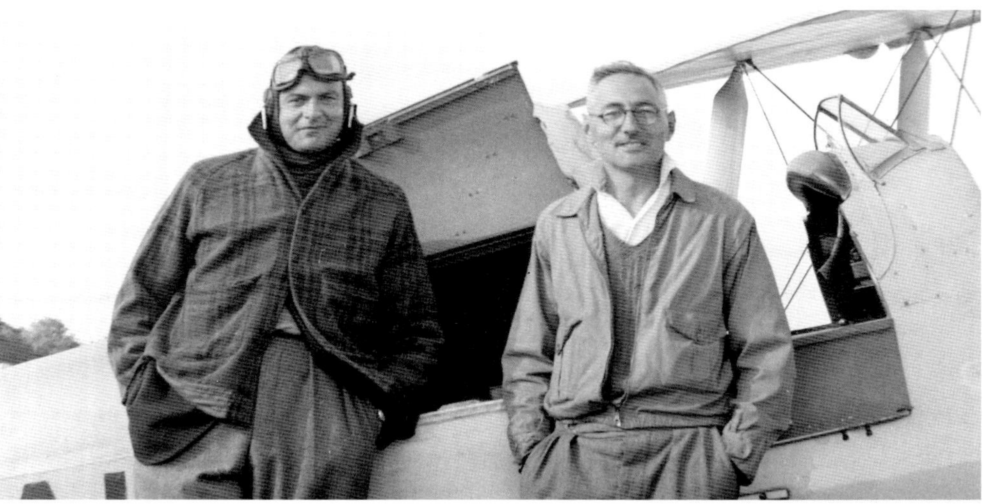

E.J.R. and A. J. Jackson have just arrived at Lympne in Southend-based D.H. 82A Tiger Moth G-AINY on 25 August to report on the Lympne International Air Races for *The Light Plane* magazine. The flights from Southend to Lympne and back took 35 minutes each way.

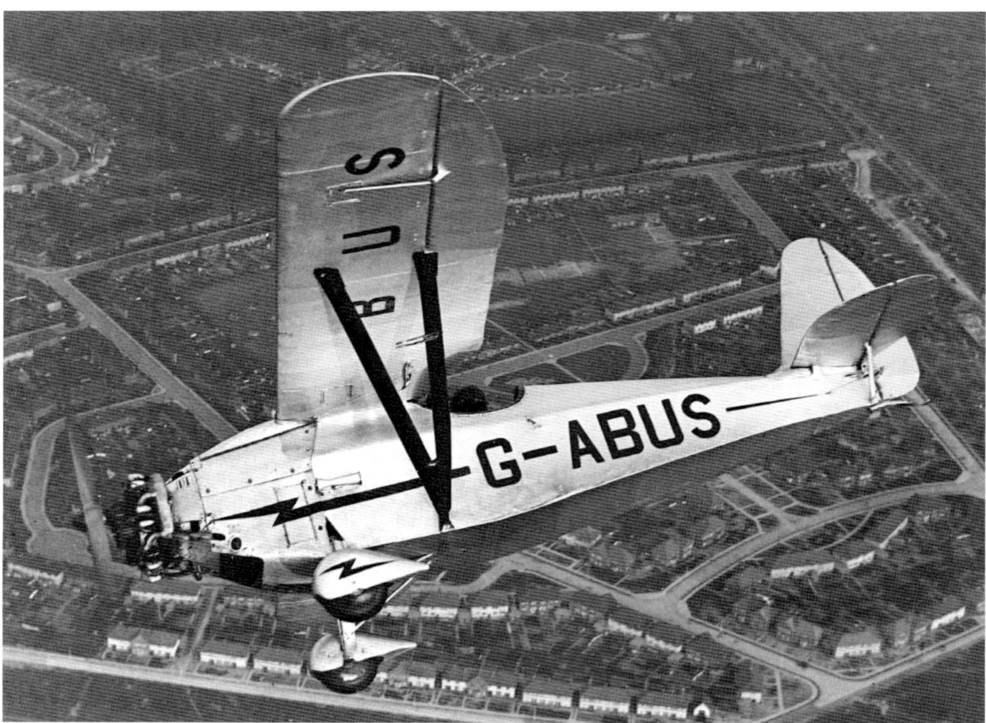

Stanley Orton Bradshaw (S.O.B) flying Comper C.L.A. 7 Swift G-ABUS from its Elstree base over Watford on 29 August. Built at Hooton Park in 1932 and first operated by Shell Mex & BP Ltd, 'US is owned currently by Roger Bailey and has been undergoing long-term restoration since the 1970s. During the immediate post-war period the Swift was painted all black and was a regular race competitor in the hands of *Throttle Benders* Tony Cole and David Ogilvy.

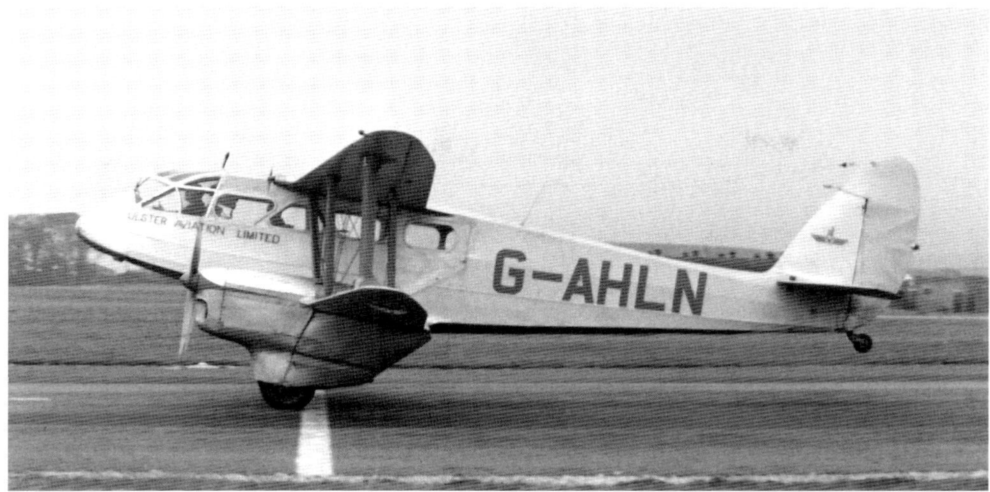

Tail up, Ulster Aviation's D.H. 89A Dragon Rapide G-AHLN takes-off from Ronaldsway Airport, Isle of Man, on 8 September. Built as a Dominie I by Brush Coachworks at Loughborough in 1944, NF883 flew with the ATA before transferring to No. 1680 Flight at Prestwick. Post-war, 'LN was with Scottish Airways and then BEA before being acquired by Ulster Aviation in April 1948. It then passed to North West Airlines, also based at Ronaldsway. In April 1953 the Rapide was sold in France as F-GBOQ, but is believed to have crashed at Toussus three months later.

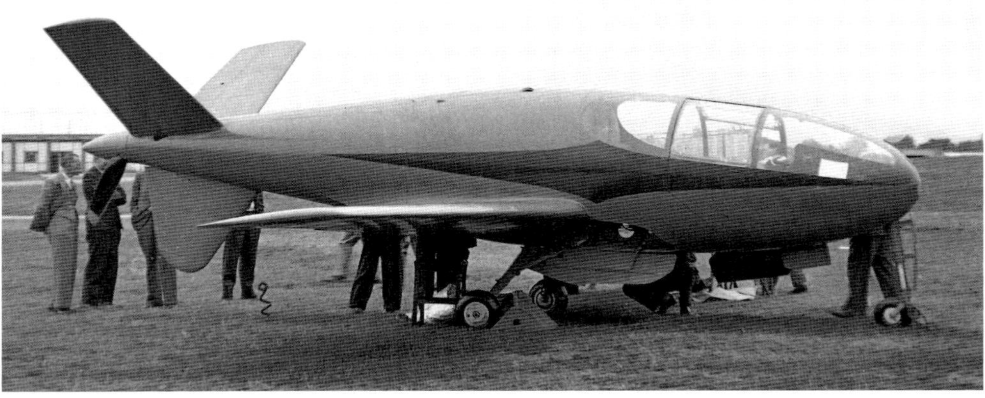

Resembling an over-sized Bede BD-5 of the 1970s, the fanciful and futuristic four-seat Planet Satellite G-ALOI, constructed of magnesium alloy and powered by a mid-fuselage mounted 250 hp D.H. Gipsy Queen 32, was a step too far too soon. Built at Croydon in 1948 and registered in April the following year, it is seen unmarked at the SBAC show at Farnborough on 9 September, where it attracted much interest. Unfortunately, despite repeated attempts to take-off, the Satellite refused to get airborne when tested at Blackbushe by Grp Capt. H. J. Wilson, losing its undercarriage in the process. It was melted down in 1958.

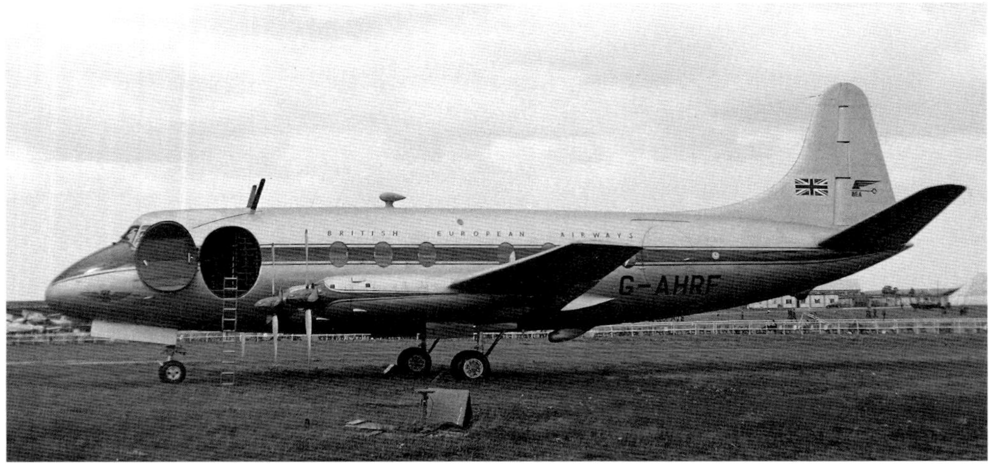

When the prototype Vickers Viscount made its first flight from Wisley on 16 July 1948 one wonders if anyone present had any inkling of the success story George Edwards' masterpiece would be. Powered by four Rolls-Royce Dart turboprops and designed initially to carry 24 passengers in pressurised comfort, the prototype was a sensation at the 1948 SBAC show at Farnborough, where it is seen on 9 September. G-AHRF flew trials as VX211 and then operated for a short period with BEA. Owned by Vickers-Armstrongs (Aircraft) Ltd when written-off whilst landing in the Sahara Desert at Khartoum, Sudan, on 27 August 1952, it is reputedly buried there!

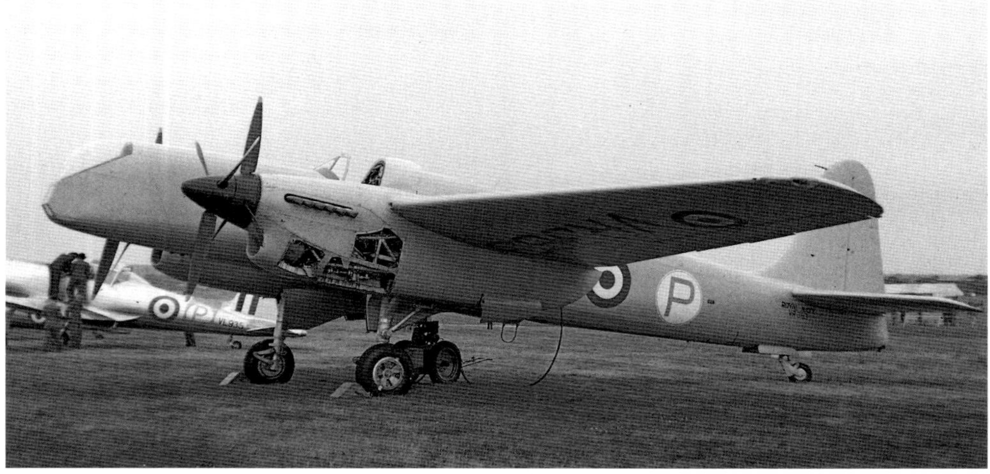

The Short Sturgeon T.T.2 was an undeniably ugly yet purposeful brute of an aeroplane that had the unglamorous task of naval target tower amongst its duties. Main differences from earlier Sturgeons were the elongated nose and deepened fuselage to allow a second crew member to crawl beneath the pilot's seat from one station to another to take photographs. In July 1951 VR363 was used to aero tow the experimental Short SB.1 tailless glider, built to test the isoclinic wing concept.

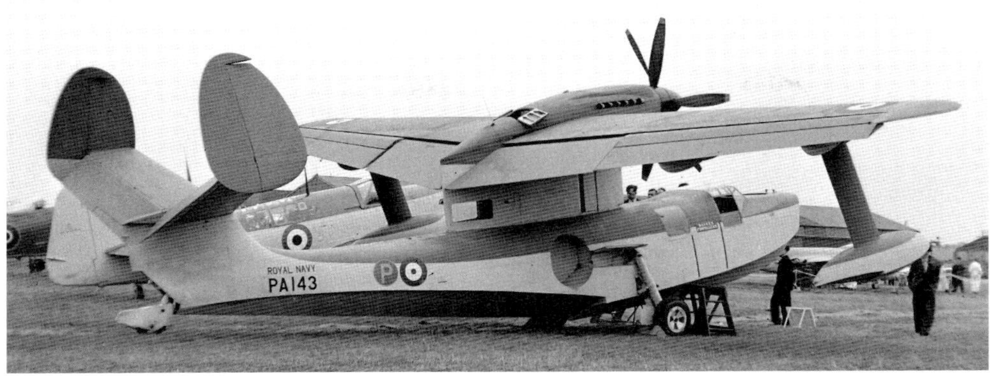

Another aircraft that only just made it to the 1948 SBAC show in September was the Supermarine Seagull ASR.I Seagull, first flown on 14 July by Mike Lithgow and demonstrated by him at Farnborough. Powered by a single 1,815 hp Rolls-Royce Griffon 29, the Seagull could get airborne from a standing start in 300 yards, making it suitable for deck operation. Trials were carried out on *Ark Royal* it was discovered that the Seagull could be flown as slow as 35 mph. Two prototypes were built, but the type was not put into production and both were scrapped in 1952, the last Supermarine flying boat.

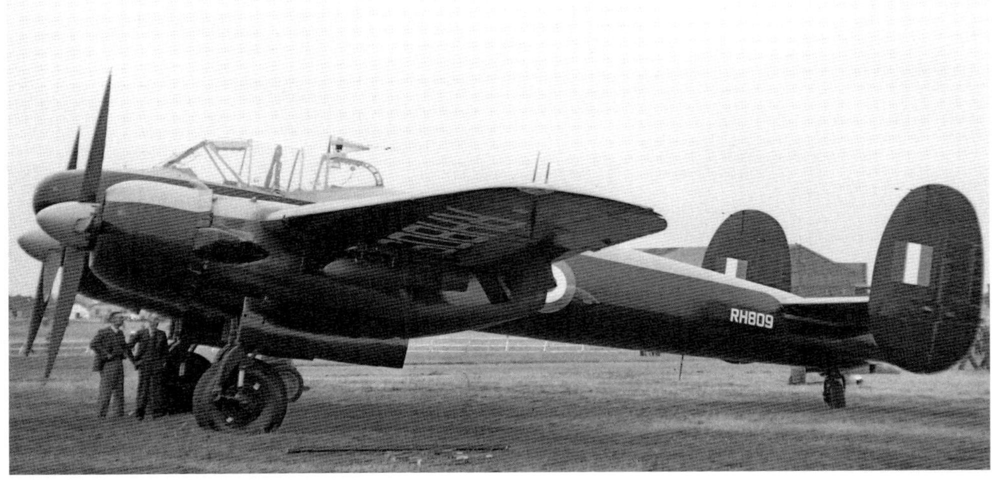

Another big brute of an aeroplane was the Bristol Brigand, this production B Mk 1 appearing at the 1948 Farnborough show carrying four 500 lb bombs, one beneath each wing and two under the forward fuselage. Brigand RH809 was part of a batch of 80 built by Bristol at Filton during 1946–49. It was delivered to No. 84 Squadron at Tengah, Malaya, but was damaged beyond repair when it lost a bomb whilst taking-off in November 1950.

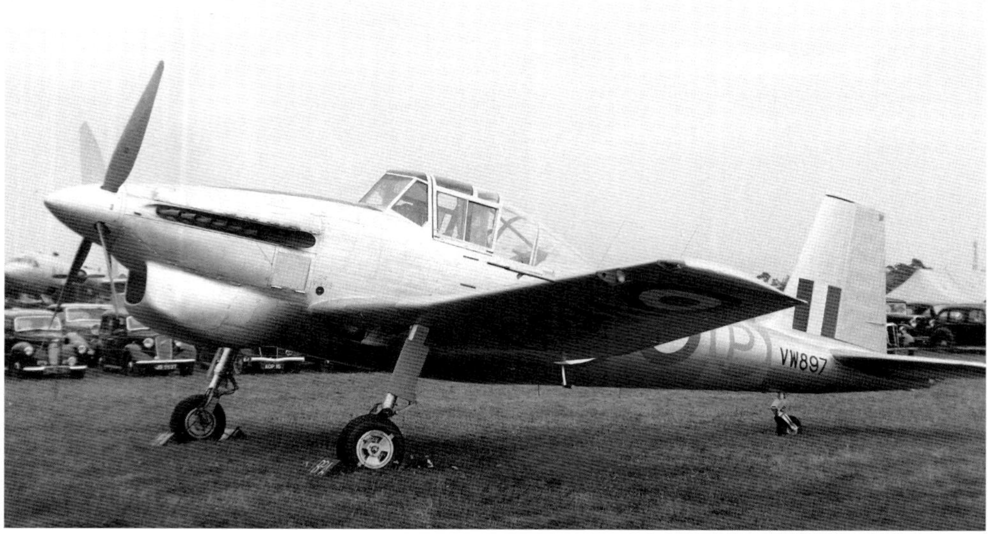

Two versions of the two-seat Boulton Paul Balliol advanced trainer were displayed at the 1948 Farnborough show. Seen here is T.2 prototype VW897, powered by a Rolls-Royce Merlin 35, having been flown a few weeks before on 10 August from Pendeford. Whilst on test on 3 February 1949 the windscreen disintegrated in a 400 mph dive, the Balliol crashing at Covern, near Wolverhampton, killing both crew. Large contracts were placed for the Balliol, but with the prospect of jet trainers on the horizon orders were cut back, production of the T.2 totalling 183.

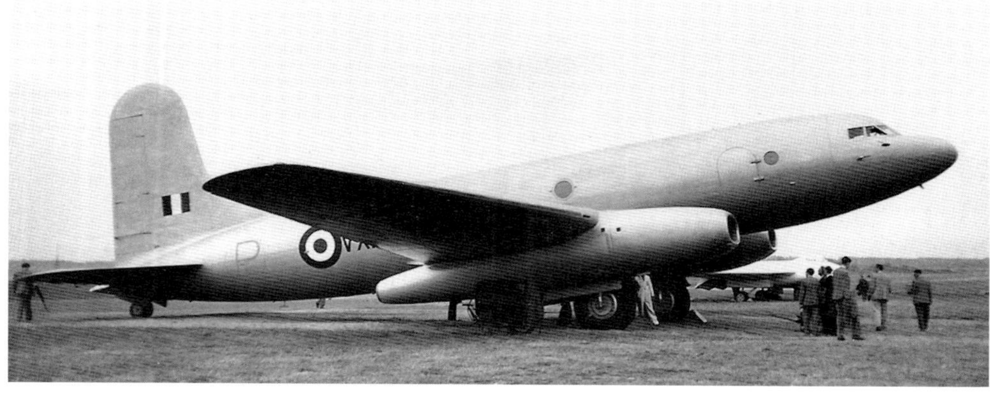

The second Avro Tudor 1 prototype G-AGST, initially TT181, went through many development stages during its short life. It was rebuilt as a Tudor 4, powered by four 1,770 hp Rolls-Royce Merlin 621s and later still fitted with four 5,000 lb Rolls-Royce Nene 4 turbojets in paired, semi-elliptical nacelles, to become the Tudor 8. Re-numbered VX195, it appeared at the SBAC Farnborough show having flown for the first time only the day before the start on 6 September; the first civil transport in the world to fly with four jet engines. Designed as part of a programme of research and development into high-altitude operation of civil aircraft, the Tudor 8 had a maximum speed 385 mph, some 125 mph faster than the original airframe! Its work done VX195 was scrapped at Farnborough in 1951.

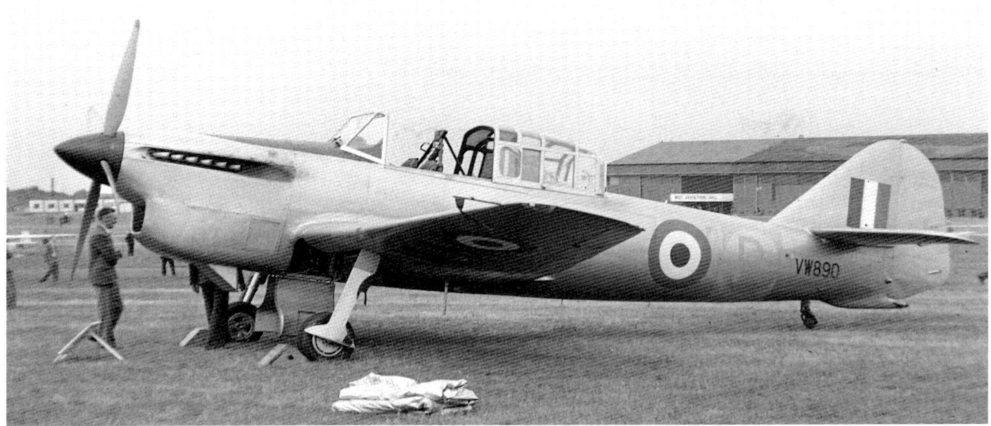

The Avro 701 Athena T.1, like the Boulton Paul Balliol, to which it bore an uncanny resemblance, was designed as a three-seat advanced trainer replacement for the Percival Prentice, The two Athena T.1 prototypes were powered respectively by Armstrong Siddeley Mamba and Rolls-Royce Dart turboprops, but as the Rolls-Royce Merlin 35 was in plentiful supply the latter was chosen instead. The greater weight of the Merlin necessitated moving the Athena's wings forward 27 inches. Two prototypes were built—VW890 and VW892. The first of them flew on 1 August 1948, in time to attend the 1948 Farnborough show where it is seen. Seventeen Athenas were delivered to the RAF, replacing the Harvard at the RAF Flying College at Manby.

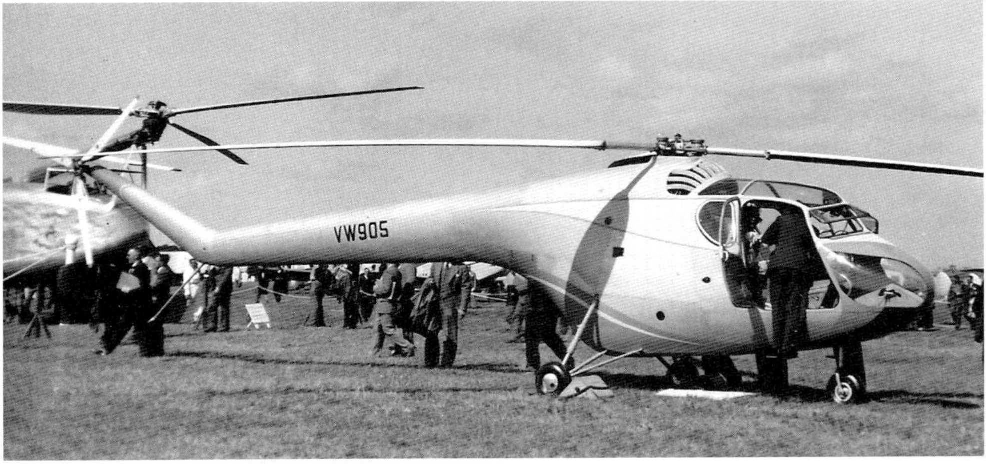

The prototype Bristol Type 171 Sycamore Mk 2 VW905 was shown statically at the 1948 Farnborough show, the Alvis Leonides-engined helicopter not flying until 3 September 1949. During early trials at Filton the rotor disintegrated in spectacular fashion, causing a delay in flight test. The sole Sycamore Mk 2, owned by the Ministry of Supply, featured two doors and accommodated two passengers on the rear seat. Although allocated the civil marks G-AJGU, the helicopter never carried them. Flight testing continued at RAE Bedford and Boscombe Down until relegation to ground testing and finally scrapping at Farnborough in December 1962.

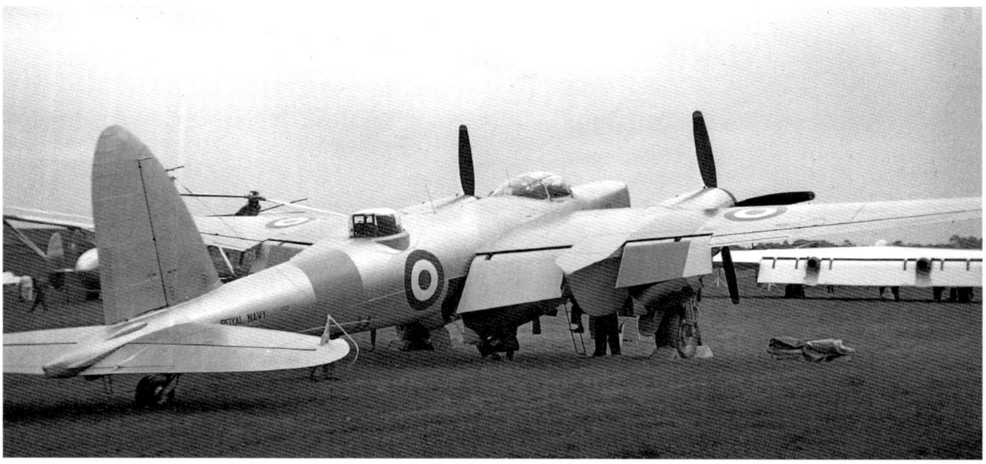

The ultimate example of the beautiful Mosquito, its perfect lines marred by a pimple on its back and a nose job! Having flown in various forms as a fighter, bomber and photo reconnaissance aircraft the Mossie was relegated finally to target towing work. PF606 was a D.H. 98 Mosquito T.T. Mk 39 shore-based naval target tug converted from a standard B Mk XVI by General Aircraft Ltd which gave it the type number G.A.L. 59. Built by Percival Aircraft at Luton in 1945, PF606 had major surgery, carried out at General Aircraft Hanworth, involving lengthening of the detachable nose and the installation of an electric winch in the bomb bay. From the jettisonable dorsal observation cupola the winch operator could keep an eye on the 16 or 32 ft target as it was being fired upon. Around 30 T.T. 39s were converted by General Aircraft.

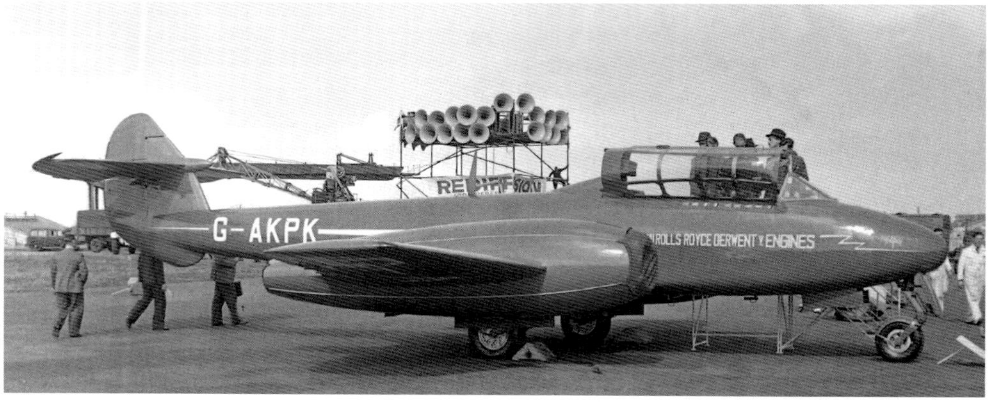

A popular attraction at the 1948 SBAC Farnborough was the carmine painted and ivory-lettered Gloster Meteor T. Mk 7 G-AKPK, powered by two Rolls-Royce Derwent 5 engines. Most of 'PK had flown previously as Meteor 4 G-AIDC as it utilised the former sales demonstrator's rear fuselage, wings and tail unit. First flown in March 1948, 'PK made a sales tour of France, Italy and Turkey in May and shortly after the SBAC show dashed from Biggin Hill to Orly, Paris, in 27.50 minutes. In November that year the T.7 was sold to the Royal Netherlands Air Force as I-1. The air forces of Belgium, Egypt, Syria, Denmark, Brazil, France, Israel and Sweden all ordered the Meteor T.7.

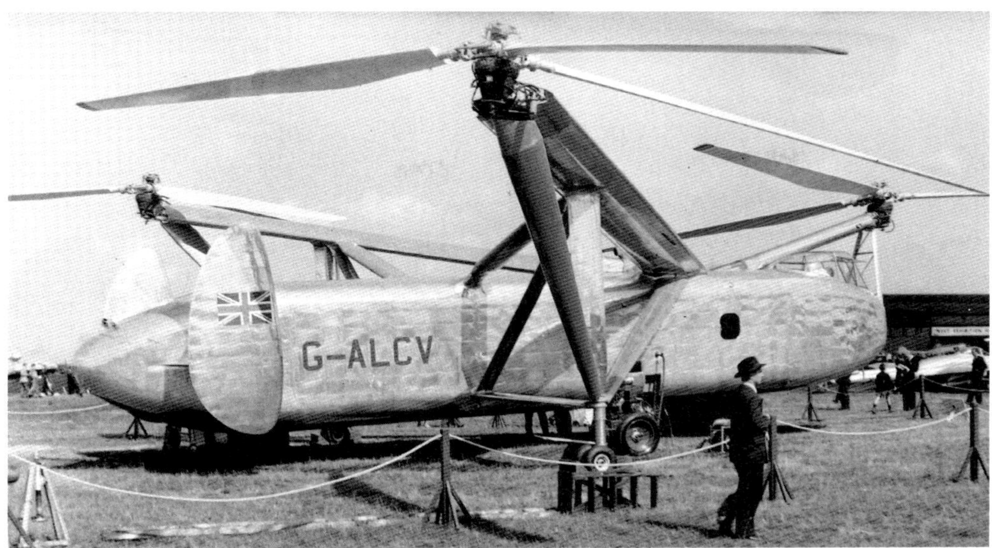

The 1948 SBAC Farnborough show played host to one of the weirdest creations in aviation, namely the Cierva W. 11 Air Horse, an experimental 24-seat or freight helicopter powered by a *single* 1,620 hp Rolls-Royce Merlin 24 engine driving three sets of rotors. Two examples were built in 1948 at Eastleigh by the Cierva Autogiro Company Ltd and the first, G-ALCV, was taken by road to the show. It was not until December 12 that year that Alan Marsh (1901–49) flew the monster, by then bearing the RAF serial VZ724. Tragically, Marsh and his crew were killed in the same machine on 13 June 1949, rotor hub fatigue failure causing the crash. For a while the Air Horse held the record for the greatest helicopter lift achieved—an all-up weight of 40,000 lb. The second Air Horse, G-ALCW/WA555, was flown and then put into storage.

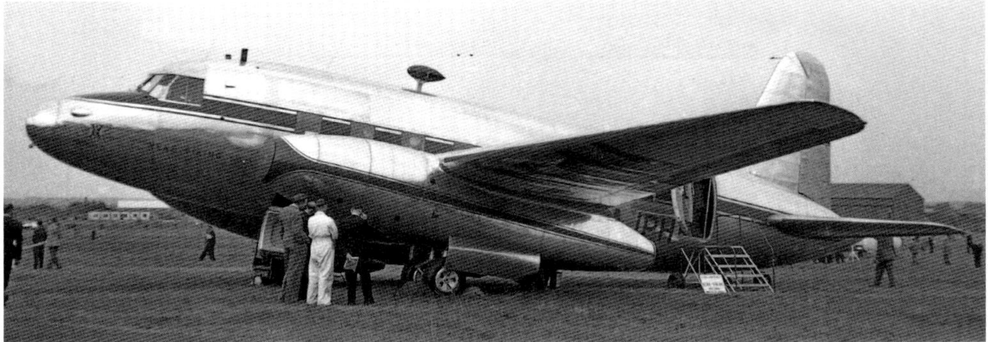

A Vickers Viking with a cruising speed of 393 mph, and a maximum speed of 457 mph? Surely not! In 1948 Vickers-Armstrongs Ltd took a standard Viking airframe from the production line and installed two 5,000 lb st Rolls-Royce Nene 1 turbojets, beefed up the tailplane and added metal-clad elevators. Registered G-AJPH/VX856 to the Ministry of Supply (MoS), the Nene Viking was first flown at Wisley by J. 'Mutt' Summers on 6 April 1948, becoming in the process Britain's first jet transport. On 25 July, the 39th anniversary of Louis Bleriot's cross-Channel flight, Summers flew 'PH from Heathrow to Villacoublay, Paris, in 34 minutes. After the MoS had completed its work the aircraft was converted to a standard Hercules piston-engined Viking 1B freighter by Eagle Aircraft Services in 1954, later upgraded to a 3B and used for trooping as XJ804. In October 1961 'PH was withdrawn from use and was dismantled for spares at Blackbushe.

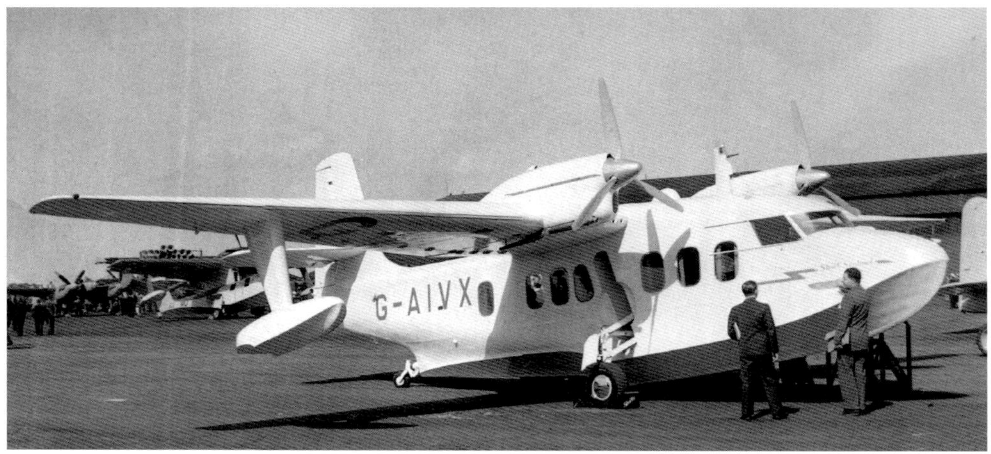

The prototype Short S.A. 6 Sealand amphibian pictured at the SBAC Farnborough show on 9 September. Built at Belfast and registered to Short Bros and Harland Ltd, G-AIVX was flown on 22 January 1948 from Belfast Lough, the first of a production batch of 24 aircraft. It was powered by two 345 hp D.H. Gipsy Queen 70-2 engines and had a cruising speed of 170 mph. After exhibition at the 1952 Farnborough show and the Paris Air Show the following year, 'VX was scrapped at Belfast in April 1954.

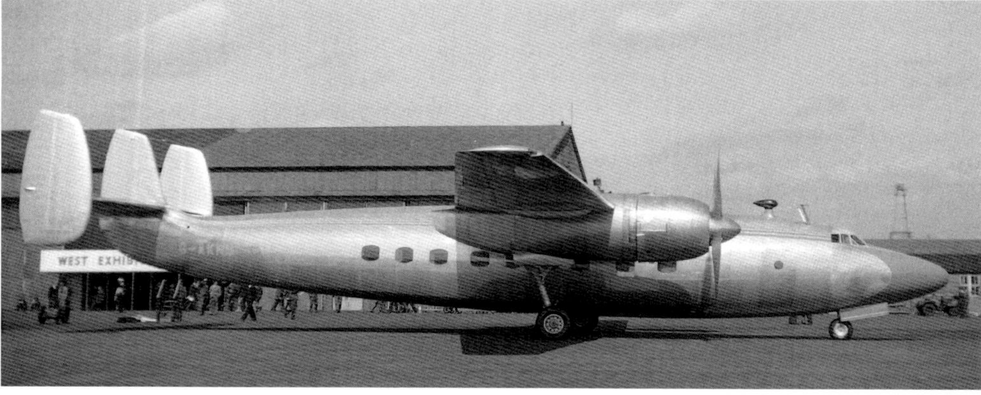

Making its first flight on 26 August 1948, the second prototype Airspeed A.S. 57 Ambassador, G-AKRD, just made it in time to appear at the 1948 SBAC Farnborough show. Fitted with two Bristol Centaurus 630 engines and featuring a fully pressurized fuselage, it was followed by 20 production aircraft for BEA's Elizabethan Class with more powerful 2,625 hp Centaurus 631 engines. BEA's first scheduled Ambassador service to Paris was flown on 13 March 1952 and the type remained in service with the airline until 1958. After trials with the Ministry of Aircraft Production 'RD joined the BEA fleet in 1951 and was named *Golden Lion*. In 1953 it became a test bed for the Bristol Proteus 705 turboprop and in August 1958 flew from Hucknall as a test bed for the Rolls-Royce Tyne, for which it bore Class B markings G-37-3. Finally, in 1961, the Ambassador swapped engines yet again, fitted with a Dart 201P and 525 and becoming known as the Ambassador P. Special. It was scrapped at Hucknall in October 1969.

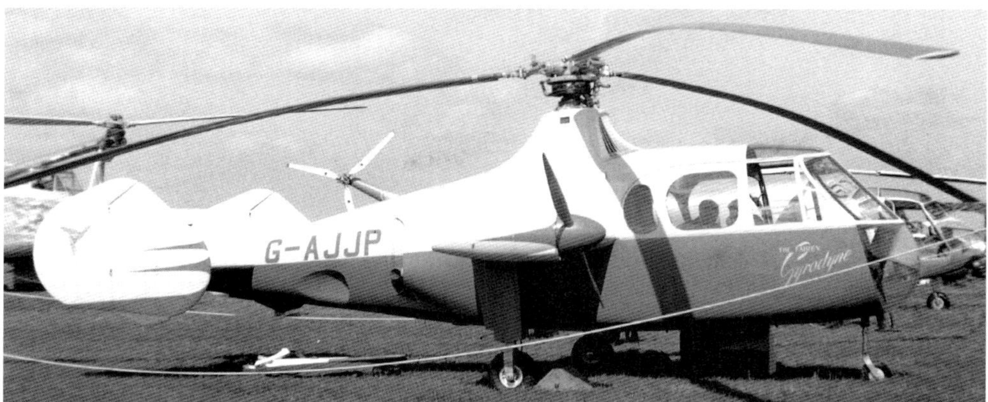

Above: G-AJJP, the second Fairey Gyrodyne, seen here at the 1948 SBAC Farnborough show, differed from the prototype only in having better interior furnishing. After the prototype crashed through rotor hub failure in April 1949 'JP was grounded, to re-appear in a different form towards the end of 1953. The main difference was the installation of fuel-burning pressure-jet units at the tips of the rotor blades. Re-named the Jet Gyrodyne and originally bearing the serial number XD759, later changed to XJ389, the four-seat helicopter appeared again at the 1955 Farnborough show. Underpowered and unable to remain airborne for more than 15 minutes, the Jet Gyrodyne nevertheless paved the way for the Fairey Rotodyne, first flown in November 1957. After retirement XJ389 was acquired by the RAF Museum but can be seen currently at the Museum of Berkshire Aviation at Woodley, Reading.

Below: Better known for the design and production of sailplanes, Elliotts of Newbury Ltd ventured into the potentially lucrative light plane market by building a wooden four-seater designed by Aviation and Engineering Projects Ltd of Feltham. The Newbury A.P.4 Eon, registered G-AKBC, was first flown from Welford near Newbury in August 1947. Its 100 hp Blackburn Cirrus Minor II delivered insufficient power so a 145 hp D.H. Gipsy Major 10 was substituted. With this and some minor other modifications the aircraft was redesignated Eon 2. 'BC is seen flying from Welford on 23 September 1948. Sadly, this promising aircraft was written off following a pilotless take-off from Lympne with a glider in tow on 14 April 1950. Fortunately, the pilot of the glider realised what was happening and vacated his mount pronto. Plans to put the Eon into limited production came to nothing and the company concentrated on sailplane production, although it produced a design study for an all-metal trainer to Air Ministry Specification T.16/48, eventually won by the Hunting Percival Provost.

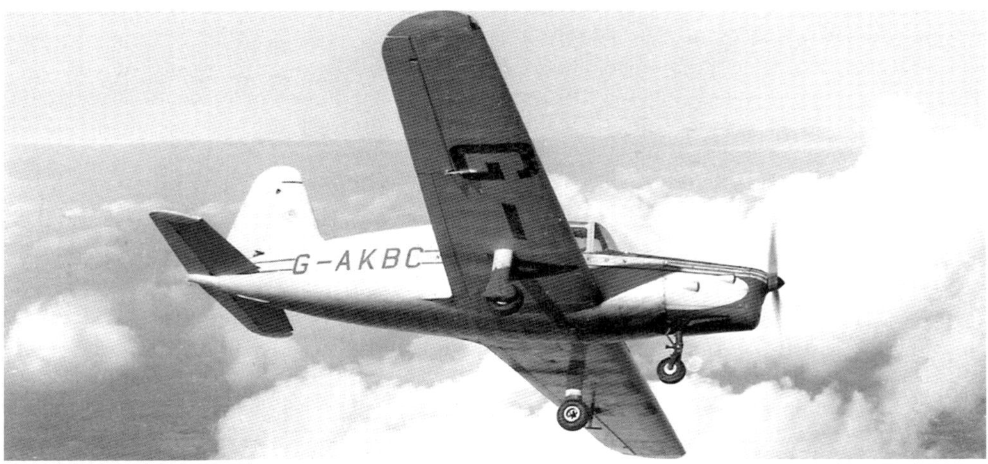

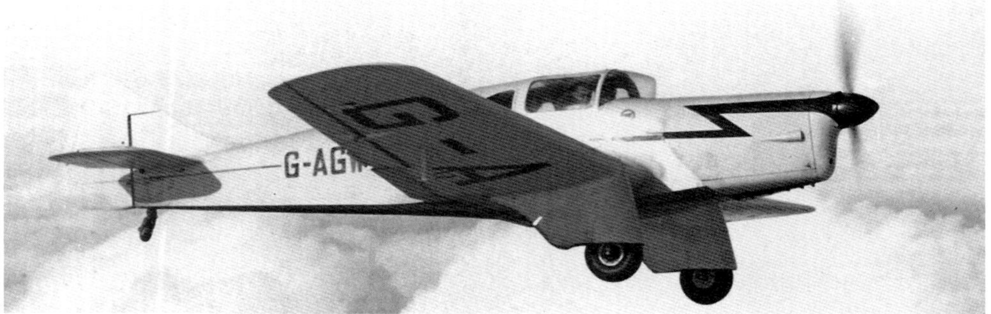

Hybrid Miles M.7A Nighthawk G-AGWT comprised a Nighthawk fuselage mated with Mohawk wings was assembled in 1940 and first flew in the Class B markings U5, later U-0225. During the war the Nighthawk flew as the company's communications aircraft and in December 1945 was registered to Miles Aircraft before being sold to test pilot Hugh Kendall (Raceways Ltd) who used it for flying jockeys to race meetings. This air-to-air view of 'WT, flown by Ian Forbes, was taken from Miles M.14A Hawk Trainer G-AIYD near Redhill on 3 October. The Nighthawk was raced extensively until June 1954 when it was sold in Kenya, becoming VP-KMM, but returned to the UK as VR-TCM in August 1961. During January 1963 'WT was on its travels again, bound for Singapore, but got no further than Lignane, near Aix-en-Provence, where it was reportedly left to rot.

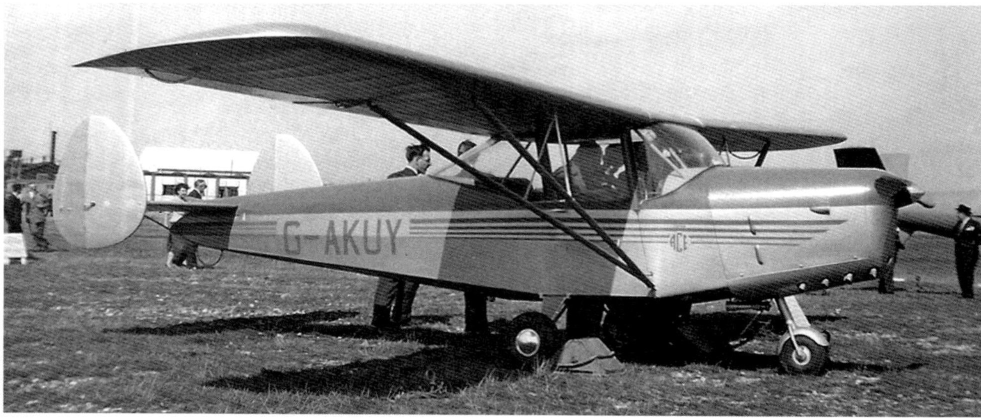

Towards the end of the 1940s the Chrislea Aircraft Company Ltd put into production at Exeter Airport a promising four-seat, twin-finned light plane with a tricycle undercarriage. In appearance it was not unlike that of a superannuated Auster. It was initially well received by private owners and flying clubs, but its revolutionary control system was to prove its ultimate undoing. Neither control column nor rudder bar was installed. Instead, a control wheel actuated ailerons, elevators and rudder— which sounds fine on paper. But instead of pushing and pulling to descend or climb, the wheel had to be moved up or down. Similarly, it had to be moved sideways for directional control. Experienced pilots found this method of control unnatural, particularly when a sudden movement was required. Consequently, pushing or pulling the wheel induced nothing but panic. Cynics referred to the aircraft as the 'Grizzly Ace'. Chrislea produced around 40 C.H. 3 Ace and Super Ace models. Seen at the 1948 SBAC show at Farnborough in September is G-AKUY, registered just in time to make an appearance. Before the end of the month this Ace had been sold in Argentina and registered LV-XAX, later changed to LV-RXV. It survived ten years before being withdrawn from use in October 1958. Had the Chrislea Ace been fitted with conventional controls from the start, and the financial climate been healthier, there is no doubt that the hundreds of orders received would have turned into solid sales.

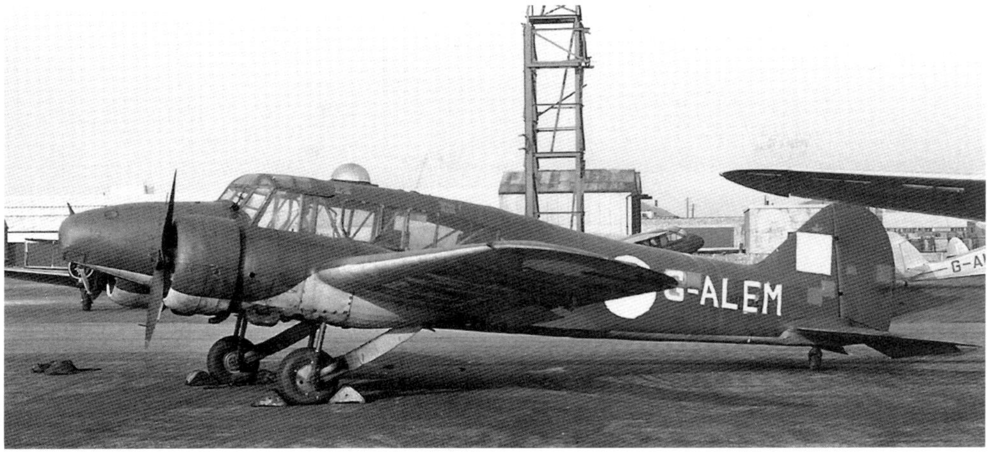

Between July 1943 and January 1944 A.V. Roe at Yeadon produced a batch of 800 Anson Is, of which MG756 was one. Delivered to No. 8 (Observers) Advanced Flying Unit at RAF Mona, a relief landing ground for RAF Valley, it was later assigned to No. 13 Operational Training Unit at RAF Bicester. The Anson was sold in October 1948 and is seen at Croydon on 6 November with its RAF marks whitewashed out and the registration G-ALEM applied temporarily after acquisition by Rollason Aircraft and Engines Ltd. Like so many of its brethren 'EM never made Civvy Street and was scrapped in 1949.

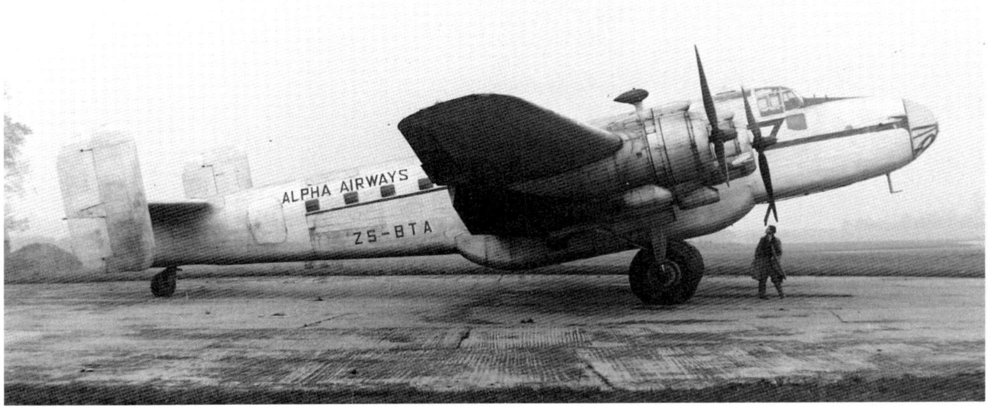

H.P. 70 Halifax ZS-BTA, previously G-AGZP (see p. ??) on 12 November at Bovingdon in the livery of Alpha Airways (Pty) Ltd, a subsidiary of LAMS. In August 1949 the Halifax was restored to the British register as 'ZP and operated by the Lancashire Aircraft Corporation Ltd from Bovingdon where it was scrapped in 1953.

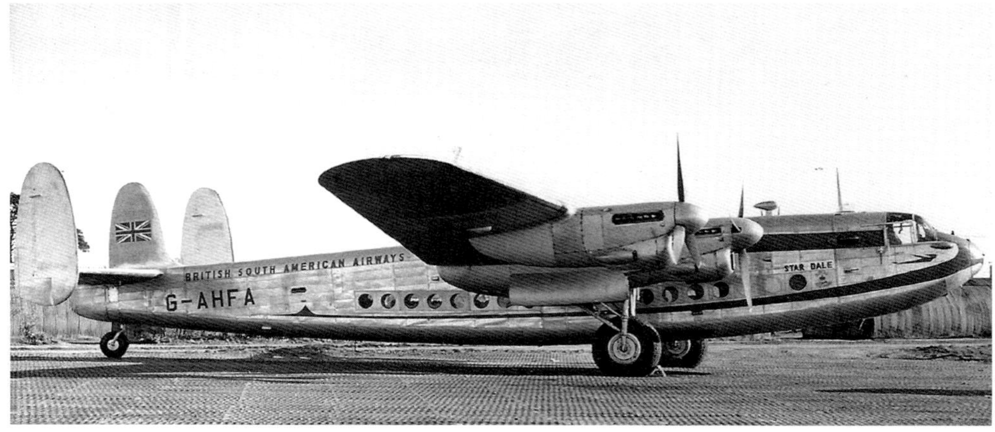

Avro 685 York G-AHFA *Star Dale,* seen at Heathrow on 26 November, was delivered new to British South American Airways, having been registered in June 1946. It was transferred to BOAC in September 1949, passed to the Lancashire Aircraft Corporation in December 1951 and was then operated by Skyways Ltd on trooping duties as WW504. On 2 February 1953 the York was flying troops from Stansted to Jamaica and during the stage from Lajes Terceira in the Azores, to Gander, Newfoundland, disappeared over the Atlantic after issuing distress signals. No sign of the York, or the 39 souls on board, was ever found.

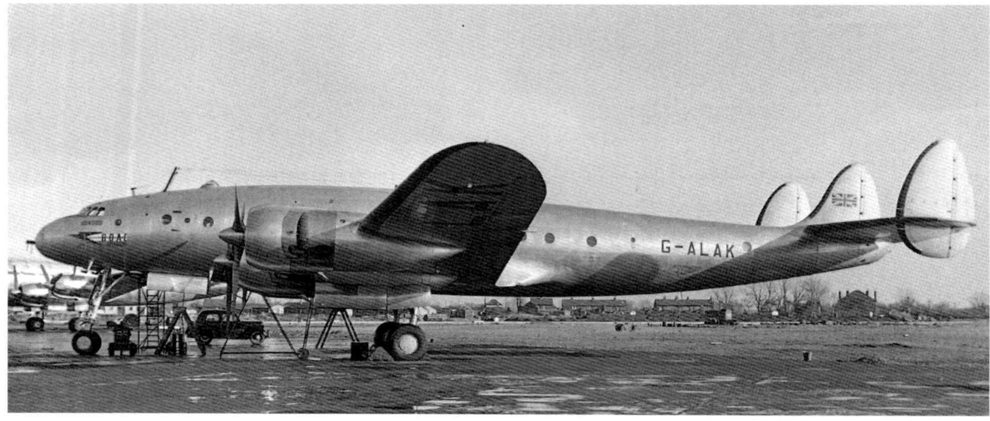

Because of the failure of the Avro Tudor BOAC needed urgently a suitable aeroplane with which to compete with US airlines on trans-Atlantic routes. The short-term solution was acquisition of five military Lockheed C-69s that were modified for BOAC use and designated Model 049E. In July 1946 BOAC began Constellation services to New York, via Shannon and Gander. It also acquired a batch of five Constellation 749As from the Irish airline Aerlínte Éireann the first going into BOAC service in December 1948. One of these was G-ALAK *Brentford,* formerly EI-ACR *St Brendan,* seen at Heathrow on 20 November. 'AK passed to Skyways in June 1959 and then to Euravia in September 1962. After a period with Ace Freighters at Coventry, in January 1968 the ageing Connie was acquired by Trans Bolivian Airways and registered CP-797, later OB-R-899. It was broken up in Peru some time in the 1970s.

5

Wings at Last
(1949–50)

On 16 June with great trepidation, I followed the A5 up to Lichfield in
Piper Cub G-AKAA, forked left at the crossroads and rattled into
Wolverhampton with the petrol gauge showing nowt.

Letter from E. J. Riding to A. J. Jackson in 1949.

The year 1949 began with visits to Northolt, Heathrow and Langley on 9 January
when E.J.R. photographed Vickers Vikings, Avro Lancastrians, Avro Tudors and
Lockheed Constellations. On the following day he dropped into Elstree where
Heath Parasol G-AFZE was being prepared for its first flight proper. The red and
silver ultralight had been built before the war by Robert Parker and tentative hops
achieved at Elstree in September 1948. 'Powered' by a 24 hp Blackburne Tomtit V
twin engine, various homemade propellers had been whittled by Parker, including
a four-blader, all painted red! On this day pilot Colin Debenham achieved one low
circuit at Elstree, but for various reasons the Parasol was refused a Permit to Fly.

News of the disappearance of BSAA's Avro Tudor IV G-AGRE *Star Ariel* with
a crew of seven and 13 passengers during a five-hour flight from Bermuda to
Kingston, Jamaica, on 17 January added to the continuing misfortunes of the
airline. The search for the Tudor was abandoned on the 21st and the Tudor IV
relegated to freight duties as a consequence, subject to certain modifications being
carried out. Undelivered airframes were sold for scrap.

On 24 January E.J.R. drove to Blackburn Aircraft at Brough, climbed into the
right-hand seat of Percival Proctor G-AHVG and took air-to-air photographs and
cine film of test pilot Peter Lawrence flying the massive, business-like Blackburn B-48
VF172, powered by a 2,475 hp, 18-cylinder Bristol Centaurus 59. After lunch and
on the following day E.J.R. had three instructional flights in Blackburn B.2 G-AEBJ.

In March E.J.R., aged 33, knuckled down to taking proper flying lessons at
Elstree in Cub G-AKAA with Wg Cdr O. V. 'Titch' Holmes and David Cotter as
his instructors.

The prototype Avro Shackleton, VW126, was flown for the first time from Woodford on 9 March in the hands of J. H. Orrell and S. E. Esler. A development of the Lincoln bomber, the ultra long-range maritime reconnaissance Shackleton, powered by Rolls-Royce Griffons, was the planned replacement for the Sunderland in Coastal Command.

On 15 March and in near darkness, David Cotter sent E.J.R. off on his first solo in Cub 'KAA from Elstree.

At the end of April BOAC, BEA and BSAA declared losses for the 1948–49 financial year of £7,805,974; £2,763,085 and £1,133,082 respectively, totalling £11,702,141.

The prototype Armstrong Whitworth A.W. 55 Apollo, VX220, made its maiden flight from Baginton, Coventry, on April 10, flown by chief test pilot E. G. Franklin and Flt Lt W. A. Else. The 31-passenger airliner, powered by four Armstrong Siddeley Mamba turboprops, was designed to the same Brabazon Committee specification as the Vickers Viscount.

On 20 April E.J.R. and Stanley Bradshaw (S.O.B) flew to Denham in Auster Autocrat G-AGXT to take air-to-air photographs and cine film of Flt Lt Harry Bilborough flying DW1 Chilton G-AFGH.

The annual Royal Aeronautical Society Garden Party at White Waltham on 8 May highlighted the slower and lighter side of pre-war light aircraft. Jeffrey Quill delighted the crowd as he hopped across the field in a 1909 Bleriot IX and Wg Cdr J. A. Kent did likewise in the 1911 Deperdussin. The flying ended with the ascent of a gas balloon piloted by M. Charles Dolfus, the well-known French aeronaut and historian. When it was realised that the balloon was drifting towards nearby Heathrow a telephone call was made to air traffic control asking if there was any objection to the balloon entering Heathrow airspace. The response was that the balloonists were very welcome, but if alighting would they kindly use Runway 2. At midnight on 11–12 May the Soviet blockade of Berlin was lifted officially, but the airlift, begun in June 1948, continued until October in order to build up stocks of foodstuffs, fuel and other essentials.

A major event in British aviation history was marked on 13 May when the prototype English Electric Canberra, VN799, was flown from Warton by Wg Cdr Roland Beamont. During the 26-minute flight Britain's first jet bomber was taken to 8,000 ft.

Eaton Bray

On 6 June E.J.R. was again at Eaton Bray, supervising the second air display to be held at the small field. Earlier, on 16 May, he had been a passenger in D. H. 89A Dragon Rapide G-AKZH during full load take-offs and landings from the field. The day before, on 5 June, he and Joan Nayler, now Mrs Douglas Russell, had been testing techniques for flour bombing and the dropping of streaming toilet rolls from Fairchild Argus G-AKGW. Later that morning he made a flight around

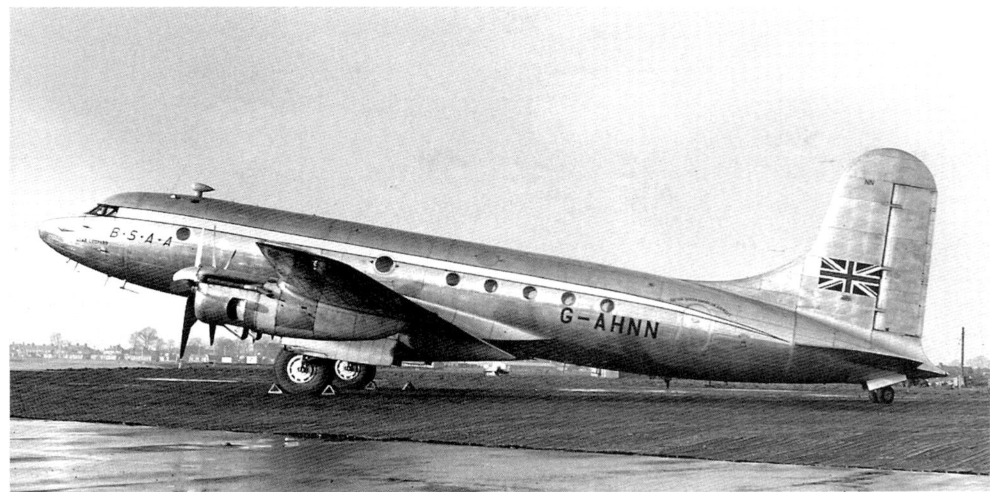

British South American Airways (BSAA) Avro Tudor 4 G-AHNN *Star Leopard* at Heathrow on 8 January 1949. By that time 'NN and sister ships 'NJ, and 'NK, had been relegated to freighting duties (hence the blocked out windows) following the loss of G-AHNP *Star Tiger* on the London-Bermuda service the previous January. After passing to the Ministry of Civil Aviation in November 1951 'NN was reduced to spares at Ringway in 1953 together with 'NJ and 'NK. The Tudor 4 was powered by four 1,770 hp Rolls-Royce Merlin 621s, cruised at 210 mph and in passenger configuration seated 32.

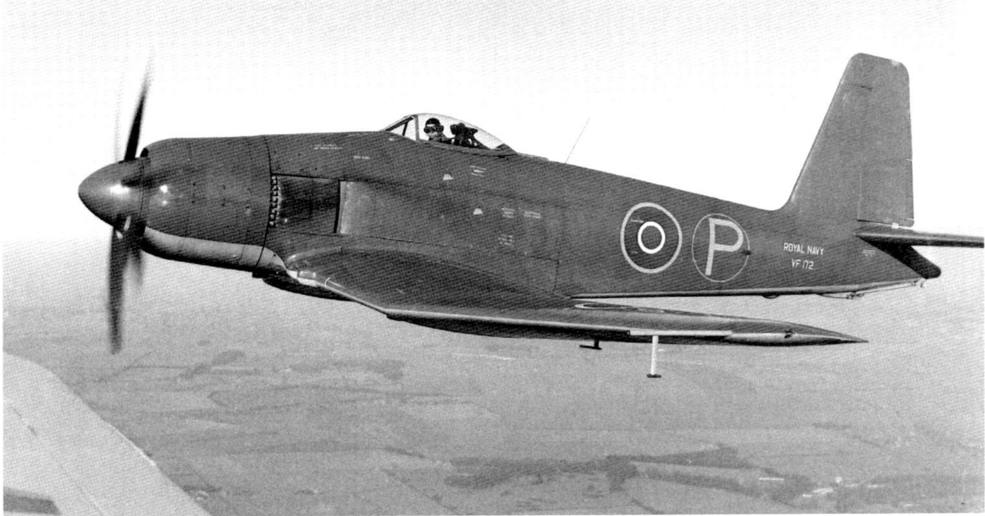

What a brute of an aeroplane! Blackburn Aircraft's chief test pilot, Peter Lawrence, is dwarfed by the bulk of Blackburn B-48 VF172 as he formates on Percival Proctor G-AHVG over Brough on 24 January. Known unofficially as the Firecrest and a derivative of the Firebrand, the B-48 was powered by a 2,450 hp, 18-cylinder Bristol Centaurus 59, giving a maximum speed of 370 mph. The aircraft had power-operated ailerons, Lawrence telling E.J.R. that they were so effective that when flying consecutive rolls he logged 50 per cent of the time as night flying because he usually blacked out when doing so! Two prototypes were produced, the first being RT651, but the type did not go into production and both were scrapped at Brough c.1950.

the local area at very low level to publicise the display in 'Maggie' G-AIUA with C. Nepean Bishop. This performance was repeated in 'Doc' Morrell's Tiger Moth G-AHRV. Eaton Bray was very important in E.J.R's life and the displays were organised in the truest barnstorming tradition of the 1930s in which he had taken part briefly—probably the happiest times of his short life.

Eaton Bray displays had a touch of the Cobham aerial circus days about them and included some turns in the programmes typifying that era. There were aerial paper chases (using toilet rolls), parachute drops and flour bombing of an old Austin Seven driven by a couple of dubious characters. The most popular event of all was announced in the programme as follows:

> When news of our Air Display got around, we were approached by a local sportsman who expressed the opinion that flying was 'kid's stuff' and that he reckoned that he could put up as good a show as any of the highly skilled pilots here today. The organisers of the Sportsdrome have always been to the forefront in the furthering of individual talent, and we have accordingly placed a machine at his disposal. A member of the staff will explain the working of the controls to him, after which he will be left alone to his own devices.

Needless to say, this was a carefully choreographed routine, carried out in a Tiger Moth by farmer Neville Browning, one of the cleverest exponents of crazy flying of the time who had 6,000 flying hours in his logbook. Anyone watching a later item on the programme, a display of aerobatics, would have made the connection between this and the apparent lack of flying skill by the 'novice'! For a quid anyone could have a flight with Neville, loops, rolls and stall turns included if requested.

At the June 1949 event legendary Hawker test pilot Neville Duke flew Hawker Tomtit G-AFTA in a 'dogfight' against a Tiger Moth, flown 'solo' by fellow Hawker test pilot E. S. 'Doc' Morrell. Morrell was 'shot down' and, as the supposed sole occupant, was seen to bail out. The 3,000-strong crowd went into a horrified hush as the 'pilotless' Tiger dived towards the horizon and disappeared. It was, however, under full control and it was Major 'Dumbo' Willans, who had remained hidden during the flight, who bailed out rather than Morrell himself. Willans returned to earth in time for him to give a demonstration of wing walking—proper wing-walking that is, not secured to a rig on the Tiger Moth's centre-section.

Another crowd pleaser was Czech Ladislov Marmol's superb demonstration of gliding, much of it inverted, in a Zlinn glider. In 1947 he had stayed aloft in another Zlinn glider for 33 hours! Later in the afternoon he was towed to Elstree by the Tomtit to give another display. Pleasure flights were given by R. A. Harris in Dragon Rapide G-AKZH, many take-offs being made from the small Eaton Bray field with nine up.

An interesting postscript to all this occurred many years later when the author was editor of *Aeroplane Monthly* and met Neville Duke for the first time at a de

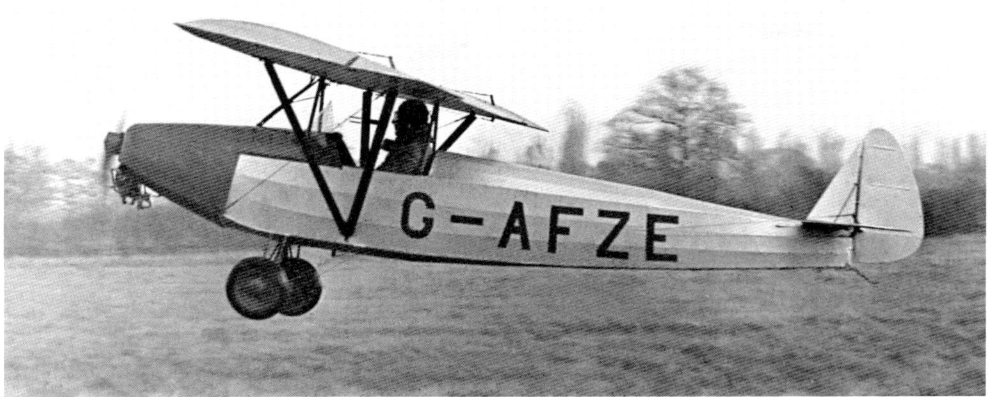

Although this American-designed ultralight was built in the UK in 1939 it did not fly until the day this photograph was taken at Elstree almost 10 years later on 9 January. Built by Robert Parker and registered G-AFZE in August 1939, the red and silver Heath Parasol was towed to Elstree from Esher where it was flown by Colin H. Debenham. Following its sale to F. G. Lowe at Redhill, the Parasol's original 696 cc Blackburne Tomtit engine was replaced with a 32 hp Bristol Cherub III. Passing eventually to F. R. Brimecombe, 'ZE was wrecked while taking off from Luton on 1 April 1966 bound for its Fairoaks home. In 1974 Desmond St Cyrien, of Sopwith Pup fame, restored the registration and the aircraft was rebuilt. Following St Cyrien's death the Parasol has since disappeared.

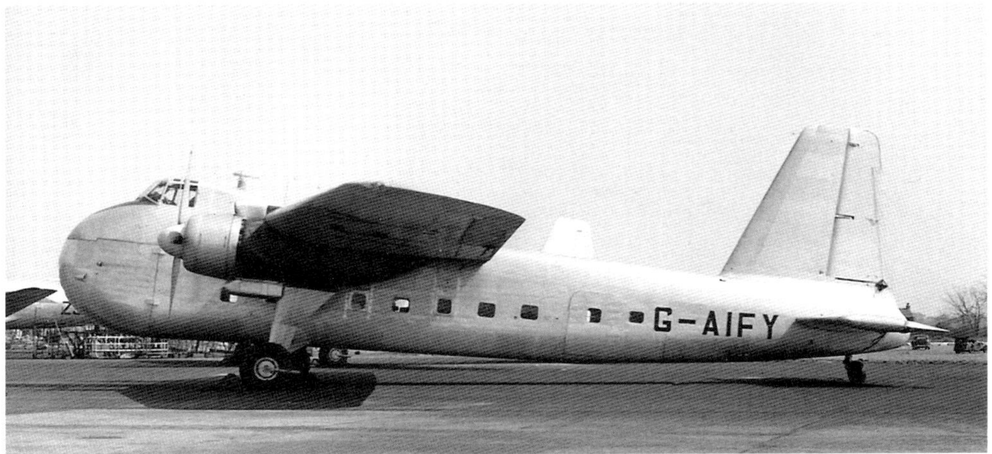

Bristol 170 Freighter Mk 21E G-AIFY was registered in January 1949 to the Secretary of State for War as G-18-62 and sold to West African Airways in April 1949 as VR-NAX. Shortly before departing for West Africa 'FY was photographed at Heathrow on 15 April. On 27 July 1951 the Freighter was wrecked when it landed short of the runway at Nigeria's Kaduna Airport.

Havilland Moth event at Hamble. During conversation the author asked Neville if he remembered giving E.J.R. a trip in the Tomtit at Eaton Bray. 'I certainly do,' he replied, 'but it was your father who *flew me.*' He had two photographs of the occasion and said that he would send copies, which he did straight away, accompanied by a letter saying how he had enjoyed the Eaton Bray meeting. It was a gesture that was so typical of that great man.

Also at the 1949 display there was an excellent exhibition of slow flying by John Fricker in the incredibly slow-flying German Zaunkoenig G-ALUA that didn't quite go to plan. John, on the editorial staff of *The Aeroplane* and the weekly magazine's 'test pilot', could not understand why the considerable crowd cringed every time he flew near them. After he landed parachutist and wing walker Willans told him that as the Zaunkoenig took off it had inadvertently picked up a glider tow rope, which then thrashed around like an angry snake in his slipstream. Had John chosen to fly really close to the crowd....

Organisation of the Eaton Bray display at an end, it was back to the day job for E.J.R. On 16 June he flew to Wolverhampton to photograph Boulton Paul Balliols for his *Aeromodeller* series. Afterwards he wrote to A.J.J.:

On 16 June, with great trepidation, I followed the A5 up to Lichfield [in Cub G-AKAA], forked left at the cross roads and rattled into Wolverhampton with the petrol gauge showing nowt—1 hour 35 minutes after leaving Elstree. After learning all about the Balliol and going through Boulton Paul's negs I went across to the club side to see what they had to offer. There were 51 aircraft in three hangars and you will be pleased to hear that so embracing is our organisation that only nine needed the attention of the Fox's Glacier Mint [the camera lens]. Coming home via Droitwich, Stratford-on-Avon and Leighton Buzzard, I clocked 1 hour 45 minutes against the south-east wind.

As a result of the visit the Balliol was the subject of E.J.R.'s *Aircraft Described* article published in the August 1949 issue of *Aeromodeller*. On 16 July he went down to Cowes to inspect construction progress of the Saunders-Roe Princess flying boat.

With 'Jock' Bryce alongside him, J. 'Mutt' Summers added to his already lengthy list of first flights with that of the prototype Vickers Varsity, VX828, at Wisley on 17 July. The Varsity replaced RAF Flying Training Command's ageing Vickers Wellington T.10s used for advanced training of pilots, navigators and bomb-aimers and was later put into service with Signals Command.

Late on 27 July the first flight of the prototype D.H. 106 Comet 1 G-5-1/G-ALVG was made by John Cunningham. An expectant press had waited all day at Hatfield to see the world's first jet airliner get airborne and had departed early and disappointed, thus missing this historic event. During the flight the Comet reached 10,000 ft. Comets were already in quantity production at Hatfield, 14 of which had been ordered by BOAC.

Three days of glorious air racing began at Elmdon, Birmingham, on 29 July, E.J.R. popping off 70 photographs during the second day of the event.

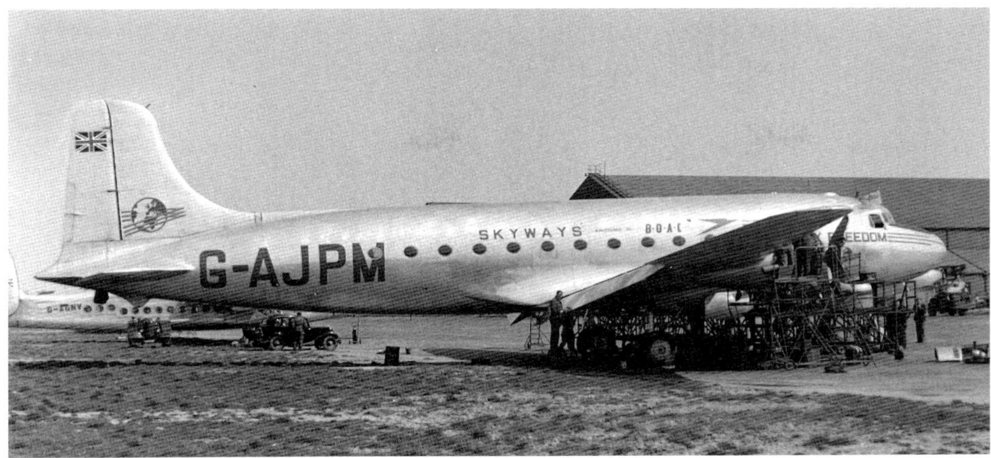

More than 1,000 Douglas C-54s, military adaptation of the DC-4, had been built in the USA by the end of the war, but restrictions on dollar purchases meant that the type was slow to reach Britain, trickling in via Europe. One of the first to arrive was KLM's PH-TBS. Re-registered in September and named *Sky Freedom*, G-AJPM was one of four acquired by Skyways Ltd, seen at Heathrow on 15 April. During early 1948 the Skymasters flew scheduled services to Bahrein for BOAC, replacing the corporation's Sunderland flying boat services. Skyways retired its fleet in 1950, though G-AJPL had been written off at Castel Benito the previous year. 'PM was sold in France as F-BELS and later became VT-DIC with Indian Airlines. On 7 May 1962 the aircraft made a wheels-up landing after the master ignition switch had been turned off in error whilst flying from Bangalore to Bombay.

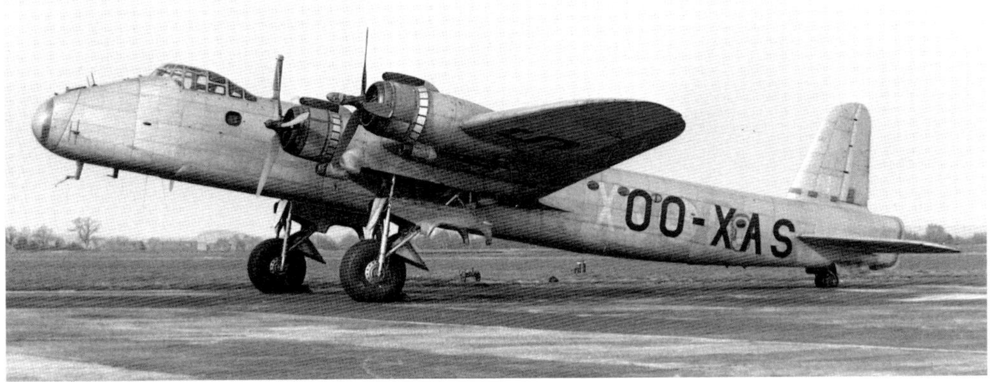

Unlike the Handley Page Halifax, the Short Stirling did not contribute much to post-war commercial aviation, but not through lack of trying. In mid-May 1947 Airtech Ltd at Thame acquired a dozen Stirling Vs from RAF Polegate, refurbishing six of them as 36-seat passenger aircraft and converting the others for cargo work. All 12 were purchased by Belgian charter company Transair of Melsbroek, Brussels, registered OO-XAK to 'XAV and put into service between Blackbushe and Shanghai. Seen at Blackbushe on 15 April is OO-XAS, formerly RAF Stirling V PK153 that had served with No. 242 and No. 46 Squadrons at RAF Stoney Cross and had been built by Short Brothers & Harland at Belfast in 1945.

The Aeroplane devoted an unprecedented 22 pages to its two-issue report. The racing encompassed the King's Cup and seven other races. The 40 or so King's Cup entrants ranged from a Comper Swift to a D.H. 104 Dove, but more than half (24) were Miles types, which triumphed spectacularly. The placings were: first, J. N. 'Nat' Somers, in Miles Gemini G-AKDC; second, Ron Paine in Miles Hawk Speed Six G-ADGP; and third, Tony Cole in Comper Swift G-ABUS.

August was notable for the first flight of the prototype four-seat J-5B Autocar, G-AJYK, from the Auster factory at Rearsby.

E.J.R. re-visited some of his pre-war haunts on the 22nd when he spent a day flying with Alec Lumsden in Miles 'Maggie' G-AIUA. They called at Ringway, Barton, Southport and Hooton and for good measure made a circuit or two of E.J.R.'s pre-war home at Chorlton-cum-Hardy, South Manchester. Landing on Southport Sands, he cadged a free ride in D.H. 83 Fox Moth G-ACCB in which he had last flown in July 1937 with the great S. N. Giroux as pilot.

From 31 August to 3 September E.J.R. and family trundled off to Dorset where the usual pilgrimage was made to Hythe (BOAC Sandringhams), Hurn (BOAC Canadair C-4s), Christchurch (Comper Swift G-ACTF and Tipsy Belfair OO-TIA) and Tarrant Rushton where he photographed tired and derelict civil registered Avro Lancasters, cannibalised to keep Flight Refuelling's remaining Lancs airborne.

The maiden flight of Avro 707 VX784, the first of a family of low-speed research deltas paving the way for the Vulcan, took place from Boscombe Down on 4 September, flown by S. E. Esler. Significant as it was, the same day this was overshadowed by the first flight of Bristol Type 167 Brabazon I G-AGPW under the command of A. J. 'Bill' Pegg. A great cheer went up as the leviathan took-off majestically from the country's then longest runway (2,700 yards) at Filton, having made ten trial runs the previous day. The 230 ft-span, eight-engine aircraft carried 4,000 gallons of fuel and reached 5,000 ft during the 25-minute initial flight.

The Tenth SBAC Show, held at Farnborough during 7–11 September was attended by E.J.R. on two of the days. The D.H. 106 Comet prototype, now wearing its G-ALVG civil registration marks and flown by John Cunningham, and 'Bea' Beamont's demonstration of the Canberra probably stole the limelight. Other contenders came in all shapes and sizes—Avro 707 delta, Short Sandringham, the giant, flailing Cierva Air Horse and the Saro SR.A/1 single-seat jet flying boat fighter. According to Oliver Stewart, editor of *Aeronautics*, the two aircraft that attracted the attention of the editorial staff beyond all others were the Comet, understandably, and the Auster J/5B Autocar! With the Comet BOAC would now be able to buy British and expect better commercial returns, the Autocar, with an estimated £1,500 price tag, because its cost would be within reach of the ordinary flyer, '... for too long, the one person nobody has troubled to think about.'

The prototype Gannet, VR546, was transported from Fairey's Hayes factory by road to Aldermaston and reassembled for its first flight on 19 September in the hands of Gp Capt. Gordon Slade, just missing an appearance at Farnborough the previous week.

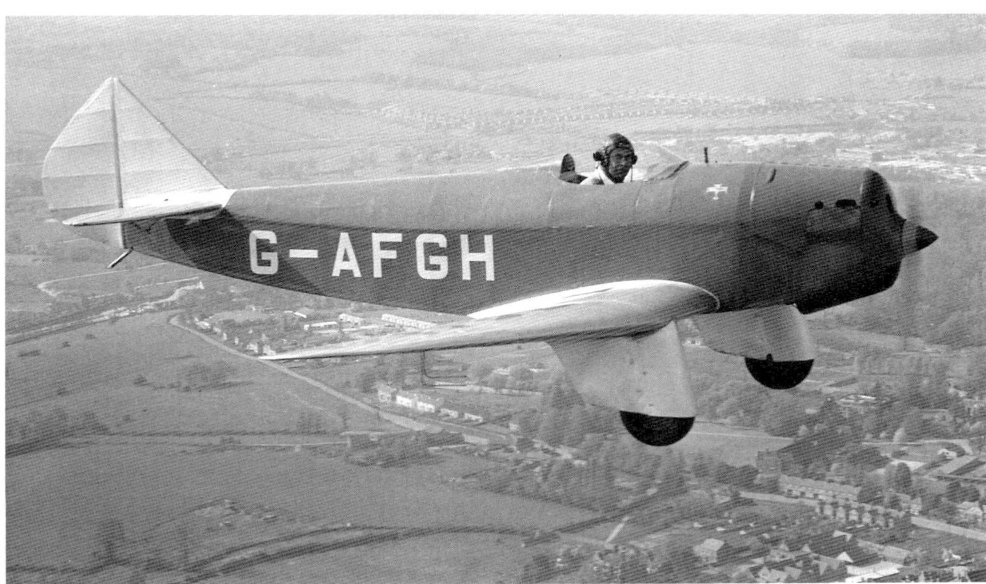

Sqn Ldr Harry R. Bilborough flying the pretty little Chilton D.W.1 G-AFGH in formation with Auster J/1 Autocrat G-AGXT in the vicinity of Denham aerodrome on 20 April. Designed by former de Havilland Aircraft Technical School students A. R. 'Reggie' Ward and the Hon. Andrew W. Dalrymple during 1936–37, the single-seat Chilton was put into limited production by Chilton Aircraft at Hungerford 'GH, built in 1938 and powered by a 30 hp Carden Ford engine, has had many owners throughout its 75 years, currently the Joseph brothers. At the time of writing Hungerford-based Newbury Aeroplane Company was nearing completion of a prolonged restoration to the aircraft's original Carden Ford configuration.

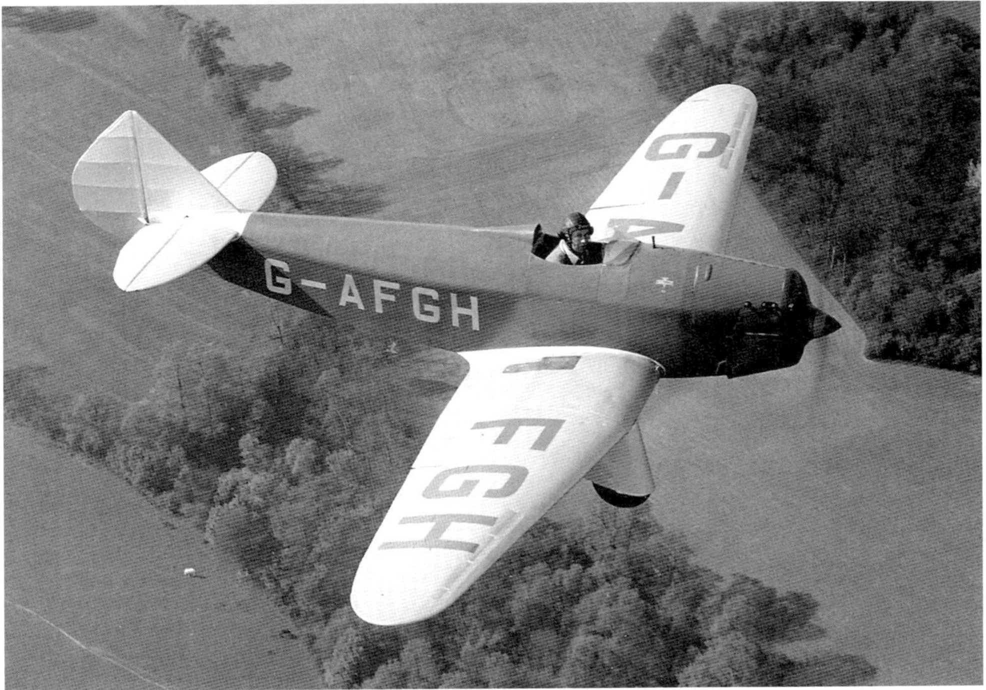

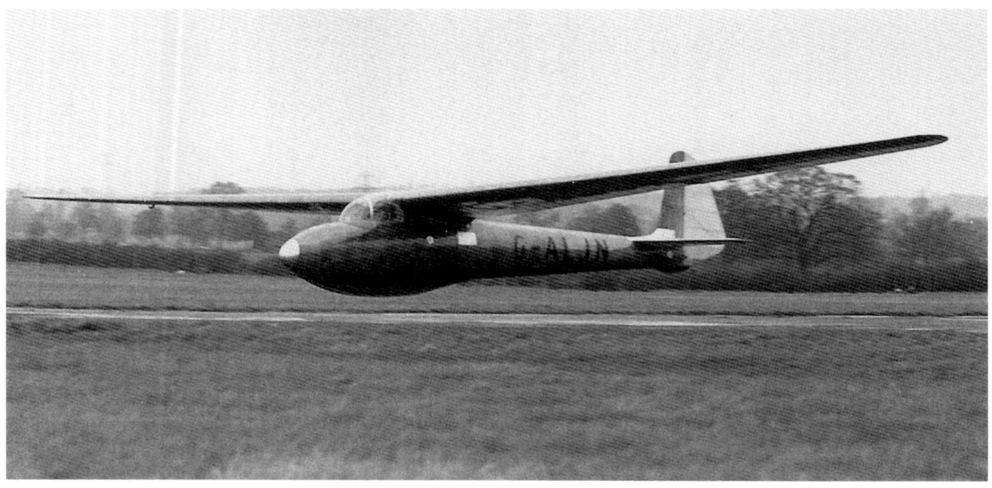

Passing at speed before E.J.R.'s camera at Elstree on 18 April is Chilton Olympia sailplane G-ALJN/BGA434 owned by Dudley Hiscox and based there for a while. On 1 April 1949 the Ministry of Aviation decreed that all gliders should be give registration letters in the same way as powered aircraft, 'JN becoming the first. Sold in Ireland in 1961, the Olympia was allocated the marks EI-103 but never bore them. After suffering damage it was scrapped in 1966.

On 15 October BOAC's first of ten Boeing 377 Stratocruisers arrived in the UK from New York after a non-stop, 10 hour 15 minute flight, averaging 350–360 mph at 28,000 ft. Shortly after, G-ALSA *Cathy* was flown to Filton for crew training and flight trials before the Stratocruiser was introduced on the corporation's North Atlantic services on 7 December.

E.J.R. flew to Hastings in Auster Autocrat G-AGXT with S.O.B. on 15 October to photograph G. R. Lush flying his Klemm L.25 G-AAHW, featured in E.J.R.'s *Aircraft Described* series in the January 1950 issue of *Aeromodeller*.

Canadair C-4 Argonauts entered service with BOAC on 2 November, replacing the corporation's much-travelled Avro Yorks, Chrislea Aircraft test pilot Donald Lowry made a two-hour first flight of Chrislea C.H.3 Skyjeep G-AKVS from Exeter on 21 November, and on the last day of the year E.J.R. called in to Heathrow to photograph BOAC's first Stratocruisers and Canadair C-4s.

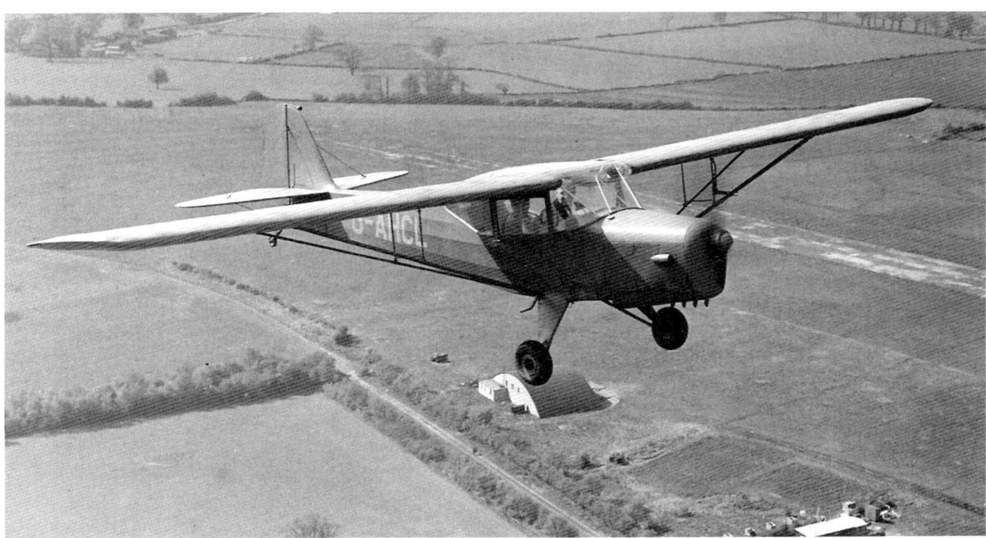

Flying over the western edge of Elstree aerodrome on 20 April is Auster J/1 Autocrat G-AHCL, photographed from another, G-AGXT. The blister hangar, once the HQ of the then Ultralight Aircraft Association and the adjacent single-storey building, have long since disappeared, the land to the left of the road now forming part of Hilfield reservoir. First registered in 1946, 'CL belonged to Jack Meaden and partners in the 1950s and was later upgraded to J/1 Alpha status. Later still, it was re-engined with a 160 hp Lycoming 0-320 and given a larger fin, so that today 'CL resembles a Beagle D.5 Husky.

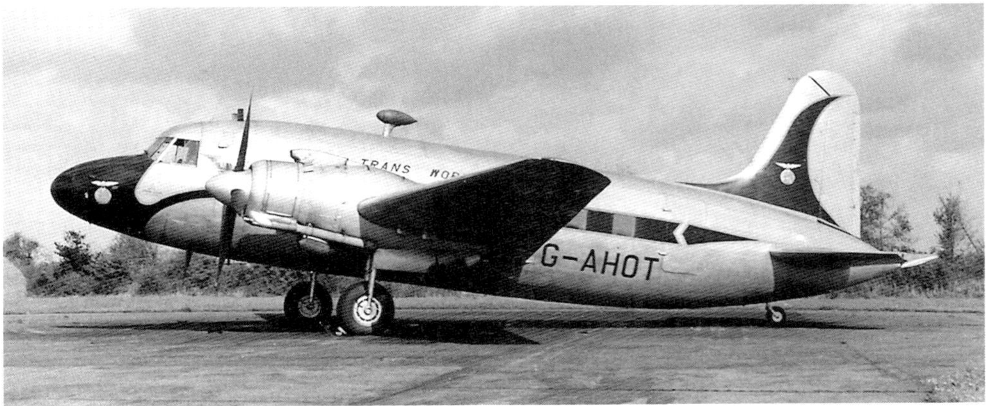

Vickers Type 498 Viking IA G-AHOT began life as part of BEA's 1946 V-Class fleet, was named *Valkyrie* and first flown in August that year. It was sold to Trans World Air Charter in January 1948, in whose livery it is seen at Bovingdon on 25 April, and used on the Berlin Airlift. In August 1952 the Viking passed to Crewsair and named *Empire Trader* before passing to Airwork for trooping duties, for which the serial number XD635 was applied. In October 1954 the Viking was acquired by newly-formed Trek Airways of South Africa and re-registered ZS-DKH, operating in the livery of Protea Airways, a Trek subsidiary. After retirement the Viking was mounted on the roof of Vic's Viking Service Station at Armadale, south of Johannesburg, but removed later for restoration by the SAA Museum Society. Nothing came of these good intentions, the nearly complete airframe probably still sitting in a neglected state at OR Tambo International Airport.

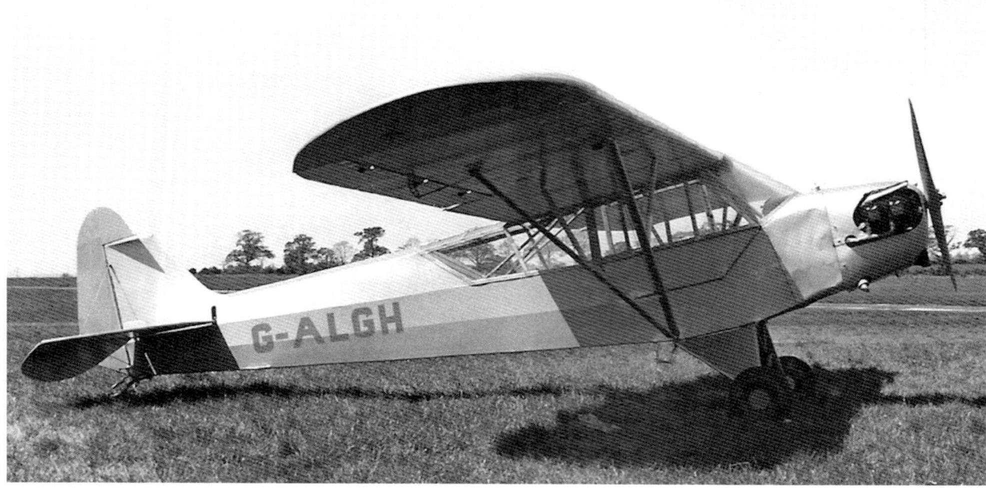

Piper L-4 Cub G-ALGH was first registered in the UK on 29 April and is seen at Elstree a couple of days later. Built as 44-80545 and sporting extra rear window area, the Cub was powered by a 65 hp Continental A-65-8S engine. 'GH was kept at Elstree by H. Tinsley before being sold in Iceland as TF-KAP. The Cub is still airworthy, the extra rear glazing having been removed as per a standard J-3 Cub.

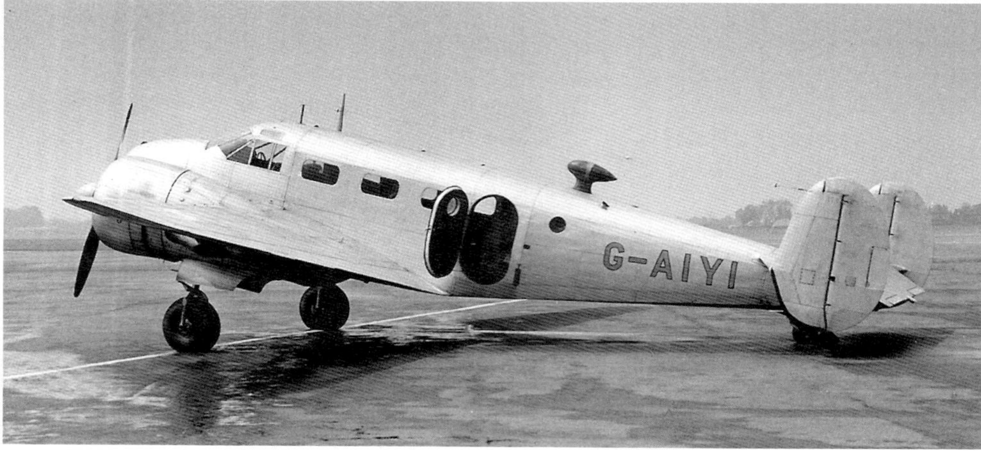

Pictured at Croydon on 7 May is Beech C-18S Expeditor G-AIYI, converted into a luxury eight-seater by Marshall's of Cambridge for Prince Aly Khan. Previously USAAF Beech AT-7-BH Navigator 42-43477, the aircraft was impressed into the Royal Navy and serialled wrongly as FE883, actually a Harvard IIB, instead of FR883. It was assigned to East Africa and then Ceylon and finished the war on the station flight at Ronaldsway, Isle of Man. Registered in June 1948, after use by Prince Aly Khan 'YI was acquired by tractor manufacturer David Brown & Sons. On 25 August 1949 it was damaged beyond repair after crashing on take-off from Sherburn-in-Elmet, West Yorkshire.

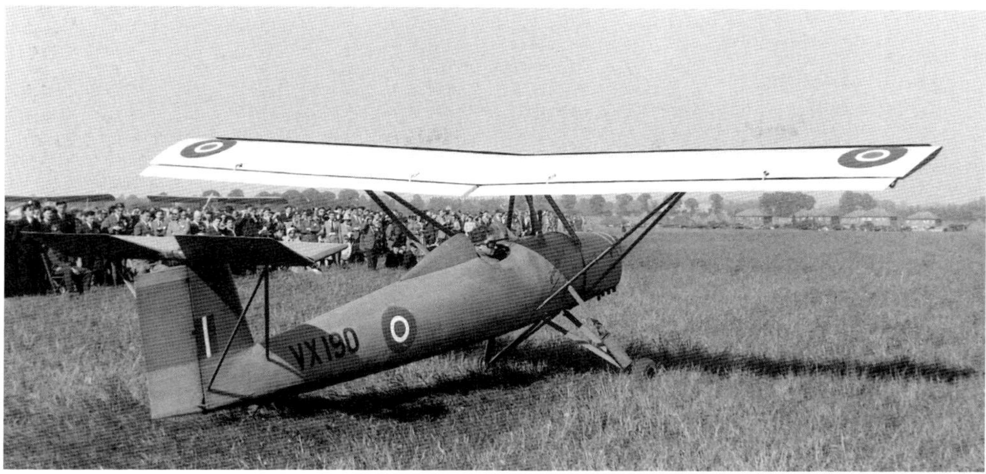

Brunswick Zaunkoenig V-2 D-YBAR was built by students of Brunswick Technical High School, Germany, to explore slow-speed flight and first flown in 1943. Powered by a 51 hp Zundapp engine, 'AR was one of four Zaunkoenigs. It survived the war in hiding and soon after arrived at RAE Farnborough as VX190, flying for a while covered in wool tufts in order to observe airflow behaviour at slow speeds. VX190 is seen at the Royal Aeronautical Society's Garden Party at White Waltham on 8 May and in the words of *The Aeroplane*: '...did its best to beat the Autogiro at its own game.' See p. ??? for a later photograph. Zaunkoenig is German for 'wren'.

1950

Although this book covers the 1940s, in reality the story finishes in early 1950. On the first day of the New Year E.J.R. eased his six-foot four-inch, 16-stone frame into the tiny cockpit of diminutive Zaunkonig G-ALUA and made a 15-minute flight from Elstree.

Shortly after his 34th birthday he made what was to be his final visit to Heathrow to photograph more BOAC Stratocruisers. The following day he drove to Filton to make preliminary drawings of the Bristol Brabazon for a forthcoming article in *Aeromodeller*. While there he also photographed more Stratocruisers, based temporarily at Filton for crew training.

On 15 February VW120, the third and final D.H.108, disintegrated in mid-air, crashing at Brickhill, Buckinghamshire and killing Sq Ldr J. S. R. Muller-Rowland of the RAE. This was the same aircraft in which John Derry exceeded the speed of sound on 9 September 1948.

First flight of the Percival Provost WE522, fitted with an Armstrong-Siddeley Cheetah 18 engine, was made on 24 February by Dick Wheldon. Production versions powered by the Alvis Leonides replaced the Percival Prentice as the RAF's *ab initio* trainer.

The penultimate images captured by E.J.R. during an air-to-air photographic sortie were on 11 March. In a follow-up letter to A.J.J. he wrote:

Have just added another type to my log book—little G-AEVS [Aeronca 100] at Denham. I was to have done the Brabazon in next month's *Aeromodeller* but they

decided it would make a good cover subject so I've been put back a month to allow
old Moore [C. Rupert Moore] to do his stuff. As a stopgap I chose the Aeronca, and
have had a trip in G-AKAA on the firm to Kidlington and also to Denham. Aeronca
'AETG's skeleton is now at Kidlington, and much to his delight and never-ending
wonder that such things could happen to him, I took George Cull in the front seat
to help me draw it. 'VS is a treat—I shall never forget the impression of a chunk
of cast iron banging and shaking up at the front end and the terribly slow initial
acceleration. Apart from that it flies very much like the Piper.

The day following air-to-air photography of 'VS, Avro Tudor V G-AKBY,
operated by Fairflight Ltd, crashed approaching Llandow airfield, Glamorgan,
when returning with Welsh rugby fans from an international in Ireland, killing
the crew of five and all but three of the 78 passengers. It is thought that the
aircraft's centre of gravity was further aft than that authorised by the Certificate
of Airworthiness.

On 31 March the two state airlines again recorded financial losses [for the
year 1949–50], BOAC, now incorporating BSAA was £9,155,481 in the red, BEA
posting a reduced deficit of £1,363,481.

The closing days

On 7 February E.J.R. flew from Elstree to Auster Aircraft's HQ at Rearsby with
S.O.B. to look at Auster Autocar G-AJYM. After taking air-to-air photographs
of the Autocar, E.J.R. and S.O.B. had a ten-minute flight in it with a chap called
Harrison. The return flight to Elstree was made in filthy weather flying at 500 ft
in rain and visibility of less than two miles.

E.J.R's next encounter with 'YM came on 6 April when, with Bradshaw as
passenger, he set off from Elstree in Cub G-AKAA for Rearsby. The plan was
for S.O.B. to collect the Autocar, return to Elstree in formation with E.J.R. and
for the two of them to head north again the following day in the Autocar for
the official opening of the Boston Aero Club. E.J.R.'s 'passenger' for the return
Rearsby-Elstree flight was a propeller destined for John 'Tubby' Simpson. E.J.R.
in the Cub and S.O.B. in the Autocar took off together from Rearsby and in the
evening sun flew in formation at 200–300 ft all the way, shooting up Eaton Bray
en route. They arrived back at Elstree just before 18.30, E.J.R. climbing into his
green Ford 10 for the drive to his home at Hendon and S.O.B. returning to his
studio at nearby Stanmore.

Next day, Good Friday, the two friends took off from Elstree in Autocar 'YM,
with Norman C. Stoneham of the Redhill Flying Club in the rear seat, headed
for Boston, Lincolnshire. They arrived in very breezy conditions to join about
30 other visiting aircraft, ranging from Dragon Rapides to the usual assortment
of Messengers, Austers, Proctors and Geminis. Guests were entertained at a
cocktail party in the new clubhouse followed by lunch in an adjacent marquee.

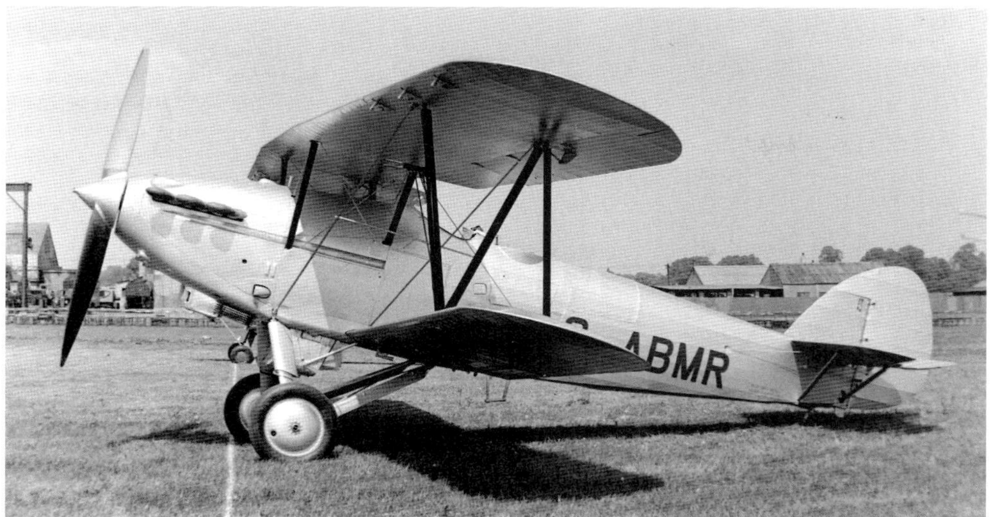

The Hawker Hart II two-seat day bomber was designed by Sydney Camm and prototype J9052 first flown in June 1928, the type entering RAF service in February 1930. The sole civil demonstrator was registered G-ABMR in August 1931 and powered by a 525 hp Rolls-Royce Kestrel IB engine. As a sales demonstrator 'MR visited 15 European countries and during the late 1930s was used extensively for air-to-air photography of new Hawker aircraft, many of the photographs featuring in the pages of *Flight* and *The Aeroplane*. During the Second World War the Hart was camouflaged and used as a company hack, after which it took on the blue and gold house colours of Hawker Aircraft. Post-war the Hart was raced regularly, notably in the 1952 King's Cup air race when, in the hands of G. F. Bullen, the old girl averaged 170 mph. After sustaining damage in a forced landing 'MR was restored and repainted to represent a No. 57 Squadron Hart and in 1972 was one of the first aircraft acquired for the newly-opened RAF Museum at Hendon. The all-silver Hart is seen at the Royal Aeronautical Society's Garden Party at White Waltham on 8 May.

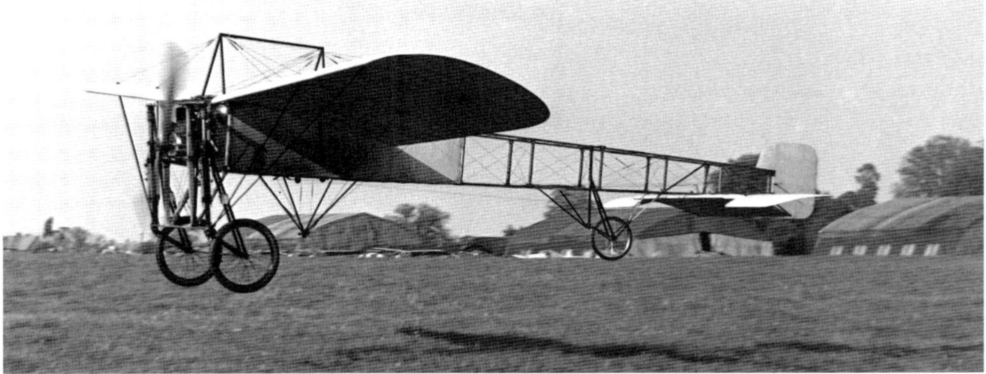

The only lull in an otherwise busy flying programme at the Royal Aeronautical society's Garden Party at White Waltham was when the Deperdussin and 1909 Bleriot IX were wheeled out to the far side of the airfield to fly, or rather hop, in straight lines. Jeffrey Quill, taking a break from flying somewhat faster hardware, coaxed the 40 year-old Bleriot several feet into the air. Like the Deperdussin, it has since been lovingly looked after by the Shuttleworth Collection at Old Warden and has the distinction of being the oldest airworthy aeroplane in the world. Not only that, its 25 hp Anzani is the world's oldest airworthy aero engine.

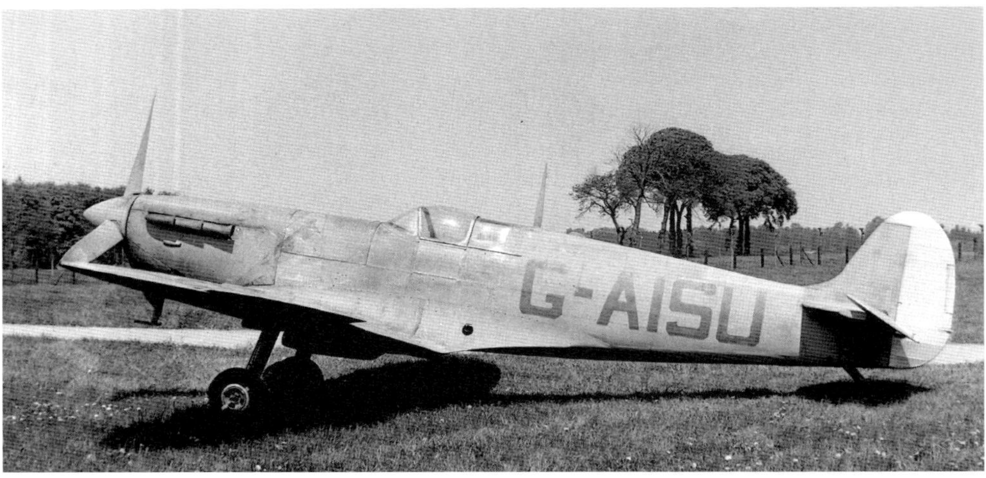

Allen H. Wheeler's Vickers-Supermarine Spitfire VB G-AISU at White Waltham on the day of
the Royal Aeronautical Society's Garden Party at White Waltham on 8 May. It was painted grey
with red lettering and powered by a 1,440 hp Rolls-Royce Merlin 45M engine. If one counts the
engine exhaust stubs the aircraft appears to have had an engine change between May and July.
Built at Castle Bromwich in 1941, further details of this Spitfire can be found on p. ??? Shortly
after this photograph was taken the Spitfire was given a new blue colour scheme and prepared
for the National Air Races at Elmdon, Birmingham, on 30–31 July.

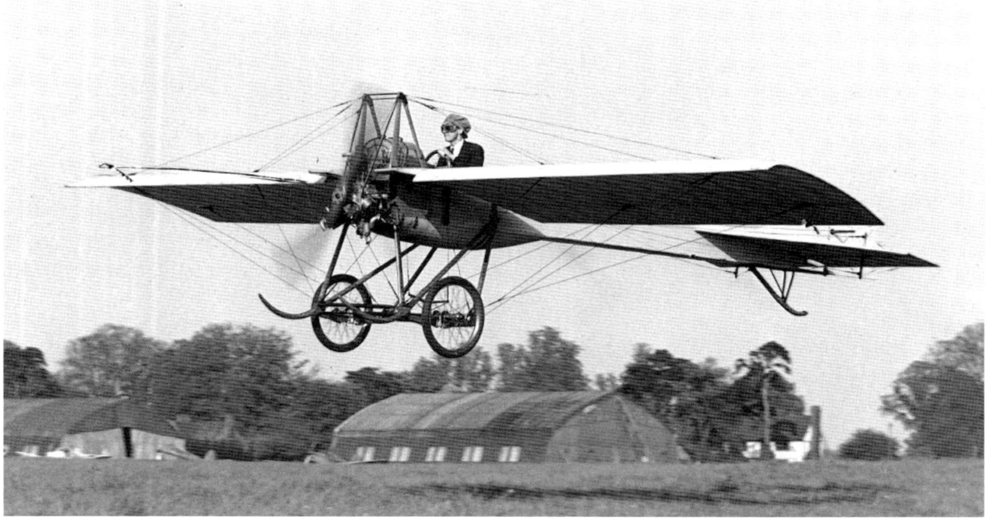

One of the highlights of the Royal Aeronautical Society's Garden Party was a flight by a 1910
Deperdussin, piloted by Wg Cdr J. A. Kent, during which it attained a height of several feet!
The Dep began life as a trainer at Hendon before the First World War until it was damaged and
acquired by A. E. Grimmer. After repair it was resold to Richard Shuttleworth in 1935. Powered
by a 35 hp Anzani engine and now more than a century old, the Dep can still be seen hopping
around Old Warden on calm evenings.

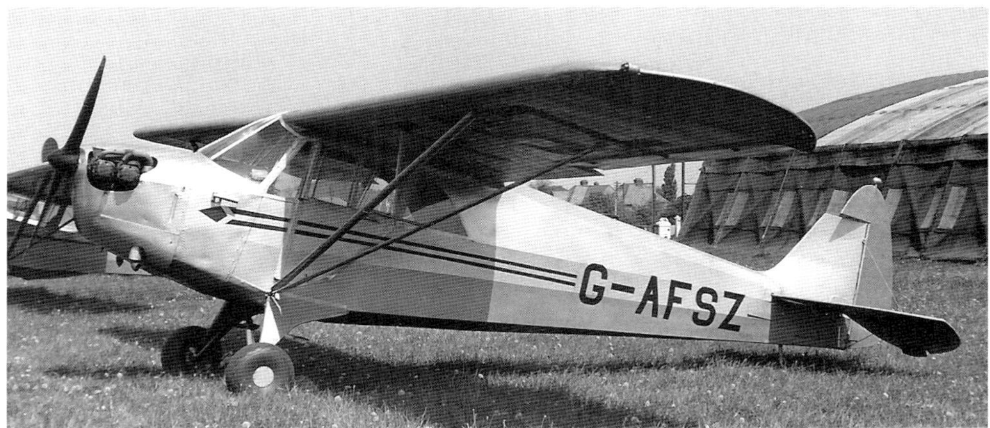

Piper Coupe J-4A Cubs, despite their more sociable side-by-side seating, were not as numerous on the British register as their tandem counterparts, fewer than 30 being imported from the USA before the war. One of the first was G-AFSZ, seen at White Waltham at the Royal Aeronautical Society's Garden Party on 8 May. First registered in May 1939 to the Wiltshire School of Flying Ltd, it was impressed as BT440 in November 1940 and flew with No. 1424 (Air Observation Post) Flight at RAF Larkhill, spending the last part of the war in storage. Re-registered in January 1946, 'FZ passed through several owners' hands before it was acquired by Edward. R. Baker and based at a strip at Cranleigh and used by the Cranleigh Flying Club. On 30 May 1962 the Coupe broke its back landing at Fairoaks and the wreckage sold to B. J. Jackson for rebuilding.

Following lunch, the Mayor of Boston performed the official opening and after encouraging the general public to get airborne did so himself accompanied by the Mayoress, in a Miles Messenger flown by the club's CFI, former Auster test pilot George N. Snarey.

Visiting pilots began to depart at around 16.00. S.O.B, with E.J.R. beside him and Stoneham occupying the rear seat, took off steeply into a gusting 30–35 mph wind. Knowing that the Autocar had a good slow flying performance, S.O.B. selected flap and headed into wind after completing a circuit of the airfield at around 500–700 ft. With a ground speed of barely 10 mph the aircraft made little headway against the wind and, teetering on the stall, the nose was seen to drop suddenly, the dark blue Autocar entering a spin. S.O.B. took instant remedial action, but although recovery was advanced the aircraft did not have sufficient altitude to make it complete. Still turning, it crashed on to the top of the banking of the Forty Foot Drain bordering the airfield, in doing so shedding a wing that ended up in a dyke at the bottom of the bank. Help was quickly on the scene. Among the first to arrive were A. Taylor of the county Police, followed closely by Dr G. R. Usmar and St John Ambulance men. But it was all too obvious that the Autocar's occupants were beyond human aid.

At the subsequent inquest, held at Boston on 3 July 1950, D. C. Douglas, a senior investigation officer with Board of Trade, gave evidence to the effect that no structural defects of any kind were found in either the aircraft or its D.H. Gipsy Major engine. He also confirmed that all cameras were in their cases,

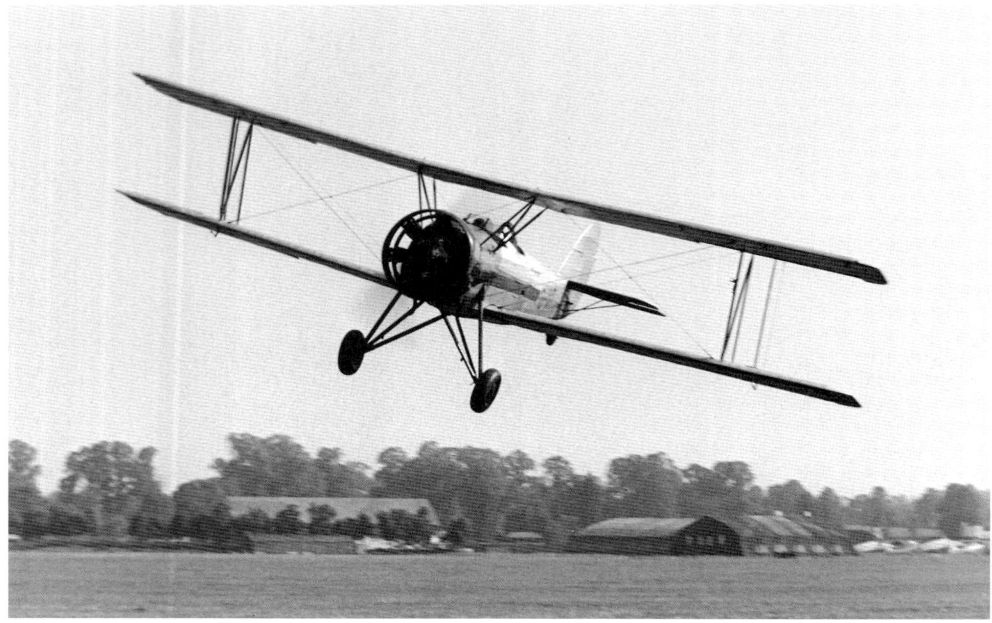

Above and below: A welcome visitor to the Royal Aeronautical Society's Garden Party on 8 May was Avro 621 Tutor I G-AKFJ belonging to the Doncaster Ultra Light Aircraft Group. This Tutor was built in 1935 and flew with No. 614 Squadron at Pengam Moors, the Central Flying School and No. 1 Flying Instructors School at Church Lawford. It was sold in August 1947, given its civil registration in December that year and acquired by Mr. Sturrock, works manager at A. V. Roe's Bracebridge Heath factory, passing to the Doncaster group in September 1948. On 30 July the following year 'FJ was destroyed after crashing on take-off from Doncaster.

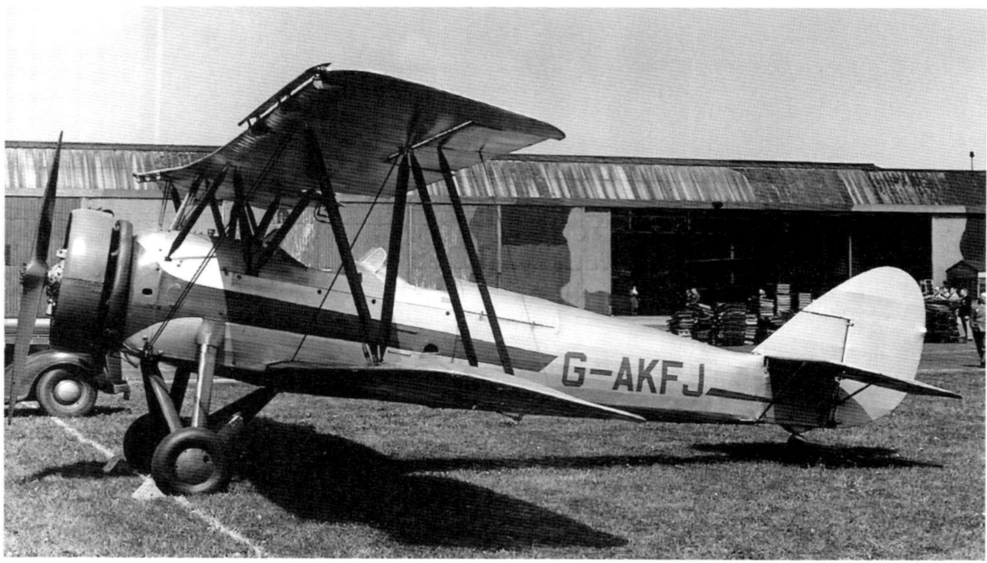

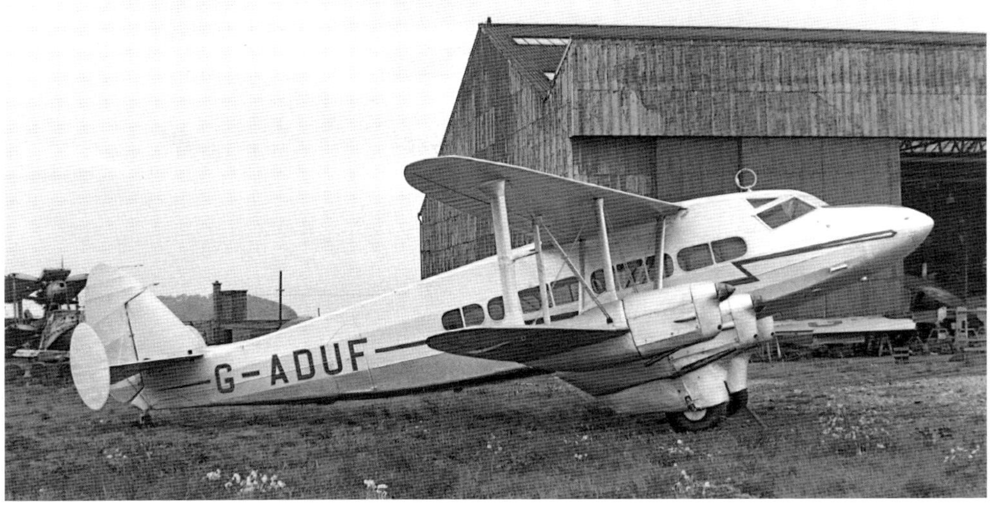

D.H.86A G-ADUF was built at Hatfield in 1936, registered to Imperial Airways Ltd and named *Dido*. With 11 other D.H. 86s 'UF was put into service on European routes and although earmarked for impressment as HK828 in November 1941 was instead used by the Egyptian airline Misrair, named *Beirut* and re-registered SU-ACR. Restored to the UK register in May 1948 and acquired by Field Aircraft Services Ltd, the '86 ended its days with Gulf Aviation Ltd and was withdrawn from use in May 1952. It is seen at Tollerton, Nottingham, on 18 May when operated by Field. Note the Walrus, with wings folded, lurking in the background.

thus refuting suggestions that the aircraft might have been 'stunting' to obtain air-to-ground photographs. Douglas stated that all three occupants were properly strapped in and confirmed that S.O.B. was the pilot, with E.J.R. seated beside him and Norman Stoneham occupying the rear seat. The jury brought in a verdict of 'death by misadventure.'

It seems reasonable to assume that S.O.B. had taken advantage of the weather conditions to demonstrate the Autocar's slow-flying qualities and for reasons unknown the aircraft stalled and spun in. S.O.B. was a very experienced pilot, having learnt to fly with the London Aeroplane Club at Stag Lane in 1926. Throughout the war he flew with the Air Transport Auxiliary and had flown some 70 types over the years. He had flown the Autocar for less than three hours and perhaps tried to get the heavily loaded aircraft to 'hover' over the airfield. Stalling speed of the Autocar with full flap was in the region of 30 mph. Flying into a headwind of 30–35 mph would give a very low speed over the ground. Richard Worcester, an experienced pilot who conducted flight tests for *The Aeroplane*, had flown prototype Autocar G-AJYK and was impressed with the type, but had this to say about the aircraft's airspeed indicator (A.S.I.):

I think that Auster should have avoided the use of the same markings on the A.S.I. in the Autocrat and Autocar. They should recalibrate the A.S.I. and instead of marking 20 and 40 mph prominently (which fits the minimum stall and approach speeds respectively for the Autocrat) they should mark 30 and 50 heavily for the Autocar. As the pitot head and the angle of attack are the same for the two aircraft the P.E.C. is similar.

One wonders if Auster Aircraft acted upon this suggestion and if not, was the A.S.I. a contributing factor? Who knows?
At the time of his death E.J.R. had flown around 66 hours solo and had 351 hours total flying time, made in 755 flights between 1929 and 1950. His funeral took place at Golders Green Crematorium on 12 April 1950.

There is a strange sequel to this tragedy. Many years later, in 1979, I attended a press preview of a collection of replica aircraft put together for Leisure Sport at Thorpe Park. During the lunch break I was approached by one of Leisure Sport's pilots, who introduced himself as Peter Newbery. He seemed rather agitated and asked if I was related to E.J.R. I told him that I was his son and he became even more disturbed. All manner of thoughts went through my mind; was he going to announce that he was my brother or some such?

What he had to say came as a complete surprise. Apparently, he was at Elstree on that Good Friday and whether by design or by chance, he had been the fourth occupant of the Autocar on its journey to Boston. When it was time to leave and return to Elstree he was offered a flight back by another Elstree pilot who had flown solo to the event. Peter told the pilot that he would have to clear it with E.J.R., which he did and in doing so escaped certain death.

On 19 May 1991 57-year old Peter's luck finally ran out when he was killed in Percival T.51 Provost G-BKOS while practicing aerobatics for the Boscombe Down Test Pilots' Display the following week. The aircraft crashed near Aldermaston, Berkshire, and caught fire.

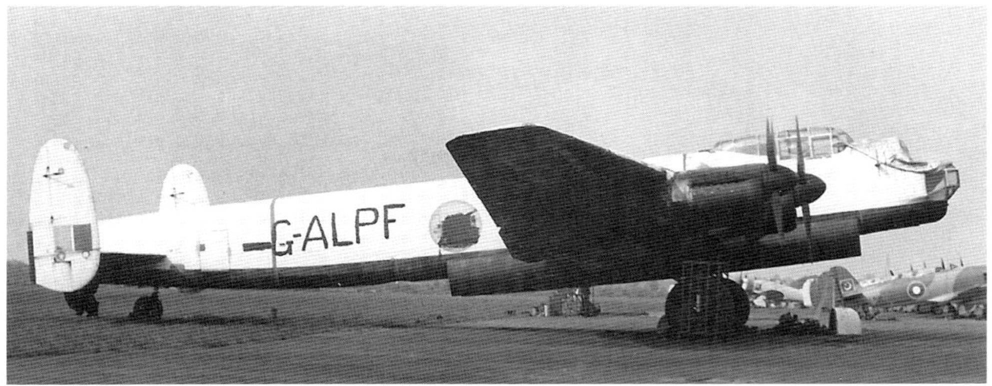

Five Avro Lincoln B. Mk 2s were converted to Avro 695 Lincolnians. This involved adding a huge ventral pannier plus a Lancastrian-type nose and tail. The work was carried out by Airflight Ltd at Langley where this photograph was taken on 21 May before conversion work had begun. Built by A.V. Roe at Chadderton in 1945, RE290 was assigned to Rolls-Royce until sold in May 1949. Registered G-ALPF and granted a C of A in June that year, 'PF took part briefly in the Berlin Airlift before acquisition by Surrey Flying Services Ltd in November 1951 when it is believed to have been kept in storage at Thame. The Lincolnian was reportedly broken up and scrapped at Southend in 1952.

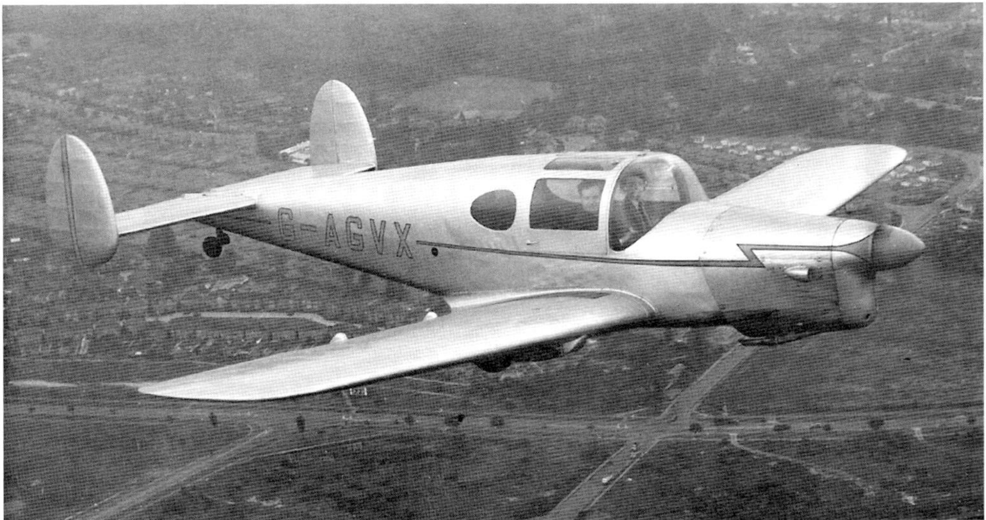

Although the type never went into production there were six marks of the Miles M.28, known unofficially as the Mercury. This photograph shows Mk 4 G-AGVX, flown by former ATA pilot Miss Roy Mary Sharpe, test and delivery pilot for W. S. Shackleton Ltd, flying from Elstree on 19 May. Built in 1944 as U-0243 and powered by a 145 hp D.H. Gipsy Major IIA engine, the retractable undercarriage appeared not to improve on the cruising speed of fixed undercarriage examples of the type. Registered to Miles Aircraft in November 1945, 'VX spent just less than a year in Switzerland with Aerotaxi A.G. Zurich as HB-EED before returning to the UK in early 1948. In 1953 the M.28 was sold in Australia and became VH-AKH.

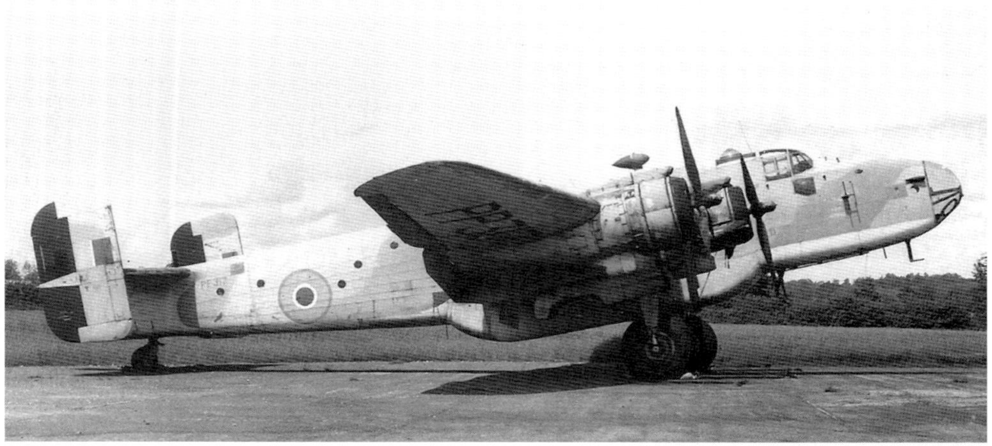

Handley Page H.P. 70 Halifax C. Mk 8 PP317 was assembled at Radlett in 1945 and reportedly registered to BOAC in September 1946 as G-AIID, only to be transferred back to the RAF in April 1947. In January 1948 it was acquired by Anglo French Distributors Ltd and delivered to Bovingdon where it is seen on 2 June, bereft of civil marks and bearing its RAF serial number and camouflage. Owned subsequently by Skyflight Ltd, the Halifax was never converted for civil use and sold for scrap in October 1949.

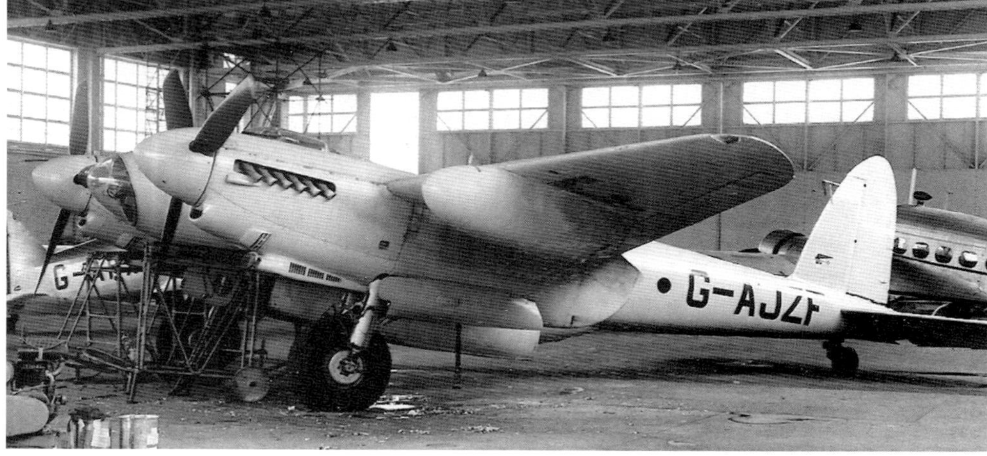

A D.H. 98 Mosquito P.R.34 with the BEA keyline logo on its fin – surely not? Built for the RAF at Hatfield in 1945, RG238 was acquired later by the Ministry of Supply and registered G-AJZF. It was loaned to BEA's Clear-Air Gust Research Unit and, with sister ship G-AJZE, based at Cranfield, where it is seen on 9 June. The Mosquito 'Gust Hunters' carried out high altitude flights over Europe, searching for clear-air turbulence over routes to be flown by the corporation's Vickers Viscounts, due to enter service in 1953. They had pressurised cabins, two 100-gallon drop tanks and operated between 20,000 and 40,000 ft, often in temperatures as low as -70°F. In August 1949, their work done, the two P.R.34s rejoined the RAF, 'ZF being struck off charge in January 1955 having been assigned to No. 81 Squadron at Selatah, Malaya. Earlier in its life, as RG238, it captured the London to Cape Town speed record when, on 1 May 1947, Sqn Ldr Harold Brownlow Martin and Sqn Ldr Edward Sismore landed at Brooklyn Airport 21 hours 31 minutes after leaving London Airport, thus beating Alex Henshaw's 1939 record by nearly 18 hours.

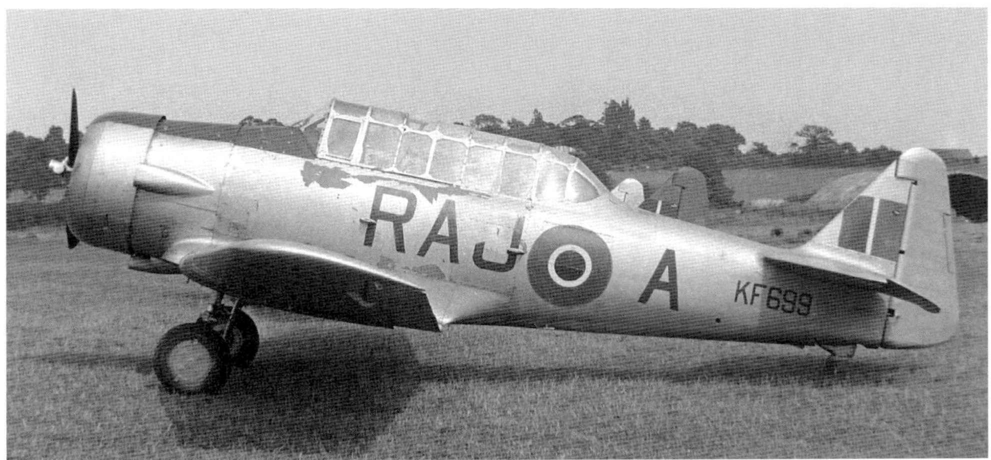

KF699 was one of 854 North American Harvard IIBs built by Noorduyn Aviation of Canada and shipped to the UK under the Lend-Lease agreement during 1944–45. It was assigned first to No. 11 Reserve Flying School at Perth, then to St Andrews University Air Squadron and finally to No. 603 Squadron at RAF Coltishall, where it was based when photographed at Redhill on 16 June, coded RAJ-A.

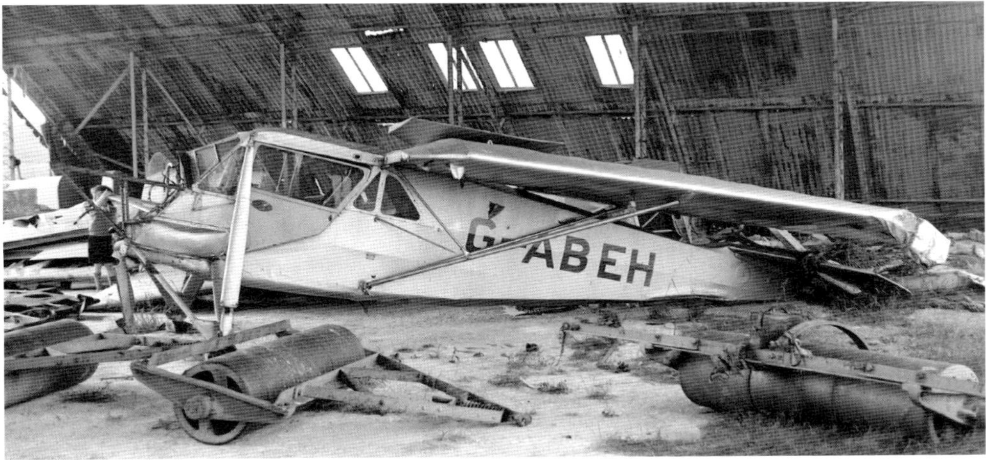

D.H. 80A Puss Moth G-ABEH, engineless and somewhat the worse for wear, at Thruxton on 12 June. First registered to Peggy Salaman in September 1930 and kept at Hanworth, it was flown into third place in the 1931 King's Cup air race by Flt Lt Geoffrey Rodd. A few months later, accompanied by Gordon Store, Rodd flew from Lympne to Cape Town in six days, six hours and 40 minutes. In February 1933 the Puss was sold in Kenya, becoming VP-KAV, but returned to the UK four months later and was owned by W. P. Taylor at the outbreak of war. Impressed into RAF service in August 1941 as HH981, it was assigned to No. 510 Squadron at Hendon before ending up in storage at RAF Kemble, where it was put up for civil disposal in February 1946. After several ownerships it was acquired by Frank G. Royce in July 1948. On 15 August Royce landed at Thruxton with the brakes on, 'EH overturning and sustaining damage that is consistent with that visible in the photograph. The Puss was never flown again, parts of its anatomy being donated to sister ship G-AAZP.

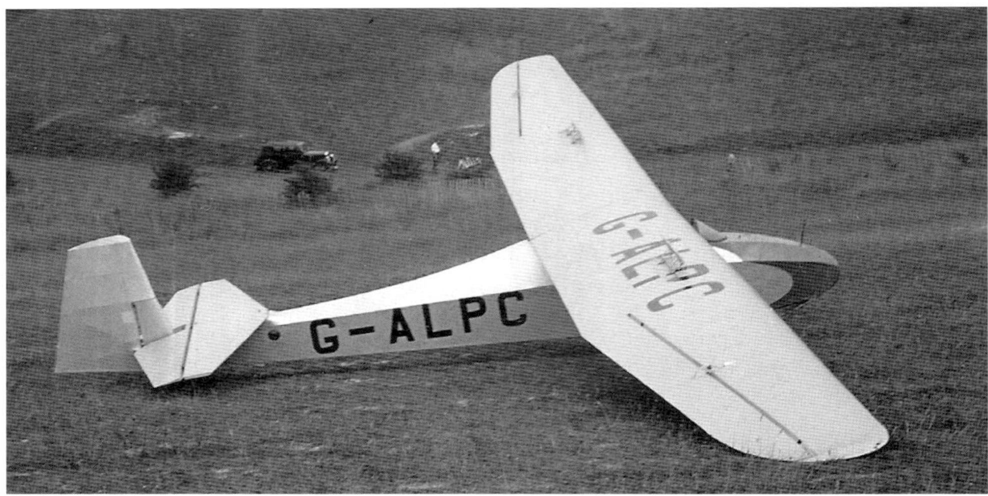

The Slingsby Type 30 Prefect was a modified Type 5 Grunau Baby, the prototype flying in June 1948. The second Prefect, G-ALPC/BGA625, is seen at Dunstable, home of the London Gliding Club, a year later. The single-seat, 45 ft span glider had a flying weight of 614 lb. Production totalled 42.

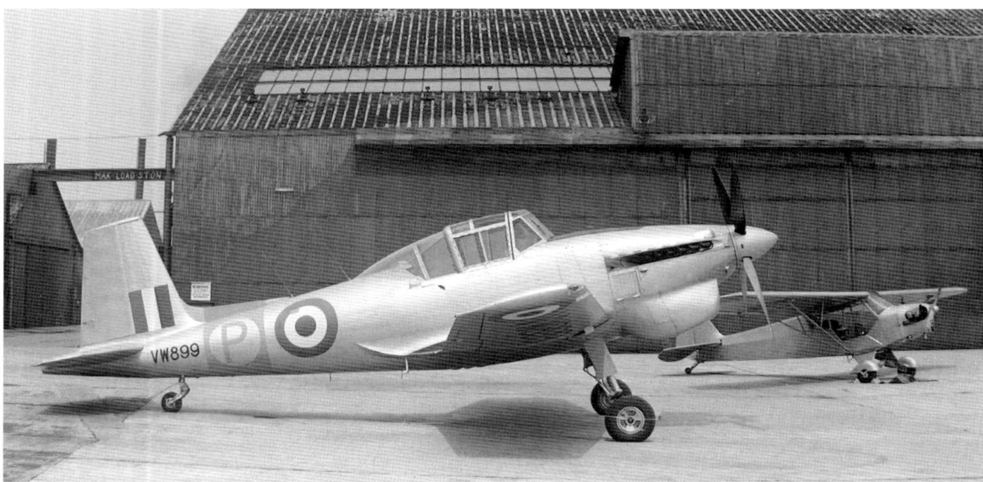

On 16 June E.J.R. flew to Wolverhampton, via Watling Street, in Piper Cub G-AKAA to take photographs of Boulton Paul Balliol advanced trainers for an article that appeared in the August 1949 issue of *Aeromodeller*. Balliol T.2 VW899, one of several Merlin-powered prototypes, is seen with 'AA in the background. Production T.2s were powered by a 1,245 hp Rolls-Royce Merlin 35. Of the 162 examples built (some sources say 183), Blackburn Aircraft Ltd produced 30 at Brough. VW897, the prototype Merlin-powered T.2, was flown for the first time on 10 July 1948 by Peter Tisshaw.

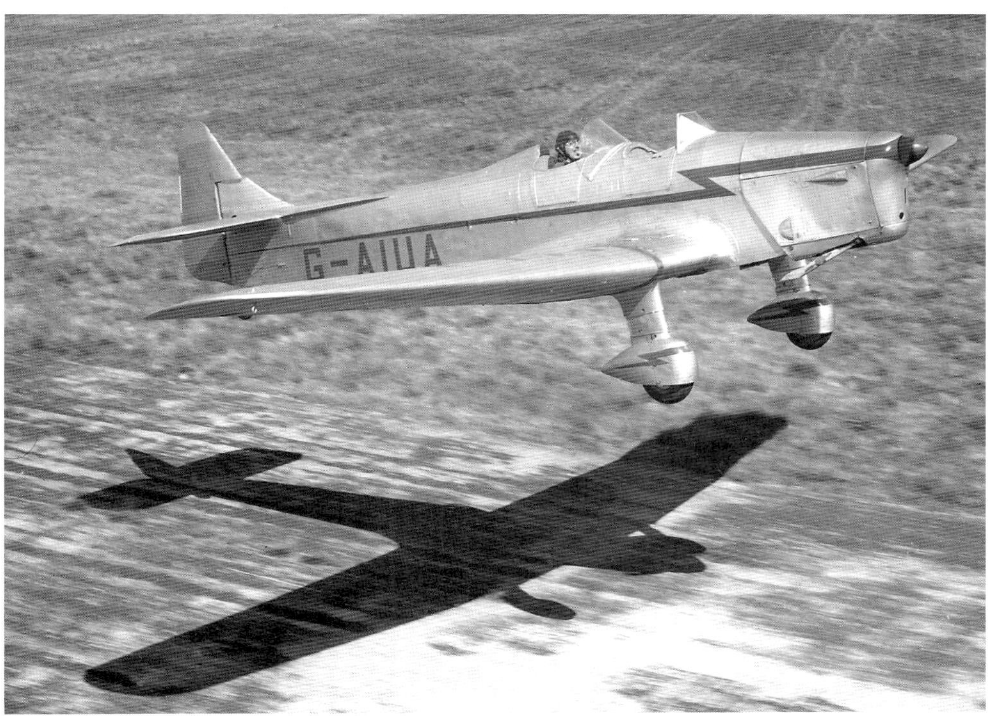

Above and below: A dramatic photograph of C. A. Nepean Bishop lifting Miles M.14 Hawk Trainer G-AIUA off Elstree's runway on 3 July, taken by E.J.R. from Auster Autocrat G-AGXT. Built at Woodley by Philips & Powis for the RAF in 1940 as Magister T9768, it served with No. 15 EFTS at Redhill, No. 7 Flying Instructors School at RAF Upavon and finally with No. 10 Air Gunners' School at Barrow. It was demobbed in November 1946 and as 'UA joined the Air Schools fleet at Burnaston, Derby, later moving south to join the company's Elstree offshoot to keep company with G-AKPF, 'PG, 'UA and 'KR. Sold to Sid Aarons *c.* 1959, 'UA was groomed for racing, its crowning glory coming when Sid's friend, W.H. 'Bill' Bailey, former Elstree CFI, flew it into third place in the 1961 King's Cup race. Following a crash at Roborough on 26 September 1965, the aircraft was stored for many years and still exists.

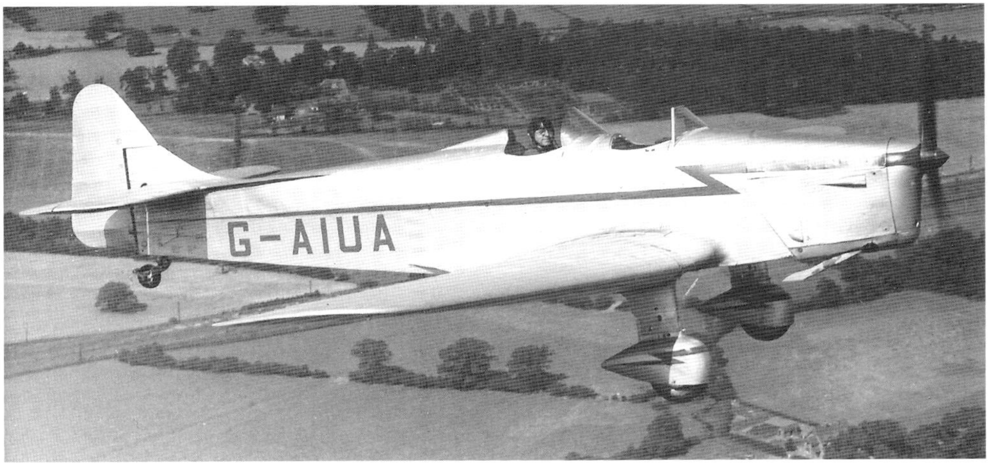

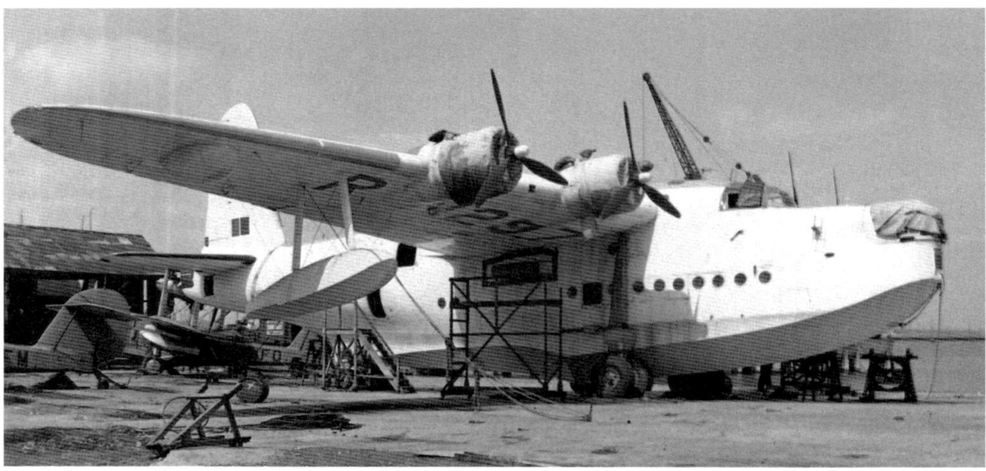

When E.J.R. visited Cowes on 16 July to photograph the Saunders-Roe Princess under construction he came across Short Sunderland V RN297, probably being used to develop the power controls for the Princess. RN297 was built by Blackburn in 1945 at Dumbarton and delivered to No. 302 Ferry Training Unit at Loch Erne. From there the Sunderland was assigned to No. 240 Squadron and thence to the Marine Aircraft Experimental Establishment at Felixstowe. The 'boat was sold in June 1953, acquired by Aquila Airways for spares and later scrapped on the 'beach' at Hamble.

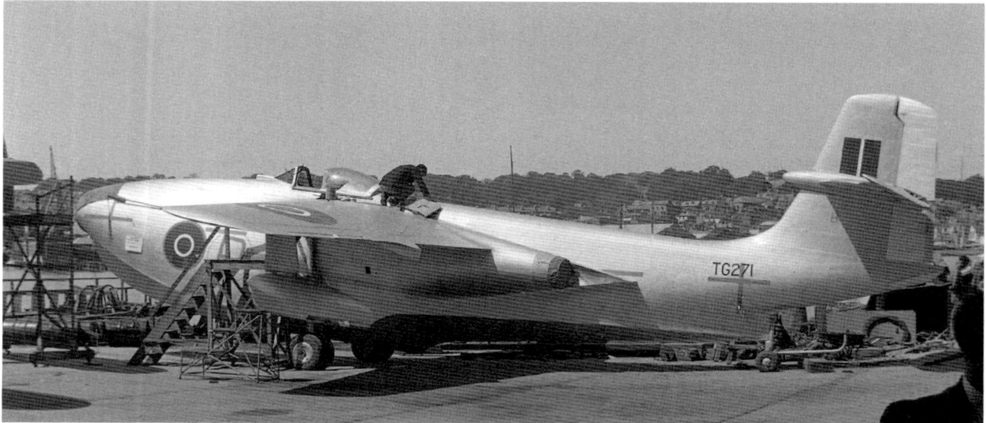

Jet-propelled flying boat fighters are almost as rare as hen's teeth, but Saunders-Roe at Cowes came up with three, the first of which flew on 16 July 1947. The SR.A/1, not named, but known unofficially as the 'Squirt', was powered by two Metropolitan-Vickers F.2/4 Beryl axial-flow turbojets and armed with four Hispano 20 mm cannon. Weighing in at 16,000 lb all up and somewhat larger than a land-based fighter, the A/1 nonetheless performed just as well, having a maximum speed of 512 mph. Three were built: TG263, TG267 and TG271, the latter seen at Cowes on 16 July and displayed in unforgettable fashion at the previous year's SBAC show when Geoffrey Tyson made a very low inverted pass during a superb aerobatic display. Shortly after this photograph was taken TG271 sank after hitting an obstruction while landing off Cowes. Amazingly, the wreckage was never found!

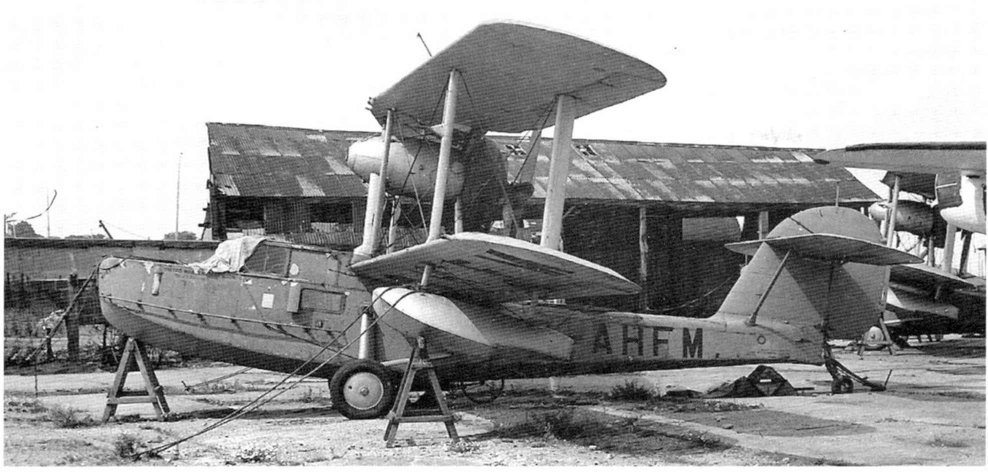

After United Whalers' Walrus Is returned from whale spotting in the Antarctic in 1947 two of them, G-AHFM *Moby Dick* and G-AHFO *Snark,* returned to Cowes where they were eventually scrapped in July 1950. 'FM is seen there on 16 July with 'FO in the background. 'FM was built as W3070 in 1942, its flying career in danger of being cut short because when being delivered from Cowes to Donibristle it crashed. Once repaired, it saw service with Nos 765, 740 and 276 Squadrons and several other units before sustaining damage during a gale at RNAS Ford. Its Service career ended in storage at No. 15 MU, Wroughton.

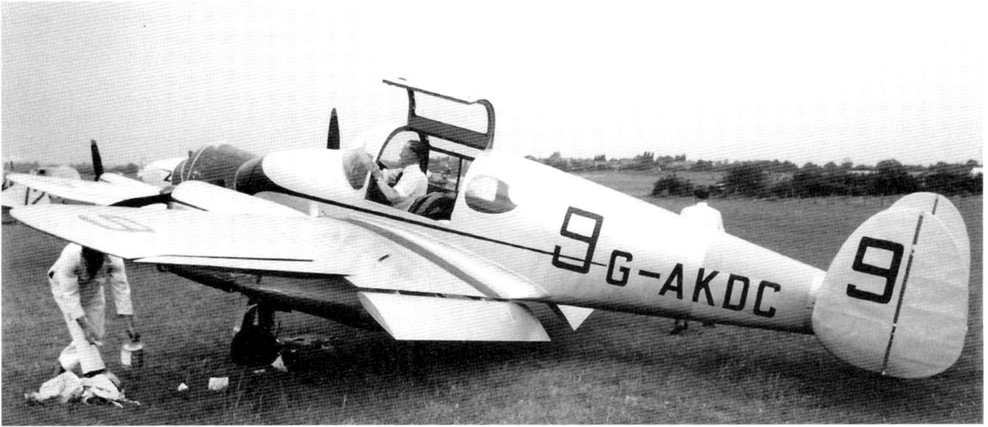

Miles M. 65 Gemini 3 G-AKDC at Elmdon, Birmingham, on 30 July while taking part in the National Air Races. In December 1957 'DC was sold in Tanganyika, becoming VR-TBP, but crashed a year later.

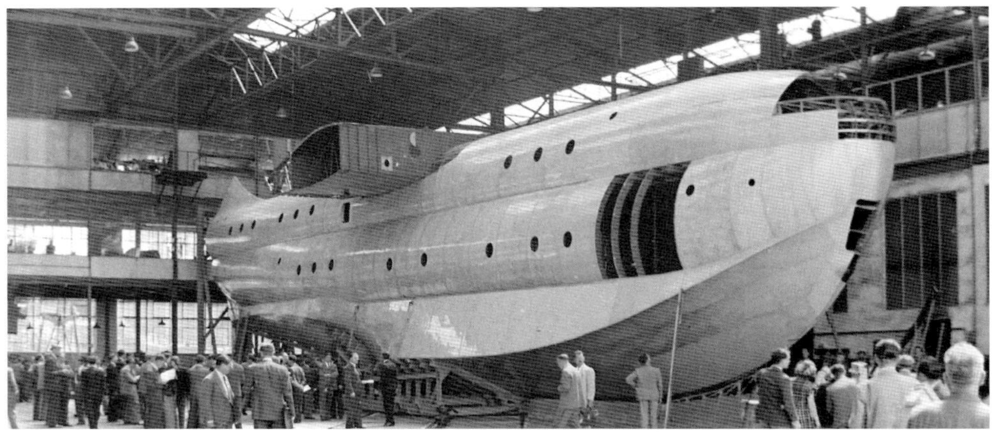

Looking massive in its hangar at Cowes is the 148-ft long fuselage of Saunders-Roe S.R. 45 Princess G-ALUN when under construction on 16 July, the first of three ordered by BOAC, but registered to the Ministry of Supply. It was to be another 25 months before the flying boat was launched and test flown by Geoffrey Tyson, just in time for an appearance at the 1952 Farnborough air show. Powered by ten 3,780 hp Bristol Proteus 600 engines and with a normal maximum weight of 330,000 lb, the Princess would have had a maximum cruise speed of 360 mph at 35,000 ft. Sadly, BOAC lost interest in this magnificent aeroplane, stating that it was out of date technically. As a consequence, the Princess programme was abandoned early in 1954. Only 'UN flew; all three Princesses ending up cocooned at Cowes. There was still great interest in a developed, more powerful version and all kinds of schemes were suggested, but they came to nothing. By the mid-1960s the airframes were deteriorating and one by one they were towed across the River Medina and scrapped.

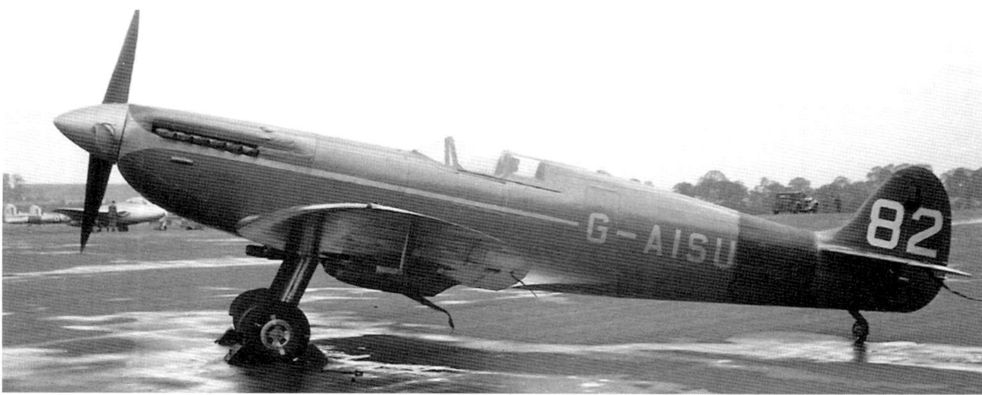

Vickers-Supermarine Type 349 Spitfire VB AB910 was part of an order for 500 of the mark produced by Castle Bromwich in 1941 and was first flown on 16 August by chief test pilot, Alex Henshaw. Delivered initially to No. 222 (Natal) Squadron, it flew with several units subsequently, ending up at the Radio Warfare Establishment at RAF Swanton Morley. The Spitfire was sold to Allen H. Wheeler (one time owner of S.E.5A G-EBQM in 1927), in July 1947 and registered G-AISU. Raced extensively, it is seen with race number 82 at the National Air Races at Elmdon on 30 July. Later in 1949 'SU was sold to Vickers-Armstrong rebuilt and repainted in camouflage and retaining its original serial number. It was given the squadron code QJ-J in honour of former Supermarine test pilot Jeffrey Quill and displayed regularly at air shows. In September 1965 AB910 was presented to the Coltishall Historic Aircraft Flight, later the Battle of Britain Memorial Flight, with which it flies today.

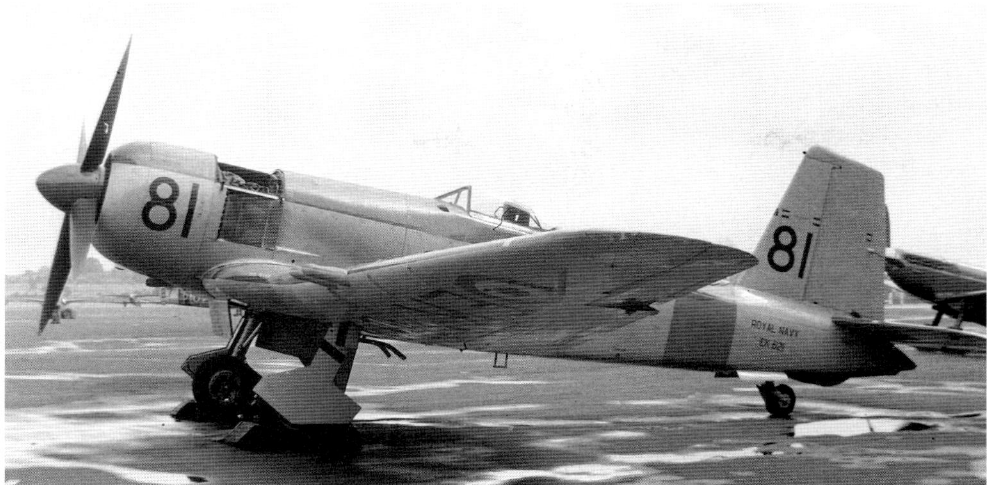

The Blackburn Firebrand single-seat, deck-landing, torpedo-strike fighter was too late to see war service even though the prototype had flown in February 1942. Final variants were the Mks V and Va for which production totalled 150. Firebrand VA EK621 was built at Brough in 1945 and delivered to RNAS Stretton in July that year. Here it is about to take part in the National Air Races, numbered 81 and flown by Blackburn chief test pilot Peter Lawrence. EK621 raced against a Boulton Paul Balliol T.2, Short Sturgeon P.R. 1, Supermarine Spitfire VB, D.H. Hornet 3 and a Hawker Sea Fury T. 20 for the Air League Challenge Cup and won, averaging 302 mph. The aircraft was scrapped at Milnathort, Tayside, in 1965.

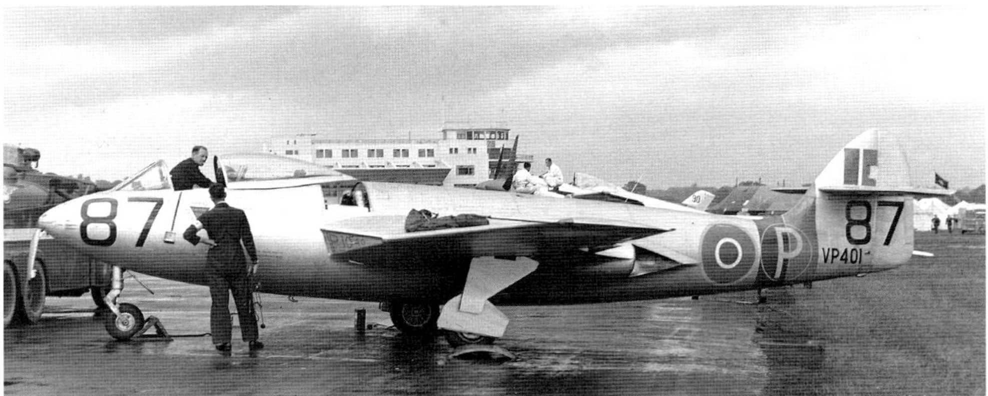

Fancy seeing a cutting edge prototype jet fighter competing in an air race! Captured at Elmdon on 30 July is Hawker P.1040 VP401, precursor of the Sea Hawk, being prepared for flight at the National Air Races. In it test pilot Sqn Ldr Trevor Wade won the SBAC Challenge Cup at an average speed of 510 mph. VP401 was first flown on 2 September 1947 by Bill Humble [grandfather of TV personality Kate], from Boscombe Down and a few days later went to RAE Farnborough for trials. Powered first-off by a 4,000 lb st Rolls-Royce Nene I, the P.1040 required modification to the jet tail pipes and an acorn fairing was added at the intersection of the fin and tailplane to alleviate tail buffet. Later, the Nene I was replaced with a 5,000 lb st Nene II. VP401 remained airworthy until retired following an incident in November 1950. More than 540 Sea Hawks were produced, the Fleet Air Arm taking deliveries from 1953.

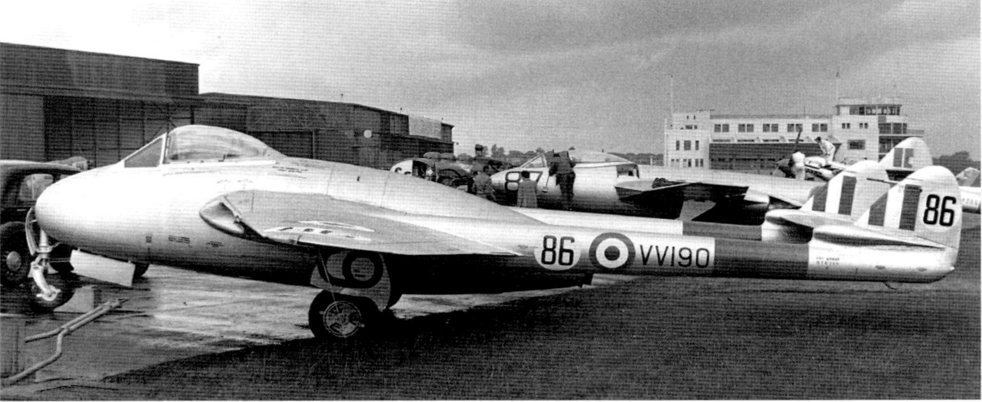

D.H.100 Vampire F.3 VV190 was built by English Electric at Preston in 1948 and after assignment to the A&AEE was retained by de Havilland for development of the D.H. Goblin 4 engine. Taking time off from development work, it competed in the Kemsley Trophy Race at the National air Races over the weekend of 30-31 July. Flown by John Cunningham, it was placed second, averaging 470 mph. It also took part in another of the races, for the SBAC Challenge Cup, again coming second (out of a field of three), and again averaging 470 mph. In January 1950 the Vampire was assigned the maintenance serial 6717M before being scrapped *c.* 1958.

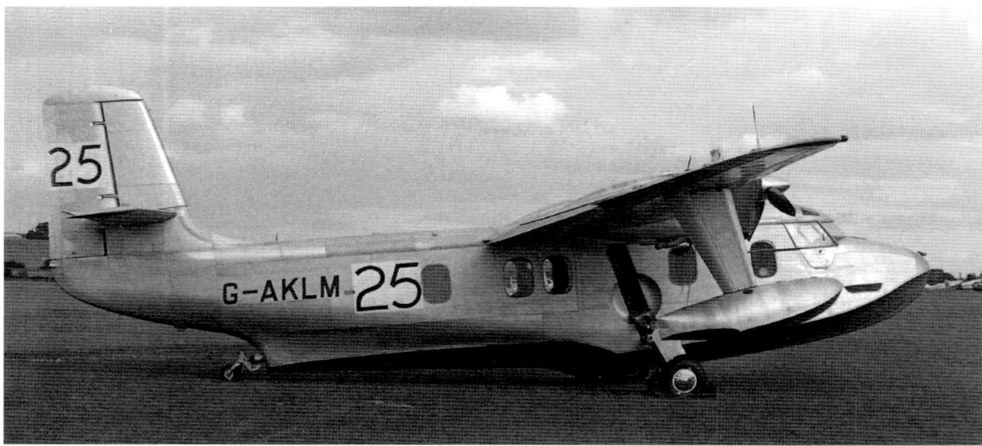

The short-lived Short S.A.6 Sealand I G-AKLM was registered to Short Bros and Harland Ltd in July 1949 and seen at the National Air Races on 30 July. Numbered 25 for the King's Cup, it averaged 169 mph flown by Tom Brooke-Smith. Tragedy struck less than three months later on 15 October when 'LM flew into a hill obscured by fog and caught fire at Lindesnes, Norway, whilst on a tour of Scandinavia. Flt Lt Denis G. McCall of the Marine Experimental detachment and his three passengers were killed.

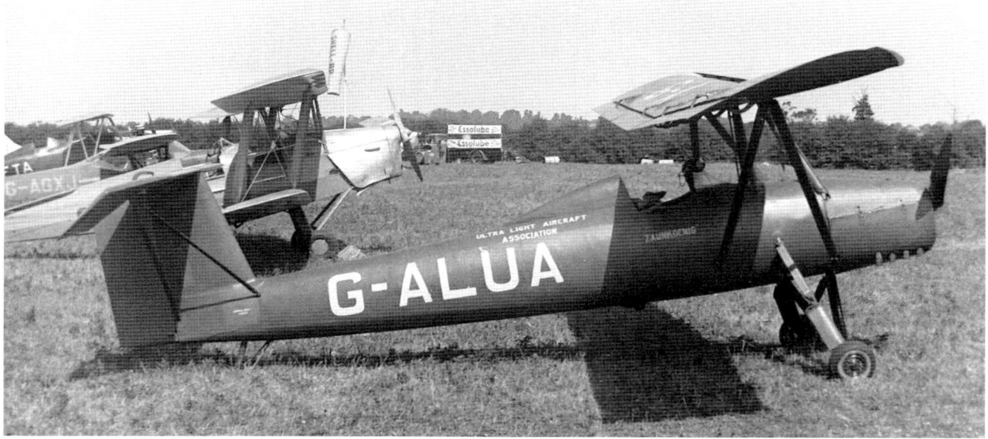

The Brunswick Zaunkoenig V-2 D-YBAR, see p.???, was built by students of Brunswick Technical High School, Germany, to explore slow-speed flight and was first flown in 1943. Powered by a 51 hp Zundapp engine, 'AR was one of four Zaunkoenigs built. It survived the war in hiding and arrived at RAE Farnborough as VX190 soon after, flying for a period covered in wool tufts in order to observe airflow behaviour at slow speeds. At the end of 1948 the Ultralight Aircraft Association, based at Elstree, got its hands on the Zaunkoenig and it was registered G-ALUA. It is seen at Eaton Bray on 21 August when demonstrated by the late John Fricker. Whilst at Elstree E.J.R. took it up on 1 January 1950. The comments column in his flying log book records: 'Take-off 40–45 mph, cruise 53 mph, approach 47 mph.' Its maximum speed was 87 mph. Over the ensuing 60 years the Zaunkoenig has changed ownership many times, spending some years as EI-AYU in Ireland before returning to Germany in 1976, to be registered D-EBCQ for preservation in the Deutches Museum, Munich.

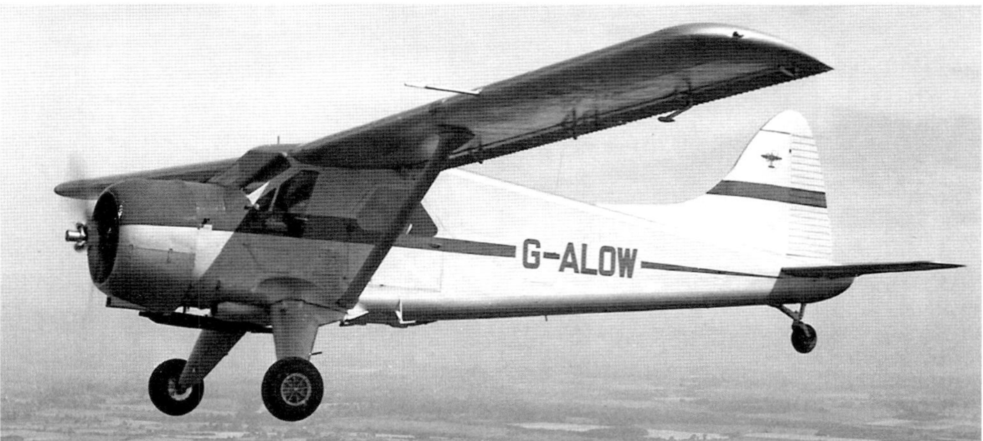

De Havilland's chief production test pilot, W. P. 'Pat' Fillingham, closes in on Percival Proctor G-AHUZ over Hatfield in D.H.C.2 Beaver G-ALOW during an air-to-air photographic sortie on 13 August. Imported from Canada, 'OW was used first to carry de Havilland personnel six at a time between the manufacturer's various factories. The all-metal, four-door Beaver was powered by a 450 hp Pratt & Whitney Wasp Junior, noted for its short take-offs and landings and the rasping engine noise during phenomenally steep climb-outs. Originally, the aircraft had a natural aluminium finish with the registration, nose apron and trim in maroon. Registered in July 1949, it was exported to Southern Rhodesia in November 1952 and became VP-YKA.

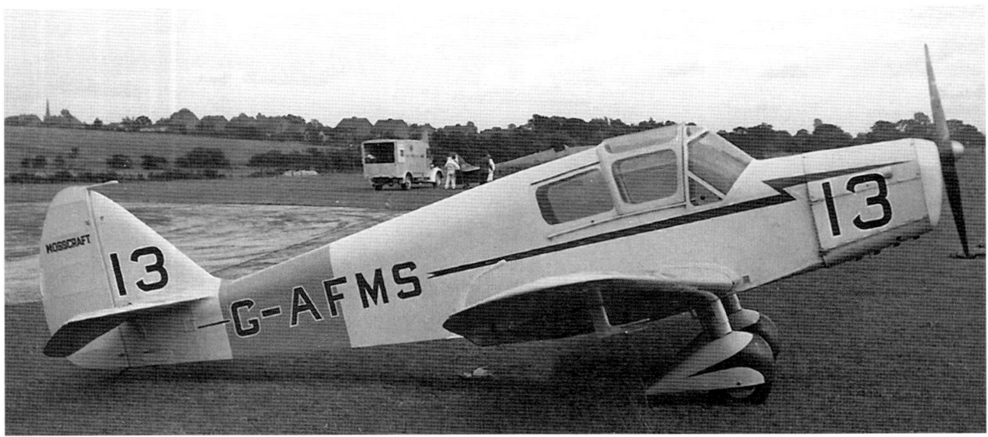

Built originally as an open two-seater in 1939 by Moss Bros. Aircraft Ltd at Chorley, Moss M.A.2 G-AFMS was powered by a 90 hp Blackburn Cirrus Minor I and soon acquired an enclosed cabin. During early 1940 its potential as an air observation post (AOP) was evaluated by the School of Army Co-operation at Old Sarum. After a Certificate of Airworthiness was granted in October 1940 the M.A.2 was shipped to Canada as CF-BUB, during which time it crossed the Rockies. Back in the UK, it was a competitor in the National Air Races at Elmdon on 30 July, flown by William Henry Moss. Sadly, Moss was killed flying Moss M.A.1 G-AEST in the following year's King's Cup air race. 'MS was sold to the Fairwood Flying Group in September 1953 and lost in a crash near Builth Wells, Wales, in July 1958.

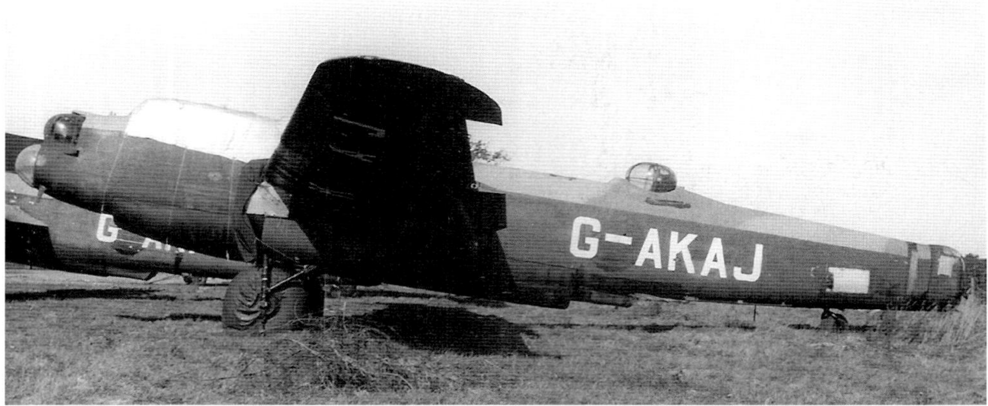

During the late 1940s Flight Refuelling's base at Tarrant Rushton, Dorset, was littered with decaying Avro Lancasters still wearing military camouflage, but bearing temporary civil registrations. One such aircraft was G-AKAJ, photographed on 4 September. Built in 1944 by Vickers-Armstrongs at Castle Bromwich as HK557 and test flown by Alex Henshaw on 20 May, this Lancaster was assigned to No. 75 Squadron at RAF Feltwell, Norfolk. After the war the Lanc was sold and registered in June 1947 to Flight Refuelling Ltd for the delivery flight to Tarrant Rushton. Over the next couple of years 'AJ gradually lost its vital parts to keep the rest of the Lancaster fleet flying and is seen bereft of its Merlin engines, tailplane and ailerons.

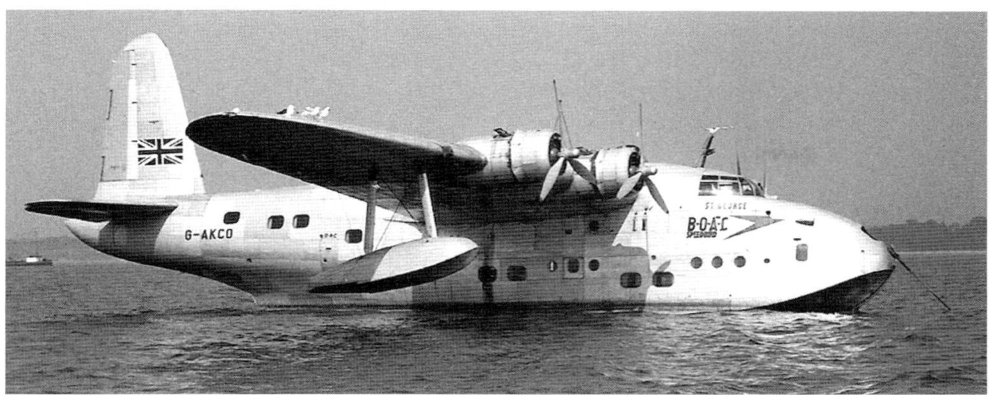

Short S.25 Sandringham 7 G-AKCO was built in 1943 by Short Bros. at Rochester as Sunderland III JM719 and converted later to Mk V configuration. It was assigned to No. 302 Ferry Training Unit, probably at Alness, Scotland, and sold in May 1957. After conversion to a 30-passenger Sandringham 7, the 'boat was registered G-AKCO to BOAC in March 1948 and named *St George*, joined by two other Mk 7s to form the Bermuda Class. It is seen off Hythe on 31 August. In October 1954 'CO was sold to Capt. Sir Gordon Taylor who flew it to Australia where it was registered VH-APG and used on South Seas flying cruises. It then passed to Réseau Aérien Interinsulaire in Tahiti in May 1958 and was registered F-OBIP. In 1979 the Sandringham arrived in Paris, courtesy of the French military, was badly damaged in a storm in the mid-1980s and is currently in storage pending restoration for display at the Musée de l'Air at Le Bourget.

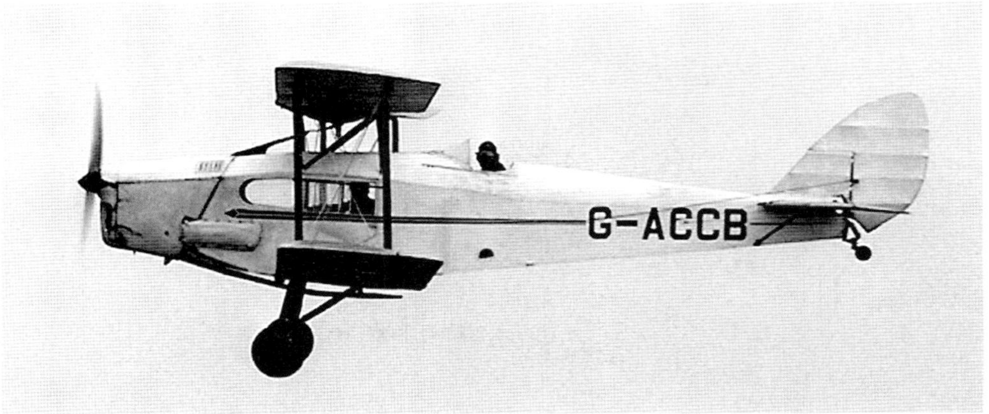

On 22 August, in company with Alec Lumsden, E.J.R. flew from Elstree in Miles M. 14A Hawk G-AIUA to land on Southport beach where he had a free ride in Giro Aviation's D.H. 83 Fox Moth G-ACCB. Previously, he had flown in the Fox Moth in July 1937 with owner S. N. Giroux. This view of 'CB, piloted by L. Knight, was taken over Southport pier the same day. The Fox Moth was first registered in February 1933, sold to Midland & Scottish Air Ferries Ltd and based at Renfrew. It was acquired by Giro Aviation Ltd in January 1936 and, in company with sister ship G-ACEJ, gave thousands of holidaymakers their first taste of flying, operating off the Southport beach during the summer season. Both aircraft somehow escaped wartime impressment, 'CB also surviving two post-war take-off accidents, one at Thruxton, the other from Southport. On 25 September 1956 its luck finally ran out when it ditched off Southport. After recovery from the sea, parts were used as spares for 'EJ which, with the remains of 'CB, had been acquired by Rollasons of Croydon. 'CB's fuselage was later put into storage by the Midland Air Museum at Coventry and then passed to a private owner for eventual rebuild.

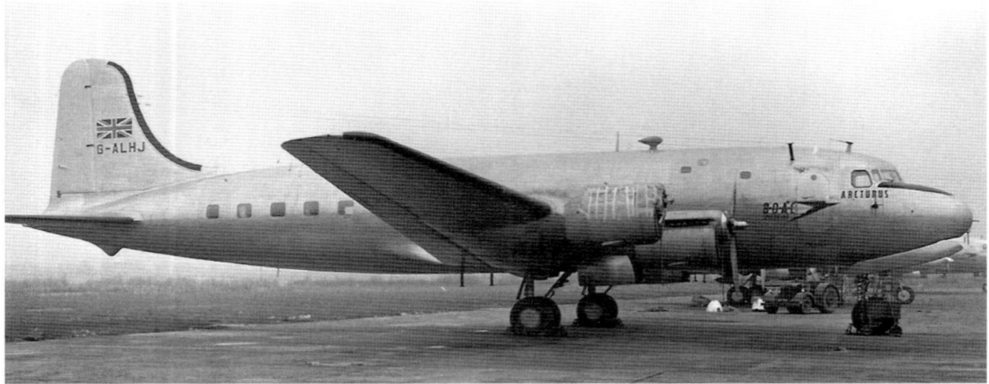

Failure of the Avro Tudor resulted in BOAC looking overseas for a suitable replacement to operate its Empire routes, settling on the Canadair C-4, a Rolls-Royce Merlin-powered version of the Douglas DC-4/C-54. G-ALHC *Ariadne*, the first aircraft delivered to the corporation from Canadair's Montreal base, arrived at Heathrow in March 1949. Known as the Argonaut, the first C-4 service was to Hong Kong, inaugurated on 23 August 1949. Seen at Heathrow on 1 September is G-ALHJ *Arcturus*, missing its starboard outer engine and not yet in service. In August 1957 'HJ went to East African Airways Corporation as VP-KOT, returning to the UK in 1964 for use at the BOAC Training School at Heathrow where it remained until scrapped in 1970.

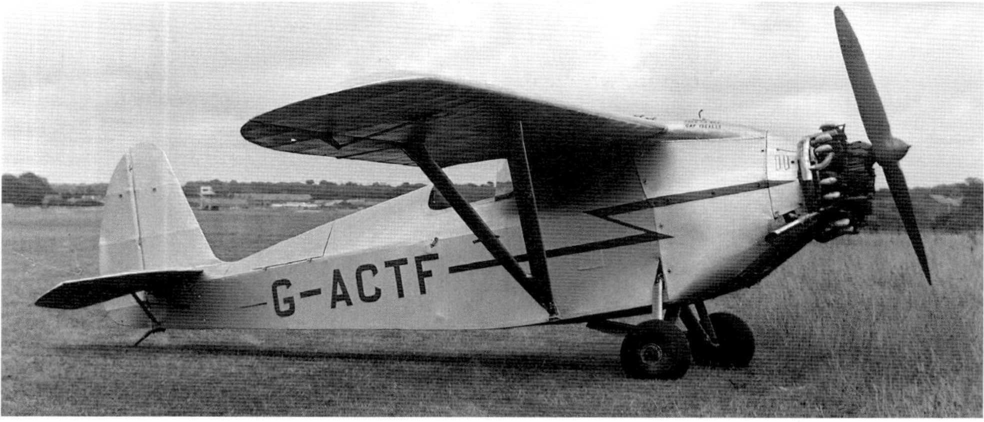

The Comper C.L.A.7 Swift designed by Flt Lt Nicholas Comper and the prototype flew in December 1929 from Hooton Park, Cheshire. Over the ensuing four years 40 or so were built several of which established a variety of records for light aircraft. G-ACTF, seen at Christchurch on 3 September, was shipped originally to India as VT-ADO and named *Scarlet Angel* by owner Alban Ali. In 1933 Ali decided to fly the Swift 'home' to Heston. On the way he competed in the Viceroy's Cup race at Delhi. Afterwards, 'DO progressed as far as Abu Sueir, Egypt, before the Pobjoy engine's greedy consumption of oil brought the flight to an end. Ali's adventures with his Swift are told in a wonderful book with the catchy title: *The Scarlet Angel— the Story of a Seven-thousand Mile Journey chiefly in a Single-seater Light Aeroplane*, published by Duckworth in 1934. The Swift was shipped back to the UK, rebuilt by Airspeed chief test pilot George Errington and registered G-ACTF. In 1951 the aircraft was acquired by Ron Clear, another Airspeed test pilot, who groomed it for racing and flew it into fifth place in the *Daily Express* Race at an F.A.I. Class Record speed of 141 mph. He also adapted it for glider towing! During the past 60 years 'TF has had had many owners, flying currently from Old Warden in the care of the Shuttleworth Collection.

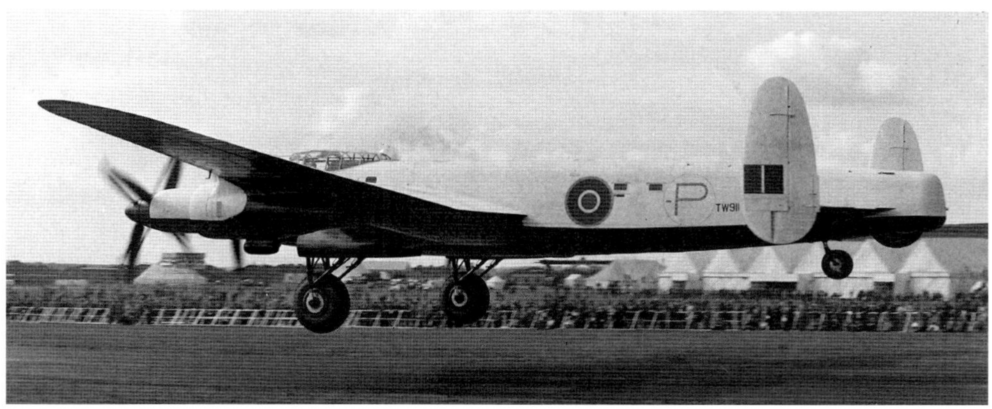

Above and below: Built as an Avro Lancaster I by Armstrong Whitworth at Baginton, Coventry, in 1945, TW911 went to Armstrong Siddeley Motors Ltd at Bitterswell for installation of two 1,610 hp Rolls-Royce Merlin 24s inboard (replacing Merlin 20s), two 3,670 hp Python I turboprops outboard and an extra 400 gallon fuel tank in the bomb bay. It is seen landing at the SBAC show at Farnborough on 9 September. The other view shows the port inboard Merlin 24 running. Note the contra-rotating propellers on the outboard Pythons. Taken off charge in January 1953, the forward fuselage was fitted to Avro Lincoln B. Mk2 RF342 and used for icing research by D. Napier & Son Ltd, for which it was equipped with two 400 gallon water tanks and given the Class B marks G-29-1. Used for all kinds of trials and testing of various aircraft parts, the Lincoln was registered G-APRJ in 1959 and appeared again at the Farnborough show that year, remaining airworthy until 1962. It then spent 25 years at the Bournemouth Historic Aircraft Museum before being dismantled and stored until purchased by the Flying Heritage Collection at Everett, Washington, where the front fuselage was restored and is currently on display.

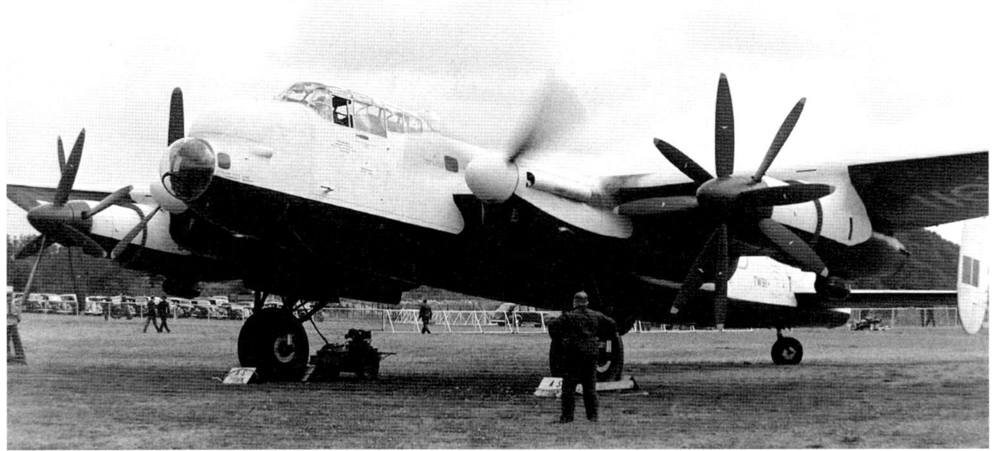

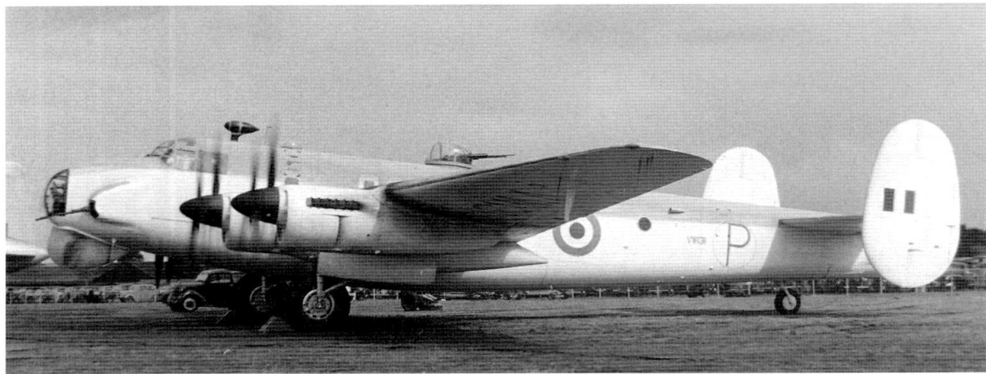

Prototype Avro 696 Shackleton VW126 flew for the first time from Woodford on 9 March 1949, designed as a land-based replacement for Second World War types in the long range maritime reconnaissance role. It utilised Lincoln main planes and undercarriage, but had a new fuselage and four 2,450 hp Rolls-Royce Griffon engines. Seen at the SBAC Farnborough show with Griffon engines running is VW131, the second prototype, first flown days before on 2 September. After a period at the A&AEE Boscombe Down it went to Napier Ltd at Luton for planned installation of the Napier Nomad E.145 engine. But the engine programme was cancelled and the aircraft stored until dismantled in 1956. Note the 20 mm Hispano cannon mounted one on either side of the nose.

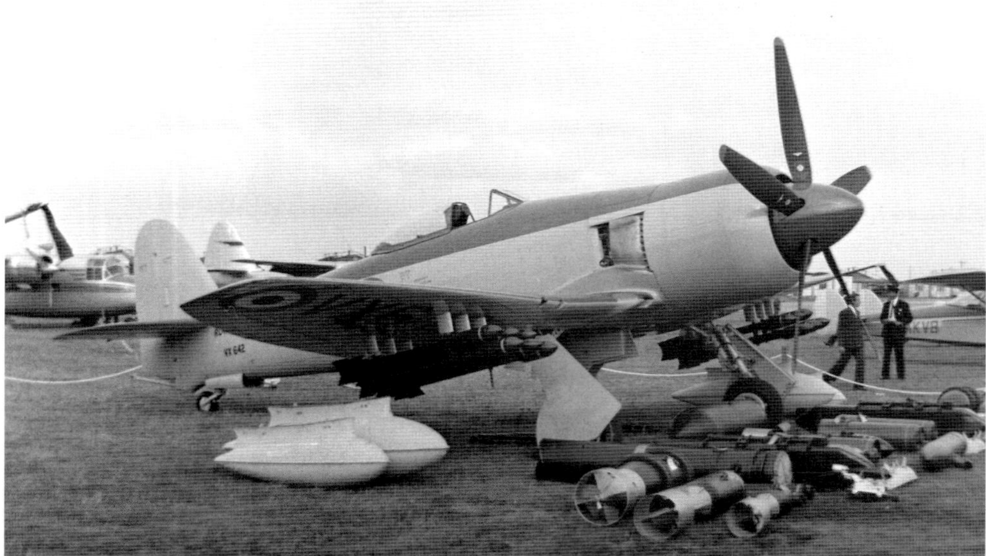

Surrounded by a veritable arsenal, Hawker Sea Fury FB.11 VX642 is pictured at the 1949 SBAC Farnborough show on 9 September. Powered by a 2,480 hp Bristol Centaurus 18 engine driving a five-bladed propeller, the F.B.11 had a maximum speed of 460 mph at 16,000 ft. Armament consisted of four 20 mm Hispano Mk. 5 guns and two 1,000 lb bombs (or 90 gallon drop tanks) accommodated on under-wing racks . VX642 was delivered to the Royal Navy in September 1949, to be taken off charge in December 1957 at Fleetlands and scrapped.

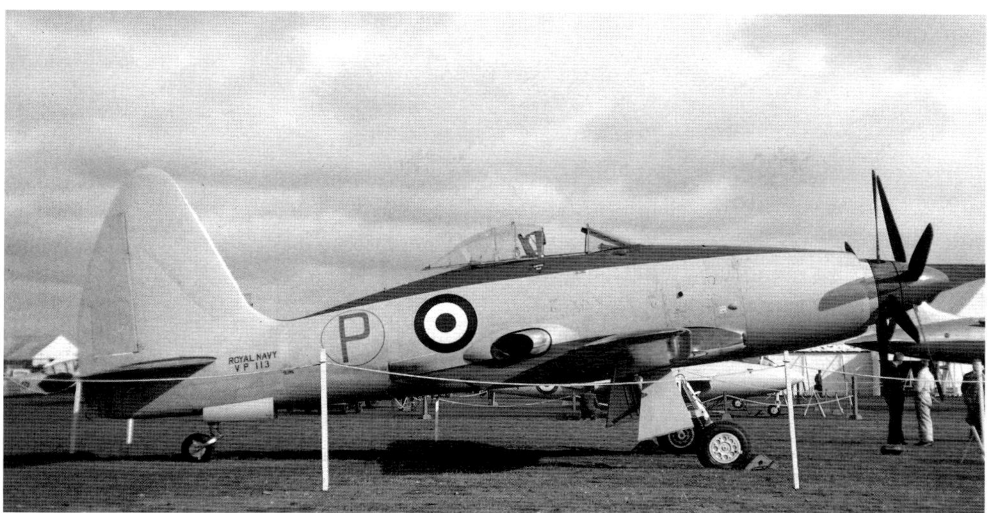

Test pilot Mike Graves put up a spirited display at the 1949 SBAC show at Farnborough in Python-engined Westland Wyvern TF. Mk. 2 VP113. *The Aeroplane* observed that it was the first occasion on which a turboprop-powered aircraft had been looped, rolled and thrown all over the sky, all the more surprising because it had flown for the first time only a few days earlier, on 20 August. VP113 returned to Yeovil for further trials, but sadly Graves was killed demonstrating the aircraft to the Air Ministry. The Python engine failed and he overshot Yeovil's grass runway during the resulting forced landing, the aircraft smashing into a house and killing the occupants.

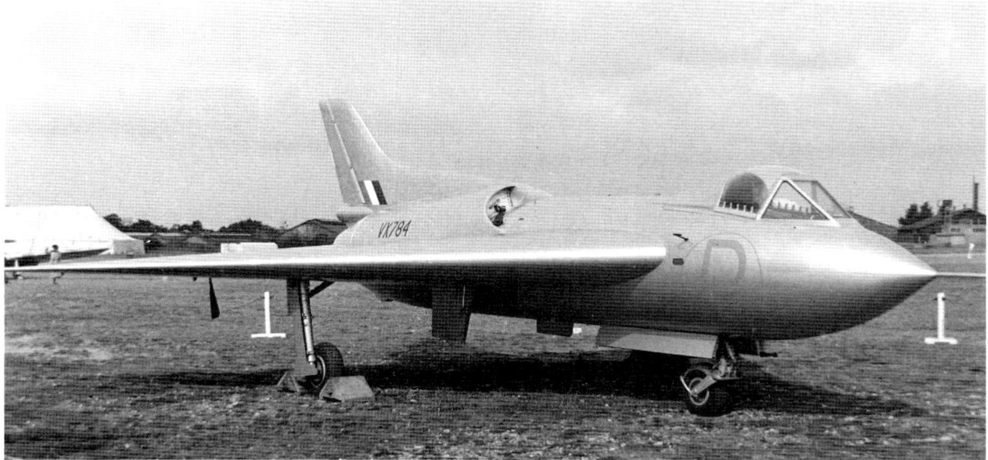

Probably the most short-lived of the aircraft exhibited at the SBAC Farnborough show in September was the first prototype Avro 707, one of five one-third scale proof-of-concept trials aircraft for the Avro Vulcan. VX784 was first flown on 4 September 1949 by deputy chief test pilot Samuel Esler, just in time to make an appearance. Powered by a 3,500 lb st Rolls-Royce Derwent 5, the 33-ft span delta continued its trials after Farnborough, but crashed near Blackbushe on 30 September, killing Esler in the process. Of the five 707s built three survive in museums.

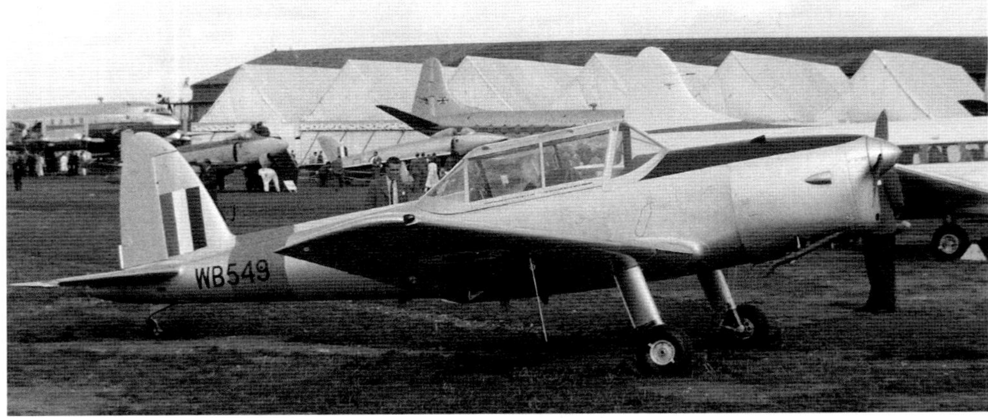

WB549, the first British-built D.H.C.1 Chipmunk, seen at the Farnborough show on 9 September. Ultimately, de Havilland received orders from 14 foreign air forces for the elementary trainer. Built at Hatfield and designated T. Mk 10, this was the first of an initial batch of 200 Chipmunks, delivered mostly in 1950. After evaluation by the A&AEE it passed to the Empire Test Pilots School, then at Farnborough. The main differences between British and Canadian versions of the Chipmunk centred on the installation of military equipment: VHF radio, accumulator stowage, cartridge starter, forward-raked undercarriage and blister rear canopy side panels. In February 1973 WB549 was sold, becoming G-BAPB in February 1979. This historic aircraft is stored currently at Tenbury Wells, Worcestershire.

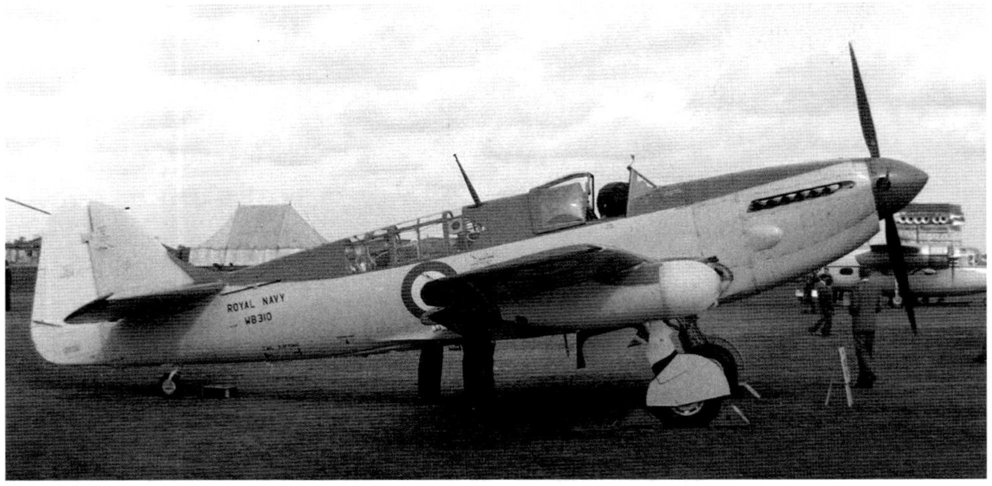

Fairey Firefly AS.5 WB310, flown by J. O. Matthews, turned many heads at the SBAC show at Farnborough when it demonstrated a rocket assisted take-off with full military load, described by *The Aeroplane* as '...looking horribly violent, but it certainly gets the aircraft into the air.' Most prolific of all the Fireflies, the Mk 5 introduced folding wings to the type, the FAA beginning to equip with the mark during 1948–49, in time to see action in the Korean War. The A.S.5 was powered by a 2,250 hp Rolls-Royce Griffon and had a maximum speed of 386 mph at 14,000 ft. WB310 was delivered to the Royal Navy in October 1949 and scrapped at Anthorn, Cumbria, in July 1957.

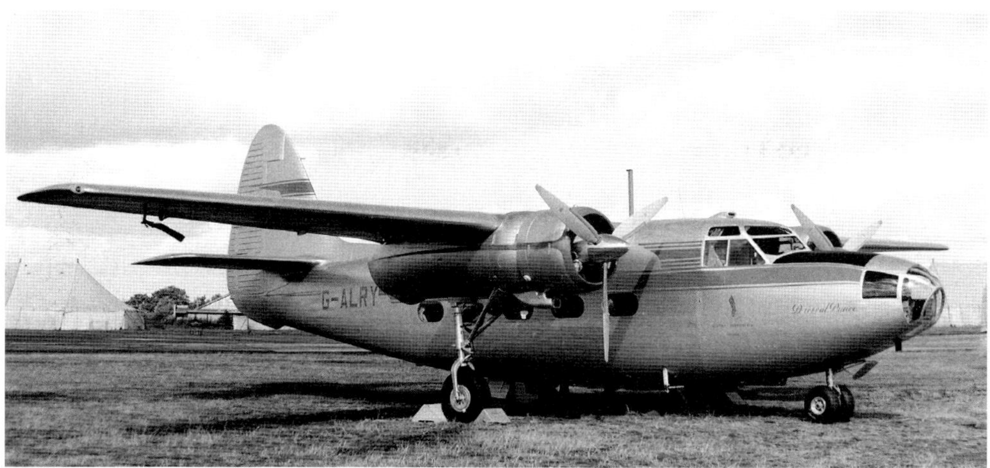

Following testing of Percival P.48 Merganser G-AHMH – (see p. 136), the prototype P.50 Prince first flew as G-23-1 on 13 May 1948 from Luton and while trials were taking place a production batch of ten aircraft was already underway. One of these, G-ALRY, was a survey version with a lengthened and glazed nose and vertical camera hatches in the belly. 'RY is seen at the SBAC Farnborough show prior to spending almost its entire career aerial surveying abroad, returning every so often to its maintenance base at Elstree. Here the author photographed it many times in various guises—VP-KNN and F-BJAJ for example—when it was seconded to various Hunting Aerosurvey associate companies. The much-travelled aerial snapper was withdrawn from use in 1966.

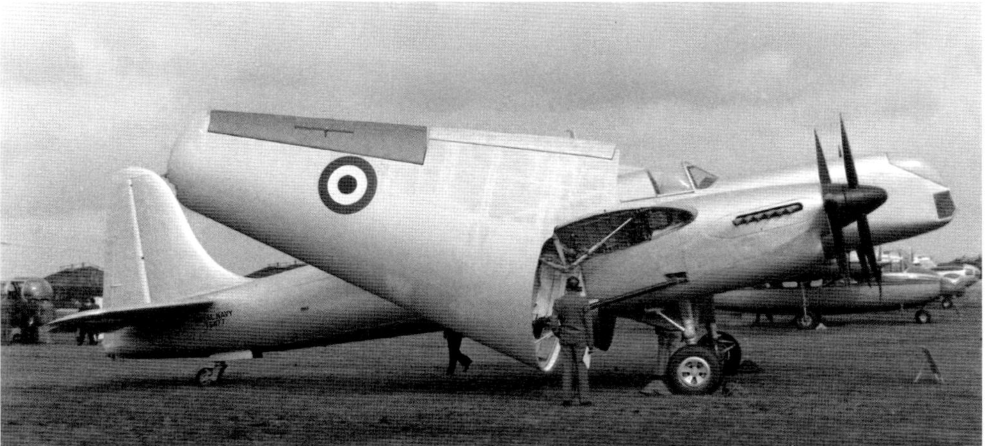

The Short Sturgeon T.T.2 high-speed, carrier-borne, target tug was a development of the Sturgeon I, intended as a reconnaissance bomber for carrier operation and first flown in 1946. The first T.T.2 made its maiden flight on 1 September 1949 and was equipped fully for carrier operation, having power-operated folding wings. Its ugly extended snout contained photographic equipment. The example displayed at the SBAC Farnborough show was TS477 from the first batch of 24 ordered for the Fleet Air Arm. Powered by two 1,600 hp Rolls-Royce Merlin 140S engines, the T.T.2 had a maximum speed of 366 mph.

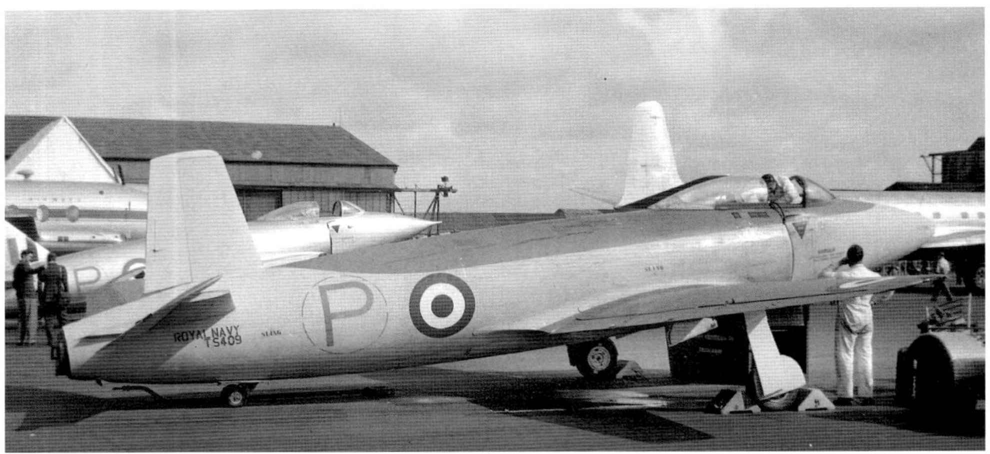

The prototype Supermarine E.10/44 TS409, later named Attacker first appeared at the 1946 SBAC show at Radlett, having been flown on 27 July by Jeffrey Quill. Powered by a 5,000 st Rolls-Royce Nene, the prototype achieved 568 mph at 15,000 ft. Its initial flight as a navalised aircraft was on 5 March 1949, appearing in this form at that year's SBAC show at Farnborough. In July 1950 Mike Lithgow won the coveted SBAC Challenge Cup in TS409, averaging 533 mph. The Attacker went into service with the Fleet Air Arm in 1951, becoming the Service's first jet fighter. As for the prototype, it was retired from RNAS Arbroath in February 1953, becoming a ground trainer before being sold for scrap in 1956.

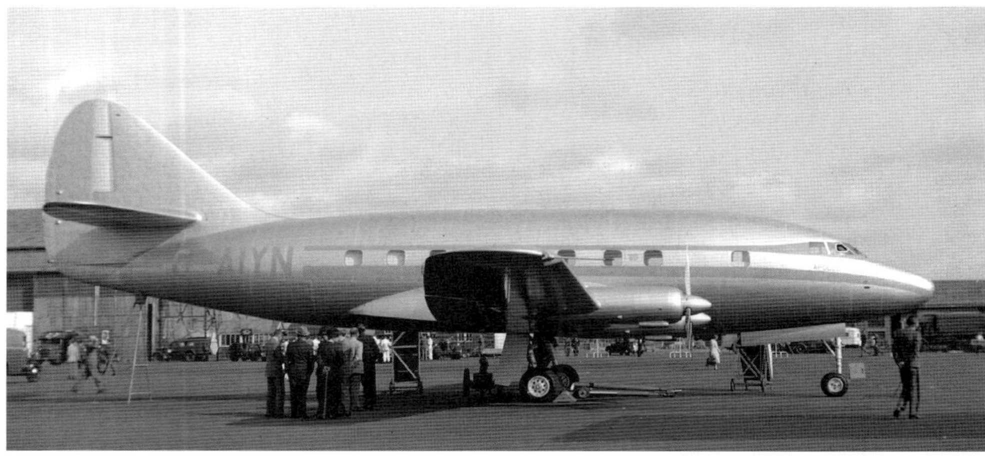

The Armstrong Whitworth A.W. 55 Apollo (originally named Achilles), a 26–31 passenger airliner, would not look out of place in the 21st century, although it was designed in 1946 and first flown as VX220 in April 1949. Powered by four 1,135 ehp Mamba A.S. Ma 1 engines, the prototype, now registered G-AIYN, is seen at the 1949 SBAC Farnborough show. A full C of A was not awarded until October 1950. Despite an intensive sales campaign no orders were forthcoming for this fine aircraft, Armstrong Whitworth deciding not to continue with its development, though a second prototype (VX224) flew in December 1952. The first aircraft was scrapped at Baginton in 1955 following trials at Boscombe Down in 1950. G-AMCH/VX224 was first flown in December 1952 and dismantled at Farnborough in 1957.

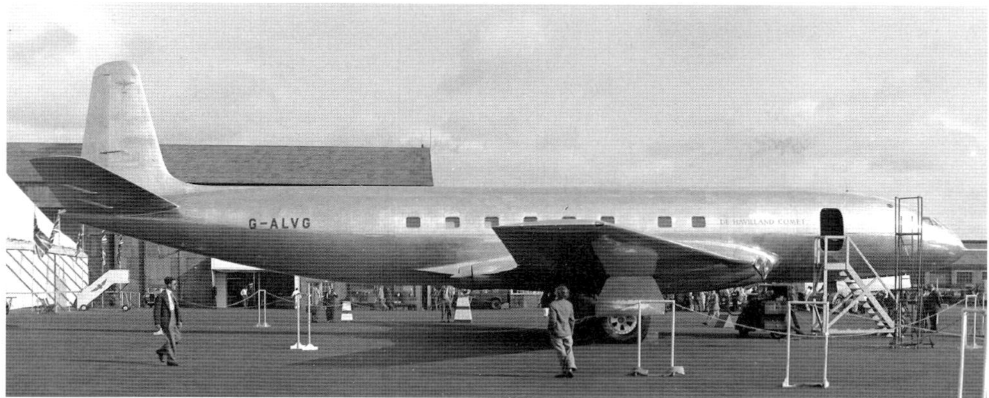

Star of the 1949 SBAC Show was undoubtedly prototype D.H. 106 Comet G-ALVG, first flown on 27 July that year by John Cunningham and about to commence flight trials involving fast overseas flights. Powered by four 4,450 lb st de Havilland Ghost 50 turbojets, the Comet ushered in a new era of air transport, becoming the world's first turbojet airliner to enter regular service on 2 May 1952.

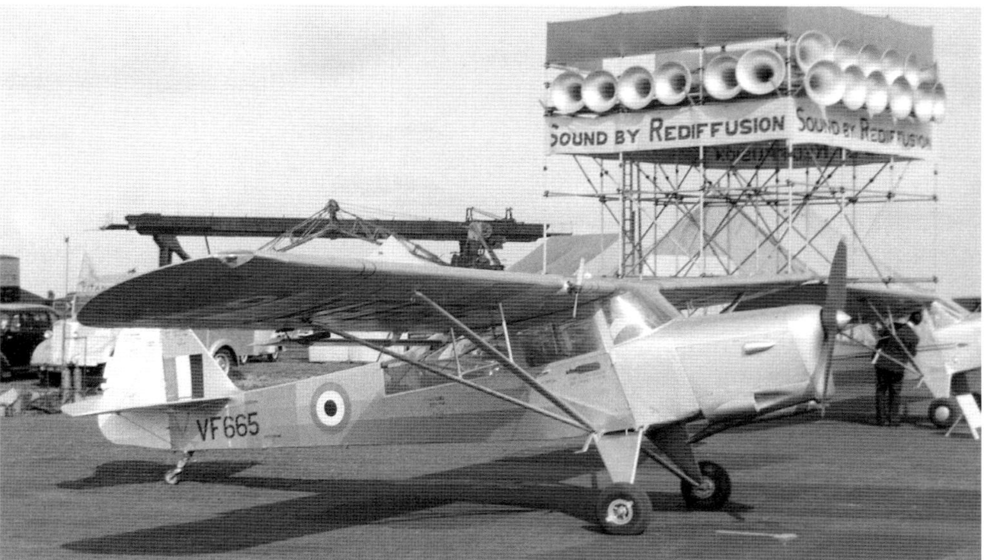

VF665 started life as a standard Auster A.O.P. 6, from the Rearsby production line before becoming the prototype Auster T.7, a dual control version of which 70 were built. In 1961 it flew in a new guise, having been acquired by Marshalls of Cambridge and, fitted with a new wing and a larger all-moving tailplane, morphed into the experimental Marshall MA.4. The wings, ailerons and flaps were perforated with holes, 200,000 in all, and connected to a suction pump driven by an auxiliary gas turbine in the fuselage, the idea being to remove the boundary layer, reduce drag and increase lift. The M.A.4 proved to be underpowered and despite further drag-reducing modifications crashed near Fulbourn, Suffolk, on 9 March 1966 after the pilot lost control. The crew of two were killed.

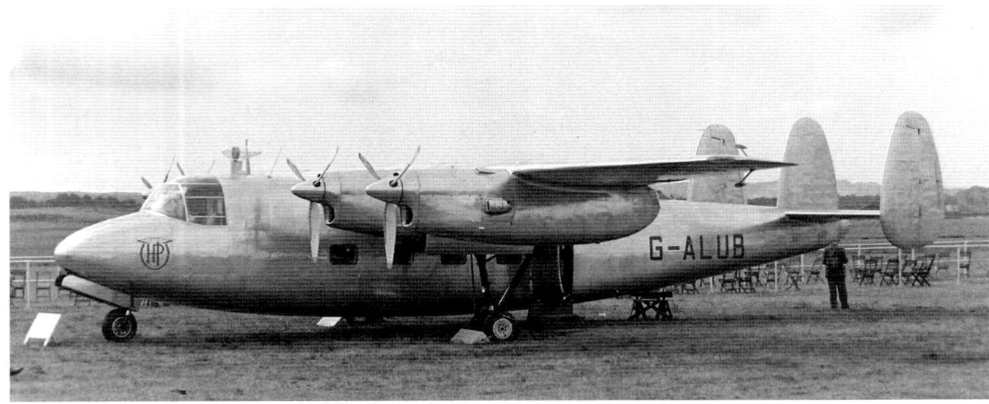

When financial difficulties overtook the Miles Aircraft Company in 1947 the company had produced two prototypes of the promising four-engine M.60 Marathon—G-AGPD and G-AILH. Because it was seen to have potential the Marathon was saved by Handley Page Ltd which acquired the Woodley factory, continued development and produced eventually 40 airframes there as Handley Page (Reading) Ltd. The first production machine, G-ALUB, left on a sales tour to Australia in January 1950 and on its return was delivered to BEA, named *Rob Roy*, and trialled on the Scottish 'Highland and Islands' routes. However, BEA deemed the Marathon unsuitable and in September 1951 cancelled its order for 25. In 1952 'UB was converted into a T. Mk 11 for the RAF and as XA249 became the first of a batch of 28 supplied during 1952-54. It flew as a navigation trainer until sold in January 1959, the type having been retired by the RAF the year before.

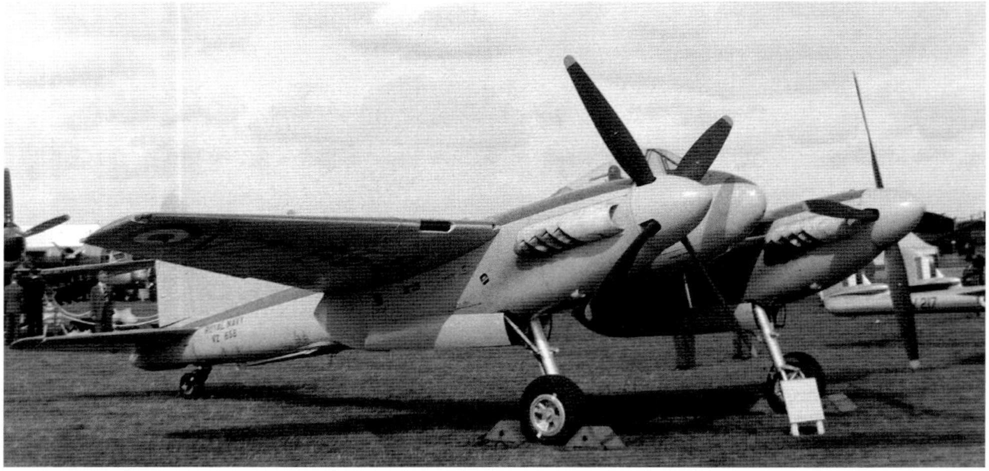

Built at Chester in 1949, D.H. 103 Sea Hornet PR.22 VZ658 was completed by de Havilland just in time to be displayed at the 1949 SBAC Farnborough show before delivery to No. 801 Squadron at Lee-on-Solent. The following year it was assigned to No. 1 Carrier Air Group on HMS *Indomitable*. Later it was sent to Abbotsinch for preservation, but tragically was instead sold for sold for scrap in July 1957. If only... Twenty-three Hornet PR.22s were delivered to the FAA. Powered by two 2,030 hp Rolls-Royce Merlin 134/135 engines, this photo reconnaissance aircraft was fitted with two F.52 and one night use Fairchild K.19B cameras.

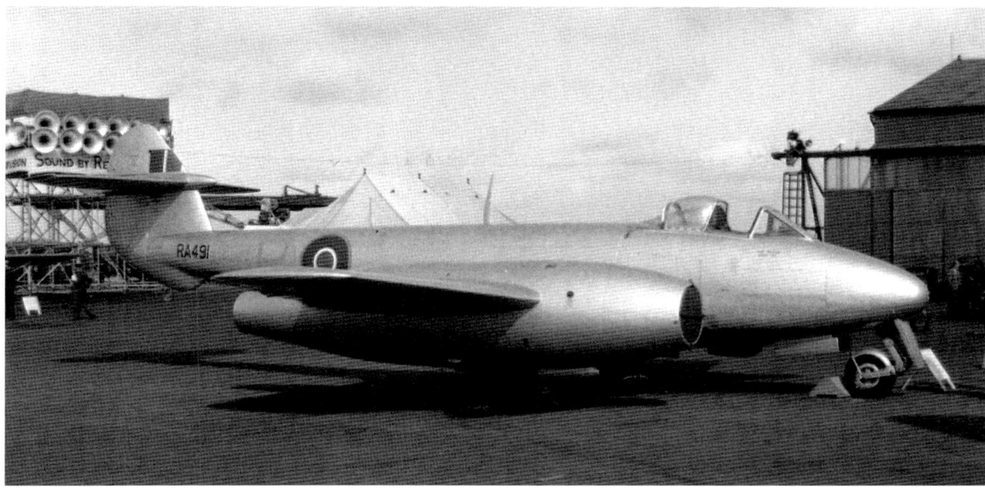

Built at Hucclecote in 1947, Meteor F.4 RA491 was retained by Gloster Aircraft before going to the National Gas Turbine Establishment at Pyestock and then to the A&AEE, to become a test bed for the Rolls-Royce Avon axial-flow turbojet. Its spectacular performance by Harvey Hayworth at the SBAC Farnborough show moved *The Aeroplane* to comment: 'He then dived from 6,000 ft to ground level—turned up, motorless, with plumes of neat fuel coming from both tailpipes, did an upward roll and then turned on the jets again on the way down. They started at once.' Later, RA491 was acquired by the French Government and fitted with two ATAR B21 turbojets and the forward fuselage of an F.8. It was not a success and was scrapped in 1952.

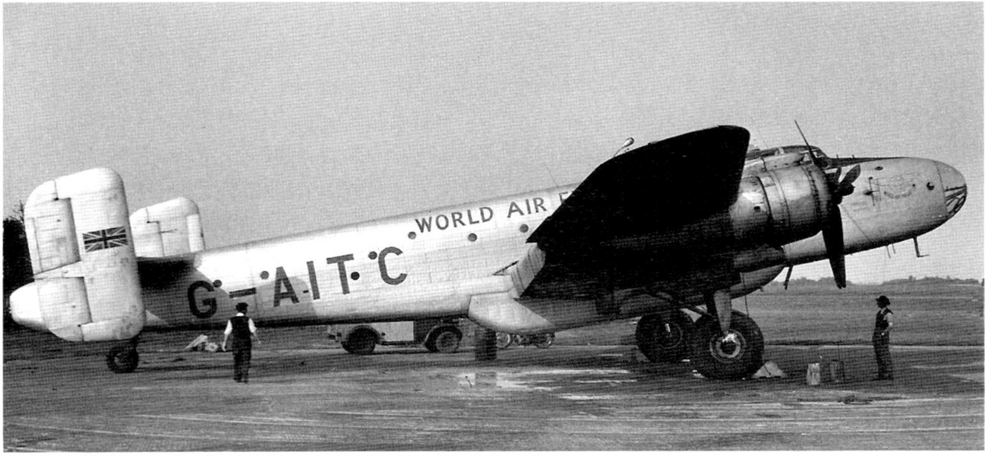

World Air Freight's (WAF) Handley Page H.P. 70 Halifax C. Mk 8 G-AITC at Bovingdon in October. Built as PP320 for the RAF, it was sold to the College of Aeronautics, Cranfield, in December 1947 and acquired by WAF in March 1949, to be based at Bovingdon. WAF operated four Halifaxes and wrote-off all of them in the space of two years, the last being 'TC, damaged beyond repair while landing at Brindisi, Italy, on 20 January 1950. With no aircraft remaining the company, not unnaturally, ceased operations!

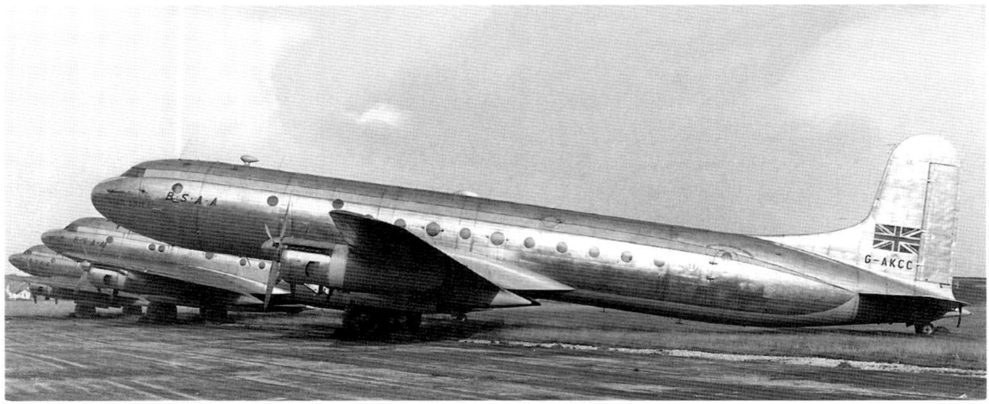

An impressive line-up of Avro 689 Tudor 5s seen at the British South American Airways' (BSAA) base at Langley in October. Nearest the camera is G-AKCC *Star Swift*, first registered in January 1949 and destined to be converted to a tanker capable of carrying nine-ton loads. It was used on the Berlin Airlift until sold to William Dempster Ltd. Named *President Kruger* and the Dempster flagship, 'CC was based at Stansted, converted to carry 52 passengers and used on charter work to and from South Africa. Damaged badly in early 1951 at Livingston Airport, it was repaired only to be written-off on 26 October after overshooting the runway at Bovingdon while landing on a flight from Castel Benito, fortunately without casualties. The 120 ft span Tudor 5 was powered by four 1,715 hp Rolls-Royce Merlin 621 engines and had an all-up weight of 80,000 lb.

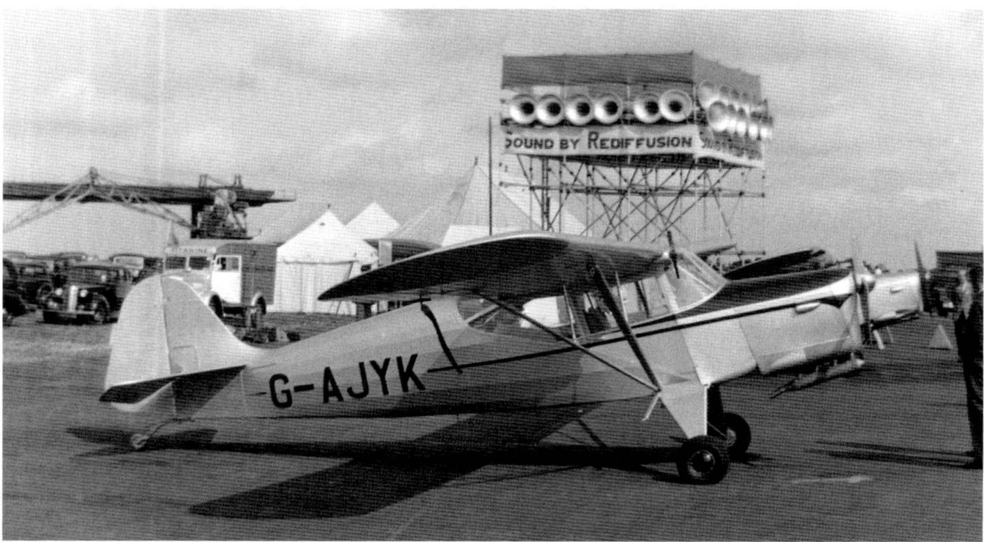

The Auster J-5B Autocar prototype seen at the Farnborough SBAC show on 9 September. Four-seat G-AJYK was flown at Rearsby the previous month and was the first of around 80 produced and exported worldwide. Powered by a 130 hp D.H. Gipsy Major 1 engine, the Autocar was characterized by its domed cabin roof to allow adequate headroom for the two rear passengers. 'YK was sold to Barton-based Airviews (Manchester) Ltd in April 1950 and used for aerial photographic work until it crashed while climbing out from Rearsby only four months later, on 18 September.

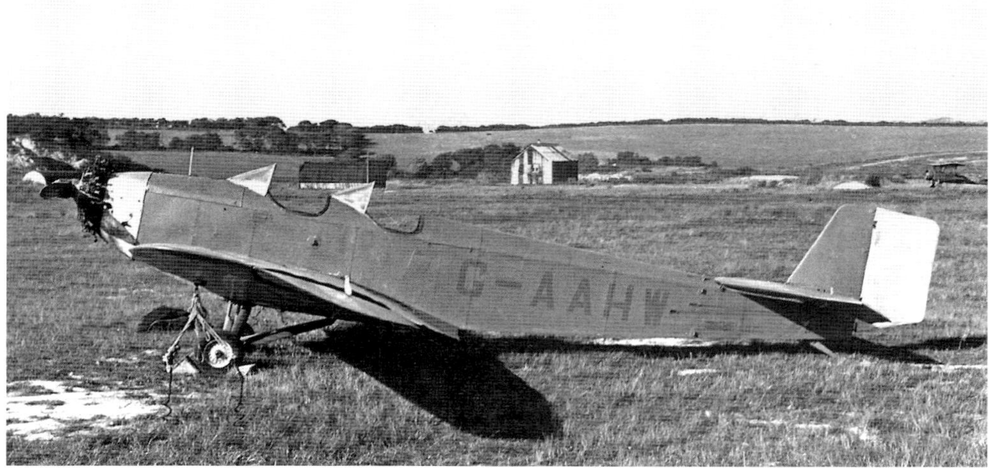

On 15 October E.J.R. flew to Pebsham airfield, Hastings, in Auster Autocrat G-AGXT to take air-to-air photographs of Klemm L.25 1A G-AAHW, owned and flown by G. R. Lush. 'HW was the 152nd example built at Boblingen and was registered first in the UK to C. W. G. Wood in June 1929, based at Croydon. In May 1983 the Klemm was sold in Germany, becoming D-ELFK, but returned to UK in January 1997, only to return once more to Germany in June 1998. E.J.R.'s flying log book notes the Klemm's performance: 'Take-off 30 mph, cruise 45 mph and landing speed 15–20 mph'—all on a 40 hp Salmson A.D. 9 radial engine.

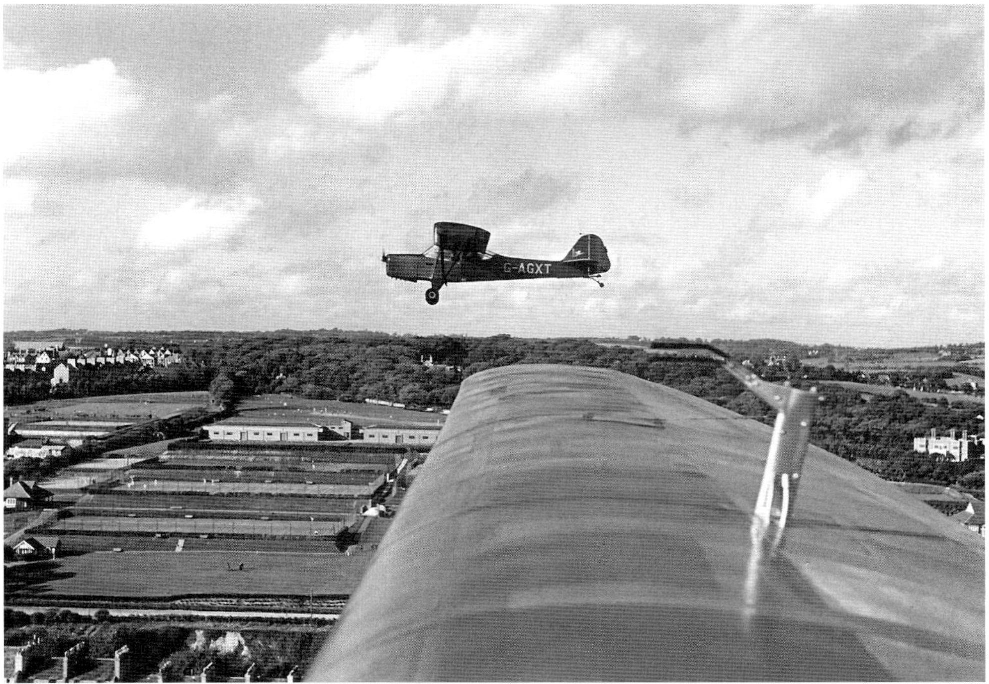

Gotcha! Me, photographing you, photographing me... While E.J.R. was busy taking air-to-airs of G-AAHW, the front seat occupant of the Klemm L. 25 was capturing shots of him in the back seat of Autocrat G-AGXT, flown by Stanley Orton Bradshaw.

M.C.A. Form 604

I.　**UNITED KINGDOM**

II.　**PRIVATE PILOT'S LICENCE (FLYING MACHINES)**

III.　Number of Licence .... 30237 ....

Particulars of holder:

IV.　Full name: .... Edwin James ....

.... RIDING ....

V.　Address: .... 17, Newark Way, ...

.... Hendon, London, NW.4. ....

VI.　Nationality: .... British ....

VII.　Signature: .... E.J.Riding ....

VIII.　Issued in accordance with the provisions of the Air Navigation Acts 1920 to 1947 and the Orders in Council in force thereunder, and with Annexe 1 of the International Convention on Civil Aviation signed on 7th December 1944.

IX.　The holder of this licence is hereby authorized to fly as pilot of flying machines in accordance with the terms and conditions specified herein, provided he also holds a current Certificate of Validity (M.C.A. Form 629A) in respect of this licence.

X.　Signature of Issuing Officer ....

Date and stamp .... 17th November, 1949 ....

XI.　**BY AUTHORITY OF THE MINISTER OF CIVIL AVIATION.**

Just as it was getting dark at Elstree on the evening of 15 March 1949 David Cotter sent E.J.R. off on his first solo, in Piper Cub G-AKAA. The flight lasted five minutes, but his second solo, consisting of circuits and bumps, lasted a whole hour. E.J.R.'s Private Pilot's Licence, No. 30237, was issued on 17 November 1949.

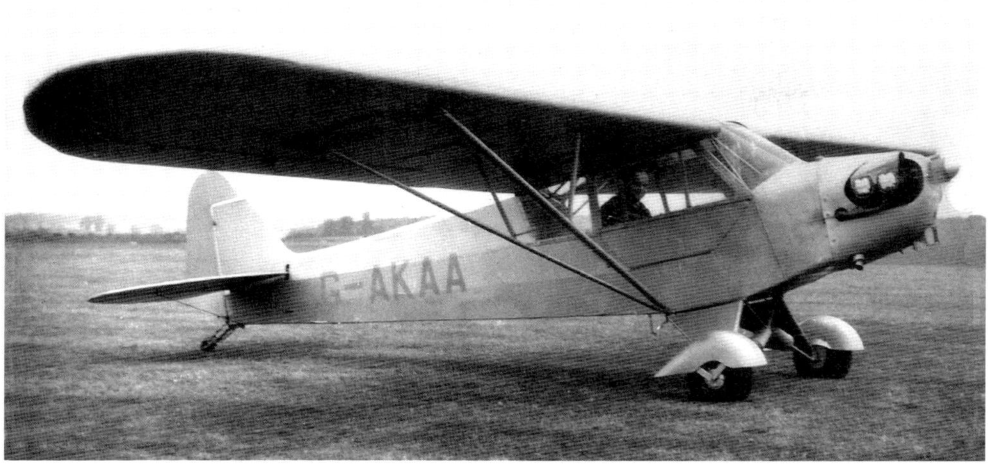

E.J.R. at Eaton Bray during one of many flying visits during 1949-50. Invariably he gave flights to *Aeromodeller* and Harborough Publishing Company staff, including C. Rupert Moore, whose colour paintings graced the front covers of that journal during the 1940s and early '50s. Piper Cub G-AKAA belonged to Wg Cdr O. V. Holmes and was kept at Elstree. As a child the author had several flights in the Cub with E.J.R. during 1949-50 and in September 1989 flew in it once again. Originally 42-29489 with the USAAF, 'KA was registered in the UK in June 1947 and sold in Spain in October 1996, becoming EC-GQE.

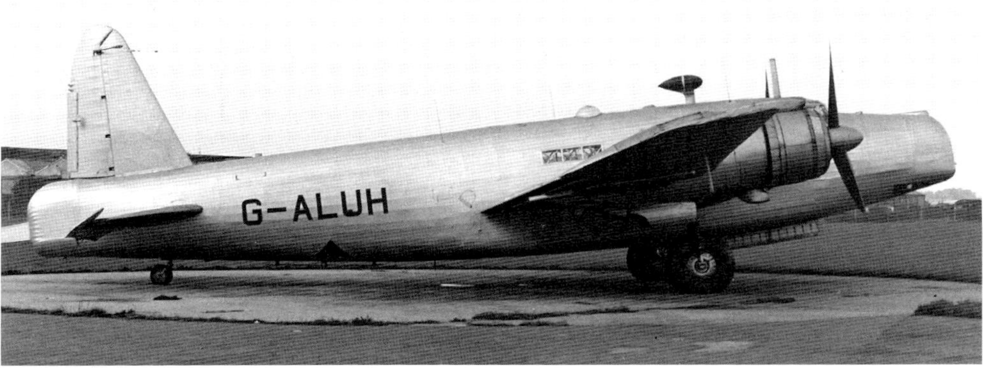

In 1945 at Blackpool Vickers produced a batch of 226 Wellington Xs and XVIIIs for the RAF. One of them became the sole British civil registered example of Barnes Wallis's long range night bomber, the first of which had made its maiden flight in June 1936. Wellington T. Mk X RP468 was registered G-ALUH in July 1949 and is seen at Langley in October, where it had the nose and tail turrets faired over and was fitted with tail boom radar equipment, tested during flights along the Norwegian coast. On completion of the tests the Wellington returned to the RAF and resumed its Service identity.

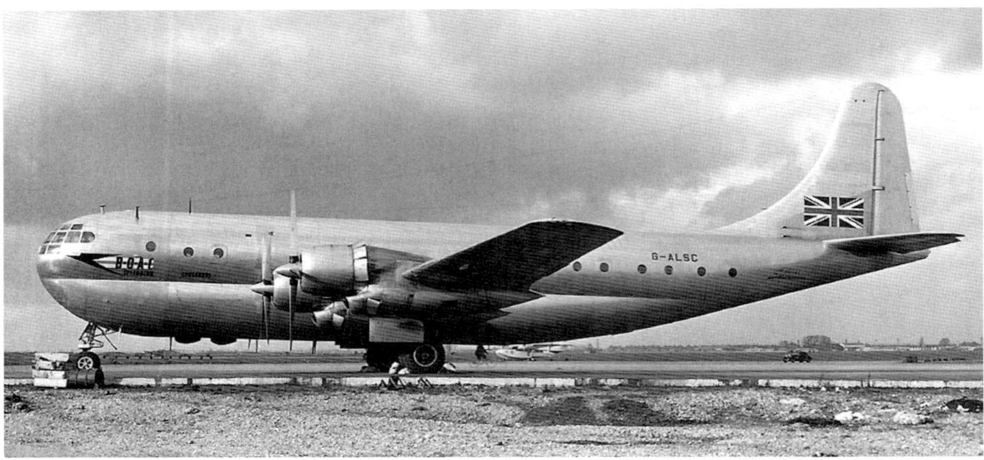

Of the 55 Boeing 377 Stratocruisers built at Seattle during 1949–50 ten were purchased by BOAC to supplement its Lockheed Constellation fleet for trans- Atlantic services. First to arrive was G-ALSA *Cathay* (named, like the others, after the legendary fleet of Empire boats.) G-ALSC *Centaurus*, seen at Heathrow on 4 February in original 'economy' livery, was registered the previous December. After nearly a decade of service with the corporation it returned to the USA as N101Q for Oakland-based Transocean Air Lines, was re-registered N406Q and subsequently broken up. Powered by four 3,500 hp Pratt and Whitney Wasp R-4360 engines giving a cruising speed of 300 mph, the Strat was famous for its double-bubble, two-deck, pressurized fuselage and lower deck cocktail bar, reached via a spiral staircase. The new standards of comfort it brought to long haul air travel gave it unrivalled passenger appeal.

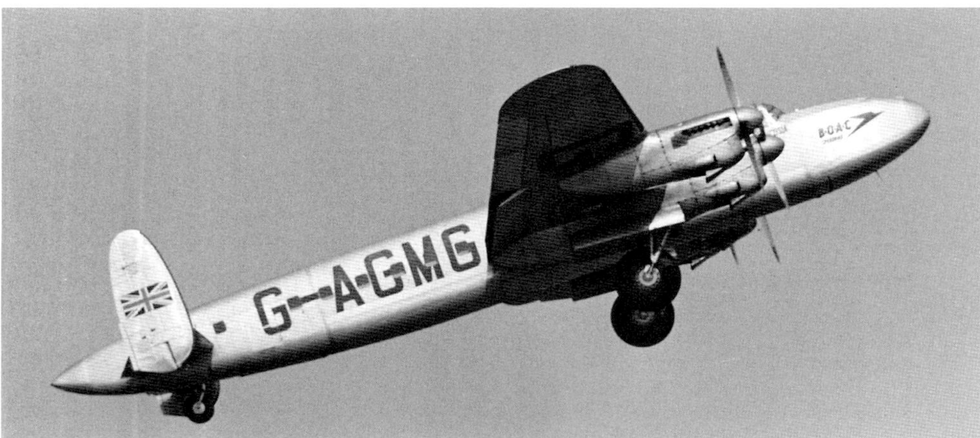

Main wheels retracting, BOAC Avro 691 Lancastrian C. Mk 1 G-AGMG *Nicocia* climbs out of Heathrow on 4 February. Built in 1945 as VF161, but delivered direct to BOAC and registered in August 1945, 'MG was used on the joint Qantas/BOAC Kangaroo service, started from Hurn in May 1945. The Lancastrians could carry only nine passengers, all seated in one row facing outwards. Just imagine the noise when sitting for hours between four thundering 1,635 hp Rolls-Royce Merlins—sounds like heaven! Under the command of the legendary Capt. O. P. Jones, 'MG made the first survey flight from Hurn to South America in October 1945 in preparation for the service that began in 1946. Along with several other BOAC Lancastrians, 'MG was scrapped at Hurn in January 1951.

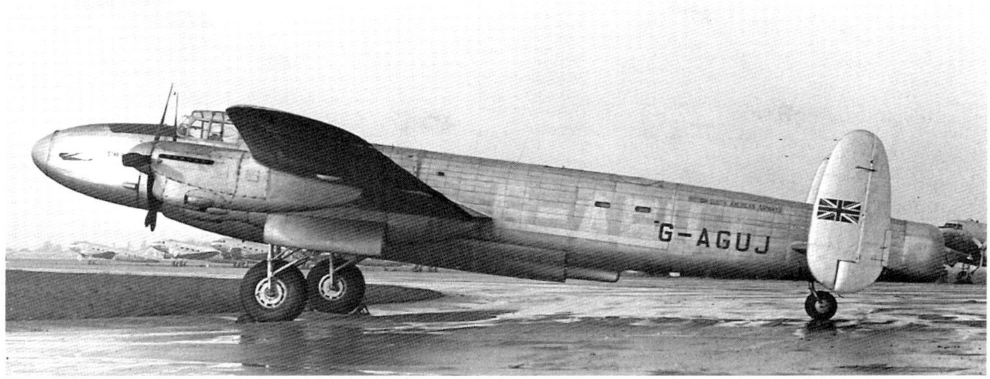

At first glance Avro 683 Lancaster I G-AGUJ appears to be a Lancastrian. In 1946 BSAA acquired six Lancasters from the Ministry of Supply, four of which were converted to freighters by A.V. Roe. Lack of fuselage windows distinguishes these Lancasters from Lancastrians and though the nose turrets were faired over those in the tail were just painted over. The converted quartet was used for flying perishable goods, but soon deemed uneconomic. 'UJ, originally allotted the RAF serial number PP689, was registered in March 1946 and named *Star Pilot*. After service with BSAA it passed to BOAC in September 1949, remaining at its Langley base where it was dismantled by the end of the year. It is seen at Heathrow on 8 January 1950. The former style of registration letters can be discerned beneath the existing registration letters.

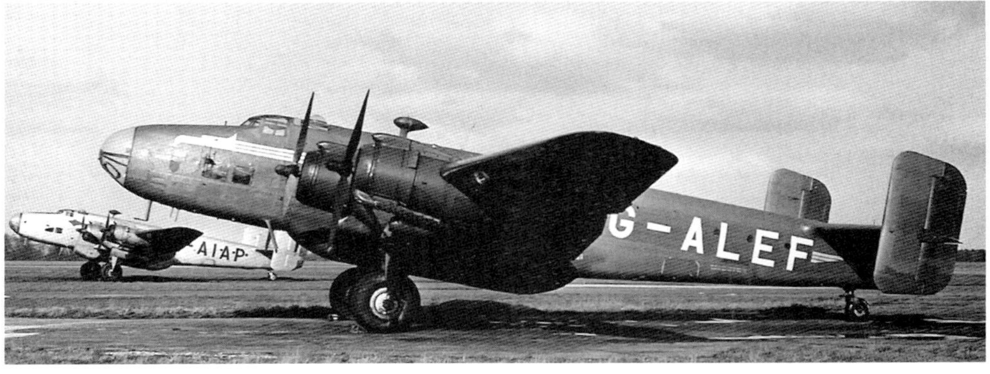

The last of some 80 or so H.P. 70 Halifax C. Mk. 8s to be allocated British civil markings, though not necessarily given Certificates of Airworthiness, was G-ALEF. It was built in 1945, formerly RAF aircraft PP337 and the penultimate C. Mk. 8 assembled at Radlett. Delivered first to Vingtor Airways of Norway as LN-OAT, it returned to the UK in October 1948, was registered 'EF to Eagle Aviation Ltd and named *Red Eagle*. It is seen at Eagle's Aldermaston base on 22 February before a move to Luton. Eagle operated six Halifaxes on the Berlin Airlift before superseded by Avro Yorks and withdrawn from use. 'EF was scrapped at Luton in 1950.

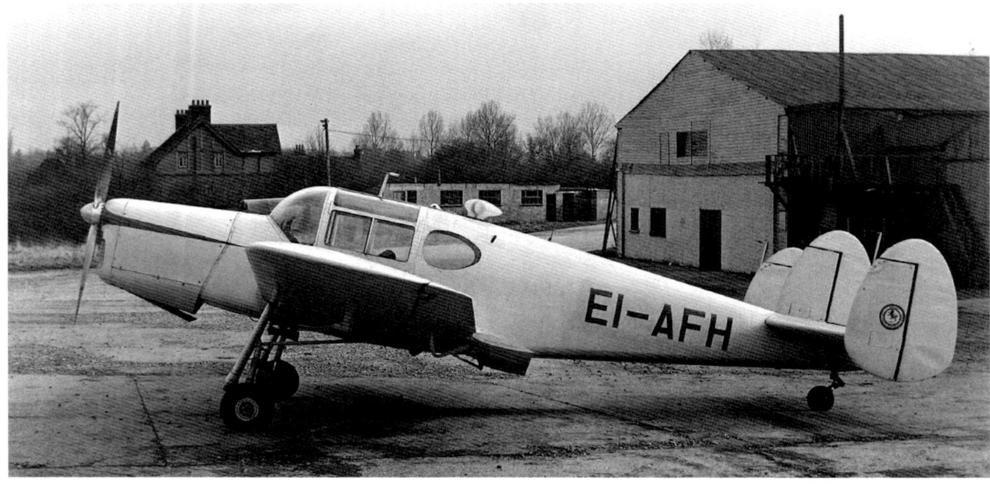

First registered in August 1947, Miles M.38 Messenger 2A G-AKBL was owned by the Smithfield Refrigerator Company Ltd and based at Elstree until re-registered in Ireland. Its new identity from February 1950 was EI-AFH, having been sold to R. Matthews-Napier, a farmer and landowner from Loughcrew, Co. Meath. The Messenger was restored to the UK register by the same owner in February 1952, but went missing over the Irish Sea while flying from RAF Northolt to Dublin on 1 April 1953. 'BL was a frequent participant in the National Air Races.

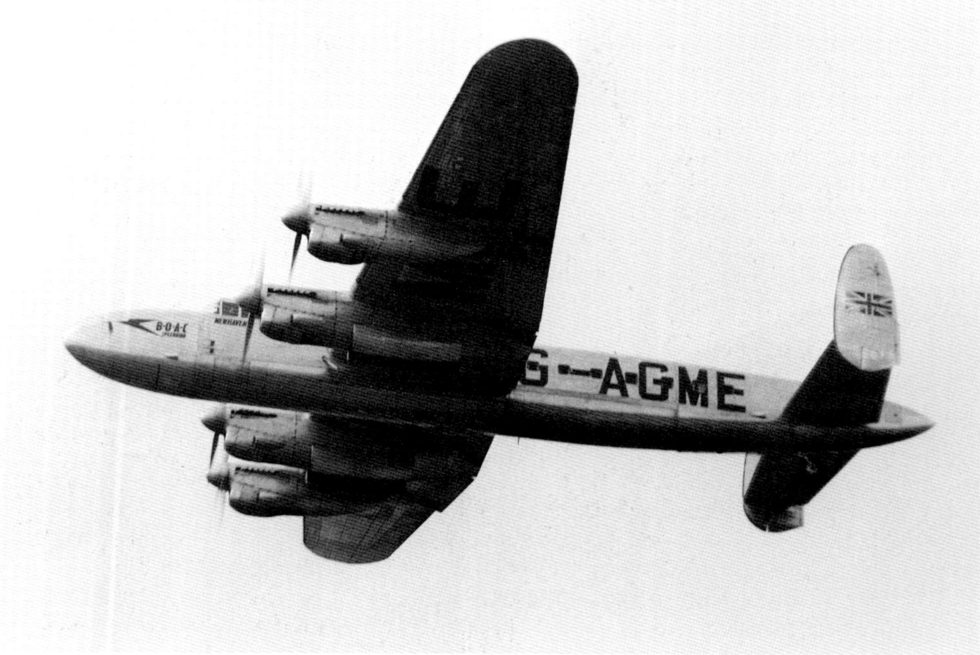

BOAC's Avro 691 Lancastrian 1 G-AGME *Newhaven,* photographed just after take-off with undercarriage doors closing. Ordered as Avro Lancaster (Special) PD165 in 1945, it was built as Lancastrian 1 VF156 and diverted to BOAC. 'ME was first registered in July 1945 and after nearly five years with the corporation was scrapped at Hurn in November 1950.

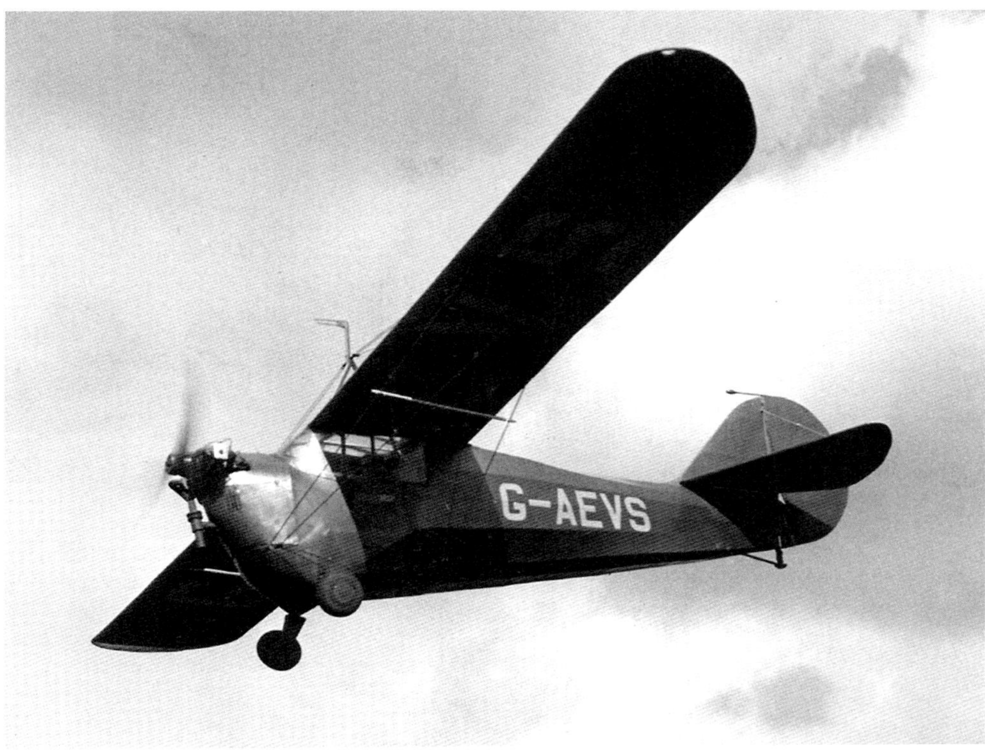

E.J.R.'s final air-to-air photographic sortie took place on 23 March when, flying in Miles M.14A Hawk Trainer G-AKKY flown by Stanley Orton Bradshaw, he photographed a Mr McNamara flying Aeronca 100 G-AEVS from Denham. Acquired originally by Aircraft Exchange & Mart in May 1937, 'VS was sold to the Speedbird Flying Club in September 1948, its owner when this photograph was taken. Beverley Snook was next, after which the Aeronca migrated north to the Yorkshire Flying Club at Sherburn-in-Elmet and then to Newcastle. Many subsequent owners later, 'VS is still airworthy.

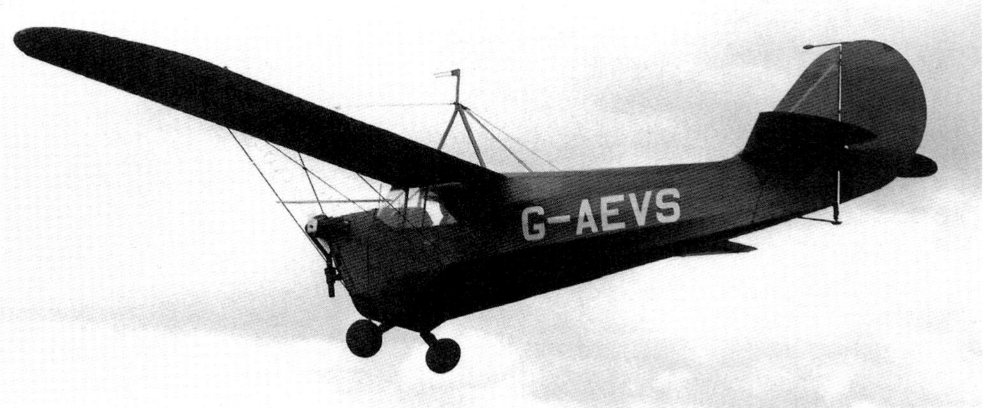

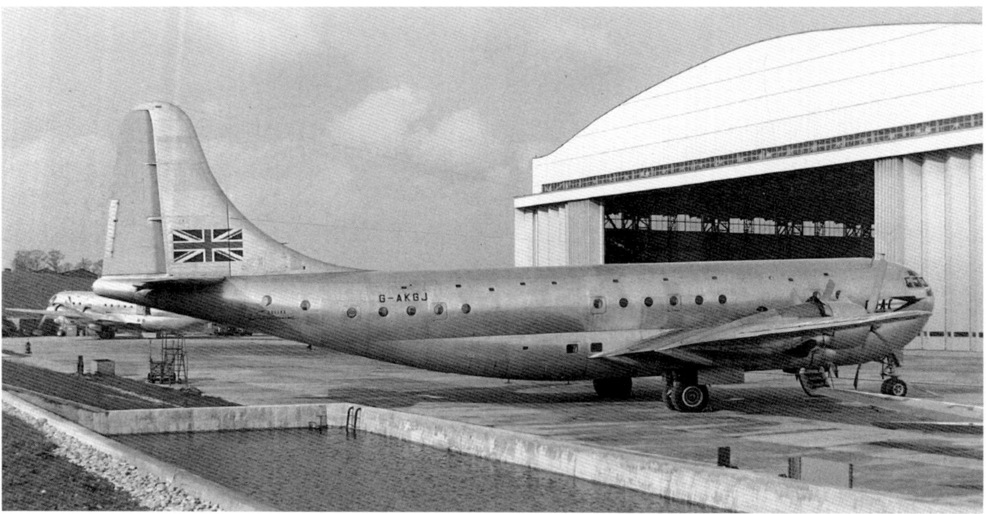

Another BOAC Boeing 377 Stratocruiser, this time pictured at Filton, Bristol, on 21 February outside the massive Brabazon hangar where the airline's Strats were maintained until the new maintenance base at Heathrow was completed. G-AKGJ *Cambria* flew on the corporation's Preswick–Montreal and London–New York routes and after almost 10 years of service returned to the USA to become N102Q with Transocean Air Lines, later becoming N407Q before eventually broken up for spares.

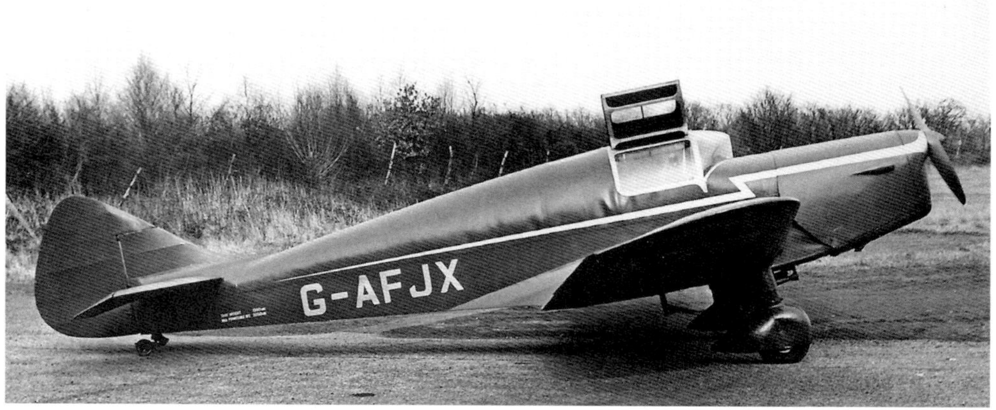

Miles M.11 Whitney Straight G-AFJX at Old Warden on 23 March. Then owned jointly by Mrs Dorothy Shuttleworth and Allen H. Wheeler, 'JX was first registered in August 1938. It was impressed into the RAF in August 1940 as BD183 and used by the communications flight at Skeabrae. On demob it went to Warden Aviation & Engineering, Old Warden, then to New Zealand, becoming ZK-AUK in 1960. Following several ownerships the Whitney Straight was badly damaged following a ground loop in June 1966 and since that date has been stored, pending restoration to airworthy condition by present owner Greg Macdonald.

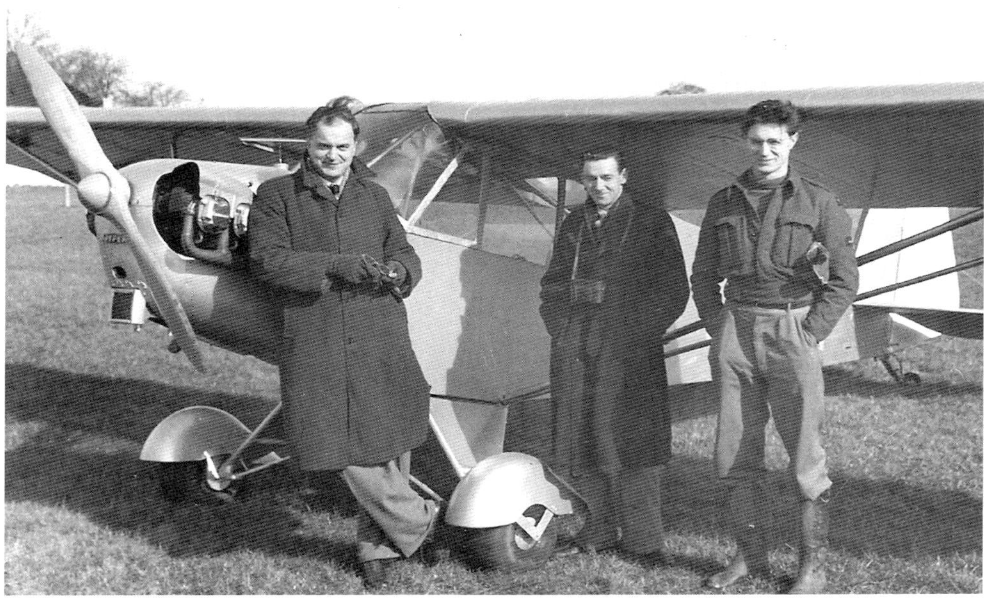

E.J.R., with Norman Eaststaff, George A. Cull and Piper Cub G-AKAA, at Eaton Bray in March during one of his frequent flying visits from Elstree. After E.J.R.'s death, the following month George Cull took over the *Aeromodeller* Aircraft Described series and, like his mentor, wrote the text, produced the three-views and photographed the subject aircraft.

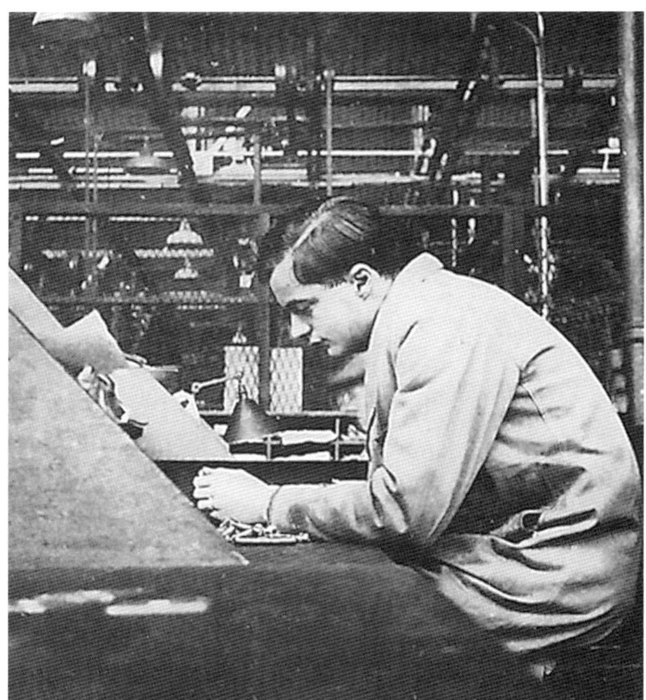

A taste of things to come. E.J.R. checking the paper work for fittings for a Blackburrn Shark at Brough. He was employed in the Works Inspection Department of Blackburn Aircraft Ltd from October 1937 until February 1938, before moving on to Martin Hearn Ltd at Hooton.

Samuel Frederick Offord
(1917–1966)

During his time with the AID, both at Fairey's Great West Aerodrome and at Leavesden, E.J.R. flew with many talented pilots—service, company and ATA. Among them—and judging from comments in his log book, a particular favourite—was Canadian Samuel Frederick Offord.

Born on 6 October 1917, Offord arrived in Britain during 1941 and on joining the RAF learnt to fly with No. 6 Elementary Flying Training School on D.H. 82a Tiger Moths operated under contract by Brooklands Aviation Ltd at Sywell, Northamptonshire. On 24 May 1941 he soloed in Tiger Moth N6808 (later G-AOEC/ZK-BNG) and was awarded his flying badge on 3 September. That month he transferred to No. 51 Operational Training Unit at Cranfield to train as a night fighter. On completion of the course in November his ability was rated 'exceptional'. On 3 September 1942 Flt Lt S. F. Offord (46533) was assigned to the General Duties Branch, RAF.

In 1942 he was posted to No. 23 fighter squadron at Ford and flew Douglas Havoc Is, Douglas Boston IIIs and de Havilland D.H. 98 Mosquito FB.6s. On 27 February that year engine trouble forced him to ditch Havoc BB900 in the sea off Margate, resulting in the drowning of his observer and friend, Flt Sgt James G. Shandley. Offord and two other crew members were picked up by the Margate lifeboat. A Court of Inquiry queried the pilot's carrying of a crew of four, three being regulation. Offord was cleared of any indiscipline, though he was no stranger to carrying unauthorised passengers. Whilst with the same squadron he took his dog, Rufus, on a local flight in a Mosquito FB.6 and later an Alsatian was a passenger with E.J.R. and Offord on a trip from Staverton to Leavesden!

Offord returned to Canada in 1943 and was posted to 36 OCU at RAF Greenwood as part of the Mosquito aircrew training programme that began in July, flying Mosquitoes and Bristol Bolingbrokes until the following year. In July 1944 Greenwood became RCAF Station Greenwood, by which time Offord had returned to England and posting to the de Havilland Aircraft Company as a Mosquito production test pilot, where he met E.J.R. Their first flight together was on 3 April 1945 in Mosquito T.III RR296 when Offord allowed E.J.R. some dual. The couple flew together subsequently on nearly 50 Mosquito flights, the last in prototype Mosquito T.33 TS449 on 5 February 1946 during which they climbed to 14,000 ft and carried out four rolls and two loops. E.J.R. left the AID later that month.

After the war Offord returned to Canada and was employed by de Havilland Canada flying Mosquitoes once more. A total 1,133 Mosquitoes were built by de Havilland Canada and by the end of the war several hundred surplus airframes were put into storage. Worth an estimated $30 million, these aircraft, together with 400 spare Rolls-Royce engines, were offered for sale in 1947. At the time China was in the throes of a civil war with the Sino-Communist Government led by Mao Tse-tung fighting Chinese Nationalists led by Chiang Kai-shek. A delegation of Chinese Nationalists arrived at Downsview Airport and a deal was completed whereby most of the aircraft and engines were acquired for a bargain price of $5 million. The aircraft were disassembled, packed and shipped off to China while the first Chinese pilots began training at Downsview with former RCAF and de Havilland Canada pilots as instructors. The Chinese pilots were used to flying nose-wheel B-25 Mitchells and found take-offs and landings in the Mosquito very difficult, resulting in numerous accidents. As a result the training programme was transferred to Shanghai, China.

Offord was amongst the de Havilland Canada personnel sent to test the reassembled FB.26s and T.29s (this is not confirmed, may have been T.27s) and to teach the Chinese pilots to fly them. With wife Madelyn, he arrived in Tachang on 17 February 1948 on a one-year contract and the couple were based at the Pacific Hotel. Madelyn worked for the base commander and Offord took her on at least one Mosquito test flight! The accident rate remained horrendous. It is recorded that 20 per cent of the Mosquitoes were written off in training accidents, many of them before the aircraft became airborne. Offord is reported to have said that the whole programme was a waste of money. He and Madelyn were among the last to leave China as the country fell to the Communists, boarding the ship home to the sound of approaching gun fire.

On returning to Canada Offord began flying Canadian-built D.H. 83C Fox Moths and Fairchild 71s in Northern Ontario for Great Northern Skyways (GNS), a bush flying company started by former US Navy pilot Keith Messenger (1920–2010) at Algoma Mills. Offord owned D.H. 83C Fox Moth CF-DIW from April 1949 until it passed to GNS in March 1951.

In the meantime Offord had resigned his RAF commission in February 1950, retaining the rank of Flight Lieutenant. In later life he became a sales executive for a shoe manufacturer. He fell victim to leukaemia and while suffering the illness fell down stairs at his home in Toronto, Ontario, on 20 January 1966 and died in hospital shortly afterwards.

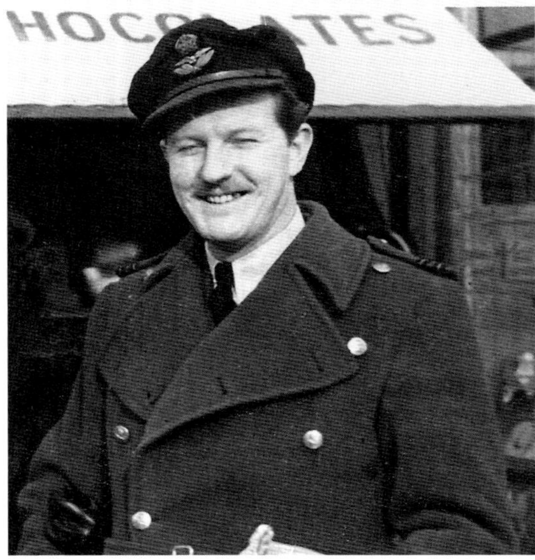

'Freddie' Offord in Watford in 1945.

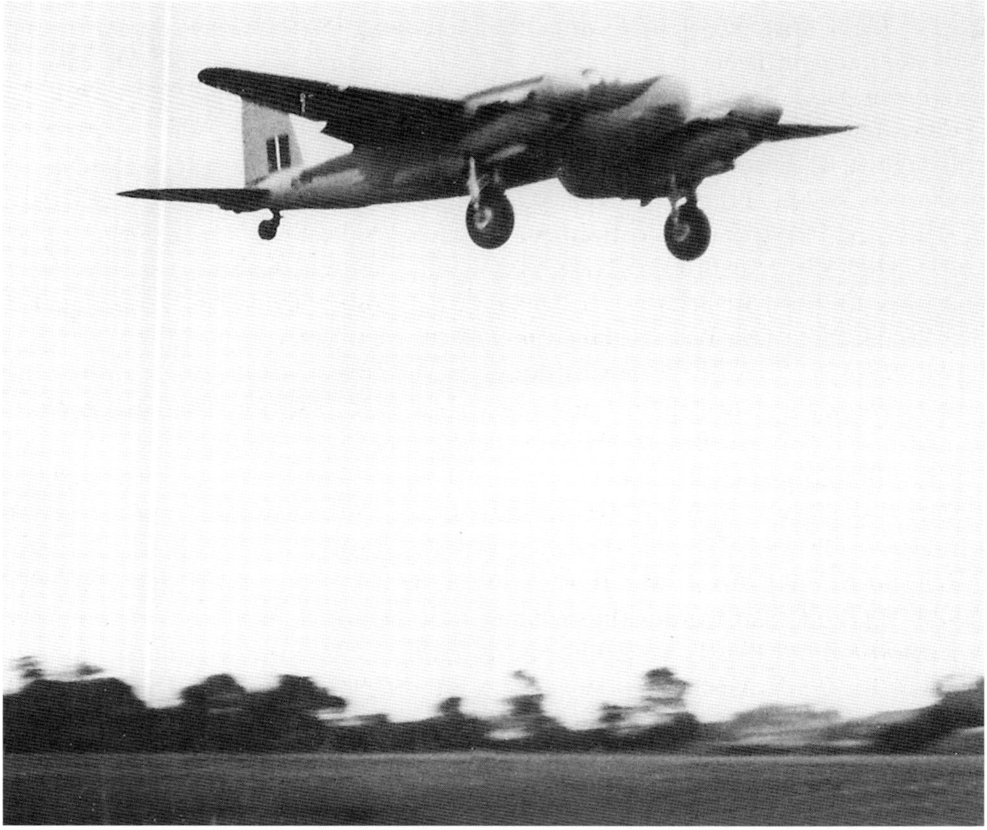

Stan Freddie' Offord returns to Leavesden on 17 August 1945 after a test flight in D.H.98 Mosquito 36 RL205.

Bibliography

Amos, Peter. *Miles Aircraft: The Early Years* (Air-Britain (Historians) Ltd., 2009)

Andrews, C. F. *Vickers Aircraft since 1908* (Putnam)

Andrews, C. F. and Morgan E. B. *Supermarine Aircraft since 1914* (Putnam, 1981)

Barnes, C. H. *Bristol Aircraft since 1910* (Putnam, 1988); *Shorts Aircraft since 1900* (Putnam, 1987)

Cheesman, E. C. *Brief Glory* (Harborough Publishing Company Ltd, 1946)

Halley, James J. Royal Air Force Aircraft J1-J9999 and WW1 Survivors, (Air-Britain (Historians) Ltd., 1987.); *The K File: The Royal Air Force of the 1930s* (Air-Britain (Historians) Ltd, 1995); *Royal Air Force Aircraft L1000-N9999* (Air-Britain (Historians) Ltd, 1993); *Royal Air Force Aircraft P1000-P9999* (Air-Britain (Historians) Ltd, 1978); *Royal Air Force Aircraft R1000-R9999* (Air-Britain (Historians) Ltd, 1980); *Royal Air Force Aircraft T1000-V9999* (Air-Britain (Historians) Ltd, 1997); *Royal Air Force Aircraft W1000-Z9999* (Air-Britain (Historians) Ltd, 1998); *Royal Air Force Aircraft AA100-AZ999* (Air-Britain (Historians) Ltd, 2000); *Royal Air Force Aircraft BA100-BZ999* (Air-Britain (Historians) Ltd, 1985); *Royal Air Force Aircraft DA100-DZ999* (Air-Britain (Historians) Ltd, 1987); *Royal Air Force Aircraft EA100-EZ999* (Air-Britain (Historians) Ltd, 1988); *Royal Air Force Aircraft FA100-FZ999* (Air-Britain (Historians) Ltd, 1989); *Royal Air Force Aircraft HA100-HZ999* (Air-Britain (Historians) Ltd, 1989); *Royal Air Force Aircraft JA100-JZ999* (Air-Britain (Historians) Ltd, 1990); *Royal Air Force Aircraft KA100-KZ999* (Air-Britain (Historians) Ltd, 1990); *Royal Air Force Aircraft LA100-LZ999* (Air-Britain (Historians) Ltd, 1991); *Royal Air Force Aircraft MA100-MZ999* (Air-Britain (Historians) Ltd, 1991); *Royal Air Force Aircraft NA100-NZ999* (Air-Britain (Historians) Ltd, 1992); *Royal Air Force Aircraft PA100-RZ999* (Air-Britain (Historians) Ltd, 1992); *Royal Air Force Aircraft SA100-VZ999* (Air-Britain (Historians) Ltd, 1985); *Royal Air Force Aircraft WA100-WZ999* (Air-Britain (Historians) Ltd, 1983)

Hamlin, John F. *Peaceful Fields: A Directory of Civil Airfields and Landing Grounds in the United Kingdom 1919-1939* (GMS Enterprises, 2007.); *The Oxford, Consul & Envoy File* (Air-Britain (Historians) Ltd, 2001)

Jackson, A. J. *British Civil Aircraft 1919–1959: Volume I* (Putnam, 1959); *Volume II* (Putnam, 1960); *British Civil Aircraft 1919–1972: Volume I* (Putnam, 1973); *Volume II* (Putnam, 1973); *Volume III* (Putnam, 1973); *De Havilland Aircraft since 1909* (Putnam, 1987); *Avro Aircraft since 1908* (Putnam, 1990); *Blackburn Aircraft since 1909* (Putnam, 1988)

James, Derek N. *Gloster Aircraft since 1917* (Putnam, 1971)

Mason, Francis K. *Hawker Aircraft since 1920* (Putnam, 1991)

Moss, Peter. *Impressments Logs, Vols 1-3* (Air-Britain 1962)

Payne, L. G. S. *Air Dates* (Heinemann, 1957)

Sharp, Martin and Bower, J. E. *Mosquito* (Faber & Faber Ltd, 1967)

Stroud, John. *Annals of British and Commonwealth Air Transport*, (Putnam, 1962); *Railway Air Services* (Ian Allan, 1987)

Sturtivant, Ray. *Fleet Air Arm Aircraft 1939 to 1945* (Air-Britain (Historians) Ltd, 1995); *The Anson File* (Air-Britain (Historians) Ltd, 1988)

Tapper, Oliver. *Armstrong Whitworth Aircraft since 1913* (Putnam, 1972)

Taylor, H. A. *Airspeed Aircraft since 1931* (Putnam, 1970); *Fairey Aircraft since 1915* (Putnam, 1974)

The Aeroplane Who's Who in Aviation 1948 (Temple Press Ltd, 1948)

Thetford, Owen. *British Naval Aircraft 1912-1958* (Putnam, 1958); *Aircraft of the Royal Air Force since 1918* (Putnam, 1957)

Thirsk, Ian. *De Havilland Mosquito: An Illustrated History Volume 2* (Crecy Publishing Ltd,) 2006)

Periodicals

Aeromodeller magazine, Vols 5–15 (Model Aeronautical Press Ltd, 1940–1950)
Aeronautics, Vols 1-22 1940–1950 (C. Arthur Pearson Ltd)
The Aeroplane, Vols for 1940–1950, (Temple Press)
The Aeroplane Spotter, Vols 1-8 1941–48 (Temple Press)
Air Review, 1945–46, (Air Review Ltd)
The Light Plane & Private Owner, 1946–48 (Light Plane Publications Ltd)

Unpublished Personal Papers, Letters and Records

Phinney, Robert. Letters relating to his uncle–Stanley Frederick Offord
Riding. E. J. *Pilot's Log Book* (Entries 1940–50); *Newspaper Cuttings of UK Aircraft Crashed (1929–1939); Correspondence from E.J.R. to A.J. Jackson (1944–1950); Flight Logs and Aerodrome Visits (1929–1950)*

E.J.R.'s personal handbook for the Fairey Albacore containing handwritten notes and drawings to aid inspection.

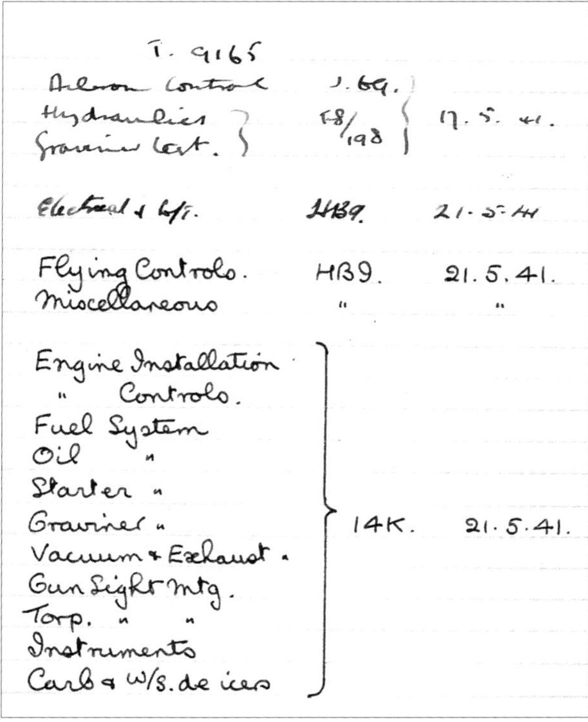

A page from a record book detailing dates of inspection of each Albacore as it came off the production line, in this case aircraft N9165. E.J.R.'s mark was A.I.D. 14.K.

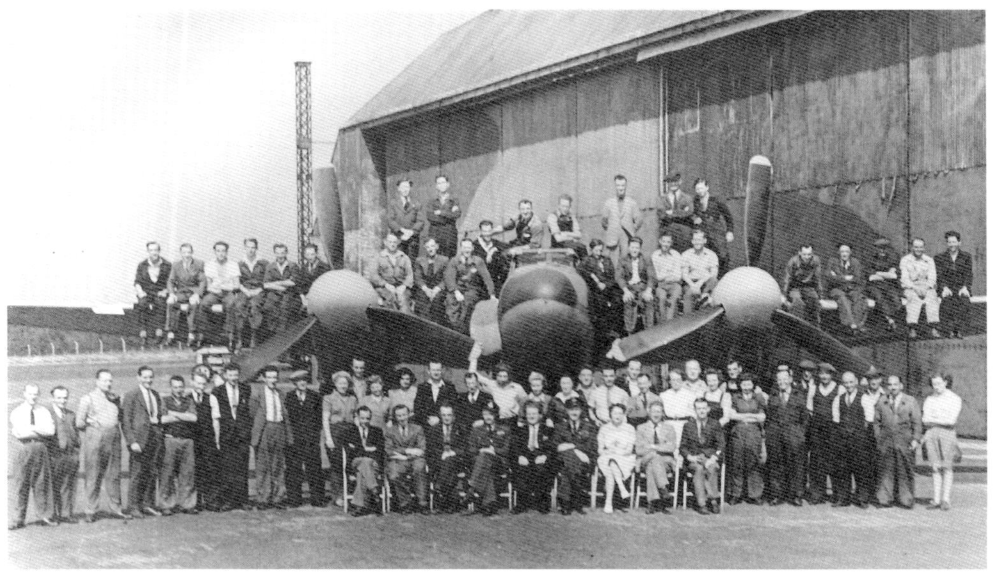

The entire Mosquito Flight Shed staff draped on and around an example of their handiwork. Stan 'Freddie' Offord is seated in the front row, fourth from the right, with John 'Tubby' Simpson on his right.

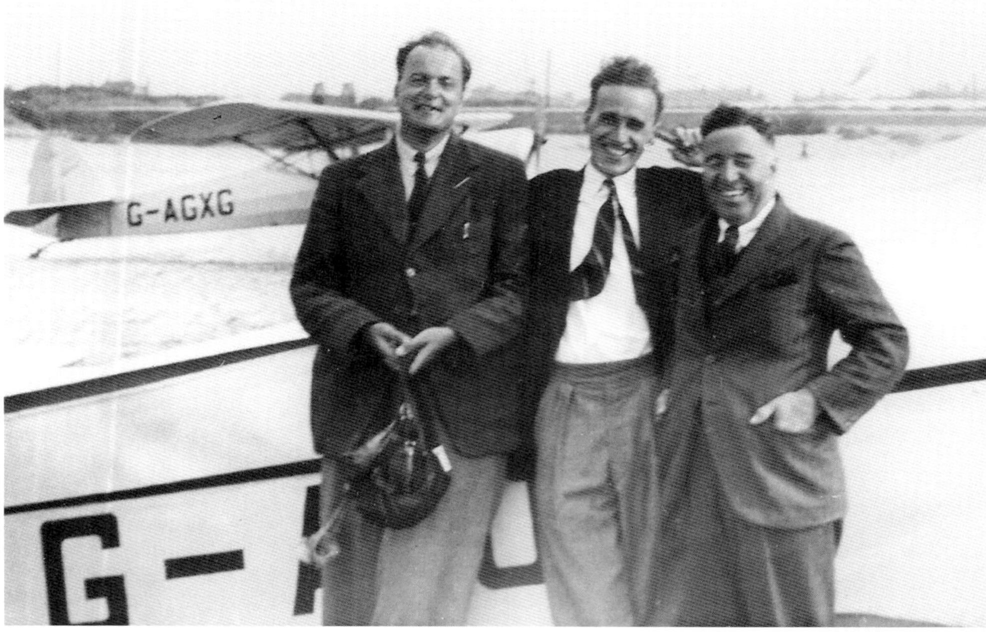

Happy days. E.J.R., Alec Lumsden and L. Knight on Southport sands on 22 August 1949. E.J.R. and Alec had flown up from Elstree in Miles M.14A G-AIUA, calling in at Wolverhampton, Ringway and Barton on the way. Afterwards L. Knight gave E.J.R. a free ride in the Giro D.H. 83 Fox Moth G-ACCB E.J.R. Stan 'Freddie' Offord at Watford in 1945.